THE WG&L HANDBOOK OF

FINANCIAL STRATEGY & POLICY

EDITOR

DENNIS E. LOGUE

AMOS TUCK SCHOOL OF BUSINESS ADMINISTRATION
DARTMOUTH COLLEGE

WARREN, GORHAM & LAMONT

COLLEGE DIVISION South-Western Publishing Co.

Cincinnati Ohio

Acquisitions Editor: Christopher Will
Production Editors: Sharon Smith and Sue Ellen Brown
Marketing Manager: Denise Carlson
Cover Designer: Lotus Wittkopf

FR60AA
Copyright © 1995
by
South-Western College Publishing
Cincinnati, Ohio
and Warren Gorham Lamont

2 3 4 5 6 MA 9 8 7 6

Printed in the United States of America

Library of Congress Cataloging-in-Publication Data

The WG&L handbook of financial strategy & policy / editor, Dennis E. Logue.
    p. cm.
  Includes index.
  ISBN 0-538-84252-0
  1. Consolidation and merger of corporations—United States.
  2. Leveraged buyouts—United States. 3. Dividends—United States.
  4. Pension trusts—United States. 5. Bankruptcy—United States.
  6. Corporate reorganizations—United States. 7. Compensation
management—United States.   I. Logue, Dennis E.
HG4028.M4W48 1994
658.15—dc20   94-20887
                                         CIP

I(T)P
International Thomson Publishing

South-Western College Publishing is an ITP Company. The ITP trademark is used under
license.

This book is printed on acid-free paper that meets Environmental Protection
Agency standards for recycled paper.

Preface

As the editor for the W, G, & L *Handbook of Modern Finance, Third Edition*, I am happy to note that South-Western Publishing Company is publishing this series of five "break-out" readings books for use in your classroom:

The W, G, & L *Handbook of International Finance*
The W, G, & L *Handbook of Financial Markets*
The W, G, & L *Handbook of Securities and Investment Management*
The W, G, & L *Handbook of Financial Policy*
The W, G, & L *Handbook of Short-Term and Long-Term Financial Management.*

These readers make a unique contribution to the classroom in that they are written primarily from the practitioner's point of view; showing students how the principles they are learning in class can be applied to real-world financial problems.

Thus they are ideally suited to supplement courses in Corporate Finance, Investments, Capital Markets, Financial Institutions, and International Finance both at the undergraduate and MBA level. They are also ideally suited for use in an executive education program.

These readers cover virtually every major technical, analytical, and theoretical financial question likely to be raised by active, inquisitive corporate financial and business executives, strategic planners, accountants (public and private), attorneys, security analysts, and bankers. They provide your students with insights for solving day-to-day business problems as well as provide guidance in long-term planning. Institutional arrangements are explained; relevant economic and financial theory and its application are presented and described. In addition, sophisticated quantitative analyses are presented in the context of real-world examples, numerous figures illustrate textual explanations, and end-of-chapter readings direct interested readers to additional technical literature in the field. The intent has been to produce a series of readings books that will help students understand the practical applications of the theory presented in their textbooks, thus helping them become better-prepared business professionals.

The W, G, & L *Handbook of Financial Policy* covers the topics of mergers and acquisitions, leveraged buyouts, divided policy, pension plans, hedging financial risk, real estate finance, bankruptcy, corporate restructuring, and executive pay, incentives, and performance. Contributors include:

Sean Boyle
Associate, Viking Graham, Inc.

Robert Case
Managing Director, Morgan Stanley, Inc.

Kate W. Cook
Vice President, Bankers Trust Company

R. Andrew de Pass
Associate, Morgan Stanley Canada Ltd.

Noreen Doyle
European Bank for Reconstruction and Development

John D. England
Principal, Towers Perrin

Steven C. Graham
President, Viking Graham, Inc.

Joseph G. May
Associate, Viking Graham, Inc.

William P. McKee
Vice-President, Viking Graham, Inc.

Christina Takoudes Morrison
Vice-President, Viking Graham, Inc.

Stephen Roulac
Managing Partner, Roulac Group

James K. Seward
Professor, Amos Tuck School of Business Administration, Dartmouth College

Dhiran Shah
Vice-President, Morgan Stanley, Inc.

Michelle J. White
Professor of Economics, University of Michigan

Arthur Williams III
Director of Retirement Plan Investments, McKinsey & Company

The editor wants to thank all of the authors who have worked so hard to produce highly focused chapters with a strong managerial slant. All are to be thanked and congratulated.

In addition to the authors, thanks must also go to Audrey Hanlon, who helped organize the work done by Tuck; Beverly Salbin of Warren Gorman Lamont, who brought so much to the party that she deserves much more recognition than this; and to Leora Harris and Vibert Gale, also of WGL, whose skills contributed so much to the final product.

Finally, I want to thank South-Western Publishing Company for bringing these readers to the college market.

DENNIS E. LOGUE

Hanover, New Hampshire
November 1993

Contents

Chapter 1
Mergers and Acquisitions

BOB CASE

DHIREN SHAH

ANDREW DE PASS

1.01 WHY MERGE?

Mergers and acquisitions (M&As) are financial transactions that involve a change in control of a company. A company that changes hands (an acquiree or target) in an M&A transaction typically experiences fundamental operating changes. At the very least, it will have a new controlling shareholder and a newly constituted board of directors. In many cases it may also experience a change in management, or a change in business strategy. Why do control transactions occur? There are as many reasons for M&As as there are M&As, but broadly speaking, companies merge and acquire because they must adapt to constantly changing markets and competitive environments.

A nonfinancial framework for understanding an M&A transaction examines the identities and objectives of the parties to the transaction. A buyer (or acquiror) will be (1) an operating company; (2) a group of managers; (3) a group of financial investors; or (4) a combination of the three. This chapter concentrates on acquisitions by operating companies, by far the most common type of transaction. Corporate buyers usually are motivated by strategic objectives—expanding an existing business, reducing costs in a business, or extending into a new line of business. Management groups, in contrast, typically acquire companies they know well in order to concentrate the benefits of improved financial performance in the hands of those who bring about the improvement. Financial groups acquire companies primarily because they identify an opportunity to earn superior financial returns by bringing about a change in the structure or business or financial strategy of a company. Financial acquisitions are typically organized as leveraged buyouts.

The principal players on the seller's side of an M&A transaction are either (1) the board of directors of the company being sold or (2) a controlling shareholder. The board may conclude that a sale is in order because the company's operating performance would be enhanced as part of a larger enterprise or under another management team. Alternatively, a subsidiary company's business may not fit with the strategic objectives of its corporate parent (and controlling shareholder), leading the parent to initiate the divestiture of the subsidiary. Finally, a controlling shareholder's objectives could be purely financial. For example, the shareholder may need to sell to achieve liquidity or may sell in response to an unexpectedly large offer from a buyer.

In theory, the fundamental financial justification for a corporation to make an acquisition is that the acquisition is expected to increase the per-share value of the acquiror over the long term. Ultimately, this comes about in only one way: the cash flows to be realized from operation of the acquired business exceed the cost of the acquisition. The fundamental reason for a company to agree to be acquired, if the transaction is for cash, is that the selling shareholders have an immediate opportunity to be paid for some of the acquisition's expected benefits. In a transaction in which the seller receives the acquiror's stock, the seller, as one of the acquiror's shareholders, will also share in the benefits of the merger over time. In other words, the selling shareholders realize a premium over the trading market stock price, which management cannot achieve on its own.

In deciding whether an acquisition will, on balance, create value for an acquiror, several rules are commonly accepted among analysts:

  1. *Pure conglomerate acquisitions do not necessarily create new shareholder value.* Shareholders of an acquiror already have the opportunity to invest in the acquisition target independently. By forcing those shareholders to make a both-or-none investment decision, management presents a less attractive investment profile to the market than if the two companies traded separately.

In order for a conglomerate acquisition to make sense, there must be some additional value created that is not present in either company on a stand-alone basis. If there is no such synergy, the combined companies will trade at a conglomerate discount, which is only eliminated when the unrelated businesses are divested or spun off. This discount reflects the difficulty of managing a diverse business. The dismantling of the Burlington Northern Railroad into an energy and transportation company has shown how value can be created by spin-offs. There have been numerous examples of this recently.

2. *Countercyclical acquisitions do not necessarily create value.* The capital market only assesses financial risk that is systematic (i.e., marketwide) in nature. Thus, mergers that tend to eliminate unsystematic (non-market-related) risk do not improve the investment profile of a company. For example, a company that sells both umbrellas and suntan lotion may have less risk in its cash flows than a company that sells only one such product. However, a combined umbrella and suntan lotion company will not experience a lower cost of capital than the independent companies. Moreover, the risk involved (sunshine versus rain) is not one for which the market will demand a higher cost of capital either. Such a merger cannot be justified on purely financial grounds, although other reasons (e.g., common management skills and operating economies) may justify it.

The argument against countercyclicality can be taken a step further. Even a combination of companies with countercyclical systematic risks (e.g., capital goods manufacturing and consumer retailing) would appear not to create new value because each investor can also achieve a risk-balanced portfolio on his or her own.

The primary circumstance in which countercyclicality does create value is where there would otherwise be underutilized assets or skills in one or both companies. For example, an umbrella company may profitably combine with a snowboat company to fill up unutilized capacity in manufacturing, sales, and distribution during the predictable off-season.

3. *The market does not reward purely acquisition-induced growth.* It is commonly recognized that companies with tremendous growth potential trade in the marketplace at earnings multiples far higher than companies with more mundane prospects. It is tempting, therefore, to conclude that a company that has exhausted its internal opportunities for fast growth can achieve equivalent results by a program of carefully timed acquisitions. The fallacy in this reasoning is that unlike the situation of an established product with growing demand, each acquisition must stand on its own in terms of its contribution to a company's earnings and cash flow. Unless the circumstances are unique (e.g., a ready supply of acquisition targets that can be bought one by one, without competition), each acquisition is a nonrepeatable event. It is not like making and selling one more widget. Investors must continually rely on the ability of the company to pick good targets and negotiate favorable transaction terms. Because the likelihood of successfully carrying out a steady, predictable series of high-return acquisitions is quite low, the market discounts the earnings of companies that grow through acquisition at a much higher rate than those of companies that happen to be in product markets offering substantial growth within an area of demonstrated expertise.

4. *Related diversification can be an important means of creating value in acquisitions.* The most successful acquisitions typically involve situations in which the assets, skills, or knowledge of one company can be applied to the problems or opportunities of the other. For example, a target may have a strong sales force in place that can market many of the acquiror's products to new customers or in a new geographic region. This would be a revenue-increasing acquisition. The target may also have a product or process uniquely suited to a need within the acquiror's business. This would be a cost-reducing acquisition. In many cases, the acquiror has the alternative of developing comparable skills, systems,

3

or products on its own, but the speed and limited risk with which an acquisition can be consummated often more than offset the savings associated with internal development. Many acquisitions are both cost-reducing and revenue-increasing.

5. *Acquisitions can be an important means of reaching a critical mass, where size is an important industry factor.* In certain industries, long-run competitive success depends largely on achieving a necessary critical mass in terms of sales, assets, customers, or some other factor. In the pharmaceutical industry, for example, research and development (R&D) expenditures are critical to long-run survival and must be funded out of the earnings of a base of successfully established products. A successful R&D program, however, requires very substantial levels that cannot be met by smaller companies. Thus, there is a strong impetus to reach a critical size or scale through acquisition. Similarly, in commercial banking, overhead costs tend to decline and margins tend to increase as a percentage of lendable assets, up to very substantial bank sizes. The principal way that the large critical mass of customers, deposits, and loans necessary for efficient operation can be reached is through acquisitions of other banks.

6. *Acquisitions are a tax-efficient means of investing excess corporate funds.* The U.S. Internal Revenue Code (IRC) provides for double taxation of corporate earnings: once at the corporate level in the form of the corporate income tax, and again at the shareholder level in the form of capital gain and dividend taxes. Shareholder taxes on corporate earnings can be deferred, however, if those earnings are retained and reinvested within the corporation. For example, a company with $100 in excess cash could pay out $100 in dividends, but that may leave shareholders with only $70 to invest (at a 30 percent marginal tax rate). A more sophisticated company would buy some of its stock back in the marketplace but, after capital gains taxes, may still only effectively distribute less than $100. On the other hand, the full $100 may be reinvested productively by means of an acquisition, and taxes at the shareholder level may be deferred indefinitely.

This is not to say that corporate management should always make acquisitions instead of paying dividends or repurchasing stock. It depends on whether there are high-return alternatives available that can be effectively managed by the corporation's executives. If there are no such alternatives, or if there is a major risk that an acquisition program will overburden management and create below-normal returns, it is better to pay out excess cash to shareholders and let them reinvest it in other opportunities.

1.02 VALUATION OF AN ACQUISITION CANDIDATE

Assume that after a lengthy search, an ideal acquisition candidate is found: Flexible Technologies Corporation. It is just the right size, fits a market niche in which there is some knowledge and which should experience attractive growth, and has capable management that would work well in the present organization. There is a controlling stockholder who is willing to sell, but it must be decided how much to offer him. How should the valuation process be undertaken?

[1] Value

There are many different concepts of value, which are largely distinguished by who the valuing party is and how the value arises. Typically, there are three different valuing parties in an acquisition: the buyer, the seller, and a potential competing buyer.

[a] **Value to the Buyer.** For the buyer, value represents the discounted present value of the net cash flows it will ultimately realize and have freely available as a consequence of making the acquisition. The cash flows could be realized by operating the business over a long period, liquidating all or part of the business, or restructuring parts of both the buyer's business and the acquired business in a way that creates synergy value in excess of that provided by the two businesses independently. The buyer's value represents the highest amount the buyer should ever pay to acquire the company in question. Payment of more than this would leave the buyer with a net economic loss for having made the acquisition.

[b] **Value to the Seller.** For the seller, value represents a similar discounted cash flow (DCF) calculation that takes into account the best available strategies for running the business. Even if the seller is more optimistic about the business's financial prospects than the buyer, the seller may value the company lower than the buyer because the seller needs cash (and so has a higher discount rate). In order for a transaction to be feasible, the seller's estimate of value must be below the buyer's by an amount larger than any taxes payable by the seller as a result of the sale. Clearly, a seller will not dispose of an asset for a price at which its net after-tax proceeds are below those realizable by retaining the asset.

[c] **Value to a Competing Buyer.** The value to another buyer must always be kept in mind by both the buyer and seller in any merger negotiation. The key issue is whether the buyer with whom the seller is dealing is the buyer who is willing to pay the highest price. To be assured of success, the buyer should offer a price that is reasonably indicative of the full value of the business to that buyer. By the same token, a smart seller will not let a buyer know he is the only suitor in the negotiation.

[2] Valuation Techniques

There are five main approaches to valuation:

1. DCF

2. Acquisition multiples

3. Premium over market trading value

4. Liquidation value

5. Replacement value

The DCF approach is the most fundamental method of measuring value, because it measures the ultimate source of value: cash. It can be used validly in most situations, provided the underlying assumptions used to project the cash flows reflect the likely course of events. Acquisition multiples are a means of establishing benchmark values for a company, based on multiples of earnings, book value, and so forth paid by other acquirors. The typical approach is "companies in the X industry trade at Y times earnings." Premiums over market trading value typically measure the percentage premium paid to public stockholders. This measure is important in drawing support from shareholders to assure the success of a tender offer or merger vote. Liquidation values measure the amount of cash that could be realized if a company sold all of its assets and paid off its liabilities in the near future. Finally, replacement values measure the cost of starting up a similar company from scratch.

In trying to make a valuation estimate, it is important to apply those methods most pertinent to the particular circumstances of the company under review. Thus, if the company has vast, underutilized resources, or other property (e.g., oil and gas, real estate, patents, copyrights, and broadcasting licenses), a liquidation approach would be material to the formation of a value judgment, even if the buyer does not plan to liquidate the company. On the other hand, if the company has little in the way of salable assets, but has an important brand name and strong management skills, a DCF analysis will be much more relevant than a liquidation analysis. The purpose of having many techniques is to be able to choose those methods that best address the nature of the company in question. A second, and equally important, reason for the several approaches to value is to allow the analyst to confirm values generated by one technique with the results of a separate analysis. No matter how methodical the techniques may seem at times, there is little question that valuation is far more an art than a science.

[3] Discounted Cash Flow Analysis

DCF analysis is doubtlessly the most fundamental method of measuring value, because it is based on the source of value: cash. The values that a DCF yields are often inappropriately referred to as "intrinsic" values. Such terminology has the unfortunate consequence of sidestepping the real issue, which is: Whose assumptions about the future should be used in estimating cash flows? A value estimate is only as intrinsic to the business as a consensus is to the likely future cash flows and the appropriate discount rate. DCF analysis has the advantage of calculating numerous different values for a company, depending on whether the underlying assumptions are those of a seller, a buyer, or another potential owner. It is only because different perceptions of value exist that exchange takes place at all.

[a] **Definition of Scenarios.** The first step in any DCF analysis is an evaluation of the historical operating characteristics of the company (e.g., growth, margins, and capital intensity) and a projection of the behavior of these characteristics in the future. The projection clearly depends on a well-developed understanding of the industry and economic environment in which the company will be operating and a feeling for the operating strategy management has adopted and will use in the future.

The objective is to arrive at a set of basic operating ratios that can be used to project cash flows for the company. A typical set of such ratios includes the following:

- Unit growth rate of sales
- Rate of price increases
- Cost of goods sold as a percentage of sales
- Depreciation as a percentage of net fixed assets
- Selling, general, and administrative expenses as a percentage of sales
- Effective tax rate

- Working capital required as a percentage of sales
- Net fixed assets required as a percentage of sales

In order to integrate these operating ratios into a more general framework of the industry and economic climate, it is useful to make explicit assumptions about the following:

- Inflation
- Industry size and unit growth rate
- Market share changes within the industry

Unfortunately, it is not generally possible to project all of these industry- and company-specific factors with a high degree of certainty. While it is technically possible to perform many sensitivity analyses of value with respect to each assumption, financial analysts find it conceptually useful to group varying sets of assumptions into scenarios that logically belong together. For example, if unit sales do not grow as fast as expected, it may be because of increased competition, a factor that should be reflected in lower margins as well. Alternatively, it may be that part of the "value creation" of the acquisition consists of more stringent management of working capital and plant efficiency. A thorough DCF analysis would examine the impact on value if such efficiencies cannot be attained.

EXAMPLE: Assume that Flexible Technologies Corporation has the following historical operating record:

	Latest Five-Year Average
Rate of unit sales growth	7.0%
Rate of price growth	6.0
Operating income (percentage of sales)	22.5
Depreciation rate (percentage of net fixed assets)	12.0
Tax rate	46.0
Net working capital required (percentage of sales)	15.0
Net fixed assets required (percentage of sales)	40.0

It is also known that over the five-year period, the average inflation rate was 4 percent (and thus, real price increases were $(1.06/1.04 - 1) \times 100\% = 1.9\%$). Industry unit growth has averaged 7 percent, and Flexible's market share has remained steady at 11 percent. Flexible's projected tax rate is 40 percent.

Two alternative scenarios are evolving in the industry. In the first, a maturity scenario, slackened demand and increasing competition will force Flexible to lower its prices and margins in order to maintain its market share. In the second, a growth scenario, high demand growth will continue for the next eight years, after which the industry should mature.

These two scenarios can be quantified as follows.

Maturity Scenario. Assuming that, in the long run, unit demand growth is tied to population growth (assumed to be 1.5 percent), in a maturity scenario, Flexible's unit sales growth declines to that 1.5 percent rate. Prices and margins must also reflect the maturity scenario. The implications of maturity can be seen by examining Flexible's return on invested capital, which has been above normal in recent years:

FIGURE 1-1

Summary of Maturity Scenario

	Year 1	Year 2	Year 3	Year 4 and Following
Unit sales growth	4.5%	2.5%	1.5%	1.5%
General inflation	4.0	4.0	4.0	4.0
Real price changes	(4.0)	(4.0)	(4.0)	0
Total price growth	0	0	0	4.0
Operating margin as percentage of sales	17.3	15.0	11.0	11.0

Pretax return on capital employed (ROCE)

$$= \frac{\text{operating income}}{\text{sales}} \times \frac{\text{sales}}{\text{capitalization}}$$

$$= \frac{\text{operating income}}{\text{sales}} \times \frac{\text{sales}}{\text{fixed assets} + \text{net working capital}}$$

$$= \frac{\text{operating income}}{\text{sales}} \times \frac{1}{\dfrac{\text{fixed assets}}{\text{sales}} + \dfrac{\text{net working capital}}{\text{sales}}}$$

$$= 0.225 \left(\frac{1}{0.15 + 0.40} \right) = 0.409 \ (40.9\%)$$

If industrial companies in mature industries generally are only able to earn unleveraged pretax returns of about 20 percent, margins can be expected to fall in Flexible's industry as well upon maturity.

Finally, it can be expected that this decline in margins would come about principally through price declines, assuming that Flexible's industry utilizes no unique factors of production whose costs will change at rates other than inflation.

$$\text{Future margins} = \frac{\text{future ROCE}}{\text{present ROCE}} \times \text{present margins}$$

$$= \frac{20.0}{40.9} \times 22.5 = 11\%$$

The extent of real price decline can then be calculated from the amount of margin compression as follows:

$$\frac{\text{Future prices}}{\text{current prices}} = \frac{1 - \text{current operating margin}}{1 - \text{future operating margin}}$$

$$= \frac{1 - 0.225}{1 - 0.110} = 0.871 \ (87.1\%)$$

In other words, a real price decline of 12.9 percent will produce the expected fall in margins. Such a real price decline can be achieved cumulatively over a three-year period at a rate of approximately 4 percent per year.

The maturity scenario assumptions are summarized in Figure 1-1, where a three-year

FIGURE 1-2

Summary of Higher-Growth Scenario

	Year 1–8	Year 9	Year 10	Year 11	Year 12 and Following
Unit sales growth	7.0%	4.5%	2.5%	1.5%	1.5%
General inflation	4.0	4.0	4.0	4.0	4.0
Real price changes	0	(4.0)	(4.0)	(4.0)	0
Total price growth	4.0	0	0	0	4.0
Operating income as percentage of sales	22.5	17.3	15.0	11.0	11.0

time period is used for a smooth transition to the "long-run" assumptions. Other operating characteristics, such as asset turnover, depreciation, and tax rates, are assumed to remain constant.

Growth Scenario. The growth scenario assumes continued high-unit growth of 7 percent for the next eight years, followed by an industry maturation period that would resemble the maturity scenario. The company's operating statistics would therefore be projected as shown in Figure 1-2. Once again, other assumptions, such as asset turnover, depreciation, and tax rates, are assumed to remain constant.

[b] Projecting Free Cash Flows. Once the scenarios are well defined, the next step is to project free cash flows (FCF) for each year. In any projected year, FCF is the excess cash that can be removed from the business after meeting all investment, spending, and other operating requirements (exclusive of financing). Specifically, levered FCF is calculated as follows:

FCF = net income after taxes + noncash charges to income (deferred taxes, depreciation, amortization of intangibles, etc.) − capital expenditures − investment in net working capital (excluding cash and short-term debt)

EXAMPLE: To calculate FCF for Flexible Technologies Corporation (under the higher growth scenario) for the first projection year, assume the previous year's balance sheet and income statement as shown in Figure 1-3. For the projection of FCF in year 1, net income is first calculated:

Item	Assumption	Projected Value ($000)
Sales	7% unit growth and 4% price growth over year 0 value of $55,000	$61,200
Operating income	22.5% of sales	13,800
Interest expense	10% of total debt	(800)
Pretax income	Net of 2 items above	$13,000
Income taxes	40% of pretax income	5,200
Net income		$7,800

9

FIGURE 1-3

Flexible Technologies Corporation Financial Summary

Financial Position, End of Year 0

Current assets	$21,500
Net fixed assets	22,500
Total assets	$44,000
Short-term debt	$ 3,000
Other current liabilities	13,000
Long-term debt	5,000
Deferred taxes	1,200
Stockholders' equity	21,800
Total liabilities and stockholders' equity	$44,000

Income Statement, Year 0

Net sales	$55,000
Cost of sales	(33,900)
Selling, general, and administrative expense	(8,600)
Operating income	$12,500
Interest expense	(800)
Pretax income	$11,700
Income taxes	(5,400)
Net income	$ 6,300

Note: Dollars in thousands.

The next step is to identify noncash income and expense items and add them back:

Noncash Expense	Assumption	Amount ($000)
Depreciation	12% of net fixed assets	$2,700
Deferred income taxes	10% of income tax expense	520
Total noncash items		$3,220

Adding noncash items to net income gives the cash provided by operations of $11,000. Finally, working capital and fixed asset investment requirements are projected:

Item	Assumption	Year-End Amount Required	Initial Amount Available	Investment Required
Net working capital	15% of sales	$ 9,180	$ 8,500[a]	$680
Net fixed assets	40% of sales	24,500	19,800[b]	4,700

[a] Based on current assets of $21,500 net of current liabilities of $13,000. Since operating requirements are calculated here, items such as short-term debt ($3,000) and excess investment cash (none available) are not included.

[b] Based on beginning amount ($22,500) less current year's depreciation ($2,700).

FIGURE 1-4

Summary Calculation of Levered Free Cash Flow

Net income	$7,800
Noncash charges	
Depreciation	2,700
Deferred taxes	520
Less: Investment in net working capital	(680)
Less: Capital expenditures	(4,700)
Free cash flow	$5,640

Note: Dollars in thousands.

As summarized in Figure 1-4, all of the components of Flexible's FCF have been calculated for year 1. It is this $5,640 cash flow that the owners of Flexible are free to dispose of as they please. The ongoing stream of such FCFs makes up the economic value of Flexible in the acquisition marketplace. The following sections review how to discount these cash flows to arrive at a capitalized value for Flexible.

[c] WACC. The owner of a company is free to vary the mix of the company's financing. Because of its fixed repayment provisions, its seniority in liquidation, and the tax deductibility of interest, debt is a less expensive source of capital than equity. Most capital-using companies therefore employ some debt financing. However, as the proportion of debt to total capital increases, so do the risks of default, insolvency, and potential loss of control of the company by the stockholders. Therefore, financial theory posits that, for every company, there is an optimum level of debt that appropriately balances the financial risk of debt with its cost advantages over equity. Experience suggests that for a large group of industrial companies, optimum is somewhere in the range of 20 percent to 50 percent debt to total capital.

"Weighted average cost of capital" (WACC) (symbolized $\bar{k}$) is defined as the weighted average cost of debt and equity:

$$\bar{k} = K_E(\% \text{ equity}) + k_p(1 - t)(\% \text{ debt})$$

where:

K_E = cost of equity
k_p = cost of debt (pretax)
t = marginal tax rate
% debt = percentage of debt to total capital
% equity = percentage of equity to total capital

The cost of debt, k_p, is typically the interest cost of medium-term to long-term borrowing. The cost of equity, however, is more difficult to calculate:

$$K_E = r_f + \beta(r_m - r_f)$$

where:

r_f = long-term risk-free rate
r_m = long-term return on the market
β = systematic risk factor of the company and its industry

11

$r_m - r_f$, the long-term real return on the market, is usually estimated at around 3 percent to 8.5 percent.

EXAMPLE: Based on studies of the cyclical risks of Flexible Technologies Corporation and its industry, an appropriate debt-to-capital ratio is 30 percent. One of several beta-estimating services is also examined, with the conclusion that Flexible's industry is slightly more cyclical than the market as a whole, so that Flexible deserves a beta (at 30 percent leverage) of 1.14. Finally, it is noted that 10-year U.S. government bonds are currently trading to yield 8 percent (which defines the medium-term risk-free rate). Therefore, Flexible's cost of equity can be calculated as

$$K_E = r_f + \beta(r_m - r_f)$$
$$= 8.0 + 1.14(6.5)$$
$$= 15.4\%$$

Assuming that Flexible's medium-term to long-term borrowing rate is 11.5 percent, the estimate for Flexible's WACC is as follows:

$$\bar{k} = K_E \ (\% \text{ equity}) + k_p(1 - t)(\% \text{ debt})$$
$$= (15.4\%)(70\%) + (11.5\%)(1 - 0.40)(30\%)$$
$$= 12.9\%$$

[d] **DCF Value Calculation.** The value of the firm in total is equal to the sum of the values of its obligations to all contributors of capital debt and equity:

$$V_{\text{firm}} = V_{\text{debt}} + V_{\text{equity}}$$

The DCF method, which employs a cost of capital representing the blended cost of debt and equity, is oriented toward valuing the entire firm, including both debt and equity. In other words, DCF calculates V_{firm}. The method of determining the value of a firm's equity as it presently exists involves a simple additional step:

$$V_{\text{equity}} = \text{DCF value} - V_{\text{debt}}$$

where V_{debt} is the market value of the debt of the firm at the time of valuation. The DCF value of the firm is calculated as:

DCF value = cash flow component + terminal component

= present value of unleveraged FCFs for each projection year (discounted at $\bar{k}$) + present value of the terminal value of the firm at the end of the projection period (discounted at $\bar{k}$)

The first component of the equation, the cash flow component, follows almost immediately from the work done to projects FCFs. The principal distinction is that unleveraged cash flows are discounted; that is, cash flows are arrived at as if the company had no debt. For any projection year:

Unleveraged FCF = FCF + (interest expense)(1 − tax rate)

Thus, for the Flexible example in year 1:

Unleveraged FCF = $5,640 + 800 (1 − 0.40) = $6,120

It is this series of cash flows that would be discounted.

> **EXAMPLE:** The higher-growth scenario assumptions lead to the unleveraged FCF calculations for Flexible as shown in Figure 1-5. Discounting these unleveraged FCFs back to the present at a weighted-average cost of capital of 12.9 percent produces a value of $52.4 million, which is the value that will be generated by Flexible's operation over the next 15 years.

The next step is to calculate the terminal value component of the DCF value. This task is a bit more subjective. Typically, the book value, earnings value, and cash flow value of the company are estimated at the end of the projection period and an attempt is made to judge what the company might be worth then. The projection period should be sufficiently long for reasonable variations in the estimation of terminal value to have only a minor impact on the total calculation.

A book value estimate is simply what the book value of all the debt and equity capital in the firm will be at the end of the projection period, assuming all the FCF has been paid out to the owners in the interim.

An earnings value estimate is simply an attempt to value by means of a price/earnings (P/E) multiple. The multiple chosen should be one typical of a low-growth company in a mature industry, since the projection period is designed to include all of the high growth years in the company's life cycle.

A cash flow estimate is an attempt to find a multiplier of FCF that will appropriately determine value. The multiplier typically used is

$$\frac{(1 + g)}{(\bar{k} - g)}$$

> *where:*
> g = rate of nominal growth of cash flows into perpetuity
> $\bar{k}$ = WACC

This multiplier is the factor that capitalizes a cash flow stream growing at rate g (not too large) into perpetuity, at a discount of $\bar{k}$.

> **EXAMPLE:** For Flexible, the projections generate the following values for year 15:

1. *Book value estimate*

Initial book value (debt and equity combined)	$ 29.8 million
Plus: Cumulative unleveraged earnings, years 1–15	176.9
Less: Free cash flow extracted, years 1–15	(123.6)
Book value in year 15	$ 83.5 million

2. *Earnings-based estimate*

Net income (unleveraged) in year 15	$11.5 million
Mature industry P/E ratio	×8.0
Implied value in year 15	$92.0 million

3. *Free cash flow multiple*

Perpetual cash flow growth rate: 4% (equal to inflation)

Cash flow multiplier: $\dfrac{1 + 0.04}{0.129 - 0.04} = 11.7$

Year 15 free cash flow	$ 7.2 million
Implied value in year 15	$84.2 million

FIGURE 1-5

Detailed Free Cash Flow Projection for Flexible Technologies Corporation (Growth Scenario)

Year	Sales[a]	Operating Income[b]	Unleveraged Net Income[c]	Net Fixed Assets Required[d]	Net Working Capital Required[e]	Depreciation Expense[f]	Deferred Income Tax Expense[g]	Cash Provided by Operations[h]	Capital Expenditures[i]	Increase in Net Working Capital[j]	Free Cash Flow[k]
1	$ 61,204	$13,771	$ 8,263	$24,482	$ 9,181	$2,700	$ 551	$11,514	$ 4,682	$ 681	$ 6,151
2	68,108	15,324	9,195	27,244	10,217	2,938	613	12,746	5,700	1,036	6,010
3	75,790	17,053	10,232	30,317	11,369	3,269	682	14,183	6,342	1,152	6,689
4	84,340	18,977	11,386	33,736	12,651	3,638	759	15,783	7,057	1,282	7,444
5	93,853	21,117	12,670	37,542	14,079	4,049	845	17,564	7,853	1,428	8,283
6	104,440	23,499	14,099	41,777	15,667	4,505	940	19,544	8,739	1,588	9,217
7	116,220	26,150	15,690	46,489	17,434	5,013	1,046	21,749	9,725	1,767	10,257
8	129,330	29,099	17,460	51,733	19,400	5,579	1,164	24,203	10,823	1,966	11,414
9	135,150	23,381	9,352	54,060	20,272	6,208	935	21,172	8,536	873	11,763
10	138,529	20,779	8,312	55,411	20,779	6,487	831	19,786	7,839	507	11,440
11	140,607	15,467	6,187	56,243	21,091	6,649	619	16,548	7,481	312	8,756
12	148,424	16,327	6,531	59,370	22,264	6,749	653	17,198	9,876	1,173	6,149
13	156,677	17,234	6,894	62,671	23,502	7,124	689	18,154	10,425	1,238	6,491
14	165,388	18,193	7,277	66,155	24,808	7,520	728	19,164	11,005	1,307	6,852
15	174,584	19,204	7,682	69,833	26,188	7,939	768	20,229	11,617	1,379	7,233

Present value at 12.9% $51,467

Note: Dollars in thousands.

[a] Sales projections based on prior year's sales, increased by previously described assumptions for unit sales growth, general inflation, and real price changes.

[b] Calculated as a percentage of sales, with the percentage declining during years 9–11, as previously described for the higher-growth scenario.

[c] Calculated as 60 percent of operating income (assuming 40 percent effective tax rate) interest expense has been ignored because the calculation here is of the amount of free cash flow available without respect to how the company is financed.

[d] Projected at 40 percent of sales.

[e] Projected at 15 percent of sales.

[f] Projected as 12 percent of previous year's net fixed assets.

[g] Estimated at 10 percent of income tax expense (the latter being 40 percent of operating income).

[h] Net income plus depreciation expense plus deferred income tax expense.

[i] Change in net fixed assets required plus depreciation.

[j] Change in net working capital required.

[k] Cash provided by operations minus capital expenditures minus increase in net working capital.

Based on these alternative estimates, a single terminal value may be pegged as the median of the three, $84.2 million. Discounting this amount by 12.9 percent for 15 years, a terminal value component worth $13.6 million today is calculated.

$$\text{DCF value of firm} = \text{cash flow component} + \text{terminal value component}$$
$$= \$51.5 \text{ million} + \$13.6 \text{ million}$$
$$= \$65.1 \text{ million}$$

Therefore,

$$V_{\text{equity}} = V_{\text{firm}} - V_{\text{debt}}$$
$$= \$65.1 - \$8^a$$
$$= \$57.1 \text{ million}$$

---

[a] At book value, which is assumed to approximate market value.

In summary, the DCF calculations show that under the higher growth scenario, the economic value of 100 percent of the equity shares in Flexible is in the neighborhood of $57 million (or nearly 2.6 times the book value of $21.8 million). A similar exercise can be performed under the maturity scenario, which will obtain significantly lower values.

[4] Acquisition Multiples

Buyers and sellers also look to other transactions in the same industry to establish valuation benchmarks in terms of the paid multiple of earnings, cash flow, book value, and so forth. Unlike DCF, this technique does not focus on the assumptions of the current prospective owner about the future. Instead, such multiples represent an index of recent market prices paid by other acquirors and accepted by other sellers. From a prospective seller's viewpoint, the multiples suggest a target price range at which other buyers have been willing to deal; conversely, for potential buyers, they suggest price ranges that are acceptable to other sellers.

Because each acquisition is unique and buyers and sellers typically do not know all the factors and motives that went into the formulation of another acquisition price, acquisition multiples often suggest a wide range of values and must be used with care. Moreover, because the acquisition market is not continuous in time, the fact that a particular multiple was paid in the past does not necessarily mean that it still applies today. Unlike the stock market, there is no current P/E benchmark other than the most recent industry transactions, which may be several years old.

Several types of multiples are usually examined. Each multiple has its uses and limitations, and the appropriate choice often depends on the industry under analysis.

[a] **Earnings Multiples.** Prices paid as a multiple of earnings are typically the most useful for a broad range of industrial companies. An important requirement for such multiples to be meaningful is that the accounting principles underlying earnings be comparable across the sample of transactions. Figure 1-6 is a sample chart that records the multiple of earnings paid in a group of acquisitions in the commercial banking industry in 1991. Column 6 (Earnings) provides data on the multiple of earnings paid in each acquisition. Column 7 shows the explicit premium over the market value prior to the announcement of the transaction.

FIGURE 1-6

Premiums Paid in Selected Mergers in the Commercial Banking Industry (1991)

Source: Morgan Stanley & Co. M&A Department Transaction Database

Dates (1)	Acquiror (2)	Acquiree (3)	Transaction Value (4)	Price Paid as a Multiple of Acquiree		
				Book Value (5)	Earnings (6)	Market Value (7)
6/24/91	Wachovia Corp.	South Carolina National Corp./Wachovia Corp.	$ 835.0	1.7×	16.2×	1.7×
7/15/91	Chemical Banking Corp.	Manufacturers Hanover Corp.	2,136.1	0.7	20.0	1.2
7/22/91	NCNB Corp.	C&S/Sovran Corp.	4,316.1	1.4	23.7	1.5
8/12/91	Bank America Corp.	Security Pacific Corp.	4,180.3	1.0	16.4	1.5
9/12/91	First America Bank Corp.	Security Bancorp, Inc.	547.0	2.8	17.8	1.8
10/28/91	Comerica Inc.	Manufacturers National Corp.	1,085.2	1.3	9.2	1.0
10/30/91	National City Corp.	Merchants National Corp.	655.4	1.9	16.7	1.8

Note: Dollars in millions; transaction value over $500 million.

Companies with lower margins, which offer some room for efficiency improvements, may appear to sell for higher multiples of past earnings. What is unknown, of course, is what level of earnings was projected as reasonably achievable by the buyer after the acquisition. A factor that may distort the comparability of earnings multiples is the amount of debt associated with an acquired company. For example, if a company with $10 million of net income and no debt were acquired for $100 million, the acquisition P/E ratio would be 10. If, however, that company had $50 million in debt on its balance sheet at an after-tax interest cost of $3 million, and the buyer therefore paid $50 million for the equity in the company, it would appear that the P/E multiple paid was 7 ($50 million paid for a company with $7 million in net income). Because a buyer and a seller usually have full control over the debt and equity financing of a company, debt on the books of an acquired company implicitly represents financing of the acquisition price. Therefore, it is often preferable to analyze acquisition precedents consistently by using unleveraged acquisition multiples—gross acquisition price (including debt assumed) divided by operating earnings (before interest expense and taxes).

Gross acquisition price = price paid for equity + market value of total debt owed by acquired company

Operating earnings = earnings before interest and taxes (EBIT)

= pretax earnings + interest expense

Cyclicality may also distort the comparability of earnings and earnings multiples. If sales and margins tend to fluctuate widely but systematically through the business cycle, the timing of a transaction within the cycle may greatly distort the multiple paid. One common approach to this problem is to normalize earnings, which typically involves the calculation of a full cycle (e.g., five-year) average operating margin (operating earnings divided by sales). The latest income statement is then recalculated as though the average operating margin had been in effect, rather than the actual one for that period.

Normalization must be used with care, however. For one thing, it is obviously based on counterfactual assumptions. For another, it depends critically on a variability in margins that is cyclical and not secular. Thus, if the industry under scrutiny is in fact in a long-term decline, it is misleading to assume that margins achieved in the past will, on average, be achieved again. Finally, a buyer will always pay less if the company is presently riding the cycle down than if the cycle is turning up, even if the seller insists that "it will all average out." This is because, in the going-down case, the strong cash flows associated with the peak of the cycle are furthest away from the acquisition date, and the uncertainties of their timing and magnitude are greatest.

[b] Book Value Multiples. Although book value (total common stockholders' equity) is an accurate accounting measure of the historical cost of the investments made by a company, it is unlikely to have a meaningful relationship to acquisition value.

There are, however, industries where book value is a meaningful valuation technique: those industries where a company's book value plays a role in determining future profitability. For example, in rate-of-return regulated industries, such as telephone, electric, and gas utilities, a company's future earnings are limited to a defined return on the company's equity. In such cases, book value plays a major role in determining acquisition value.

Another example is financial institutions such as banks, insurance companies, and securities firms. In these industries, the balance sheet values of most assets and liabilities are reasonably close to market values, so that book value represents a sort of liquidation value. Because such institutions typically have a franchise value in excess of what would be realizable in a liquidation, they are usually sold for a premium to book value that is much more systematic than any multiple of earnings. Column 5 in Figure 1-6 presents book value multiples paid in commercial banking mergers in 1991.

A variation on this technique that compares prices paid for companies with their replacement cost book values is often used. The concept involves revaluing all of a company's assets and liabilities to replacement cost or market value, and making the corresponding adjustment to book value. Analysis would then center on the premium (or discount) paid relative to replacement value in a series of comparable transactions.

[c] Cash Flow Multiples. In some industries, so-called cash flow multiples are a common form of valuation. It is important, however, to define the term "cash flow" in this context. Accountants and stock market analysts typically refer to cash flow as meaning "cash flow from operations": net income plus noncash charges (depreciation, amortization of intangibles, and deferred tax expense). This value is the denominator of a cash flow multiple. It is primarily in industries where cash flow from operations is close to the free cash flow of the DCF analysis (i.e., minimal required ongoing investment in working capital and plant and equipment) that cash flow multiples tend to be useful.

What industries are these? Typically, they are industries that undertake project-type investments (e.g., real estate and oil and gas). In these industries, massive amounts of capital tend to be invested initially (e.g., building an office complex or finding and developing a well), after which a steady stream of earnings and operating cash flows results, with relatively small investments required to maintain them. To the extent that companies in such industries spend massive amounts of capital year after year, they are investing in new projects that are not required to maintain the stream of cash flows from existing projects. Therefore, multiples of cash flow from operations can be a relatively accurate guide to the value of such companies if the value of assets and projects that are not yet past the start-up point is excluded.

[5] Premium Over Market Trading Value

When an acquisition candidate is publicly traded, the market price of the stock is very important to the determination of a feasible acquisition price. Clearly, the buyer must pay a premium to market; otherwise no shareholder would tender his shares. How much of a premium is required? The answer depends on the attitude of the company's management (friendly or hostile to the acquiror) and the regulatory climate.

Before the Williams Act was passed in 1969, acquirors were typically able to buy companies successfully at premiums of 32 percent above the "unaffected" market price. (It is important to examine trading values that prevailed 30 to 60 days in advance of an acquisition announcement to be sure that the stock was not affected by acquisition rumors.) In that unregulated period, tender offers took place in very brief time spans, usually a matter of days, which did not allow target company management to do anything other than capitulate.

Under the Williams Act, much longer periods were mandated for tender offers; for example, a bidder now cannot purchase shares until four weeks after commencement

FIGURE 1-7

Average Acquisition Premium Offered Over Unaffected Market (1978–1992)

	Successful Bid	Unsuccessful Bid	Success Rate
Friendly bidder (agreed transaction)	53%	50%	81%
Hostile and unsolicited bidder	49	48	41

Note: Through August 31, 1992.

of the offer. These longer time periods allow management greater flexibility in seeking a higher price through negotiation, litigation, or by finding a competing bidder willing to pay more (a white knight). In this era, acquisition premiums have increased to an average level of about 50 percent.

Figure 1-7 reflects the average premiums to market offered by successful and unsuccessful bidders in hostile and friendly acquisitions. As expected, the success rate for hostile bidders is much lower than for friendly bidders. It would appear that target shareholders receive essentially full value for their companies whether a transaction is friendly or hostile. Tactically, it is valuable for a bidder to position a proposal as a friendly one rather than a hostile one due to the higher chances of success. Market trading values are also useful as a benchmark in calculating the value of a privately held company or division. If a seller wishes to divest such a company, one alternative would be to evaluate how much might be realized in a secondary public offering. Assuming that such an offering is feasible, the trading value of the shares in the company represents a minimum level of value that the seller should be willing to accept. Conversely, a buyer may not be willing to pay more than the fully distributed trading value of such a company, plus a reasonable acquisition premium, because that is the price at which other alternatives might be available in the market.

[6] Liquidation and Replacement Values

Two other valuation benchmarks that buyers and sellers look to are the liquidation and replacement values of a company. Liquidation value represents the amount of proceeds that could be realized by a stockholder if a company ceased operations, if all assets were sold at prevailing market prices, and if all liabilities and tax obligations were satisfied. Replacement value, on the other hand, represents the cost that would be incurred if one tried to replicate all of the assets and liabilities of a company by building them or purchasing them on the market. Broadly speaking, liquidation value represents a minimum value for a company, because the liquidation alternative is always available to its owner, whereas replacement value represents a maximum value for a company, the point at which an acquiror would build rather than buy.

In practice, the replacement value concept is awkward. What does it mean to build the equivalent of a 10-year-old plant with outmoded technology and capacities? What does it mean to replace a strong brand name and customer base? The best thing to

FIGURE 1-8

Sample Calculation of Liquidation and Replacement Values

	Book Value	Liquidation Value		Replacement Value	
		Amount	Comment	Amount	Comment
Assets					
Cash	$ 50	$ 50	100% of book	$ 50	100% of book
Accounts receivable	100	90	90% of book	100	100% of book
Inventory	80	56	70% of book	80	100% of book
Prepaid expenses	20	—	0% of book	20	100% of book
Total current assets	$250	$196		$250	
Net plant and equipment	$300	$150	Distress sale value	$500	Replacement cost
Investment in Hi-Tech Industries, Inc.	10	200	Hidden asset	200	Hidden asset
Goodwill	60	—	No value	90	Franchise value
Total assets	$620	$546		$1,040	
Liabilities					
Current liabilities	$150	$150	100% of book	$150	100% of book
Long-term debt	100	100	Redemption value	90	Market value
Deferred taxes	40	—	Separate tax calculation	—	No deferred taxes at start-up
Unfunded pension liability	—	20	Termination value	—	No pension liability on start-up
Total liabilities	$290	$270		$240	
Taxes on liquidation	—	50		—	
Net value to stockholders	$330	$226	Liquidation value	$800	Replacement value

do is guess at the acquisition values of such items. Liquidation value is much more straightforward because it is a realistic alternative for most companies.

Figure 1-8 represents a sample analysis of liquidation and replacement value. The methodology is straightforward; each asset and liability should be revalued to market value (which may differ between the liquidation and replacement alternatives), and any additional "hidden" assets or liabilities not reflected in the balance sheet should be added or subtracted. For liquidation values, taxes must be paid on the difference between realized proceeds and the tax basis of each asset. The calculation of capital gain, recapture, and ordinary income tax liabilities, or the avoidance thereof, resulting from the liquidation is a technical subject not addressed here.

[7] Excess Assets and Liabilities

The previous subsections have shifted back and forth between valuation techniques based on periodic flows (earnings and cash flows) and those based on momentary positions (balance sheets). No single technique captures all of the others; an integrated picture of a company's value must be built based on all the techniques. An important requirement for integrating the values derived from the various techniques is to determine what elements of value any given technique leaves out, and to try to assess those items separately.

For example, assume that a company has a $10 million operating profit each year ($6 million after tax), and the appropriate P/E multiple is 10. The initial value estimate is $60 million. However, assuming there is also $5 million in excess cash on the balance sheet, not necessary to the business, as long as the interest earned on that cash is not already included in the $6 million profit figure, the company is actually worth $5 million more, or $65 million. If there is an unfunded vested pension liability of $3 million, that amount (adjusted for taxes) would reduce the value. In general, if there are excess assets or liabilities of a company that play no part in determining the earnings or cash flows on which the basic valuation is made, such assets and liabilities must be separately added to (or subtracted from) the basic value estimate.

1.03 FINANCING AN ACQUISITION

Competitive acquisition markets and ready availability of financing have typically allowed sellers to demand, and receive, payment in cash for most acquisitions. Transactions today deviate from cash payment only when an alternative form of consideration can achieve a superior result for both parties. The driving factors for noncash payment are principally taxes, accounting, regulatory requirements, contingent payments, and financing ability. Each factor is discussed in the following sections, along with the payment medium it leads to.

[1] Obtaining Tax Deferrals

If a seller has a low tax basis in the business to be sold, a cash transaction would impose a high tax cost on the seller and might ultimately deter him from consummating the sale. There are well-established means of deferring the recognition of tax gain on the sale of a business, providing the seller receives equity (common or preferred) in the acquiring company.

[2] Obtaining Pooling Accounting

The pooling of interests method of accounting can often have favorable effects on the reported earnings per share (EPS) of an acquiror. This is particularly true when the target is being acquired for a high multiple of its earnings since, in the absence of pooling treatment, the acquiror would probably face significant dilution to EPS owing to the amortization of goodwill created by the acquisition. A fundamental requirement of a pooling transaction, however, is that the merger be for common stock of the acquiror.

[3] Meeting Minimum Capital Requirements

In certain regulated industries, such as banking, thrift institutions, and utilities, regulators require minimum levels of equity capital for industry participants. Such regulation can force buyers to issue equity as part of the transaction in order to obtain approval for the transaction, or to avoid an unacceptable downgrade in credit rating.

[4] Setting Contingent Payments

Occasionally in a transaction, the parties will have difficulty in coming to a mutually acceptable price because of an identifiable difference of opinion (e.g., the performance of a newly patented product or the amount to be recovered in a pending lawsuit). In such cases, the buyer and seller can sometimes bridge the price gap by agreeing on a contingent payment as part of the purchase price. When the contingency is resolved, the contingent payment can be made to the seller based on the outcome. Contingent payment arrangements can pose problems, however, when the sellers are the thousands of shareholders of a public company. In such cases, the buyer may issue contingent payment certificates, which are publicly traded until they are redeemed or expire.

[5] Difficulty Obtaining Financing

Traditionally, the principal reason for a seller to accept noncash consideration from a buyer is that, for some reason, no buyer can obtain sufficient financing to pay cash. Typically, this might involve an extremely large acquisition, or an acquisition by a buyer with limited financial resources (such as a management-led buyout). Sellers have then been forced to accept some unusual forms of securities (often referred to as wallpaper), such as highly subordinated debt and preferred stock, or even securities that will not pay cash interest or dividends for several years. When issued directly to selling stockholders, such securities typically lack liquidity and sell for deep discounts.

The extensive development of new-issue markets in high-yield securities in the 1980s greatly reduced the need to burden selling stockholders with wallpaper securities. Except for very large (several billion dollars or more) and relatively small (under $30 million) transactions, the high-yield markets have the capacity to finance many acquisitions that are sensibly priced in terms of underlying cash flow.

1.04 FEDERAL INCOME TAX ASPECTS OF ACQUISITIONS

Federal income taxes can have important effects on the parties to an acquisition transaction, and therefore must be carefully considered. There are two principal issues that must be resolved: (1) whether the selling shareholders are going to pay a tax on the gain they have realized upon sale (i.e., taxable versus tax-free transaction) and (2) whether the transaction should be designed to trigger a corporate level of tax based on the gain embedded in the assets.

[1] Taxable and Tax-Free Transactions

The IRC provides that in carefully defined circumstances, an acquisition can be accomplished without triggering income tax liability on the part of the selling shareholders. Such transactions are technically referred to as tax-free reorganizations and, broadly speaking, include the following types of acquisitions. (For clarity, the acquiror is X, the target is Y, and S is a dummy subsidiary of X that exists for the purpose of consummating the transaction.)

- *A reorganization (merger).* Y merges into X under state law, and the former shareholders of Y retain a continuity of interest in the new XY corporation (i.e., at least 40 percent to 50 percent of the aggregate consideration paid for Y consists of equity securities, preferred or common, of X).

- *B reorganization (stock purchase).* X purchases at least 80 percent or more of the voting stock of Y, using only voting stock of X in payment.

- *C reorganization (asset purchase).* Y transfers substantially all of its assets, with or without Y's liabilities, to X in exchange for voting stock of X.

- *(a)(2)(D) reorganization (forward triangular merger).* Y merges into S. X retains 100 percent of the ownership of S. Y's former shareholders receive equity securities in X in sufficient quantity (40 percent to 50 percent) to satisfy the continuity-of-interest test.

- *(a)(2)(E) reorganization (reverse triangular merger).* S merges into Y. X receives all of the voting securities of Y as a consequence of the merger. Y's former shareholders receive solely voting stock in X.

Probably the most commonly used structures for tax-free acquisitions are the last two triangular mergers, because they are generally more flexible than the other forms, do not commingle the assets of the target with the assets of the acquiror, and generally do not require approval by the shareholders of the acquiror. The reverse triangular merger, however, is more restrictive in that it must be accomplished "solely for voting stock." (Technically, this applies only to the first 80 percent of shares acquired, but it is a rare occasion when this in practice does not mean all shares.) Therefore, the most common type of triangular merger is the forward merger, in which equity securities of the acquiror (voting or nonvoting, preferred or common) may be used for as low as 40 percent of the aggregate acquisition price.

What happens to the selling shareholders in a tax-free reorganization? Generally speaking, if a shareholder receives an equity security in the acquiror, he maintains carryover basis in the new security. If he receives cash or debt, he owes a capital tax on his gain. If he receives a mixture, however, he may have dividend treatment the cash portion. This is a complex area, best addressed by tax experts.

Recognition of gain or loss by shareholders will have no tax impact company. Typically, the target's tax basis in its assets will remain the the fact that the assets may be written up for accounting purposes. In a tion, the acquiror may step up the tax basis of the assets in the target election under Section 338(g) of the IRC. In this event, however, the a corporate tax measured by the difference between the tax basis i their fair market value. As a result, a 338 election is rarely justified has significant net operating losses.

[2] Subsidiary Divestitures and Section 355 Structures

In recent years, companies have often elected to undergo restructurings that involve the disposition of major lines of business, but not "substantially all assets" and that therefore are not eligible for "C" reorganization treatment. An important issue in such cases is whether the disposition can be completed in a tax-free or tax-deferred manner.

Section 355 of the IRC allows a company to distribute a subsidiary to its stockholders in two principal manners: (1) a spin-off, wherein the shares in the subsidiary are distributed as a pro rata dividend to the company's common stockholders, or (2) a split-off, wherein one or more stockholders of the company exchange their shares for shares in the subsidiary, on a non–pro rata basis.

Section 355 transactions are subject to some very significant restrictions requiring both the distributing company and the subsidiary to have conducted an active trade or business for five years preceding the date of the transaction, and not to have been acquired during that period. The distribution transaction must transfer at least 80 percent control of the subsidiary from the company to its stockholders. In addition, the transaction must be supported by a nontax corporate business purpose.

The principal difficulty with Section 355 as a general tax-saving device for divestitures is that the divesting company cannot arrange to sell the subsidiary to a third party. Hence, it is difficult to realize an acquisition premium for the subsidiary until well after the subsidiary shares have been issued to the distributing company's shareholders. In addition, the distributing company receives no cash consideration for its equity in the subsidiary and is effectively shrinking its capitalization in the process.

Spin-offs can be used as a divestiture technique in cases where an all-stock transaction is contemplated. In this transaction, referred to as a reverse spin-off, a company would contribute all of the businesses that are not targeted for sale into a new company. The new company would be spun off to shareholders and the "old company" would be acquired in an all-stock transaction. This transaction requires careful tax planning.

[3] Stock Sale Versus Asset Sale

Suppose X Corporation has a subsidiary, S Corporation, which it wishes to sell for cash in a taxable transaction. Further assume that X's basis in the stock of S is $50 million, while S's underlying assets (A) have a basis of $30 million. A buyer has offered X a purchase price of $200 million for S. Should X sell the stock of S or the assets, A?

On the surface, it would appear that X would be better off selling the stock of S, since the taxable gain in this approach of $150 million ($200 − $50 stock basis) is $20 million less than the gain on an asset sale of $170 million ($200 − $30 asset basis). This conclusion, however, would be incorrect. In the case of the asset purchase, the buyer would obtain a higher basis in S's depreciable assets than if it bought stock. So, if the assets had a depreciable life of five years, the asset buyer would enjoy additional depreciation of $34 million annually (($200 − $30) ÷ 5 years). As a result, the buyer would be willing to pay more for the assets than the stock. Both parties would be better off if they used an asset-sale structure and the buyer increased the price so that the seller's net proceeds in an asset purchase would be greater than or equal to a stock sale. For example, if the buyer paid $215 for the assets, the after-tax proceeds for the seller would be $152 ($215 − 30 = $185 gain × 0.34 = $63 tax) versus $149 in after-tax proceeds on a $200 sale of stock.

In addition, it is usually possible to obtain the tax benefits of an asset-sale structure while actually transferring legal title to the stock by making an election provided for in Section 338(h)(10). This can be especially useful in cases where the subsidiary has assets or obligations that are difficult to transfer to a buyer without a third-party consent (e.g., licenses, contracts, or debts).

The decision to sell stock or assets also has critical significance when selling a high-basis business. Recent Treasury regulations make it extremely difficult to claim a tax deduction on the sale of a subsidiary's stock at a loss. Losses on sales of assets are fully deductible.

1.05 ACCOUNTING TREATMENT OF ACQUISITIONS AND PRO FORMA ANALYSIS

One of the most important, and most misunderstood, reasons behind the decision to proceed or to reject an acquisition opportunity is the accounting impact the acquisition will have on the acquiror. More precisely, managers ask, "What effect will the acquisition have on my reported earnings per share?" and "Will my credit rating be affected?"

Efficient-market economists are inclined to argue that the market sees through accounting conventions to the underlying reality of an investment. This may be true, but if an otherwise attractive acquisition can be structured in two ways, one offering 30 percent initial earnings dilution and another offering only 8 percent, a good manager will choose the latter structure. Managers are very sensitive to an acquisition's impact on reported earnings, and they believe that the market expects them to behave in a manner that does not lead to drastic earnings declines. This is not to say that all acquisitions that improve earnings are good. The point is that few acquisitions that seriously impair earnings are feasible, even if desirable for other reasons.

There are two principal methods of accounting for acquisitions of control of a company. They are the pooling method and the purchase method. The pooling method applies exclusively to acquisitions using the acquiror's common stock. The purchase method, which is far more prevalent, applies to all other forms of acquisitions. The pooling method is the simpler of the two.

[1] Pooling Method Accounting

The theory behind pooling accounting is that the two shareholder groups of the merged companies have fused their respective stakes, with a view to sharing jointly the benefits and risks of the combined venture thereafter. This may sound obvious, but it has very important consequences for the rules that determine when an acquisition must be treated as a pooling. The principal requirements of generally accepted accounting principles (GAAP) for when pooling treatment can, and must, be used are as follows:

1. *No subsidiaries.* Each of the combining companies must have been an autonomous corporation (not a subsidiary or a division of another corporation) for two years prior to announcement of the merger.

2. *Mutual independence.* No merging company may control more than 10 percent of the other prior to merger.

3. *Timely completion.* The plan of merger must be consummated within one year, and all in one event.

4. *90 percent rule.* At consummation, the acquiror must issue its own voting common stock for at least 90 percent of the outstanding stock of the acquiree.

5. *No equity changes.* Neither merging company may have changed the interests of its voting common stock for two years prior to announcement of the merger in contemplation of the pooling (no recapitalizations, unusual dividends, or the acquisition of a significant amount of treasury stock prior to the transaction, for example).

6. *Repurchases.* Stock repurchases after the pooling are limited to "normal" amounts, but stock may be repurchased for the purpose of effecting another purchase or business combination.

7. *No voting realignments or restrictions.* Each shareholder's vote must remain proportionate to that of other shareholders in a combining company after the pooling. Shareholders in the combining companies may not have their voting rights restricted in any way.

8. *No contingent earnouts.* The consideration exchanged generally must be fixed at the transaction consummation date and no contingent consideration agreements based on future earnings or share price levels can exist.

9. *No plan to dispose of significant assets.* The combined enterprise cannot, at the time of the merger, plan to sell off or otherwise divest a significant operation or asset within a two-year period following the merger.

10. *No other financial arrangements.* The combined enterprise cannot enter into other arrangements that in effect negate the exchange of equity securities.

Assuming that a transaction satisfies these strict requirements, a financial manager in the position of evaluating the transaction must determine its pro forma impact on the earnings and balance sheet of the acquiror.

Figure 1-9 offers a relatively simple example of the pooling of balance sheets. The pooling method is a very straightforward consolidation method: Balance sheets are simply added together, line by line. The only adjustment commonly arising is the elimination of any intercompany investments, which are treated as treasury stock. The income statement effect of a pooling is also simply calculated, as shown in Figure 1-10. Comparable income statement items, down to net income, are simply added (assuming that each company prepares its statement according to the same accounting principles).

The key statistics for merger analysis can be derived from the combined income statement and balance sheet. The first is pro forma EPS. While earnings in the aggregate are additive in a pooling, the number of shares outstanding after the combination depends on the exchange ratio of the merger (i.e., the number of shares issued by the acquiror for each share of acquiree stock). Thus, in Figure 1-10, if acquiror A has 40 million shares outstanding, acquiree B has 8.3 million shares outstanding, and A offers an exchange ratio of 2:1, then the combined AB will have 56.6 million shares outstanding after the acquisition. As Figure 1-10 shows, EPS of A are reduced from $1.20 per share with no transaction to $1.02 if the transaction takes place. This is dilution: EPS are diluted by 15 percent, pro forma, as a result of the acquisition. Ordinarily, managers will examine combined forecasted EPS for several years into the future to determine when, if ever, EPS dilution disappears and pickup (the opposite of dilution) emerges.

FIGURE 1-9

Pooling of Interests Example: Balance Sheets

	Prior to Merger A	Prior to Merger B	Merged A + B
Assets			
Current assets	$200	$100	$300
Net plant and equipment	200	100	300
Goodwill	100	50	150
Total assets	$500	$250	$750
Liabilities and Shareholders' Equity			
Current liabilities	$ 50	$ 30	$ 80
Long-term debt	100	100	200
Deferred taxes	100	40	140
Total liabilities	$250	$170	$420
Common equity	250	80	330
Total liabilities and shareholders' equity	$500	$250	$750

Note: Dollars in millions.

If a transaction promises no pickup for the foreseeable future, there are probably serious questions as to either the price or the financial structure of the transaction.

Credit statistics (i.e., debt ratio, interest coverage) are the other ratios to be examined. The financial planner must know just how much financial flexibility is being gained or lost as a result of an acquisition. Figure 1-10 calculates the "before and after" credit statistics. In a pooling, because the acquiror is issuing equity, the credit position of the combined entity is never worse than that of the weaker party to the transaction. Nevertheless, the acquisition of a much weaker company could impair the credit rating of a strong acquiror. As a general rule, however, poolings create the least concern for the credit position of the acquiror.

[2] Purchase Method Accounting

If an acquisition does not fall into the pooling category, it must be treated as a purchase. The theory behind purchase accounting is that an investment has taken place on the part of an acquiror, and that the investment must be recorded at the acquiror's full cost. The cost of an investment must be allocated among the assets acquired as follows:

1. Adjust each acquiree balance sheet account to its fair value. Under Statement of Financial Accounting Standards No. 109, deferred taxes must now be shown at their projected undiscounted value, based on current tax rates.

2. Any excess of purchase price over net fair value (fair value of acquiree's assets minus fair value of liabilities, including any liabilities attributable to the target's unfunded pension and postretirement medical benefit plans) is recorded as goodwill.

FIGURE 1-10

Pooling of Interests Example: Income Statements

| | Prior to Merger | | Merged |
	A	B	A + B
Sales	$300	$120	$420
Cost of sales	(100)	(50)	(150)
Selling general and administrative expense	(100)	(40)	(140)
Interest expense	(20)	(14)	(34)
Income before taxes	$ 80	$ 16	$ 96
Income taxes	(32)	(6)	(38)
Net income	$ 48	$ 10	$ 58
EPS	$1.20	$1.20	$1.02
Dividends per share	$0.50	$0.30	$0.50
Number of shares outstanding (millions)	40.0	8.3	56.6
Market Assumptions			
Stock price per share	$ 12	$ 24	$ 12
P/E ratio	10	20	11.8
Total market value	$480	$200	$680
Dividend yield	4.2%	1.3%	4.2%
Credit Statistics			
Long-term debt capitalization (see Figure 1-9)	29%	56%	38%
Interest coverage	5.0	2.1	3.8

Transaction Assumptions

A acquires B.

Each share of B is converted into two shares of A (i.e., exchange ratio is 2A:1B).

Note: Dollars in millions, except per-share amounts.

3. If the purchase price is below net fair value, noncurrent assets should be reduced proportionately. Negative goodwill is ordinarily not recorded.

4. Assuming the acquisition involved more than 50 percent of the target, the revalued target balance sheet is consolidated with that of the acquiror. However, the revaluation takes place only to the extent of the percentage interest purchased by the acquiror.

The acquisition and the revaluation process have implications for the earnings of the combined companies beyond the mere sum of the independent earnings streams:

1. Revaluations that alter the recorded value of depreciable assets of the acquiree must be amortized against future earnings according to the remaining life of the asset.

2. Goodwill must be amortized against future earnings over a period not to exceed 40 years.

3. Revaluations of liabilities (most commonly, bond discount or premium) must also be amortized into earnings over an appropriate period.

4. In each case, it is important to ascertain the tax effect of the particular adjustment to earnings. For example, goodwill incurred is not currently tax deductible and therefore reduces net income directly. Recent U.S. tax proposals would permit a tax deduction for goodwill amortization in certain situations. Additional depreciation charges may also be nondeductible if the transaction is not structured as an asset purchase.

Figure 1-11 is a self-explanatory example of the balance sheet adjustments associated with purchase accounting. The principal noteworthy facts of the example are that the unfunded vested pension liability is recorded as a liability, and deferred taxes are adjusted by the book/tax differences created by the purchase accounting process.

Figure 1-12 shows the corresponding combined income statements for a purchase. Each balance sheet revaluation creates a related income statement adjustment. The most important change, of course, is the interest on acquisition debt. Net income after the acquisition is less than that of the acquiror before the acquisition, and thus dilution takes place both in the aggregate and on a per-share basis. The credit impact of the transaction is also shown in the figure.

[3] Stock Price Impact

An interesting and useful analysis for both purchase and pooling transactions is to estimate the stock price impact the acquisition will have on the acquiror. If the acquiree is much smaller than the acquiror, the effect is usually minimal. On the other hand, a major acquisition can have a dramatic effect on the stock market's perception of a company.

An elementary fallacy is to assume that if a high P/E company acquires a low P/E company, the acquiror's P/E will be applied to the acquiree's earnings, thus boosting the value of the combined entity above the sum of the values of each company separately. At least in recent years, the market has not been fooled by such transparent devices. In reality, if there are no synergies or other improvements made as a result of an acquisition, the combination of two unrelated companies can often reduce the value of the combined enterprise below the sum of the values of the two taken independently, because the market has difficulty in assessing the true nature of the combined businesses. This is generally known in financial circles as the conglomerate discount.

One way to analyze the effect of an acquisition on a company's stock price is to calculate a weighted average P/E for the combined company based on the pre-acquisition P/Es of the two merging companies. The weights to use typically are the percentage contributions of each company to the pre-interest operating earnings of the combined enterprise. The weighted average P/E is applied to the pro forma EPS to generate a hypothetical stock price.

1.06 LEGAL AND REGULATORY ASPECTS OF MERGERS

In the United States, corporations are private entities established at the behest of their founding shareholders, and governed in the context of a system that includes the following:

- A body of state statutory and judicial corporation law that enables a corporation's formation, recognizes its rights as a legal entity, and offers default rules for internal governance.

FIGURE 1-11

Purchase Accounting Examples: Balance Sheets

	Prior to Merger		Adjust B to Fair Value	B as Adjusted	Purchase Price Allocation	Combined A and B
	A	B				
Assets						
Current assets	$200	$100	10[a]	$110	(100)[h]	$210
Net plant and equipment	200	100	50[b]	150	—	350
Goodwill	100	50	(50)[c]	—	130[i]	230
Total assets	$500	$250		$260		$790
Liabilities and Shareholders' Equity						
Current liabilities	$ 50	$ 30	—	$ 30	—	$ 80
Long-term debt	100	100	(10)[d]	90	100[h]	290
Pension liability	—	—	5[e]	5	—	5
Deferred taxes	100	40	25[f]	65	—	165
Total liabilities	$250	$170		$190		$540
Common equity	250	80	(10)[g]	70	(70)	250
Total liabilities and shareholders' equity	$500	$250		$260		$790

Transaction Assumptions

A acquires B.

Each share of B is exchanged for $24 cash.

Total transaction size is $200, which A raises by issuance of $100 in long-term debt and $100 in excess cash.

Since the transaction is a stock purchase, A retains B's old tax basis in its assets.

Note: Dollars in millions.

[a] Since B is on LIFO, B's balance sheet understates the value of B's inventory by $10.

[b] B's fixed assets are worth 50 percent more as a result of long-term inflation effects.

[c] Goodwill incurred by B in its own past acquisitions has no identifiable value and therefore is eliminated.

[d] B's outstanding fixed-rate debt is worth less today because of general interest rate rises. It therefore must be revalued at a discount.

[e] B's unfunded vested pension liability is added.

[f] B's deferred tax liabilities are increased by the tax effect of timing differences arising from valuation adjustments a, b, d, and e. The net valuation adjustment is a debit of $65, which creates an additional deferred tax provision of $25 (at a 38 percent tax rate).

[g] This is a balancing adjustment reflecting the net effect on the fair value of B's common equity.

[h] Transaction price of $200 is financed by $100 in excess cash and $100 in new long-term debt.

[i] Goodwill incurred is aggregate price paid ($200) less fair value of net assets acquired ($70).

FIGURE 1-12

Purchase Accounting Example: Income Statements

	Projected Income Statements in Absence of Merger		Purchase Accounting Adjustments	Combined A + B
	A	B		
Sales	$300.0	$120.0	(10.0)[a]	$410.0
Cost of sales	(100.0)	(50.0)	8.4[b]	(158.4)
Selling, general, and administrative expense	(100.0)	(40.0)	1.6[c]	(141.6)
Interest expense	(20.0)	(14.0)	11.0[d]	(45.0)
Income before taxes	$ 80.0	$ 16.0		$ 65.0
Income taxes	(32.0)	(6.0)	(11.8)[e]	(26.2)
Net income	$ 48.0	$ 10.0		$ 38.8
EPS	$ 1.20	$ 1.20		$ 0.97
Dividends per share	$ 0.50	$ 0.30		$ 0.50
Number of shares outstanding (millions)	40.0	8.3		40.0
Market Assumptions				
Stock price per share	$ 12.0	$ 24.0		$ 12.0
P/E ratio	10	20		12.4
Total market value	$480.0	$200.0		$480.0
Dividend yield	4.2	1.3		4.2
Credit Statistics				
Debt ratio (see Figure 1-11)	29%	56%		54%
Interest coverage	5.0	2.1		2.4

Transaction Assumptions

A acquires B.

Each share of B is exchanged for $24 cash.

Total transaction size is $200, which A raises from $100 in excess cash and $100 in new long-term debt.

Since the transaction is a stock purchase, A retains B's old tax basis in its assets.

Note: Dollars in millions, except per-share amounts.

[a] Interest income forgone on $100 of excess cash (at 10 percent).

[b] Increased depreciation on B's fixed assets' $50 increase, amortized over remaining life of six years.

[c] Net change in B's goodwill amortization, assumes prior amortization of $1.7 per year and 40-year life for amortization of new goodwill ($130).

[d] Increased expense: $100 new debt, financed at 10 percent. In addition, amortization of debt discount will generate another $1 of interest expense.

[e] Income tax effect of all purchase accounting adjustments other than goodwill at 40 percent.

In choosing a state of incorporation, a founding group of shareholders chooses that body of law that best suits the needs of their corporation and its shareholders.

- Articles of incorporation, or the corporate charter, which define the basic rules of corporate governance and supplement or override the default provisions of state law.
- Bylaws that provide rules of governance for the board of directors, in some detail.

This section describes the legal mechanics of a business combination of two Delaware corporations, which is perhaps the single most common type of combination. Other state laws governing combinations generally parallel the Delaware rules.

[1] Mergers and Consolidations

The most basic form of combination is achieved through a merger or consolidation. In a merger, two corporations, A and B, combine as follows:

1. The directors of corporations A and B approve an agreement of merger, which specifies, among other things:
   - The terms and conditions of the merger;
   - Designation of one corporation, e.g., A, as the survivor;
   - The number of shares of A or other consideration (e.g., cash) into which each share of B is to be converted as a result of the merger; and
   - The timing and means by which the merger is to be carried out.
2. The shareholders of each corporation hold meetings at which the proposed merger is approved. The percentage of each corporation's outstanding shares that must approve the merger is 50 percent plus one vote, unless the charter specifies a higher percentage.
3. The surviving corporation files a certificate of merger with the secretary of state of Delaware.
4. As a result of filing, B ceases to exist and each share of B becomes a right to receive the consideration provided in the agreement of merger.
5. All assets and liabilities of B by operation of law become assets and liabilities of A, the survivor.

A consolidation is simply a merger in which there is no designated survivor but, rather, a newly created corporation that represents the combined A and B.

In the merger process just outlined, the most cumbersome aspect tends to be the requirement that each corporation obtain a vote of its shareholders to approve the merger. In addition to certain state law requirements, the New York Stock Exchange (NYSE) requires shareholder approval if common stock or convertible securities are to be issued in a transaction (other than a public offering) where such securities will have voting power equal to 20 percent or more of the voting power outstanding before the issuance of such securities or the stock to be issued will equal or exceed 20 percent of the common stock outstanding before the issuance. Therefore, an acquiror, A, planning to use its equity as consideration in a merger, must carefully assess whether it will need approval from its shareholders in order to complete the acquisition.

On the side of the target, B, the shareholder approval requirement is more difficult to circumvent in the context of a merger. If the target, B, is a subsidiary of another company, the formalities of a public shareholder meeting can be avoided because the directors of *B*'s parent can approve a merger of *B*. If *B* is publicly held, however, the only real alternative open to the acquiror is a purchase of stock, typically by means of a tender offer. A tender offer, however, does not usually garner 100 percent of the target's stock, and therefore is usually followed by a merger to squeeze out the laggard or nontendering shareholders. In many states, if 90 percent of the shares are acquired, the merger can be effected without shareholder approval.

Some interesting factors come into play if *A*, the acquiror, owns a majority of *B* before the merger, as in a merger following a tender offer. *A* is then a controlling shareholder and controls the board of *B*. This type of transaction is generally referred to as a squeeze-out merger, because it represents a majority shareholder squeezing out the remaining shareholders from their position of ownership in *B*. While squeeze-out mergers serve many useful purposes, there is a great potential for unfair treatment of the minority. That is because *A*, as a majority shareholder, is assured of success in the vote among *B*'s shareholders to approve the merger. Moreover, if *A* owns more than 90 percent of *B*, *B* need not even hold a shareholder meeting to permit *A* to merge out the minority under the short-form merger laws of many states (including Delaware). To assure that the consideration offered is fair, most states impose some substantive fairness requirements and mandate appraisal rights for dissenting shareholders in such situations. Where *A* has been a controlling shareholder for a substantial period of time, the Securities and Exchange Commission (SEC) also requires extensive disclosure of the nature of such transactions under its Rule 13e-3.

[2] Tender Offers

A tender offer is a solicitation made broadly to shareholders of a target company requesting tenders of shares for purchase by the bidder. The consideration offered is usually cash; if it is another security, such as stock of the bidder, the offer is referred to as an exchange offer. Tender offers may be partial offers (seeking less than 100 percent control of the target) or offers for all shares (seeking 100 percent control).

A bidder may also establish conditions under which it will not purchase tendered shares, such as if fewer than 50 percent of the outstanding shares are tendered or the target company's board fails to revoke a "poison pill" plan, and so forth. A tender offer seeking 100 percent of the shares with no minimum condition is referred to as an "any-and-all" offer.

Tender offers are extensively regulated by the SEC under the Williams Act. Some of the more important elements governed by these regulations are:

- *Prorationing*. In a partial tender offer, the offerer must accept all shares tendered on a pro rata basis from each shareholder. For example, if the bidder is seeking 50 percent of the target's shares, and 80 percent is tendered during the proration period, each tendering shareholder will have five eighths of his share taken up under the offer.

- *Withdrawal*. An offeror must allow tendering shareholders to withdraw their shares for the entire period the offer is open, including any extensions.

- *Minimum offer period*. Under current rules, a bidder must keep its offer open for a minimum of 20 business days.

- *Amendments*. A tender offer is required to remain open for 10 business days after a change in the percentage of shares being sought or the consideration being offered.

FIGURE 1-13

Sample Timetable for Any-And-All Cash Tender Offer

Date	Event
D-5–D-1	Bidder *A* announces its intention to make a tender offer for target B at a specified price
D-day	Commencement of offer Tombstone advertisement of offer is published in national newspapers. Schedule 14D-1 is filed with SEC. Offer to Purchase and transmittal documents are mailed to shareholders. Filing is made for premerger anti-trust review of the offer under the Hart-Scott-Rodino Act.
D + 15 calendar days	Hart-Scott-Rodino Act waiting period expires unless government requests supplemental information, in which case waiting period expires 10 days after compliance.
D + 20 business days (D + 26 to 28 calendar days)	Offer expires at midnight, unless extended. Withdrawal rights expire along with the offer. Bidder commences purchase of tendered shares.
Thereafter	Assuming success, bidder and target prepare proxy statement for shareholders' meeting at which nontendered shares are merged out of existence. If bidder holds 90 percent of ownership, short-form merger process may be available (which eliminates the need for a target shareholder meeting).

- *Purchases outside the offer.* A bidder is prohibited from purchasing stock of the target during the tender offer except pursuant to the offer or upon its expiration.

Unlike a merger, a tender offer does not require the approval of the board of directors of the target corporation. Instead, the offer is made directly to the shareholders, the ultimate owners of the corporation. The tender offer is therefore the means of accomplishing a hostile takeover, in which the board and management of the target company oppose the acquisition. Tender offers are quite flexible, however, and can be used in friendly acquisitions as well. Where an acquiror is afraid of a competing offer, the tender offer presents the fastest route to ownership of the target, because no proxy statement is prepared and no shareholder vote need be obtained. A tender offer is also less risky than a merger, because if an acquiror does not obtain a majority vote in a merger, it has nothing. It must completely reinitiate the proxy solicitation to raise the price. However, if an acquiror makes a tender offer, and receives about 40 percent of the shares, it has the option of amending the offer by increasing the price, leaving it open for 10 business days, and potentially increasing the number of shares tendered to a majority. A typical tender offer timetable is shown in Figure 1-13.

[3] Asset Sales

The third principal method for effecting a business combination, the asset sale, is typically used when the business to be sold represents less than all of the businesses of a larger corporation (e.g., a single division). In some cases, the division's assets and liabilities are held in a separate subsidiary, in which case the only asset sold is the stock of the subsidiary. In the true asset sale, however, a buyer, *A*, agrees to buy specified assets and to assume specified liabilities of the seller, *B*. Because the only assets and liabilities transferred are those specifically agreed to in the purchase and sale agreement, that agreement becomes a critical document in the process. It often proves extremely difficult to negotiate the scope of the asset purchase agreement, especially when there are assets shared with other divisions of the seller, and where certain asset categories (e.g., inventory and receivables) can fluctuate significantly in amount prior to closing. In addition, many such sales require approval by third parties (e.g., secured lenders, other creditors, lessors, and holders of significant contracts), which will be transferred to the buyer as part of the sale. The combination of all of these factors causes asset sales to be the least preferred form of business combination. In pure outline, however, the concept is straightforward, and shareholder approval is often not necessary for either the buyer or the seller.

The steps involved in a typical asset sale are:

1. Buyer and seller reach agreement in principle with respect to the sale of a division. The agreement specifies broadly the price to be paid, principal terms and conditions of the transaction, and general principles for the determination of assets and liabilities to be transferred to buyer.

2. Buyer and seller negotiate and execute purchase and sale agreement.

3. Boards of buyer and seller approve purchase and sale agreement.

4. Buyer and seller file for antitrust clearance under the 1976 Hart-Scott-Rodino Antitrust Improvements Act (30-day waiting period).

5. Any necessary third-party waivers and consents (e.g., to *A*'s assumption of *B*'s obligations) are obtained.

6. Assets and liabilities of seller's division are transferred to buyer, and buyer makes payment, at closing.

[4] Antitrust Review

While antitrust factors generally do not affect the design or valuation of a merger, they can have an important effect on the success or failure of an acquisition attempt. The typical scenario is to determine in advance whether a proposed transaction is likely or unlikely to be challenged as a violation of the antitrust laws. If it is likely to be challenged, the proposal may either be dropped or substantially revised to include divestitures.

To assist businesses in planning mergers and acquisitions, the Department of Justice (DOJ) and the Federal Trade Commission (FTC) have published detailed guidelines, which can be applied to a given-fact situation, and which are intended to indicate how the agencies are likely to react to a given-merger proposal. In early 1992, the DOJ and FTC issued new Horizontal Merger Guidelines, significantly revising the DOJ's 1984 Merger Guidelines and the FTC's 1982 Statement Concerning Horizontal Mergers. The joint issuance of these Guidelines marks the first time the two federal antitrust agencies have formally subscribed to a single statement of horizontal merger enforcement policy. The new guidelines describe the framework that both agencies will use to analyze the antitrust legality of horizontal transactions (i.e., mergers, acquisitions, tender offers and joint ventures between and among competitors).

The principal factor involved in analyzing a horizontal merger (one between competitors in the same industry) is whether the transaction is likely to create or enhance market power, or to facilitate its exercise. For example, a merger is deemed to enhance market power if, as a result of the merger, the merged firm would be able to raise and maintain prices above the level that would exist if the market were competitive. To answer this question, the new guidelines provide a five-step analytical process. First, the agencies define the relevant markets affected by the transaction and determine whether the transaction would significantly increase concentration in a concentrated market. (The postmerger Herfindahl-Hirschman Index (HHI) is used to measure industry concentration. The HHI is calculated as the sum of the squares of the market shares of all producers in an industry. Thus, if an industry had three producers with shares of 60 percent, 30 percent, and 10 percent, the HHI would be $60^2 + 30^2 + 10^2 = 4,600$.) Second, if the transaction exceeds the guidelines' concentration thresholds, the agencies assess whether, in light of various market characteristics, the transaction is likely to facilitate coordinated and unilateral anticompetitive effects. Third, if anticompetitive effects appear likely, the agencies attempt to determine whether entry by new competitors would be timely, likely, and sufficient either to deter or to undermine these effects. Fourth, if such entry does not appear likely, the agencies examine any claims of efficiency gains that reasonably cannot be achieved by means other than the transaction. Fifth, the agencies assess whether either party to the transaction is likely to fail, causing its assets to exit the market, if the transaction is not consummated.

The 1992 guidelines do not explicitly cover nonhorizontal mergers. The standards for such mergers (which are rarely challenged) can be summarized as follows:

1. *Vertical mergers.* The DOJ will ordinarily not challenge vertical mergers (transactions involving companies in a customer-supplier relationship) unless it creates barriers to entry, facilitates collusion, or is designed to evade rate regulation.

2. *Conglomerate mergers.* Conglomerate mergers will ordinarily be challenged only if they involve the elimination of a potential entrant, and (a) the industry HHI exceeds 1,800; (b) entry is difficult; (c) there are fewer than three other potential entrants; and (d) the market share of the acquired firm exceeds 5 percent.

The DOJ and the FTC evaluate proposed mergers through a prenotification procedure enacted in 1976 under the Hart-Scott-Rodino Antitrust Improvements Act. The procedure requires parties to a merger or acquisition to file economic data once they have reached an acquisition agreement. The government is required to permit the transaction to proceed within 30 days after filing, unless it makes a request for supplemental information or takes action to oppose the transaction. In the case of a cash tender offer, the 30-day review period is shortened to 15 days.

1.07 HOSTILE TAKEOVERS AND DEFENSE

[1] Why Hostile Takeovers Occur

In the modern corporation, the separation of corporate ownership from corporate control is great, and for good reason. The providers of equity capital consist of individuals, who use the stock market as a high-return use of savings, and institutions, such as insurance companies, mutual funds, and pension funds, which have substantial financial assets requiring investment. Institutions hire professional portfolio managers, who aim to maximize their investment portfolios' values over relatively short periods. Portfolio managers and individual investors have a strong interest in the quality of management in each company in which they have invested because management's choice of policies and the implementation of them can greatly affect a company's value in the stock market. Portfolio managers and individual investors, however, have very little interest in actually heading a major corporation or directing the use of its physical assets and hired labor. In general, investors are relatively passive and shift their capital to those companies that appear to be adopting policies that generate the highest economic returns.

Corporate managers, on the other hand, have very substantial control over corporations and their policies, but often have very small ownership stakes in their companies. While the mandate of corporate management is to maximize the long-run value of the company, the separation of ownership and control permits managers to deviate somewhat from value maximization, resulting in opportunity costs identified by economists as "agency costs." Agency costs can be actual expenditures that are unnecessary or excessive, or they can represent the value of lost opportunities. For example, a manager might cause the expenditure of a large amount of funds on a monumental headquarters building, which he or she would not do if the funds employed were his own and not those of a diverse and somewhat distant shareholder body. More seriously, a manager can make fundamental errors of corporate policy if he or she ignores the guidance of the capital markets, guidance that an owner-manager can hardly avoid. For example, he or she might embark on a new-plant-expansion strategy involving the commitment of billions in capital when underutilized capacity already exists in the industry that can be purchased and renovated at a fraction of the cost. Or he or she might fail to adopt any clear strategy at all and, as a result of changing business conditions, find his or her company outflanked by the competition in a few years.

The capital markets serve to protect against corporate mismanagement in several ways. Poorly managed companies obtain a low stock price (i.e., a low P/E or price/book value ratio) relative to the industry. Such companies are thereby effectively denied access to additional equity capital, except at exorbitant cost and may become targets of opportunity for hostile takeovers. An acquiror that identifies a company with entrenched management and underutilized assets or skills can create substantial value by replacing that management with better operators. To do so, however, the acquiror must buy control of the company from its shareholders by offering the shareholders a premium to sell their shares. In so doing, the acquiror splits the value it will be creating with the existing owners of the company. An entrenched management that expects to be ousted after an unsolicited acquisition usually opposes the acquiror's efforts, and thus, the situation develops into a struggle for control, referred to as a hostile takeover attempt. In spite of its bad publicity, the hostile takeover has many redeeming virtues. In particular, the hostile takeover can do the following:

- Create new wealth in the hands of the shareholders of both the bidder and target companies

- Cause control over assets to be transferred to better managers (or at least to managers who perceive themselves as better and are willing to stake a great deal of money on it)

- Cause assets themselves to be shifted to higher and better uses on a large scale

- Equitably share the benefits of such better management or better use of assets with the selling stockholders

- Cause all corporate managers to focus attentively on adopting policies that will maximize their companies' stock prices, in order to avert hostile takeovers

- Induce greater accountability of management to shareholders

This analysis might be deemed the classical explanation for the hostile takeover. Its main defect is that it assumes target managements to be incompetent, or at least not very good at reading the signals of the capital and product markets. However, an acquiror may have many other good business reasons for advancing the acquisition proposal (e.g., business synergies, product line fit, and useful technology). The acquiror may wish to have the target management stay on, although if senior management departs, the acquisition would still be attractive. Cases like this still create important economic value, even if the value is unrelated to a change in management. The mere fact that some hostile takeovers involve situations in which a target company was rather well managed does not disprove the thesis that hostile takeovers create new wealth in the hands of bidder and target shareholders that, in the aggregate, did not exist before.

[2] Reasons for Defensive Measures

The previous discussion of the merits of hostile takeovers is not intended to imply that defensive measures on the part of target managers are inappropriate. Managers of all companies are pledged to act in a manner that, in their business judgment, is in the best interest of their shareholders. Even the manager whose only goal is to maximize his or her stockholders' wealth, when faced with an unsolicited offer, will employ some defensive tactics to obtain negotiating leverage on behalf of his or her numerous and unorganized shareholders. The appropriateness of a particular defensive action turns on the net gain that it is estimated to produce for target shareholders. That net gain is the probability-weighted increase in offer price resulting from the defensive action.

> EXAMPLE: Assume that target company T has received an unsolicited acquisition proposal at $25 per share. Prior to the proposal, the stock of T was trading in the marketplace at $20. The board of T believes that if it takes defensive action X, either the offeror or a third party will make an offer for T at $28 (70 percent probability) or all offers will be withdrawn (30 percent probability). The expected net gain resulting from taking action X therefore is
>
> Gain × probability of gain) − (loss × probability of loss) = ($28 − 25) (0.70) − ($25 − 20) (0.30) = $0.60
>
> Because there is a positive net gain, the board is justified in taking action X in spite of the risk it creates that the only offer in hand will be withdrawn.

In addition to a purely theoretical analysis of legitimate defensive measures, there are other reasons for a board of directors to reject or oppose an offer. Some are legitimate and some are not. ("Legitimacy" refers to commonly accepted reasons for a defensive action, especially reasons that are more likely than not to be accepted in a court of law reviewing a board's exercise of business judgment in taking defensive action. This summary is not intended to represent the state of law in any jurisdiction, however.)

Some legitimate motives for defensive actions include the following:

- Belief that target shareholders would realize greater value over time if they hold on to their stock instead of accepting a bidder's offer
- Belief that a higher offer can be obtained in the near future
- Belief that the bidder's offer is less than it appears, because it involves difficult-to-value securities, it is for less than all target shares, or it involves conditions that have a material risk of not being satisfied (e.g., regulatory approval)
- In situations where target shareholders would hold a continuing financial interest in the company, belief that the new management would impair the value of the company

Motives that probably do not support a business judgment to take defensive action, denying shareholders the power to decide to sell to a bidder, include the following:

- Desire of senior managers to retain their jobs, status, and perquisites
- Belief that the company should remain independent when shareholders will clearly be worse off over the long term than by accepting the offer

[3] Advance Preparation

The key to an effective takeover defense is advance preparation. There simply is not enough time, once a bid has been made, to prepare for all the actions that might be desirable in executing a good defense. Some of the best defenses that can be prepared in advance are structural devices that leave the board of directors in control of any decision to sell the company and with sufficient flexibility to provide the board with economically attractive alternatives to succumbing to the hostile bid.

[a] Poison Pill Plan. A poison pill or share purchase rights plan is a device that has achieved great popularity since its general legality was ratified by the Delaware Supreme Court in 1985. The plan has the effect of forestalling a bidder from purchasing more than a threshold level (frequently 20 percent) of a target's stock because of the dire consequences that would result (hence the name "poison pill"). All plans, however, permit the target company's board of directors to neutralize the pill under certain circumstances (usually before a 20 percent purchase and sometimes shortly thereafter). A pill thus allows a board to run a controlled auction for the company, removing the pill only when the highest bid has been obtained.

Poison pills generally operate as follows: Upon implementation of the plan, the company declares a dividend distribution of 1 right per common share. Each right initially represents a 10-year warrant to buy one share of common stock of the company, at a very high (out-of-the-money) price, designed to have little financial value. Initially the rights do not trade separately from the common stock, and may be redeemed by the company for a nominal amount (e.g., $0.05 per right). In the event that a third party purchases more than 20 percent of the outstanding common stock, the rights separate from the common stock, and trade separately (i.e., become distributed).

Once distributed, rights acquire valuable new characteristics that are harmful to the bidder. In flip-over plans, the distributed rights become exercisable for purchase of the bidder's common stock at a 50 percent discount from market price, in the event the target company is merged. In flip-in plans, the rights become exercisable for purchase of the target's common stock at a 50 percent discount from market price, in the event the bidder purchases more than, perhaps, 30 percent ownership in the target. In addition, the bidder is usually precluded by the terms of a plan from exercising flip-in rights. Many companies have combined flip-in and flip-over plans.

The net effect of a poison pill is to make it prohibitively costly for a bidder to purchase control of a company without obtaining approval of the target's board. Thus, the board retains a strong hand in determining whether control of the company is sold, and if so to whom and at what price.

[b] Takeover-Resistant Charters. The fundamental determinant of a successful takeover effort is whether the bidder achieves control of the target's board. Recently, bidders (such as AT&T in the NCR situation) will mount a proxy contest to take control of a target's board while their tender offer is outstanding. Such contests, in addition to traditional challenges at an annual meeting, may include the following actions:

- Bidder calls a special meeting of the target's shareholders at which bidder proposes to remove target's board and replace it with its own slate; or
- Bidder solicits action without a meeting, which removes the target's board and replaces it with the bidder's slate.

Defensive charter provisions tend to be ones that make these processes more difficult for a bidder to initiate unless it owns a substantial amount of the company's stock. Typical defensive charter provisions include:

1. *Supermajority removal provisions.* These provisions require the vote of more than 50 percent of the outstanding shares (e.g., 80 percent is an almost unattainably high voting requirement) to remove the board of directors unless the target has approved the bid in advance. Such provisions are primarily directed toward preventing an unsolicited bidder from making a tender offer for less than 100 percent of a company.

2. *Classified boards.* Such systems group the directors into three classes, so that only one third of the board is up for election each year. Removal of directors not up for election is prohibited except for good cause. The effect of this system is that it will take a hostile bidder two annual meetings to elect a majority of the board, and thus deter those who would take control by exercising the influence of substantial minority (15 percent to 30 percent) blocks.

3. *No action without a meeting.* Denying shareholders the right or imposing a higher percentage requirement on shareholders to call a special shareholder meeting frustrates a bidder's ability to replace the board. This allows a target more time to play out its defensive strategy.

All of these provisions have a tendency to create delays in the speed at which a bidder can achieve board control. Ultimately, it would be unrealistic to expect board members not to resign in the face of a majority shareholder. However, a delay can make the difference in the success of certain defenses, such as a pac-man defense or finding a white knight.

Other defensive charter provisions are designed to deter would-be acquirors by interfering with important steps in their acquisition plans. For example, hostile takeovers are usually structured as a tender offer followed by a merger to obtain the remaining shares. Charter provisions aimed at interfering with this process include:

1. *Supermajority merger provisions.* Such provisions require high percentage votes (e.g., 80 percent) for shareholder approval of a merger following a hostile tender offer (typically defined in the charter as a tender offer made without the approval of the board prior to the acquisition of a 10 percent foothold). Thus, if the bidder received 60 percent of the shares in the hostile tender offer, it would still need approval of half the remaining nontendered shares (20 percent out of 40 percent) in order to complete the merger under an 80 percent supermajority provision.

2. *"Majority of the minority" provisions.* Such provisions require a merger following a hostile tender offer to be approved not only by a majority of shares, including the bidder's shares, but also by a majority of shares not owned by the bidder. In a sense, this provision deprives a controlling shareholder of the voting power necessary to cause corporate action. For example, if the bidder owned 56 percent as a result of a hostile tender offer, a vote of more than 22 percent of the disinterested 44 percent of shareholders would be needed to approve the merger. The similarity in result to supermajority provisions is apparent. These are effectively "floating" supermajority provisions.

3. *"Fair value" provisions.* Such provisions are oriented toward assuring that the price paid in the second-step merger is at least equal to that paid in the initial tender offer. They are a reaction to bidders' tactics of encouraging quick tendering by offering more to those who sell early and do not wait to be merged out. Fair value provisions are designed to persuade shareholders not to tender into a hostile tender offer, because a better offer may come along shortly. Even if the initial bidder is successful, nontendering shareholders will be made whole in the second step. Shareholders can then be encouraged to hold out for a better offer and, if enough shareholders fail to tender, a hostile offer can be defeated. Fair value provisions operate like supermajority merger provisions, in that they apply a supermajority vote requirement to the approval of any second-step merger in which the value paid is less than that paid in the preceding tender offer.

4. *Unequal voting rights.* A more exotic form of defensive strategy requires more long-range planning, involving the creation of two classes of stock: voting and nonvoting. The voting stock typically is held by a small group of founding family members or another trusted group (e.g., an employee stock ownership plan), which effectively retains control over the sale of the company. Nonvoting (or low-voting) stockholders provide substantial additional equity capital and participate on an equivalent basis in any dividends or other distributions with the voting stockholders. Regulatory requirements make it difficult for publicly listed companies to create or modify an unequal voting stock structure.

[c] State Law Defenses. A number of states have modified their corporate governance statutes for companies incorporated in their jurisdictions in order to restrict hostile takeovers. Reincorporation in a state with more restrictive takeover rules is a possibility in the early stages of defensive planning. However, reincorporation is such a drastic step requiring strong shareholder support that it usually cannot be used once a company has become widely regarded as a potential takeover target.

There are three major types of state antitakeover laws in common use today. Except for the Control Share Law, which was validated by the U.S. Supreme Court in 1987, there remain questions as to the constitutionality of these types of statutes.

1. *Control share law.* This type of law removes the voting rights from shares accumulated in excess of various thresholds (20 percent, 33 percent, and 50 percent). A shareholder who is accumulating in excess of these thresholds must obtain the approval of the disinterested shareholders in order to reinstate his voting rights (and hence his ability to control the target company). States following this approach include Indiana, Ohio, Minnesota, and Missouri.

2. *Merger moratorium statute.* This provides that a statutory merger cannot be accomplished under state law with a 20 percent shareholder for a lengthy period of time (typically five years) after the shareholder purchased 20 percent of the target company. The principal exception to this moratorium is if the target's board approved the merger before the 20 percent purchase. States adopting this approach include New York, New Jersey, Kentucky, Indiana, and Missouri. Delaware, importantly, has adopted a weakened version of the moratorium statute. Under the Delaware approach, the merger moratorium is for three years, and can be avoided by the bidder reaching the 85 percent ownership level in a single step (e.g., a tender offer) starting from less than 15 percent, or with the ratification of the bidder's merger proposal by vote of two thirds of the disinterested shares during the moratorium period.

3. *Cash-out law.* This law allows target shareholders to "put" their shares to a bidder once a bidder has crossed an ownership threshold (e.g., 30 percent). Pennsylvania, Maine, and Utah have adopted this approach.

Nothing in the previous discussion of takeover defense is intended to recommend that companies generally rush to adopt "shark repellent" policies wholesale. Such policies, when used in quantity, can prove addictive and, in the long term, lead to lethargic company performance. There is a good deal of evidence to suggest that the presence of significant legal barriers to takeover leads to a lower stock valuation and a higher cost of capital: the best defense against a hostile bid is a high stock price.

[4] Responses to a Hostile Offer

Once a hostile approach has been made, there are a number of tactics at a board's disposal for taking defensive action.

[a] Negotiate for a Higher Price or a Standstill Agreement. If a defense program has not successfully maintained the independence of the target, it may still be powerful enough to permit some negotiating leverage against the bidder. The target's board may determine that an acquisition by the bidder is acceptable if a full and fair price can be achieved on behalf of the shareholders. Alternatively, the board may choose to be firm on maintaining the target's independence, and seek to prevent additional bidder stock purchases by means of a standstill agreement. In such an agreement, a bidder commits not to make further purchases of the target's stock for some period of time. In return, however, the target must usually make some concessions, such as a board seat for a representative of the bidder. Such arrangements typically only work successfully when the bidder has obtained a stake as large as 20 percent to 30 percent of the target, and where the bidder is comfortable with its level of influence over the company, although still distant from actual control.

[b] Seek a White Knight. Often the only way to prevent shareholders from tendering into a hostile offer is to find them a better one. An offeror that comes in at the behest of target management to rescue a company from a hostile tender offer is commonly referred to as a white knight. Managements usually begin seeking white knights as soon as a hostile offer is made because it often requires a great deal of effort, persuasion, and provision of information to find a company willing, on the basis of a quick analysis, to make a competing tender offer at a level higher than that of a hostile bidder. It is also important to have a white knight make its bid as soon as possible, in order to assure that it is not seriously disadvantaged in timing with respect to the initial offer. Of course, the board's decision to agree to a white knight's offer is a difficult one, as it requires giving up any prospect of maintaining the company's independence.

[c] Dispose of Key Assets. An important defensive technique, which is consistent with maximization of value to shareholders, is the sale of significant corporate assets to third parties. The basis of this defense is that if the asset disposed of is a principal factor in the bidder's pursuit of the target, the bidder may withdraw from the contest. On the other hand, if the asset was not essential to the bidder, the bidder may view such a sale more as a convenience than a discouragement, as it makes the target more liquid and easier to take over. An important aspect of an asset disposition involves the fairness of the value received by the seller for the asset. It is critical that the directors of the target believe that the price they are realizing for the asset enhances the value of their company for its shareholders. If the disposal is not at a fair price, then it is a waste of assets for which directors risk liability.

An integral part of a large asset disposal (or restructuring) defense is the distribution of the proceeds to the stockholders. An extraordinary dividend of the cash proceeds, or a self-tender, can result in the delivery of cash that, when combined with the residual value of the shares afterwards, exceeds the value of the hostile bid.

[d] Recapitalize. In addition to distributing the cash proceeds from asset disposal programs, a target can attempt a recapitalization by raising cash through increased bank lines and the issuance of public debt securities. This tactic usually results in the target's credit rating falling below investment grade, resulting in increased borrowing costs and less certain access to both debt and equity capital until the target's debt leverage is reduced. In some cases, a recapitalization can involve the distribution of such high-yield debt securities to the target's shareholders, who would then be faced with an alternative to the hostile offer consisting of cash, fixed income securities, and a stub equity stake in the company. An assessment of the fully distributed value of the fixed-income securities and the stub equity share is the most critical element in comparing the package value of the recapitalization alternative to the hostile offer.

[e] "Pac-Man" Defense. A 1980s innovation in the tender-offer area was the utilization of a reciprocal hostile offer, more commonly known as the pac-man defense (named after the popular electronic game in which the pursued becomes the pursuer). In a pac-man defense, the target threatens that unless the bidder withdraws (or raises its offer price), the target will proceed to acquire the bidder and oust the bidder's management. A necessary condition for the success of a pac-man defense is that the target have financial resources comparable to those of the bidder, or have a deep-pocket ally willing to lend its credit and credibility to the enterprise (as United Technologies did for Martin Marietta in 1982). In essence, a pac-man defense acknowledges the appropriateness of merging the two companies but challenges the determination of which management will control the new enterprise.

Despite the game-like appellation, the decision to embark on a pac-man defense should only be undertaken with the most serious study and care. Such actions can obviously pose grave risks to the financial health of a target company if it succeeds in acquiring its pursuer.

[f] Litigate. Both as an area for implementing a tender offer defense and as a strategic weapon in itself, litigation pervades virtually all hostile takeover situations. The principal strategic aim of litigation is to obtain an injunction, temporary or permanent, or a temporary restraining order against the bidder's offer. The basis of the injunction is usually some alleged violation of law on the part of the bidder. Typical bases of litigation are

- *Securities laws.* The bidder, in making its offer, has arguably violated one of the many laws governing the making of tender offers: disclosure of nonpublic information, or one of the many rules governing trading in the securities markets.

- *State tender offer laws.* The bidder has arguably violated (or failed to comply with) one of the complex state laws affecting takeovers, such as the Control Share Statute.

- *Antitrust laws.* A target is permitted to argue that the proposed combination would probably violate the U.S. antitrust laws and, therefore, should be enjoined.

Other less-common legal defenses arise in regulated industries (e.g., banking and insurance, transportation, communications, defense, and energy), where there is public interest in the identity and reputation of the acquiror. In addition, federal antiracketeering laws have been stretched by targets in an effort to include within their scope acquirors that, either in the past or in the tender offer itself, have arguably committed multiple securities law violations. In modern takeover battles, however, managements are usually only able to use litigation as a delaying tactic. The fundamental strategy must be to obtain an economically superior alternative for the stockholders.

Chapter 2
Leveraged Buyouts

KATE W. COOK

NOREEN DOYLE

FIGURE 2-1

Going-Private Transactions: Aggregate Dollars Paid (1982–1991)

Source: Mergerstat^{SM} Review

Year	Total Going Private	Total Dollar Value Paid	$100MM or More	$1,000MM or More	Average Purchase Price	Median Purchase Price
1982	31	$ 2,836.7	11	—	$ 91.5	$ 29.6
1983	36	7,145.4	14	1	198.5	77.8
1984	57	10,805.9	26	—	415.6	66.9
1985	76	24,139.8	28	6	317.6	72.6
1986	76	20,232.4	29	4	281.0	84.5
1987	47	22,057.1	26	7	469.3	123.3
1988	125	60,920.6	57	10	487.4	79.8
1989	80	18,515.4	30	3	231.4	52.8
1990	20	3,539.9	8	1	177.0	36.9
1991	9	334.2	0	0	37.1	28.2

Note: Dollars in millions.

2.01 INTRODUCTION

Few issues permeated the business and financial community over the latter half of the 1980s as much as the leveraged buyout (LBO). Once used primarily to recapitalize smaller private firms, LBOs became a major tool for the restructuring of U.S. business, both large and small, during the mid- and late 1980s. Familiar and respected U.S. public firms such as Burlington Industries, Inc., Owens-Illinois, Inc., Beatrice Co., Northwest Airlines, Inc., and RJR Nabisco, Inc. became private companies through buyouts. Figures 2-1 and 2-2 show the number of and consideration paid in going-private transactions during each year since 1982. Other firms, such as Owens-Corning Fiberglass and Phillips Petroleum, took on massive amounts of debt and used the proceeds to repurchase their own stock in order to protect their companies and prevent LBOs by outsiders.

The number of going-private transactions, the number of deals over $100 million, and the aggregate dollar value of the market peaked in 1988. The aggregate dollar value of announced going-private transactions in 1988, almost $61 billion, was more than double that in any other year. Almost half of the 1988 announced deal volume consists of a single transaction, RJR Nabisco, the largest LBO ever at $26.2 billion, which closed in 1989. In 1989, the market was still fairly strong; however, transaction activity fell off precipitously in 1990 and 1991, with only nine deals completed in 1991. No deals totaled over $100 million in 1991, and the aggregate dollar value was only $334 million, less than the average purchase price of a single transaction during the most active years of the 1980s.

LBO activity was slowed by a number of factors. Some of the largest, most visible transactions in the 1980s were precipitated by companies being ''put in play'' by a corporate raider or an LBO specialist seeking to capitalize on the difference between a company's publicly trading value and its value in private hands. In the late 1980s,

FIGURE 2-2

Going-Private Transactions: Valuation (1982–1991)

Source: Mergerstat^{SM} Review

Year	Price/Earnings Ratio Paid		Premium Paid Over Market Price	
	Average	Median	Average	Median
1982	11.2	11.0	41.4%	38.6%
1983	18.6	13.8	36.7	31.3
1984	14.2	12.6	36.3	33.7 .
1985	17.2	14.7	30.9	25.7
1986	21.0	17.4	31.9	26.1
1987	22.0	20.3	34.8	30.9
1988	21.1	17.9	33.8	26.3
1989	17.8	15.5	35.0	22.7
1990	15.5	13.6	34.3	31.6
1991	13.2	10.7	23.8	20.0

changes in the protections available to companies to thwart raiders, such as poison pill provisions, shifted the advantage in takeover situations to the company, thus discouraging unwanted advances. Also, strong stock market rallies increased the purchase price of many companies, reducing the benefit of going-private transactions. In addition, debt financing for leveraged transactions became much scarcer after 1989. The high-yield debt market was affected by the bankruptcy in 1990 of Drexel Burnham Lambert, one of the largest purveyors of non-investment-grade debt (junk bonds), and by regulatory scrutiny of some of the largest purchasers of this debt, including the savings and loan institutions. Bank regulators also increased the focus on bank loans to leveraged companies by defining highly leveraged transaction (HLT) parameters that determined which loans would be designated as HLTs, thus requiring special disclosure on banks' HLT portfolios.

LBOs continue to be organized and financed during the 1990s on the same principles as during the 1980s, but on a much smaller scale. Supporters of buyouts suggest that the focus on cash flow created by high debt levels, combined with the incentives created by making company managers major shareholders in the corporation, makes leveraged companies stronger, more valuable, and more focused. Companies streamline operations, cut costs, refocus their strategies, and improve asset utilization in efforts to improve cash flow and thereby create shareholder value.

Critics suggest that buyouts (and threats of buyouts) create little but short-term thinking. They argue that research budgets and capital investments are cut and that near-term financial results are emphasized at the expense of long-term strategies. Debt-laden companies are forced to focus so exclusively on cash flow and debt reduction that any long-term strategy is ignored. Critics also suggest that there is little economic rationale for LBOs other than the enrichment of the financial institutions and buyout firms that assemble the deals (primarily with other people's money) for fees and portions of the equity of the acquired firm. Asset value is moved around rather than created.

2.02 OVERVIEW OF LEVERAGED BUYOUTS

Simply stated, an LBO is the purchase of a company's stock (or assets, in certain cases) by a highly leveraged entity, with the acquiror using extensive amounts of debt financing based solely on the value of the company to be acquired. Relatively small amounts of equity can be invested by the acquiror, allowing small firms to purchase and control much larger corporate entities. In the RJR Nabisco LBO, only $1.5 billion in equity was invested by the sponsor in a $26.2 billion LBO transaction. Although in the 1980s it was not unusual for transactions to be completed with only 10 percent to 15 percent equity, the amount of equity required in the 1990s has increased significantly as debt financing has became more scarce, and transactions with 30 percent to 40 percent equity are not unusual. The key to the LBO is debt financing and, specifically, the ability to issue debt based solely (or primarily) on the value of the company to be acquired and not the acquiror.

In the mid-to-late 1980s, many large buyouts were sponsored by relatively small buyout firms, such as Kohlberg Kravis Roberts & Co. (KKR) and Forstmann Little & Co., often in concert with the company's management. The buyout firm supplied equity capital from its own funds or arranged third-party equity from an LBO fund, itself made up of funds invested by large institutional investors such as pension funds and college endowment funds. Management is generally offered some equity interest as an incentive to operate the business successfully. The buyout firms do not guarantee any debt, nor do they generally have any other continuing financial obligation beyond their equity commitment once they have made their commitment.

The financial structure of a large-scale LBO generally consists of equity, subordinated debt, and senior debt. Senior debt is often provided by banks and is usually secured by assets of the firm or by the stock of the firm being acquired. Sometimes privately placed or publicly issued high-yield fixed-rate senior notes also provide a portion of the senior financing. This debt may be equivalent in rights to the bank debt, but it is almost always of longer maturity and usually has significantly fewer rights than the banks in terms of financial and other covenants. Also, it often has less security than the bank debt. Senior lenders provide debt to the extent that the cash flow and/ or collateral is sufficient to insure their repayment under nearly all foreseeable and reasonable circumstances. While the amount of financing varies significantly from one transaction to another, banks often finance approximately 40 percent to 60 percent of the purchase price. Subordinated debt ranks below senior debt and is less likely to be repaid if the firm has financial difficulty. Subordinated debt, the often-maligned junk bond, is sold publicly or arranged privately with insurance companies or other investors. Subordinated debt often is not secured and has limited covenant protection, but it has a high return to investors to compensate for the heightened risk. There may be different levels of subordinated paper, such as junior and senior subordinated tranches, and some subordinated tranches are zero coupon or have other deferred interest payment mechanisms. Sometimes a preferred stock layer is also involved. Subordinated lenders generally provide up to 25 percent of the necessary financing. Such financing is frequently referred to as mezzanine financing. The cash flow of the purchased company pays the interest on the debt incurred for the transaction as well as paying down principal. As the amount of total debt on the company declines over time and the total value of the company increases owing to earnings growth, the value of the equity investment increases rapidly. Typically, sponsors have an investment horizon of approximately five years, after which time they pursue an exit strategy and seek to realize their equity gains.

FIGURE 2-3

Debt and Cost of Capital

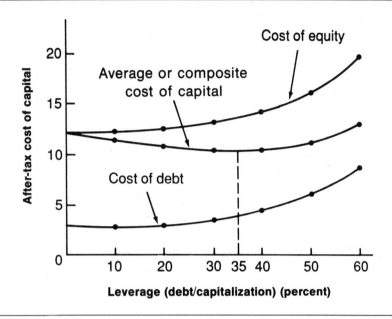

2.03 CORPORATE FINANCIAL THEORY AND THE OPTIMAL CAPITAL STRUCTURE

Lenders must get comfortable with the high levels of debt associated with LBOs, given that lenders take less risk when companies are less leveraged. In some cases, companies may have been underleveraged prior to their buyouts. Also, lenders may view the high debt as a transient event that can be reduced through cash flow generated from the company's operations or from planned asset sales. Corporate financial theory suggests that there is an optimum capital structure for every business based on the financial and operating risk inherent in that business. Since debt is normally less expensive (after tax considerations) than equity to the issuing company, higher levels of debt result in a lower cost of capital to a firm. However, the cost of equity (as well as the cost of debt) rises with the amount of debt owed by a company because of the increased financial risk associated with higher levels of debt. At some point, the higher equity cost, combined with higher interest rates on the debt and the added burdens associated with the covenants on the debt, begins to overwhelm the savings from debt financing. Thus, additional debt creates a higher cost of capital, not a lower cost. The point at which the cost of capital curve is at its lowest is the optimal capital structure for that firm. Figure 2-3 illustrates this point. Also, at some level of leverage, lenders become unwilling to tolerate the increased risk.

Historically, optimal capital structures have varied with the risk of the company and its industry. Public utilities, which have been considered low-risk companies, were able to support debt of approximately 50 percent of capitalization, a relatively high level of debt compared to the proportional amount of debt financing in industrial companies. Cyclical firms in automobile production or chemical processing, which have much greater earnings and cash flow volatility, have historically had debt of only 10 percent to 20 percent of capitalization. These firms would not be able to support higher debt levels in slack periods, resulting in intolerable financial risk. Thus, the optimal capital structure for a cyclical firm includes a lower level of debt than for a public utility.

The extremely high leverage of an LBO, however, appears to violate the theory of the optimal capital structure. Traditionally, no companies have been considered able to support 80 percent or more of their capitalization in debt. There are certain factors that explain this conflict.

One factor is the risk of the firm involved in a buyout. Many of the LBO target companies are in industries that are more stable and predictable in terms of cash flow than other industries. Businesses such as supermarkets, consumer products companies, and some industrial segments have had more than their share of buyouts. The stable cash flows of these businesses can support high levels of debt financing; that is, the optimal capital structure curve should allow relatively high debt. This implies that existing management of the firm was not moving the company toward its optimal capital structure curve, and hence the firm was underleveraged prior to the buyout. However, even if companies in these businesses had been able to lower the overall cost of capital by incurring more debt, this theory does not explain the wide discrepancy between LBO leverage and the capital structures of these companies' peer group or comparably stable businesses. Also, there have been businesses in cyclical industries that have undergone leveraged buyouts and incurred large debt burdens for a transitional period.

There are two major factors that explain the tolerance for high leverage. First, the high debt levels are viewed as temporary, with the company having the capability of reducing leverage in a fairly short time frame.

The majority of lenders to LBOs do not consider the firms to be optimally leveraged after the buyout. Instead, they view the high leverage as a transient situation. Lenders are willing to accept a more highly leveraged capital structure for a short, specified period than what they would consider to be optimal from a long-term perspective. Lenders typically look at the cash flow of the firm under various business scenarios to determine how much debt they are willing to approve, appropriate interest rates to charge, and when debt can be paid down to more supportable levels. Typically, bank lenders require a structure that permits bank debt, which represents a significant portion of total leverage, to be repaid within five to seven years. Even where total debt is not projected to decline significantly in the first few years of a deal, perhaps owing to accrual of interest on non-cash-paying securities or because capital lease financing is to be used to fund capital expenditures, these companies are expected to become relatively less leveraged as they build cash flow and firm value by investing in growth. From this perspective, buyouts require the confluence of economic stability, growth, successful corporate strategy, and stable financing costs. If and when this does not occur, the buyout is in trouble.

The second major factor that explains the tolerance for high leverage in LBOs is that the equity investors are seeking high returns for their greater risk, and while the cost of capital may not be less for these companies than for less-leveraged peers, the returns for investors are greater. The following comparison illustrates this point:

	Optimally Leveraged Company		LBO Company	
	%	After-Tax Cost	%	After-Tax Cost
Debt	40	4.5%	80	7%
Equity	60	13.0	20	35
Blended		9.6%		12.6%

The cost of capital for the LBO is one third higher than for the optimally leveraged company. Lenders have been willing to take increased risk for increased return. Subordinated lenders, which bear the highest level of risk among the various classes of lenders, have charged yields in the range of 13 percent to 15 percent for 10-to-12-year bonds. (The comparison assumes that short-term, low-risk interest rates are about 7 percent). Tax-deductibility of interest costs shelters equity investors from bearing the full burden of these higher interest rates, but in return for their increased risk, equity investors require expected returns that are truly spectacular.

A review of the major corporate buyouts over the past several years suggests that operating and financial inefficiencies as well as inappropriate strategies at companies lead to LBOs. Historic underleveraging is just one factor. At the same time, nearly all LBO transactions are overleveraged in a traditional sense and require significant debt reduction for the company to return to an optimum capital structure.

2.04 DEVELOPMENT OF THE LEVERAGED BUYOUT

The LBO began as a mechanism for smaller, privately held companies to cash out the founder or owner. Generally, owners have several choices in this situation. For example, they can sell the company to another company. Such a sale generates cash (or securities) immediately, but it takes the control of the company away from the owner (or his or her family). Owners of small businesses that sell out to other firms generally retain little control over the firm. (An owner should sell the company when he or she wants to get out cleanly and has no interest in passing control to management or family.)

The initial public offering (IPO) is another method by which owners can make liquid their holdings. The advantage of the IPO is that the owner can retain control through selling a percentage of his holdings to provide liquidity or to raise capital for expansion. However, the IPO has drawbacks. Once a company becomes public, significant expenses must be incurred to service shareholders. These include compliance costs with the Securities and Exchange Commission and costs associated with the preparation of periodic reports to shareholders. Additionally, public companies lose some of the flexibility in operating decisions that exists with private firms. The IPO, like the sale of a company, is not a mechanism for insuring management succession or estate planning.

Initially, the LBO option provided a means for owners to transfer ownership to management or family where those individuals did not have access to extensive amounts of capital. To the extent that the owner had built up sizable value in the business, the managers or his or her family most likely could not raise equity to purchase the company without forgoing control. They could, however, engage in an LBO. Generally, a bank was brought in to estimate the value of the assets of the firm and to provide financing. Banks would often lend higher amounts than the assets commanded, based on knowledge of the firm's operations and history, good cash flow, and confidence that existing management would continue to run the business. LBOs were used primarily for these purposes during the 1970s.

The next step in the development of the LBO came with the breakup of many of the conglomerate companies that were assembled during the 1970s. The conglomerate rage ended in the 1980s. The diverse pieces did not fit together, and managements felt that it was better to focus on specific business lines. Furthermore, it appeared that the market was unable to properly evaluate all of the diverse pieces. (The stock market was valuing companies at less than the sum of the parts.) The managers of these firms began to sell off pieces of these businesses. Such a sale is called a spin-off. The LBO became a tool for management of these spun-off pieces or for outside investors to take control of the new firm.

The breakup of the conglomerates provided an opportunity for LBO technology to be utilized on larger firms. Whereas buyouts of smaller firms involved tens of millions of dollars, conglomerate spin-offs resulted in deals of hundreds of millions of dollars. This attracted new investors and intermediaries to the market. Investment banks, particularly the now defunct Drexel Burnham Lambert, focused on this market, and money center banks and insurance companies recognized the profit opportunities in lending to and investing in these situations.

The final step in the development of the LBO came with the low stock prices of the early and mid-1980s. The Dow Jones Industrial Average was only 964 at the end of 1980 and 1,211 at the end of 1984. Company stocks looked cheap compared to the perceived value of the firm. Firms such as KKR began buying public companies and taking them private through LBO technology. What followed was the buyout phenomenon of the late 1980s and the rise of the modern LBO.

2.05 TYPES OF TRANSACTIONS

There are several distinct types of transactions that are now collectively referred to as LBOs. These are the LBO, the management buyout (MBO), the recapitalization, and the leveraged acquisition.

[1] Modern Leveraged Buyout

In the modern LBO, a buyer representing the equity interests organizes the buyout of the company and arranges for the placement of the equity, subordinated or other mezzanine debt, and the senior debt. The traditional form that the LBO takes is the establishment by the sponsor (LBO firm or fund) of a new corporation (Newco) that is capitalized with sufficient funds to purchase the stock or assets of the target company. The capital structure has a significant proportion of debt (senior and/or subordinated). A typical capital structure of the 1980s follows:

Senior debt (bank loans)	60%
Subordinated debt (public or private)	25
Equity	15
	100%

It is more difficult to generalize about capital structures in the current market, but typically 25 percent equity is considered a minimum for a new deal, with 30 percent to 40 percent equity quite common. Bank debt and other senior debt may comprise 40 percent to 60 percent of the capital structure, with subordinated debt making up the balance.

The equity financing is provided by the sponsor and/or its investment fund. Many LBO sponsors have raised funds in advance from investors so that equity is available for opportunities as they are identified. While the sponsor owns the majority of the equity, a portion is typically made available to the management of the target company for purchase at the same purchase price available to the sponsor or through options. The subordinated debt can be raised in the private or the public market, at the discretion of the sponsor, depending on which market is more attractive with respect to interest rates, timing, and flexibility. The sponsor generally employs a securities firm to underwrite the subordinated bonds or place them privately. The senior financing is generally provided by a bank or a syndicate of bank lenders with an agent or agents selected by the sponsor to negotiate terms on behalf of the syndicate.

Senior financing may also take the form of senior notes that can be privately or publicly placed through securities firms.

An LBO is normally a two-stage transaction when a publicly owned company is involved. In the acquisition phase, a new holding company is formed by the acquirer to purchase the stock or assets of the company being acquired in a tender offer. Generally, the holding company borrows acquisition financing to supplement its equity and allow it to purchase the stock of the company to be acquired. Once sufficient shares have been acquired, the holding company is merged into the acquired company.

Sometimes shareholders that did not sell their shares to acquirors in the tender offer receive "cramdown" securities in lieu of a cash payment for their remaining shares in the merger. Often cramdown securities are comprised of subordinated debt or equity securities. During the 1980s, it was not unusual for banks to provide all of the premerger acquisition financing. Upon the completion of the merger, bank bridge loans were repaid through subordinated debt issued by the merged company and the remaining bank debt was assumed by the merged company. In the late 1980s, a number of investment banks began to provide the bridge financing for subordinated debt that they planned to place as banks became less willing to provide all of the premerger financing. A number of these bridge loans created significant credit problems for these investment banks, which were unable to place the permanent securities in a timely fashion.

Buyouts of smaller firms and transactions involving privately owned companies are usually simpler than the buyout just described, but they have the same general structure: a high level of secured debt, a high level of subordinated debt or preferred stock, and a relatively small amount of common equity.

The corporate structure is a concern of the organizer and the lenders. The lenders, particularly the senior bank lenders, have a distinct preference for lending funds at the operating entities, as close to the assets of the company as possible. The typical corporate structure of the leveraged company is shown in Figure 2-4. The new debt and equity are raised at Newco, but the lenders look to the cash flow and assets of the target company when making credit decisions with respect to the debt. Normally, the senior debt is secured with 100 percent of the stock of the target at the acquisition phase and, when the target has been merged into Newco, with the assets of the company and the stock of all of its subsidiaries. The objective of the senior lenders is to take all collateral available. The subordinated lenders may obtain second liens on some of the assets upon which the senior lenders have first liens, but they are often unsecured. The subordinated lenders are relying, as are the senior lenders, on the future

FIGURE 2-4

LBO Corporate Acquisition Merger Stage Structure

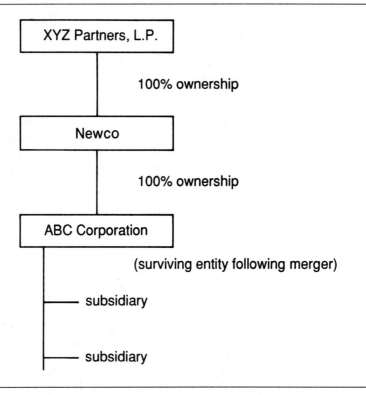

cash flows of the target. In addition to lending at one corporate entity (the borrower), often the senior lenders receive guarantees from other corporate entities, including the parent holding company and the borrower's subsidiaries. These guarantees insure that the lender has a claim for repayment against all entities. The guarantors also may pledge their assets in support of the debt. Sometimes subordinated lenders receive subordinated guarantees.

[2] Management Buyout

In contrast to the LBO as just described, an MBO is initiated by the management of the company. Very often, the motivation for the transaction is the same as for the LBO: The market does not perceive the same future value of the firm as does management. Furthermore, management may believe that without public ownership it can manage for cash flow and not for current earnings. This initiation of a buyout by management does not necessarily mean that management can control the transaction, as was shown in the RJR Nabisco transaction. In that case, management initiated the transaction at a price higher than the company's stock was trading for on the New York Stock

Exchange. However, the proposed buyout attracted other buyers, and in the end the company was purchased by KKR after a bitter struggle. MBOs have been more the norm in the European market and in the smaller, private company transactions in the United States than for large public companies in the United States.

[3] Recapitalization

The term "recapitalization" (recap), in general, refers to any restructuring of the capital of the company. More specifically, a recap is usually done by leveraging the company and paying the shareholders a special dividend but without a change in ownership. Alternatively, a company can buy back shares of its stock with the proceeds of a debt offering or initiate an exchange offering, where a package of new debt and equity securities is offered to shareholders. In an exchange offer, the shareholder ownership may change and may include an LBO firm that has initiated the transaction. Colt Industries and Union Carbide are two companies that repurchased the majority of their common shares through recaps. Quantum Chemical and Sealed Air Corporation paid special dividends, with debt funding, to effect their recaps.

[4] Leveraged Acquisition

The leveraged acquisition transaction is often categorized as a different sort of LBO. A leveraged acquisition is usually the acquisition of an existing business by a strategic buyer using significant amounts of debt financing. The new debt generally relies on the cash flow and assets of both the target company and the acquiring company for its repayment. The basic difference between the LBO and the leveraged acquisition is that the lenders to the leveraged acquisition have an additional credit basis in the acquiring company, as well as reliance on the target. Also, in a leveraged acquisition, the acquiror is generally making a strategic as well as a financial decision in purchasing the new business and may integrate the businesses, bringing to bear the strength of an existing balance sheet and operating business.

2.06 EXPECTED RETURNS

From the perspective of investment and credit evaluation by the potential equity owners, subordinated lenders, and senior lenders, all four types of transactions described are evaluated in the same manner. The investors and lenders are concerned with future cash flows, interest coverage, the value of the underlying assets or business, the structure of the transaction, and the prospective economic and business cycles. In looking at each potential transaction, the investor and lender review the critical variables that will influence cash flow and model the future performance of the company. The important variables to consider are company and industry growth rates; operating margins and the internal and exogenous factors that affect them, capital expenditures that are necessary for growth and/or required to maintain existing business; working capital requirements; and tactical options, such as assets that may be available for sale and opportunities for reduction of expenses.

The investor's strategy is evaluated in terms of highest potential for overall return.

Generally, the LBO investor expects to realize this return in any one of a number of ways: through the sale of the stock in a public or private offering, through the sale of the company and consequent return of investment to the shareholder, or through long-term ownership and dividends. For the lender, the expected outcome is to hold the loan or note until its scheduled maturity under the assumption that it will meet its principal and interest payments as scheduled, or, if the company is sold or refinanced prior to debt maturity, to be prepaid from the proceeds of the sale of the business or the issuance of debt or equity. Lenders typically seek a "second way out." In the event of a default by the borrower, lenders may seek repayment of the loan or note through the sale by the company of assets or businesses, attempt a reorganization of the company and repackage the debt to match the new businesses, or restructure the debt instruments to match the changed outlook for the company. Essentially, the equity investor evaluates upside potential while the lender looks at downside risk. The equity investor's return is unlimited, while the best lenders can do is receive payment of their principal and contractual interest.

Each of the participants in the LBO capital structure—the senior debt, the subordinated debt, and the equity—has a different financial objective and a different perspective on the critical issues in structuring the transaction and in assuring the achievement of its return. The senior lender is usually a bank group that provides anywhere from 40 percent to 70 percent of the total capitalization. Banks lend at a spread over their cost of funds. For LBO transactions, banks normally expect a spread over cost of funds of 2.5 percent to 3 percent. Also, banks require fees to make LBO loans, generally in the range of 1 percent to 2.5 percent on a onetime basis, to help cover their costs of evaluating and committing to the financing. Agent banks receive fees on top of these amounts for structuring the credit, documenting the loans, and arranging for a syndicate of banks. The key issues for the bank lender are interest coverage (earnings before interest and taxes (EBIT) to interest cost should be at least 1.5 times), principal and interest repayment in full within 5 to 7 years, a possible second source of repayment in addition to cash flow (e.g., asset sales) should the company fail to meet projected performance, collateral to secure its extension of credit, and financial covenants. The usual financial covenants include but are not limited to a minimum interest coverage test, a minimum net worth test, and an earnings test, each measured quarterly; a limitation on the incurrence of additional debt; a limitation on the dollar amount that may be spent on capital expenditures; restrictions on any fundamental changes in the company's business or operations; prohibitions on the payment of dividends or prepayment of subordinated debt; restrictions on investments; and prohibitions on the sale of any material corporate assets. In addition, to protect against adverse changes in the cost to the company of borrowing, senior lenders may require the company to hedge its floating rate debt (and currency exposures, if applicable). Essentially, these covenants are designed to come into effect if the company deviates in any material way from the projections as presented at the time of the transaction. This gives the bank the opportunity to evaluate the current circumstances and determine whether any additional steps should be taken.

The subordinated debt represents about 25 percent to 40 percent of the typical capital structure of an LBO. The subordinated debt can take a number of different forms. Generally, subordinated debt returns a fixed interest rate, payable in cash semiannually. Where cash flow is low but is expected to improve, zero-coupon or pay-in-kind (PIK) bonds are used. In the 1980s, PIK bonds were an attractive source of financing for LBOs because interest was paid not in cash but in additional securities, usually for three to five years (the bond equivalent of paying stock dividends in lieu of cash dividends). This permitted the company to direct cash flow to the repayment of the more senior securities and had the additional benefit of being a noncash, tax-deductible expense. In the late 1980s, tax deductibility of noncash interest was regulated, and the demand by investors for high-yield bonds virtually disappeared. As a result, deferred interest bonds were rare in transactions even after the high-yield market recovered in late 1991. As to hierarchy, all subordinated debt is beneath senior debt in the capital structure and is junior with respect to payments. There may be various layers of subordinated debt, such as senior subordinated, subordinated, and junior subordinated debt. Complex transactions involve all three layers.

The final maturities on the subordinated debt are generally staged over a 10-to-12-year horizon, with no amortization prior to the scheduled final maturity of the senior bank debt. Historically, subordinated debt enjoyed very limited financial covenants. More recently, subordinated lenders have demanded more stringent covenants, including limitations on additional debt of the company, provisions offering them redemption privileges should the ownership of the company change, and other covenants protecting their rights in the event of changes in control of the company. In some circumstances, subordinated lenders impose financial covenants to come into effect if the company's financial condition deteriorates. For example, if net worth falls below a certain level, the company may be required to repurchase a portion of the bonds. Some subordinated debt has fixed-charge coverage tests. The subordinated lenders have a financial objective of a return of 2.5 percent to 5 percent over the corresponding Treasury note. If the coupon on their debentures does not provide sufficient return, they may require a portion of the equity to achieve their objective.

Sometimes LBOs also include a layer of preferred stock. Preferred stock may be issued to selling shareholders to bridge a difference in purchase price between buyers and sellers. Preferred stock typically has no covenants, although it typically pays a contractual dividend, which in some cases may be PIK at the company's option. One advantage of preferred stock is that if cash flow gets tight in the company, preferred dividends may be suspended and will cumulate without creating a default. One disadvantage with preferred stock is that the dividends are not tax deductible. Some preferred stock therefore has an exchange feature that permits the company to exchange the preferred stock for debt.

The equity investors typically represent 25 percent to 40 percent of the capitalization of the LBO (in the 1980s, it was as low as 10 percent) and have expectations for returns in the range of 25 percent to 35 percent on their investment. Equity returns are realized by the holder through dividends paid (usually after senior debt has been substantially repaid) or through the sale of the company either to another buyer or in a public offering. The smaller the proportion of equity of the capitalization of a transaction, the greater the equity return. Equity investors typically have an investment horizon of about five years, after which they hope to be able to realize their equity gains. The value of the equity investment increases from the repayment of debt over time as well as from increases in the value of the firm. For example, assume that a sponsor buys a company for $100 million, or five times the operating cash flow before interest, and contributes 25 percent equity. If operating cash flow increases 5 percent per year, the total value of the company will be $128 million in five years for a sales price at the same multiple of five of cash flow. If debt has been paid down by $50 million (to $25 million) over the five years, the equity is now worth $103 million ($128 million total value less $25 million of debt), representing an annual return of 33 percent. If the investor contributes 40 percent equity to the initial transaction, the exit value is $118 million but the annual return is only 24 percent. Therefore, equity investors will attempt to structure an LBO with as high a proportion of debt as is feasible, usually preferring low-cost bank debt.

2.07 PARTICIPANTS IN THE MARKET

As mentioned previously, the LBO sponsor is the initiator of most of the transactions. The sponsor identifies opportunities, creates the structure, and establishes the price at which the buyout is to be executed. Sponsors also raise equity funds, primarily from pension funds, insurance companies, banks, and other institutional equity investors. The fund is available to the sponsor when a transaction is to be made. The investor, in the interim, has the use of his funds but also pays a fee to the sponsor while the funds are available to the sponsor. The investor, once committed to the fund, typically has no discretion over its investments and must supply funds to the sponsor when called on to do so. The fund generally has certain guidelines governing the kinds of transactions and investments it may consummate.

The subordinated debt and high-yield senior notes may be privately placed or registered and publicly distributed. The major investors in subordinated debt have been insurance companies, pension funds, high-yield mutual funds, and other institutional funds. During the 1980s, thrifts and savings and loans (S&Ls) were also major buyers of high-yield paper. The large junk bond portfolios of the S&Ls, which declined dramatically in value with the collapse of the high-yield market in the late 1980s, are partially blamed for precipitating the S&L crisis. Thrifts and S&Ls are no longer major participants in the high-yield market. Underwriting and placement of the subordinated debt has been done by securities firms (investment banks or the securities subsidiaries of commercial bank holding companies). Usually, the mandate to place this debt was awarded to an investment bank that provided an underwriting commitment to "place or purchase" the securities. In the mid-1980s, Drexel Burnham Lambert, based on its respected distribution capability, was able to substitute a "highly confident" letter for the underwriting commitment. This letter was a commitment to place the securities without the obligation to commit its capital to purchase the securities through a formal underwriting. Because of its distribution network, the firm was nearly always successful in placing securities for which it issued a highly confident letter, and Drexel became the major investment bank in the high-yield subordinated debt market.

In an attempt to regain some of Drexel's formidable market share, some competitors began to offer subordinated bridge loans, which were also a response to banks' decreasing willingness to provide all of the acquisition financing for a transaction. Traditionally, banks would bridge the placement of subordinated debt, which usually occurred upon consummation of the merger of the acquisition company and the target company. Some investment banks offered subordinated bridge loans, making interim loans of their own funds prior to the placement of the permanent securities. Typically, these loans had escalating interest rates, usually subject to some ceiling on the cash interest rate, if they were not replaced as expected by permanent fixed-rate debt. Drexel reacted by marketing "increasing rate notes" (IRNs), under which investors would provide interim loans with escalating interest rates to bridge permanent financing. When the high-yield market collapsed in the late 1980s, these bridge loans and IRNs created problems for the companies that issued them as the rates began to escalate, and the bridge loans created problems for the investment banks that held them. As can be seen in Figure 2-5, the high-yield market recovered in late 1991 and 1992, with dollar

FIGURE 2-5

Nonconvertible High-Yield Issues (1980–1992)

Source: Securities Data Company, Inc.

Year	Proceeds	Number of Issues
1980	1,374.2	45
1981	1,247.2	34
1982	2,466.7	53
1983	7,406.4	95
1984	14,002.7	131
1985	14,190.8	175
1986	31,905.6	226
1987	28,140.1	190
1988	27,718.8	160
1989	25,091.6	129
1990	1,394.9	10
1991	9,971.0	48
1992[a]	33,397.8	196

Note: Dollars in millions.

[a] Through October.

volume through mid-October 1992 surpassing full-year totals in the mid-1980s. However, much of the current volume is for refinancing debt at existing leveraged companies, as opposed to new LBOs.

The senior debt is generally provided by a syndicate of banks. In smaller LBOs, one bank may commit to the entire amount of the loans required and may hold these loans on its own books or choose to syndicate the loans to one or more other banks. For the larger transactions, several large money center banks may commit to the entire transaction and then syndicate it to a wider group of financial institutions. Purchasers of senior loans for LBOs include foreign banks (European and Japanese), domestic regional banks, insurance companies, finance companies, Japanese leasing companies, certain mutual funds, and credit companies. An institution can purchase a bank loan in one of two ways: on the basis of an assignment where it has the full rights and obligations of a direct lender or on the basis of a participation where its rights and obligations are limited by the contract it signs with the selling institution. In the late 1980s, regulatory pressure to disclose banks' exposure to LBOs adversely affected banks' appetite for LBO loans. With some loosening of regulatory scrutiny and deals being structured with less leverage than during 1980s, some lenders have returned to the market, although there are still fewer institutions extending new LBO loans than during the mid-1980s.

2.08 ADVANTAGES OF LEVERAGED BUYOUTS

Analysts have cited numerous reasons for the boom in LBOs. Critics believe the major motivation for LBOs has been the greed of the market participants, including deal sponsors, investment banks, and investors. While greed may have created the impetus for many LBOs, the advantages to a leveraged company and its prior shareholders include the benefits of private ownership, low public equity valuation, and tax effects.

[1] Public Versus Private Ownership

In a large, publicly held corporation, management is hired, in theory, to build shareholder wealth while making the necessary decisions to operate the company efficiently and productively. In practice, managements may have vastly different interests from shareholders, which results in firms' being operated in a manner that does not necessarily enhance shareholder value. The common complaint about public companies is that management (which has little equity ownership) operates for its own interest and benefit and not for that of shareholders, as evidenced by increasing management compensation (regardless of shareholder value created), consolidation of power in the hands of senior management rather than placement of power with the board of directors or major shareholders, and increasing perquisites available to managers (e.g., large, plush quarters, corporate jets, and art collections).

Many of the benefits companies realize after undergoing a LBO could and should have been introduced by management prior to the LBO. The leveraging event often causes management to undertake beneficial strategies owing to three major factors.

The first factor is the discipline imposed by the high level of debt. The need to generate cash flow to pay down the debt and remain in compliance becomes a powerful motivator. Management must focus on minimizing investments in working capital, selling nonproductive or nonstrategic assets, reducing costs, and cutting unnecessary expenditures. In a well-structured LBO, these cuts should not require reductions in necessary research and development, capital expenditures, or marketing and advertising. These activities build the franchise value of the company, and if they are neglected, the value of the company and the levels of future cash flow can be impaired. Neither should the cash flow requirements in a well-structured LBO be so onerous that there is no cushion for an unexpected downturn in business or for unanticipated expenditures.

The second major factor motivating sound management practices in an LBO environment is the focus on cash versus book accounting. For example, to a leveraged company the logic of selling a non-cash-generating business for less than book value is compelling. However, a publicly held company, where management is concerned about reporting quarterly profits, may avoid taking this step. Leveraged companies often embrace the tax-shielding benefits of recognizing a loss and endure the adverse effects on book earnings and book net worth of noncash expenses, such as stepped-up depreciation and goodwill amortization, caused by the LBO. Most lenders and equity investors view these noncash effects as irrelevant to any assessment of how the company and its management are performing.

The third and perhaps the most important factor is the benefit realized by tying the economic stake of key managers to the success of the transaction. Management is usually given the opportunity to invest or earn a significant stake in the company. Through the compounding effects available through leveraging, managers of successful LBO companies often amass significant personal fortunes much greater than they would simply as paid employees. Managers' own incentives to realize the potential equity returns are combined with the active oversight of the majority shareholders, the sponsor groups, which are much more active in influencing major corporate undertakings and reviewing company performance than is typical in the publicly held arena.

Thus, the combination of private ownership (including giving management a significant equity share) and high leverage is a powerful way of improving a company's operations.

[2] Low Equity Valuation

In theory, a firm will not be subject to a buyout by another party if the price that must be paid is higher than the full value of the firm. "Full value" must be defined as full value to the most efficient operator, which may not be present management. However, the public equity market only gives a value for the firm based on its most likely valuation, which may not be the maximum potential value of the firm. Full value is not given to a firm's equity securities if full value is not warranted; that is, full value will not be given when the firm is not performing up to its potential. Securities analysts examine the firm and provide a valuation based on their view of how the firm will perform in the future. If they believe that management will operate the firm at suboptimal potential and that management will not be changed by the board of directors, the value they place on the firm's equity securities will reflect that belief.

Securities analysts may believe that the performance of the firm can be improved, yet they may not be in a position to act on that belief. LBO sponsor firms, on the other hand, can improve the firm by buying it and changing management or strategy. The LBO firm places a value on the firm based on how well they think it can be operated. As long as the purchase price for the firm is below that level, LBO sponsors are encouraged by the profit motive to acquire the poorly performing firm.

In order to induce the majority of shareholders to sell stock of a publicly held company, the buyer generally must offer a premium over the quoted price. This premium is usually in the 20 percent to 25 percent range. Existing public shareholders benefit from the opportunity to sell their stock at a price that would not have been realized for many years if it continued as a public company. This "control premium" paid by purchasers of publicly owned companies is a factor whether the buyer is an LBO sponsor or another acquiror. In either case, by taking majority ownership, the purchaser will be able to set corporate policy and strategy.

[3] Tax Effects

Clearly, the most obvious tax benefit of an LBO is the deductibility, for tax purposes, of interest on borrowed money. This is another reason why buyout firms attempt to maximize the amount of leverage in purchasing a business. Historically, both interest paid in cash and interest accrued but not currently paid in cash (i.e., PIK or zero-coupon securities) were allowed to be deducted for tax purposes as expense items by the borrower. However, when the concerns over the problems created by LBOs reached a crescendo in Congress in the late 1980s, measures were undertaken to limit the amount of noncash interest that could be expended. For example, noncash interest on newly issued debt that accrues at a rate higher than 5 percent over the comparable Treasury note or that is not paid in cash within five years is not deductible. Tax-deductibility of noncash interest on existing PIK securities and zero-coupon securities was grandfathered.

Most firms that have undergone LBOs pay little or no income tax after the buyout. The interest deduction on the debt securities generally reduces taxable income to zero or below (new tax rules notwithstanding), thus eliminating income taxes. For example, in 1988, RJR Nabisco reported a provision for income taxes of $893 million, which included current U.S. federal and foreign tax liability of $678 million. For 1989, from February 9 through September 30 (the period after the LBO), the tax liability of RJR Nabisco Holdings, the new parent company, was -146 million, with a -96 million being current liability. On an annualized basis, nearly a billion dollars of cash previously paid in taxes is now available for debt service.

2.09 TRENDS FOR THE 1990s

As LBOs developed, their characteristics changed. In the early days of this phenomenon, the companies that were purchased in leveraged transactions were basic, predictable, recession-resistant businesses with very stable cash flows. Buyers offered five times cash flow, and the debt-to-equity ratios of the resultant companies were in the range of 5.0 to 6.0. In addition to good cash flows, the businesses generally had assets that provided comfort to the lender in the event of changes in circumstances. Management was also key, as the LBO investors were not staffed to run the businesses and expected to motivate existing management by bringing them in as shareholders.

In the 1980s, the composition of the LBO changed, as mentioned earlier. Rather than smaller private firms, large public companies or their subsidiaries become the target of the LBO transaction. Relatively low stock market prices and low debt costs combined to allow sponsors to pay high prices for companies. The result was an explosion of buyout activity in the late 1980s, culminating with the $26 billion RJR Nabisco LBO in early 1989.

By the end of 1989, the buyout binge appeared to be coming to an end, at least temporarily. Various factors contributed to this change. In the aftermath of defaults by a number of LBO bond issues, the high-yield junk bond market declined sharply, and the ability to raise money in this market all but stopped in 1990. In late 1991, this market recovered strongly, and it had its highest volume ever in 1992. However, high-yield investors are requiring transactions with less leverage (more equity) and more cash flow coverage than in the 1980s. A continuing strong stock market, coupled with concerns about recession, caused LBO sponsors to be wary of investing in new deals at high prices when earnings and cash flow continued to be curtailed by economic conditions. Several large planned LBOs collapsed in late 1989, including the United Airlines transaction, indicating that the markets and the banks felt that the transactions could not be financed. This was an indication that prices for companies were too high for successful buyouts. Congress began to feel that the tax deductibility of interest provided too much incentive for HLTs. While the only legislative restriction actually imposed was a restriction on interest deductions for PIK bonds under certain circumstances, the threat of other congressional action cast a pall over the LBO arena.

In 1990, the banking regulators declared a uniform definition of HLTs. Prior to this standard definition, each bank defined for itself which loans to report as HLTs. These loans, under the newly imposed designations, were reported both to the regulators and in public financial statements, permitting both regulators and analysts to make judgments as to the risk composition of a bank's loan portfolios. The new definition captured loans that resulted from a financing transaction that involves the buyout, acquisition, or recapitalization of an existing business and met one of the following criteria: (1) The transaction doubled the company's liabilities; (2) the transaction resulted in a leverage ratio of higher than 75 percent; or (3) the agent designated the

FIGURE 2-6

Standard & Poor's 500 Stock Index

Date	Close
12/31/85	211.28
12/31/86	242.17
12/31/87	247.08
12/30/88	277.72
12/29/89	353.40
12/31/90	330.22
12/31/91	417.09
10/20/92	415.48

Note: Numbers shown are index numbers.

transaction as an HLT. This standardization forced each bank to review its entire portfolio when year-end 1989 numbers were released. The reviews showed much higher aggregate numbers than had been previously reported for many of the banks.

As of June 1992, the federal bank regulatory agencies discontinued the use of the HLT definition for regulatory reporting purposes. This was in response to criticism that the definition had created an unintended "credit crunch" affecting the pricing and availability of credit to certain highly leveraged buyers. In addition, in the early 1990s many fewer leveraged transactions were occurring and many companies were improving their credit standing by deleveraging and issuing equity. The agencies felt that the HLT designation had served its purpose by causing lenders to structure and monitor credits more carefully given the increased risks. However, bank lenders continue to be wary of extending HLT loans. Pricing on LBO bank loans has increased, and some institutions have withdrawn from the market owing either to bad experiences in terms of losses on loans to poorly performing LBOs or concern about regulatory scrutiny.

Many of the factors that contributed to the growing number of LBOs in the 1980s have changed. The stock market is at near-record-high levels, showing strength and resiliency following the crash of 1987 and the mini-decline of 1989, as shown in Figure 2-6. Corporate profits (and cash flow) appear to be falling off or at least not showing the robust growth that powered the rise of the stock market in the late 1980s. Improvements in the efficiency and productivity of many firms are reducing the need for and effectiveness of buyouts.

If stock prices were to decline, a pickup in buyout activity would presumably result. Investor funds continue to be available to LBO sponsors to organize these transactions, and the high-yield market has recovered. However, debt financing from the bank market has become harder to obtain for buyouts, and all lenders have increased their credit criteria. In the current environment, LBOs continue to occur but not with the same frequency or on the same scale as in the 1980s. At this juncture, it appears unlikely that activity level of the 1980s will be repeated, but the principles and benefits of LBOs continue to be applied in the current market.

APPENDIX 2.1   SAMPLE LEVERAGED BUYOUTS

George Stable Corporation

George Stable Corporation (Stable) is a major manufacturer of a diversified line of basic disposable household products. The company is the largest domestic producer of these products. Historical financial statements for the company are shown in App. Figure 1. In September 1988, the company agreed to be acquired by an investment firm in an LBO at a purchase price of approximately $53 per share, or about $3.9 billion. Prior to the offering, the stock of the company was trading at approximately $36 per share. The agreed-on purchase price was approximately 50 percent above the prevailing market price of the stock prior to the buyout. The stock had previously traded at over $60 per share but had declined with the overall market over the year prior to the buyout.

The sustainable cash flow of the company from operations before financing costs (operating income plus noncash depreciation and amortization charges less capital expenditures, known as EBIDT − C) on an annual basis was approximately $380 million. This was determined in the following manner. As shown in App. Figure 2, historical EBIDT − C was $135 million for the first six months of 1988. On an annual basis, therefore, EBIDT − C would be $270 million (if there is no seasonality). However, two adjustments were made to determine the cash flow available to support the LBO. First, capital expenditures were thought to be excessive for current operations, and a reduction to $100 million per year from the $168 million anticipated for the year was considered to be not only feasible but also sensible. It was further estimated that operating and administrative costs could be reduced by approximately $40 million annually through better management of the company. These two items would improve cash flow by approximately $110 million and result in total expected annual EBIDT − C of approximately $380 million in the first year after the buyout.

As mentioned previously, the purchase price of the company, including fees and expenses, was $3.9 billion, or just over 10 times the cash flow. While this is a high acquisition multiple for this type of company, the company's growth potential and stability of earnings will allow future debt service to be accomplished easily. Furthermore, the buyer realized that certain assets of the company could be sold at advantageous prices. The receipts from these sales would be used to retire a portion of the indebtedness accumulated from the buyout, allowing the retained parts of the company to support the remaining (much reduced) debt burden.

As an alternative to looking at the purchase price as a multiple of cash flow, the analyst can compute the discounted cash flow return. The discount rate that results in the present value of future benefits equaling the purchase price is known as an internal rate of return (IRR). In order to compute the IRR, refer to App. Figure 2, the pro forma financial summary for the company. Adjusted EBIDT − C was $380 million for the first year after the buyout, as determined earlier. It was assumed that cash flow will grow at 7 percent per year, approximately equal to previous growth experience. A terminal valuation for the company equal to seven times cash flow (a conservative acquisition multiple) is used at year 10. The present value of the projected pretax cash flow plus the terminal value is $3.9 billion if a discount rate of 13 percent is used. This equals the purchase price, so 13 percent is the IRR.

In 1988, this IRR was considered by the buyers, in light of their other opportunities and the degree of leverage employed, to be appropriate for a company of this type. The ability to sell some assets at high cash flow multiples provided some offset to the

APP. FIGURE 1

Historical Financial Summary

Financial data	Six Month		Annual			
	June 30, 1988	June 30, 1987	1987	1986	1985	1984
Sales	$930.0	$867.0	$1,758.0	$1,549.0	$1,363.0	$1,339.0
Cost of sales	(673.0)	(601.0)	(1,233.0)	(1,082.0)	(889.0)	(899.0)
Gross income	$257.0	$266.0	$ 525.0	$ 467.0	$ 474.0	$ 440.0
SG&A	(101.0)	(101.0)	(205.0)	(196.0)	(170.0)	(173.0)
Operating income	$156.0	$165.0	$ 320.0	$ 271.0	$ 304.0	$ 267.0
Interest expense	(14.0)	(16.0)	(31.0)	(15.0)	(11.0)	(17.0)
Other expense or income	(3.0)	1.0	(1.0)	20.0	(1.0)	(3.0)
Income before taxes	$139.0	$150.0	$ 288.0	$ 276.0	$ 292.0	$ 247.0
Income taxes	(56.0)	66.0	(129.0)	(130.0)	(135.0)	(114.0)
Net income	$ 83.0	$ 84.0	$ 159.0	$ 146.0	$ 157.0	$ 133.0
EBIT	$153.0	$166.0	$ 319.0	$ 291.0	$ 303.0	$ 264.0
Depreciation and amortization	66.0	61.0	126.0	102.0	83.0	72.0
EBIDT	$219.0	$227.0	$ 445.0	$ 393.0	$ 386.0	$ 336.0
Capital expenditures	(84.0)	(89.0)	(186.0)	(355.0)	(198.0)	(157.0)
EBIDT − C	$135.0	$138.0	$ 259.0	$ 38.0	$ 188.0	$ 179.0
Coverage ratios						
EBIT/total interest	10.9	10.4	10.3	19.4	27.5	15.5
EBIDT/total interest	15.6	14.2	14.4	26.2	35.1	19.8
EBITD − C/total interest	9.6	8.6	8.4	2.5	17.1	10.5

Note: Dollars in millions.

APP. FIGURE 2

Pro Forma Financial Summary

	1988	1989	1990	1991	1992	1993	1994	1995	1996	Terminal Value
EBIT	$348.0	$372.4	$398.4	$426.3	$456.2	$488.1	$522.3	$558.8	$597.9	
Depreciation and amortization	132.0	135.0	140.0	145.0	150.0	150.0	150.0	150.0	150.0	
EBIDT	$480.0	$507.4	$538.4	$571.3	$606.2	$638.1	$672.3	$708.8	$747.9	
Capital expenditures	(100.0)	(100.0)	(100.0)	(100.0)	(100.0)	(100.0)	(100.0)	(100.0)	(100.0)	
EBIDT − C (Pretax free cash flow)	$380.0	$407.4	$438.4	$471.3	$506.2	$538.1	$572.3	$608.8	$647.9	$4,535.5[a]

Note: Dollars in millions.
[a] Terminal value is set at seven times last year's EBIDT − C.

perceived risk of the firm. The high acquisition multiple and low discount rate suggest that cash flow is low for the price paid, and some innovative financing will be required to finance a portion of the acquisition, thus allowing for an exceptionally high return on the equity investment.

The transaction was financed in two phases: the initial acquisition phase and the later merger phase. In the acquisition phase, the stock of Stable was acquired through a tender offer, with financing coming from bank loans, subordinated bridge loans, and equity. These bridge loans were provided by investment banking firms, either from their own funds or from a private placement with investors, and were to bridge the financing until longer-term subordinated bonds could be sold. Once the buyer completed the acquisition of stock, the acquired company was merged into the acquisition company. At this point, the merger phase, permanent long-term subordinated debt financing was sold to refinance the bridge debt. The bank debt is often restructured at this time as well.

The first consideration in debt financing of LBOs is the determination of the amount of funds that the banks will lend on a senior basis. Maximizing bank debt is important because it is generally the type of debt that carries the lowest interest cost that is available for LBO transactions. At the time of this LBO, banks provided loans if the interest coverage for senior debt (EBIDT − C, or in some cases, EBIT divided by bank interest expense) was at least 1.4 or 1.5 times. Also, banks liked to see that the capital structure had no more than approximately 60 percent bank debt (banks generally lent on a secured basis for LBOs, and collateral value played an important, although secondary, role in determining the amount of bank debt that could be raised).

For Stable, banks provided $2.4 billion in financing for the acquisition phase, which was 62 percent of the amount necessary to complete the transaction. An 11 percent interest rate was assumed on the bank debt, which resulted in $264 million of interest expense and senior interest coverage of 1.4 times. During the merger phase refinancing, bank debt was reduced to approximately $2 billion, which reduced bank interest cost to $220 million and improved interest coverage to a more comfortable 1.7 times for the banks.

With the total acquisition cost of $3.9 billion, bank debt was clearly insufficient to finance the acquisition fully. The next step was to sell as much subordinated debt as possible (generally, for larger transactions, different tranches of subordinated debt, such as senior subordinated and junior subordinated, are used to reduce the cost of issuing this debt). Separate tranches and special provisions help to segment the market for debt, thus allowing the borrower to design instruments that will be unusually attractive for certain investors. Subordinated lenders will provide funds that are at greater risk than bank funds because of the higher interest rate that they receive. Generally, subordinated bonds can be sold with interest coverage of 1 to 1.1 times. In this case, it was decided to issue approximately $1.5 billion of various subordinated securities. If the subordinated debt interest rate was 14 percent, subordinated debt interest cost would be $210 million, resulting in total interest cost of $430 million. This posed a serious problem, however, as interest expense was now projected to be $50 million in excess of cash flow.

There were several ways to solve this problem. Total debt could be reduced by increasing the amount of equity used in the financing (whatever portion of the purchase price is not funded with some form of debt must be funded with equity). From the standpoint of the equity owners, however, this was the least desirable course of action. In the case of Stable, the equity owners wished to minimize their investment so as to maximize their potential return on the limited equity contributed.

APP. FIGURE 3

Capitalization Summary

Bank debt		
Revolving credit	$ 230.0	
Term loan	1,800.0	
Total		$2,030.0
Subordinated debt		
Senior subordinated notes	$ 383.9	
Subordinated debentures	383.9	
Junior discount debentures[a]	364.6	
Junior debentures[b]		
	352.7	
Total		$1,485.1
Equity		$ 429.6
Total financing		$3,944.7

Note: Dollars in millions.

[a] The junior discount debentures are zero-coupon bonds.

[b] The junior debentures are PIK bonds.

The alternative would be to structure a portion of the debt securities as deferred interest obligations. Approximately $700 million in bond indebtedness was issued as zero-coupon or PIK debt for Stable. Zero-coupon bonds are issued below par value with no cash interest paid currently. However, the value of the bond increases each year toward par value (known as interest accretion) based on an assumed interest rate, specifically, the market rate for this type of bond at issue. At maturity, the bond is redeemed at par value, and the investor's profit results from the difference between the purchase price and the par value. PIK bonds are similar to zero-coupon bonds, except that PIKs are issued at par, with interest payments made by sending the holders the appropriate amount of identical bonds, not cash. The amount of additional bonds is determined as if it were an interest rate. Thus, if $1 million worth of 14 percent PIKs was issued, the holder would receive $140,000 worth of new bonds each year that the bonds are outstanding. Holders also get additional "interest" on the bonds received as payment.

The use of zero-coupon and PIK bonds resulted in a $100 million reduction in cash interest cost, from $430 million to $330 million, and this total is $50 million below available cash flow. Cash interest coverage was 1.15 times, which was deemed acceptable to bondholders.

Interest not paid currently on zero-coupon and PIK debt is accrued, however, and must eventually be paid. Deferred interest debt is a time bomb that continues to accrue and eventually becomes a cash obligation. Deferred interest obligations are best used in situations in which the current cash flow is particularly depressed or significant growth in cash flow is expected. The goal is to retire such bonds as soon as possible.

The financing structure actually used at Stable is shown in App. Figure 3. Total debt raised from the banks and the bond markets was approximately $3.5 billion, still $400 million below the financing requirement. As noted earlier, the remaining amount of financing had to be equity, and it was provided by the LBO buyer.

American Standard Inc.

The transaction that is examined here is the American Standard Inc. acquisition by Kelso & Company. In January 1988, the Black & Decker Corporation initiated an unsolicited cash tender offer at $56 per share for all shares of American Standard. After resistance from the company, Black & Decker increased its offer to $77 per share. Management and the board of American Standard attempted to pursue a recapitalization of the company but in February elected to put the company up for sale to third parties. In March, Kelso submitted an offer to the Board of American Standard, and the offer, at $78 per share, was approved by the Board. Kelso formed ASI Acquisition Company, which commenced a tender offer for all shares of American Standard. ASI Acquisition was capitalized as follows for the tender phase of the transaction:

Senior debt (banks)	$1,580
Subordinated bridge loan	920
Equity	180
	$2,680

Note: Dollars in millions.

These funds were used to pay for the purchase of shares ($2.387 billion in total), to escrow sufficient cash ($144 million) to pay interest on the senior and subordinated debt over the maximum estimated period (six months) that it might take to effect the merger, and to pay expenses of the acquisition and merger ($149 million).

Kelso is a private investment banking firm that specializes in LBOs. Prior to the American Standard transaction (Kelso's largest deal at the time), the firm had completed over 75 LBOs. Funds for the equity financing were provided by an LBO fund previously raised by Kelso and by additional equity investors found by Kelso. By the completion of the tender offer, 95 percent of the shares of American Standard had been purchased. On June 29, 1988, ASI Acquisition was merged into American Standard. (See App. Figure 4 for a diagram of the corporate structure.) The resulting capital structure was as follows:

Senior debt (bank)	$1,719
Preexisting senior debt	208
Senior subordinated debt	550
Junior subordinated debt (PIK)	350
Equity	250
	$3,077

Note: Dollars in millions.

American Standard is a leading producer of air conditioning, plumbing, and transportation products. Its operations are worldwide and it manufactures and sells products in 30 countries. For the year ended December 31, 1987, the company reported net sales of $3.4 billion, income from continuous operations of $133 million, and net income of $127 million.

In order for the company to hedge its foreign-source income, a portion of the senior bank debt was structured as a multicurrency term loan (in U.S. dollars, deutsche marks, U.K. pounds, and Canadian dollars). The remainder of the bank debt was denominated in U.S. dollars. The final maturity of the term loan was eight years.

APP. FIGURE 4

Kelso–American Standard Transaction

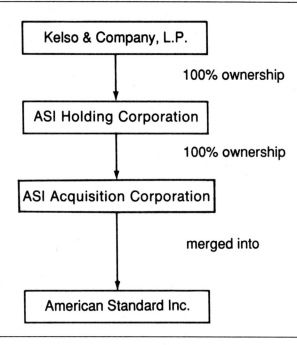

Principal covenants on the debt included maintenance of a minimum current ratio and a minimum consolidated net worth, limitation on leverage (defined as the ratio of senior liabilities to consolidated net worth plus subordinated debt), maintenance of interest coverage (defined as the ratio of consolidated EBIDT to consolidated cash interest expense), and an EBIDT − C test. The senior bank debt was secured by a pledge of stock of all of the domestic securities of American Standard, mortgages and liens on domestic property, and (where legal and practicable) pledges of shares of the principal foreign subsidiaries and mortgages and liens on foreign properties. Pricing on the senior debt was at the London interbank offered rate (LIBOR) plus 2.5 percent, with a facility fee of 1.5 percent on the total aggregate commitment, with additional fees paid to the agent bank.

The $920 million subordinated bridge financing (at the tender phase) was provided by an investment firm and was priced at LIBOR plus 5 percent, with a 3 percent fee to the firm for arranging the placement deal. The permanent subordinated debt, which refinanced this bridge, was publicly placed. The rate on the senior subordinated debt was at 12.875 percent with a maturity on June 30, 2000, and the junior subordinated debt was placed at a 14.34 percent coupon (PIK for five years) to June 30, 2003. Principal covenants on the subordinated debt included a limitation on incurrence of additional debt and a restriction on use of proceeds from asset sales. Kelso and the company agreed to a plan that provided for the reduction of debt through improved cash flow from operations as well as through the sale of certain noncore assets and businesses.

Since the LBO in April 1988, the company has accomplished the sale of several noncore businesses as well as its headquarters building. Proceeds from these sales were approximately $300 million, about $70 million higher than the company had estimated. For the year ending on December 31, 1989, the company's EBIT improved 19 percent over EBIT for the comparable 1988 period, for a net increase of 9 percent. For the nine months ending on September 30, 1989, net sales were modestly ahead of plan, and EBIT was about 5 percent ahead of plan (and about 16 percent ahead of EBIT for the comparable 1988 period).

As of September 30, 1989, the company's long-term debt was reported at $2,143 million and its stockholders' equity at $83.9 million. The stockholders' equity account was compressed as follows:

Capital surplus	$253.1
Retained deposit	(73.4)
Foreign currency	
Translation effects	(95.8)
	$ 83.9

Note: Dollars in millions.

Chapter 3
Dividend Policy

STEVEN C. GRAHAM

SEAN M. BOYLE

JOSEPH G. MAY

WILLIAM P. MCKEE, JR.

CHRISTINA TAKOUDES MORRISON

3.01 INTRODUCTION

"Dividend policy" refers to the method of distribution of past years' or the present year's earnings to shareholders. Dividend distributions may take the form of cash, stock, and, in very rare circumstances, company products or property. This chapter highlights the most common ways publicly held C corporations distribute cash to common shareholders; although the majority of information presented relates to publicly held C corporations, additional information is provided concerning cash distributions from S corporations or partnerships. This information regarding S corporations is particularly relevant in light of the increasing number of business owners electing this corporate form.

The arguments presented are not expanded to include the effects on total shareholder wealth when the receipt of a dividend (assuming the market price of the stock does not change after the dividend distribution and assuming the shareholder does not sell any shares) and the receipt of proceeds from the sale of stock (where the shareholder has sold shares before the announcement of a dividend distribution) are compared.

The view of dividends by U.S. corporations as well as investors has shifted significantly since 1950. Prior to 1950, it was not unusual to have dividend yields on stocks in excess of bond yields (bonds, not corporate stocks, were preferred by investors). The reluctance of investors to own stocks resulted from the economic depression of the 1930s and the accompanying lack of confidence in the future of the economy. Therefore, publicly held corporations used high dividend payments to entice investors to buy stocks. It was not until the mid-1950s, when investors' views of the economy began to change, that corporate stocks gained favor and dividend yields began to decline.

Since the early 1980s, corporate dividend policy has undergone significant changes. Prior to this period, management would almost always state its confidence in future earnings by regularly raising the company's dividend. During the 1980s, however, shareholders became more concerned with the double taxation of dividends (once at the corporate level, and a second time at the individual level), and began preferring that the company reinvest its excess cash rather than distribute it to shareholders. As a result, management has more often communicated future earnings confidence to investors by reinvesting cash flow into the business or by repurchasing a portion of the company's shares.[1]

3.02 KEY TERMS

[1] Dividends

A dividend is the distribution of past years' or the present year's earnings to shareholders. A dividend is generally distributed in the form of cash or additional shares of stock and is prorated by the type of stock security (common or preferred). In most cases, the amount of the dividend is determined by management, approved by the board of directors, and then announced to shareholders. The day of the announcement

---

[1] A.J. Cohen and S.G. Einhorn, "Valuation Update," *Goldman Sachs Portfolio Strategy* (Aug. 19, 1992), p. 3.

is known as the declaration date, and the announcement includes the holder-of-record date and the payment date. A typical announcement might read: "On July 18, 1992, the directors of ABC Corporation met and declared a dividend payment of $1 per share, payable to shareholders of record on August 25, 1992, with payment to be made on October 1, 1992."

[a] Regular Dividends. The vast majority of dividend-paying companies distribute earnings to common shareholders at regular intervals, usually quarterly. Companies that establish regular dividend payment policies are generally reluctant to reduce or omit the dividend for fear that such an action will be perceived negatively by investors. Therefore, regular dividends tend to become viewed by management as a fixed disbursement and will rarely be cut except in the most serious circumstances.

[b] Special Dividends. Once earnings for an entire fiscal year are known, a company may elect to make a distribution in the form of a onetime special or extra dividend. The onetime payment may be used to share higher than expected earnings with stockholders. The irregular occurrence of this type of dividend alerts shareholders that the payment should be treated as a onetime event and not a regular dividend. This tactic permits the company to convey some good news and distribute earnings to shareholders without increasing the regular dividend to a level that may not be sustainable. A company that routinely pays no regular dividend may occasionally choose to pay a special dividend.

[c] Stock Dividends. A stock dividend is a noncash distribution and is similar to a stock split in that it increases the number of shares outstanding without affecting the wealth or the ownership interest of the current shareholders. For example, in a 10 percent stock dividend, the owner of 100 shares of stock will receive an additional 10 shares at no cost. The shareholder now owns 110 shares, but earnings-per-share and price-per-share figures have decreased in proportion to the dividend, effectively having no impact on the value of the holdings. Despite the similar effects of stock dividends and splits, the events are treated differently on the balance sheet. Figure 3-1 illustrates the accounting treatment of the two transactions.

[2] Share Repurchase

As an alternative to paying a cash dividend, a company may choose to distribute earnings to its shareholders by repurchasing its own shares. A share repurchase is often chosen when management believes that the stock market has undervalued its shares or that its shares are the company's best currently available investment opportunity. Share repurchases have also been used by corporate management to defend against unwanted takeovers. In many cases, a share repurchase will increase the share price of the remaining outstanding shares. This type of distribution effectively distributes cash to shareholders in the form of capital gains rather than dividends.

[3] Dividend Yield

The dividend yield is the annual dividend payment divided by the stock price. Usually, dividend yield is computed at a point in time by annualizing the current quarterly

FIGURE 3-1

Accounting for Stock Dividend Versus Stock Split

Before a Stock Split or a Stock Dividend

Common stock (3,000,000 shares authorized, 2,500,000 shares outstanding, $1 par)	$ 2,500,000
Additional paid-in capital	5,000,000
Retained earnings	77,500,000
Total common stockholders' equity	$85,000,000

After a Two-For-One Stock Split

Common stock (6,000,000 shares authorized, 5,000,000 shares outstanding, $0.50 par)	$ 2,500,000
Additional paid-in capital	5,000,000
Retained earnings	77,500,000
Total common stockholders' equity	$85,000,000

After a 20% Stock Dividend

Common stock (3,000,000 shares authorized, 3,000,000 shares outstanding, $1 par)[a]	$ 3,000,000
Additional paid-in capital[b]	44,500,000
Retained earnings[b]	37,500,000
Total common stockholders' equity	$85,000,000

[a] Shares outstanding are increased by 20 percent, from 2.5 million to 3 million.

[b] A transfer equal to the market value of the new shares ($80 per share) is made from the retained earnings account to the additional paid-in capital and common stock accounts:

Transfer = (2,500,000 shares)(0.2)($80) = $40,000,000

Of this $40 million, ($1 par)(500,000 shares) = $500,000 goes to common stock and $39.5 million to paid-in capital.

---

dividend and dividing by the current stock price; that is, if the current quarterly dividend is 25 cents and the stock price is $20, the indicated annual dividend is $1 and the dividend yield is 5 percent per annum.

[4] Dividend Payout Ratio

The dividend payout ratio is the proportion of earnings the company pays to shareholders in the form of dividends and is usually calculated on a per-share basis. For example, if earnings are $4 per share for the year and dividends are $1 per share for the year, the payout ratio equals 25 percent. Although a company may elect to pay out a constant percentage of earnings, this policy is rarely selected by management owing to the fluctuation in dividends caused by changes in earnings. The historic five-year average dividend payout rates of the Standard & Poor's (S&P) 500 Index are shown in Figure 3-2.

FIGURE 3-2

Payout Rates of S&P Composite Stocks in Five-Year Spans (1936–1985) and Goldman Sachs S&P 500 Update for Three-Year Period (1989–1991)

Source: Compiled from Standard & Poor's Statistical Service, *Security Price Index Record* (New York: 1986), pp. 118–121; Goldman, Sachs & Co. *Valuation Update* (Aug. 19, 1992), p. 3

Period	Percent
1936–1940	71
1941–1945	64
1946–1950	52
1951–1955	55
1956–1960	56
1961–1965	57
1966–1970	55
1971–1975	46
1976–1980	41
1981–1985	49
1989–1991	59

3.03 ISSUES AFFECTING DIVIDEND POLICY AND STOCK VALUE

[1] Impact of Dividend Policy on Stock

[a] Bird-In-Hand Theory. Prior to 1961, eminent thinkers and analysts, including Graham and Dodd[2] and Gordon,[3] argued that more liberal dividend payouts were likely to be rewarded by investors willing to pay higher prices for a company's common stock. Part of this reasoning was based on investors' perceptions about the corporation's ability to pay a dividend. At the time, investors believed that it was important for corporations to show dividend-paying capabilities. In addition, investors believed that the higher the dividend component of total return (dividends plus capital gains), the lower the volatility of the stock. All things being equal, investors were willing to pay a premium for shares with a higher dividend component of total return. This "bird-in-hand" theory gains additional support through Graham and Dodd's argument that past experience has taught investors to be skeptical of the future dividends and capital gains promised to them by management, and, therefore, shareholders prefer to have management pay regular dividends.

The bird-in-hand theory, which argued for the certainty of current dividends versus the uncertainty of future dividends (or capital gains), seemed to be supported empirically by a strong statistical correlation between high dividend payouts and high price/earnings (P/E) ratios. However, the theory overlooked companies whose future cash flows are uncertain and represent a high-risk investment, such as start-up or growth

---

[2] Benjamin Graham and David Dodd, *Security Analysis: Principles and Techniques,* 5th ed. (New York: McGraw-Hill, 1988).

[3] M. Gordon, "Dividends, Earnings and Stock Prices," *Review of Economics and Statistics* (May 1959), pp. 99–105.

companies. These types of companies generally pay out a lower level of dividends, opting instead to conserve cash and reinvest earnings in the company. If a company fits this description, the bird-in-hand theory implies that the company's stock will have a low P/E ratio, which in practice is not always true. Conversely, the theory states that companies whose investments yield more consistent returns (i.e., are less risky) can safely afford a higher dividend payout rate. Although the theory might overlook low-payout companies, it is important to understand the period and economic climate (early 1930s through 1950) in which Graham and Dodd published much of their work.

[b] Dividend Policy as Irrelevant to Share Price. In October 1961, Modigliani and Miller[4] argued that dividend policy should have no impact on a company's stock market value. Their underlying assumption was that a company's investment policy decisions are made independent from its dividend policy decisions. Thus, dividend policy is irrelevant to share price, as long as the firm's investment decisions are unaffected by the decision to pay (or increase) dividends.

A study by Black and Scholes[5] published in 1974 supports Modigliani and Miller's conclusion that expected returns on high- and low-payout stocks of equal risk are not significantly different and that stock value is unrelated to dividend yield.

A 1989 study by Jose and Stevens[6] supports the irrelevancy of dividends theory in determining stock values as originally published by Modigliani and Miller in 1961 and supported by Black and Scholes. The Jose and Stevens study concentrated on the relationship between dividend policy and the value of the company. Their findings indicated that valuation premiums are linked to stable, consistent, and positive dividend-per-share trends, irrespective of the dividend payout ratio. Also, higher dividends without increased earnings failed to enhance share value.

In addition to these theories, there are several other issues that may or may not effect dividend policy and the stock market value of a company's stock. Some of these issues will be discussed in the following three sections and will include the tax effect, clientele effect, information effect, and agency theory.

[2] Effects of Tax Treatments

What effects, if any, should taxes have on investors' preference for capital gains or dividends, and should tax treatments cause investors to prefer one form of payout to another? Do taxes affect the shareholder in a C corporation differently from the shareholder of an S corporation? How is the total return of a C corporation shareholder different from the total return for a shareholder in an S corporation or partnership? Is this difference in total return significant?

---

[4] M. Miller and F. Modigliani, "Dividend Policy, Growth and the Valuation of Shares," *Journal of Business* (Oct. 1961), pp. 431–433.

[5] F. Black and M. Scholes, "The Effects of Dividend Yields and Dividend Policy on Common Stock Prices and Returns," *Journal of Financial Economics* (May 1974), pp. 1–24.

[6] M.L. Jose and J.L. Stevens, "Capital Market Valuation of Dividend Policy," *Journal of Business Finance and Accounting,* Vol. 16 (UK) (Winter 1989), pp. 651–662.

[a] TRA 1986. Prior to the changes enacted in the Tax Reform Act of 1986 (TRA 1986), Litzenberger and Ramaswamy,[7] in a 1979 study, argued that the higher tax on dividends actually makes investors dividend-averse and that a dollar of dividends is therefore worth less than a dollar of capital gain, resulting in a relative market discounting of high-dividend-yielding shares versus low-yielding shares.

Following the full implementation of TRA 1986, dividends and capital gains earned by individuals were taxed at the same rate. However, even with the elimination of preferential treatment of long-term capital gains, at least two reasons remain for taxpaying individuals to favor capital gains over dividend distributions. First, dividends are taxable in full in the year they are received, but capital gains are not taxed until the investor chooses to liquidate the investment. Second, an investor pays tax on the entire dividend, while taxes are paid only on the portion of the proceeds from a sale of stock that exceeds the tax basis or cost. Therefore, on the receipt of equal cash amounts, the tax liability on receiving a dividend payment will be greater than on receiving the proceeds of a stock sale.

A 1991 study published by Bolster and Janjigian[8] focused on the effects of TRA 1986 on shareholder wealth and dividend policy. Their results indicated that high-dividend-yielding stocks significantly outperformed low-dividend-yielding stocks once the tax reforms were finalized. They did not find evidence however, that corporate management, in reaction to TRA 1986, had materially changed its company's dividend policy.

The long-standing argument as to whether investors prefer high-, low-, or no-dividend yields is likely to continue for some time. In a 1983 study using a sample of firms that had paid no dividends for at least 10 years, Asquith and Mullins[9] concluded that announcements of unanticipated dividends resulted in a short-term increase in shareholder wealth.

Because empirical studies seek to evaluate investor preferences by measuring yields and total returns over many years, it may be that the preferences of investors in 1983 were different from those of investors in 1933. Preferences may be evolving as investor concerns become more sophisticated (such as the increased concern over the double taxation of dividends), or preferences may be, at least in part, cyclical in response to changing economic conditions and expectations.

[b] S Corporation Tax Treatment. In the case of an S corporation, double taxation under current tax law is not an issue. Tax on all annual income generated by an S corporation is the liability of each individual shareholder based on its portion of the company's income and is only taxed at the individual level. The S corporation shareholder then realizes an additional advantage in that under current tax laws, individual tax rates (maximum 31 percent) are lower than corporate tax rates (34 percent), allowing the shareholder to retain a greater portion of income. In contrast to a publicly held

---

[7] R. Litzenberger and K. Ramaswamy, "The Effects of Personal Taxes and Dividends on Capital Asset Prices, Theory and Empirical Evidence," *Journal of Financial Economics* (June 1979), pp. 163–195.

[8] P.J. Bolster and V. Janjigian, "Dividend Policy and Valuation Effects of the Tax Reform Act of 1986," *National Tax Journal,* Vol. 44 (Dec. 1991), pp. 511–518.

[9] P. Asquith and D. Mullins, Jr., "The Impact of Initiating Dividend Payments on Shareholders' Wealth," *Journal of Business,* Vol. 56 (Feb. 1983), pp. 77–96.

FIGURE 3-3

Total Return to Shareholders in Different Corporate Scenarios

C Corporation Paying Dividends

Annual income		$1,000	$1,000	$1,000	$1,000	$1,000
Corporate tax rate	34%	(340)	(340)	(340)	(340)	(340)
After-tax cash distributed to shareholders		660	660	660	660	660
Individual tax rate	31%	(205)	(205)	(205)	(205)	(205)
Shareholders' after-tax cash		455	455	455	455	455
After-tax return on reinvested dividends	6.9%		31	65	101	139
Cumulative after-tax total return		$ 455	$ 942	$1,463	$2,019	$2,614

C Corporation Reinvesting Cash

Annual income		$1,000	$1,000	$1,000	$1,000	$1,000
Corporate tax rate	34%	(340)	(340)	(340)	(340)	(340)
After-tax cash reinvested by company		660	660	660	660	660
After-tax return to company on reinvested cash	6.6%		44	90	139	192
After-tax total return to company		660	1,364	2,114	2,913	3,765
Individual tax rate	31%					(1,167)
Cumulative after-tax total return						$2,598

S Corporation or Partnership

Annual income		$1,000	$1,000	$1,000	$1,000	$1,000
Corporate tax rate	0%	(0)	(0)	(0)	(0)	(0)
After-tax cash distributed to shareholders		1,000	1,000	1,000	1,000	1,000
Individual tax rate	31%	(310)	(310)	(310)	(310)	(310)
Shareholders' after-tax cash		690	690	690	690	690
After-tax return on reinvested cash	6.9%		48	99	153	211
Cumulative after-tax total return		$ 690	$1,428	$2,216	$3,059	$3,960

C corporation, S corporation shareholders are not taxed on the cash distributions they receive.

Figure 3-3 provides a simplistic analysis of the total returns to shareholders in (1) a C corporation that distributes annual dividends; (2) a C corporation that reinvests excess cash internally; and (3) an S corporation or partnership that makes annual distributions to shareholders or partners. The example assumes that all reinvested excess cash, whether it is reinvested by the shareholder or the company, earns a pretax return of 10 percent. It also assumes that the reinvesting C corporation distributes all of its accumulated earnings to shareholders in year 5 and that the corporate and individual tax rates are 34 percent and 31 percent, respectively. Individuals who invest in publicly held C corporations through institutional investors such as mutual funds, pension plans, and trusts, will realize an even smaller return than those who invest directly in a publicly held C corporation owing to the payment of management and other related fees.

[c] **Clientele Effect.** The clientele effect refers to the difference among investors that prefer high- or low-dividend-yielding stocks depending on their individual investment philosophy and tax position. For example, generally 70 percent of dividend income for corporate investors is not taxed under current law, but a similar exclusion does not exist for capital gains. Moreover, some of the largest investors, which today account for a significant proportion of share ownership (e.g., pension funds, mutual funds, and other trusts), are not taxed on either dividends or capital gains and may not care which they receive, concentrating instead on total return.

With the universe of shareholding opportunities providing the investor with an equities "supermarket" in which high-, low-, or no-dividend-paying stocks may be purchased, investors may shop for the shares that provide them with the particular values they are seeking. If a company were to make a significant change in its dividend policy, two events would probably occur. First, there would most likely be an adjustment in the stock market price of the company's shares depending on whether the company was eliminating (reducing) or commencing (increasing) dividend payments, and there would probably be a change in the makeup of investors or clientele holding the company's shares.

[3] Effect of Information on Stock

Securities and Exchange Commission (SEC) regulations prevent corporate management of publicly held companies from revealing certain inside corporate information to outside investors. Therefore, dividend policy has historically been used as a means to convey some of this private information to the investing public. A dividend increase has historically been viewed by investors as a positive sign because it implies a higher level of sustainable earnings. The information effect has little or no relevancy to an S corporation because the stock is not publicly traded and often the majority of shareholders are members of management and already have knowledge of the company's private information and financial position.

Because common stock dividends must be paid from earnings, dividends tend to rise irregularly over time. Generally, there is a lag between an increase in earnings and a subsequent increase in dividends, indicating that companies are unwilling to increase the dividend until the board is convinced that the earnings increase is sustainable. This conclusion is supported by empirical evidence that unsustainable spurts in earnings are usually not accompanied by significant increases in the regular dividend (although a onetime or special dividend might be declared). Also, once a dividend level is established, companies are unlikely to reduce it, owing to the negative effects on the stock price, although further increases may be reduced or deferred if earnings growth is unsustainable.

The history of the earnings and dividends per share of the fictional ABC Corporation

FIGURE 3-4

ABC Corporation's Earnings and Dividend History

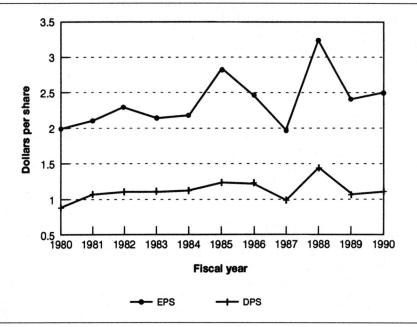

Fiscal year

EPS   DPS

for the period 1980–1990 are shown in Figure 3-4. They are consistent with the previous comments. Although earnings increased in 1982, the dividend increase was much less dramatic. Also, when earnings dipped in 1983, the dividend was not cut. Not until a substantial decline in operating earnings was reported for fiscal 1986 did the company lower dividends.

The practice of raising dividends in response to earnings increases is attributed to the information effect of dividend announcements. By increasing the dividend, management may be implying that the company's growth in earnings and cash flow will be sustainable and can be expected to continue into the future. Therefore, the company can afford to raise its dividend payout now and sustain the dividend payout level into the future.

Empirical studies indicate that dividend-paying companies tend to establish a target range for the payout ratio while not trying to distribute precisely the same percentage of earnings each quarter or each year. Given a target payout ratio, the lag in dividend increases compared to earnings increases supports the argument that management is reluctant to increase dividends out of concern that such an increase may not be sustainable into the future.

The existence of the information effect of dividends is also supported by empirical evidence that cuts in dividends are uncommon even when earnings have actually declined. As shown in Figure 3-2, during the period 1989–1991, when U.S. corporate profits were declining,[10] the dividend payout ratio increased from the previous period.

---

[10] Cohen and Einhorn, *op. cit.*

Concern about the information effect may result in the investor's overlooking the underlying earnings figure. A review of corporate annual reports reveals instances where dividends were actually increased in the face of declining earnings, apparently to convey management's confidence that it perceived the earnings decline to be temporary.

In certain industries, a strong belief in the information effect might be misleading to investors in predicting earnings. There have been several instances in which the industries with the worst profit performances have increased their dividends the most.[11] This pattern directly contradicts conventional thinking that increased dividends are the result of higher earnings or anticipated higher earnings that management believes will be sustainable now and into the future.

[4] Agency Theory

Agency theory was first advanced by Jensen and Meckling[12] in 1976, and arises from the conflict of interest between corporate managers, outside shareholders, and bondholders (which are not addressed in this section). In a study originally presented in 1987 and published in 1989, Crutchley and Hansen[13] examined the validity of agency theory and the steps suggested to reduce its impact on the relationship between shareholders and management.

Agency theory recognizes that the majority of shareholders in publicly traded companies are outsiders holding fairly well-diversified stock portfolios that have delegated the control and decision-making process to corporate managers. It is assumed that these stockholders, in general, own many different stocks in an attempt to diversify risk away from any one holding. Corporate managers, however, may have their own interests that do not coincide with those of the shareholders. The difference in interests between shareholders and corporate managers creates agency cost, which helps contribute to dividend policies.

When outside shareholders control a majority of the outstanding shares of a publicly held company, their objectives and financial goals may conflict with those of management. To avoid this conflict, the agency theory recommends an increase in management's share ownership, which, in theory, would better align management's interests with those of the outside shareholders.[14] A second recommendation is that management pay dividends or increase the current dividend payment to shareholders, which, in theory, will force management to consider how it will continue to pay dividends and move the company forward. If management elects an increase in the dividend payment, and if the increase is large enough to require additional external capital, management has in effect engaged outside third parties whose interests are more in line with those of the shareholders to review its performance. As part of their job of raising additional capital, these outsiders will review management's actions, and if

---

[11] R.M. Cahn, "Economic Comment," *First Boston Weekly: Insights, Equity Research* (Aug. 24, 1992), p. 17.

[12] M.C. Jensen and W.H. Meckling, "Theory of the Firm: Managerial Behavior Agency Costs and Capital Structure," *Journal of Financial Economics* (Oct. 1976), pp. 305–360.

[13] C.E. Crutchley and R.S. Hansen, "A Test of the Agency Theory of Managerial Ownership, Corporate Leverage, and Corporate Dividends," *Journal of Financial Management*, Vol. 18 (Winter 1989), pp. 36–46.

[14] *Ibid.*

these actions are thought to be detrimental to shareholder goals and objectives, management will have to refocus and align itself more closely with its shareholders.[15]

Agency theory recognizes the possible conflict of interest between corporate managers and outside shareholders and recommends reducing the conflict by having managers better align themselves with the outside shareholders of the company and/or pay dividends. In an S corporation or partnership, where shareholders are often also the managers, agency conflicts are minimal, if they exist at all.

[5] Dividend Irrelevancy

Academicians and other theorists have argued compellingly that beyond the very short term, management cannot influence stock prices through dividend policy. Some argue that dividends should not be paid except to communicate information that would otherwise not be available to investors. Others simply believe that the prevalence of dividend payments by U.S. corporations, in and of itself, shows that the remittance of dividends is not an irrational or ill-advised use of earnings.

Many studies support the basic tenet of Modigliani and Miller's 1961 study that the profitability resulting from a company's investment decisions is the prime factor affecting its stock price. It is critical that dividend policy be considered only after investment policy has been established and that forgoing a profitable investment in order to pay or maintain a dividend is never justified.

In writings and seminars, Stern[16] argues that investors at large are dividend neutral and the few investors that require income from their securities should either hold bonds (yielding higher returns with less risk) or periodically sell a portion of their stock portfolio to generate the cash income they need. Stern argues that since corporations are reluctant to reduce dividends, they become the equivalent of a fixed charge and inhibit management's financial flexibility. In other words, dividend payments tend to be maintained, even in light of lower earnings, potentially causing rejection or deferral of a profitable investment.

Stern and his supporters contend that in the setting of dividend policy, less is better than more and none is best. However, they stop short of advocating that the traditional payers of generous dividends abruptly eliminate them. Rather, they support a reduction in the rate of increase or even maintaining the current dollar level, which reduces the payout ratio as earnings rise. The proponents and practitioners of the no-dividend (or low-dividend) strategy claim that clear and ample communication of dividend policy is most important.

3.04 DETERMINING DIVIDEND POLICY

Management should never take for granted those elements of investor expectations within its control, especially dividends. Dividend policy should only be considered within the framework of the overall financial strategy of the company.

The value of a company's shares and the attractiveness of those shares to investors

---

[15] *Ibid.*

[16] Joel Stern, *Analytical Methods in Financial Planning,* 4th ed. (New York: Chase Manhattan Bank, N.A., 1980), pp. 8–10, 65–68, 79.

depends on the investors' expectations. Investors are averse to unpleasant surprises, particularly with respect to company earnings and investment returns. They need to believe that management is in control, conducting operations consistent with well-thought-out investment, business, and financial strategies. In this context, dividend policy is important because the cash resources used for shareholder remittances could alternatively be allocated to capital investment. Also, the level and method of funding dividends can affect a company's debt-to-equity ratio and cost of capital, underscoring the need for attention to dividend policy within the overall financial policy.

[1] Factors Affecting Corporate Dividend Policies

Lintner[17] concluded from a series of interviews during the 1950s that corporations try to maintain a target payout ratio, although dividend increases typically are less than the proportional increase in earnings. Because dividend increases do not usually match earnings increases, a dividend cut will not be automatic if a company experiences an unexpected decline in earnings. In a 1972 study, Higgins[18] related dividend payout to funding requirements for capital investment. If investment opportunities are such that capital needs and dividend payments exceed the company's capacity for internal financing, more generous dividend payouts will result in greater external funding. If debt financing is used to replace dividend earnings, the company's debt-to-equity ratio will increase.

Studies by Rozeff[19] use multiple regression analysis to test the relationship of several variables to the target dividend ratios of a large sample of U.S. companies. Rozeff assumed that the target payout ratios equaled their actual average ratios over a seven-year period. He then demonstrated significant correlation between the target ratios and three independent variables: (1) actual and forecasted growth; (2) risk as measured by beta coefficients; and (3) the proportion of shares held by insiders. Industry grouping was shown not to be a significant determinant of dividend policy in Rozeff's study: instead, it appears that companies in a given industry may independently arrive at common dividend payout policies owing to similar characteristics of growth, risk, and ownership, as shown in Figure 3-5. Rozeff concludes that dividend payout ratios are not randomly distributed and that more rapidly growing companies having greater investment expenditure levels tend to have lower dividend payouts. Companies exhibiting greater financial and operating leverage also have lower payouts, and higher dividend payouts tend to be evidenced in companies whose equity is held by a greater number of outside, nonmanagement shareholders, as shown by the agency theory.

The exhibited phenomenon of higher dividend payouts when there is a significant percentage of ownership by outside shareholders could result from a number of factors. Management may feel that a greater number of shareholders with proportionately less control over the business demand greater dividend payout in return for surrendering control (agency theory). Conversely, in restricting dividend payout, insiders may be acknowledging the tax burden demanded from their own pockets caused by receiving

---

[17] J. Lintner, "Distribution of Incomes of Corporations Among Dividends, Retained Earnings and Taxes," *American Economic Review* (May 1956), pp. 97–113.

[18] R. Higgins, "The Corporate Dividend-Saving Decision," *Journal of Financial and Quantitative Analysis* (Mar. 1972), pp. 1527–1541.

[19] M. Rozeff, "How Corporations Set Their Dividend Payout Ratios," *Chase Financial Quarterly* (Winter 1982), pp. 69–83.

FIGURE 3-5

Industry Differences in Payout Ratios

Source: A. Michel, "Industry Influence on Dividend Policy," *Financial Management,* Vol. 8 (Autumn 1979), p. 26

Industry	Five-Year Average		Ten-Year Average
	1967–1971	1972–1976	1967–1976
Life insurance	20.1%	25.5%	22.8%
Aerospace and aircraft	32.8	25.4	29.1
Building materials	41.5	31.1	36.3
Business equipment	34.9	38.5	36.7
Paper and paper products	45.7	32.2	38.9
Oil	47.9	34.6	41.2
Drugs and health care	49.7	38.9	44.3
Metals and mining	49.9	38.9	44.4
Steel	53.8	37.3	45.6
Textiles	48.5	44.9	46.7
Chemicals	55.3	42.3	48.8
Foods	57.0	47.3	52.1
Electric utilities	68.5	69.5	69.0
Average	46.6	39.0	42.8

dividends now rather than capital gains later. Also, C corporation owners who are employees can take salary increases, which are tax deductible for the firm, in lieu of dividend payments, which are not. (Owner-shareholders of an S corporation should be indifferent regarding their form of compensation. The Internal Revenue Service (IRS) views all salary and distributions received by an S corporation shareholder as self-employment income and subject to all federal income taxes and all applicable payroll withholding taxes.)

Another possibility is that ownership dispersion is a function of a company's life cycle. A young, high-growth company will be more inclined to reinvest in itself, whereas a more mature, slow-growing company will have fewer capital investment alternatives and more cash available for distribution. In addition, the young company may find its shares held by fewer shareholders, while the share ownership of a mature company may be distributed among a greater number of individuals.

The managements of many publicly held C corporations prefer dividends to share repurchases because most companies forbid managers from tendering their shares in a repurchase. Therefore, dividends become the primary vehicle by which managers can receive a cash distribution from their holdings, and managers may be willing to impose a current tax liability on themselves and all shareholders (because of dividend payments) to receive the cash.

[2] Integration With Investment and Financial Policy

To put dividend policy ahead of investment policy is to say that, at least under certain circumstances, a profitable investment in the business could be deferred in order to permit the dividend disbursement to be maintained or even increased. Most studies published in the past 30 years support the conclusion that investment returns, not dividends, are of primary importance in determining stock price and shareholder wealth. To accept this conclusion is to accept that dividend policy must be secondary to investment policy. Since management wants to reduce both volatility and financial risk, dividend policy's proper place is as one component of the overall financial policy of a company.

[a] **Residual Method.** The residual method for establishing dividend payout is one way to assure the proper integration of dividend policy with financial policy. Simply put, the residual method implies that dividends should only be paid out of excess cash and attempts to determine the excess cash available for distribution to shareholders.

Management should first examine the availability of attractive investment projects and the projected internally generated funds flow available to finance the desired investments. A target capital structure or debt-to-equity ratio should be established that, together with the resulting measures of creditworthiness provides management with sufficient financial flexibility in the face of business and economic uncertainty. The target capital structure is one determining factor in the cost of capital. "Attractive investments" may therefore be defined as projects with investment returns that exceed the cost of capital. With the investment level and internal funds flow projected over a horizon of 5 to 10 years and the debt-to-equity ratio also pegged to an appropriate target level,[20] the proportion of earnings available for dividends may be calculated as a residual. Since both projected and actual cash and investment requirements can fluctuate from year to year, it would be wise to set dividend payout levels lower than the total residual cash available.

The residual method for determining the amount available for dividends assumes that all external financing is in the form of debt. Of course, it is possible to issue new stock to replace the equity lost through shareholder remittances. The net effect would be the replacement on the balance sheet of retained earnings with capital stock and surplus, minus transaction costs. Also, the residual method calculates the amount available for dividends, not the amount that should be paid out. A discussion of the pros and cons of actually paying dividends appears later in this chapter.

[b] **Using the Residual Method to Determine a Dividend Policy.** If management is able to project both cash and funds requirements with sufficient certainty, the residual method may be used to set dividends, as shown in the following example.

The current debt and equity levels, earnings, and investment requirements for the fictional ABC Corporation are shown in Figure 3-6. As also shown in the figure, management projects that ABC Corporation will earn $1,310 during the next five years, and capital investment requirements are expected to be $1,480. The pattern of annual earnings and investment flows illustrates two facts: (1) the unlikelihood that management will forecast an earnings downturn and (2) that management's predicted capital investment requirements will be more accurate in the early years than in the later years, when investment projects have yet to be identified. For simplicity, capital investment includes changes in both working capital and investment in new plant and equipment.

---

[20] The so-called target debt-to-equity ratio is also only one component of an overall financial policy, which supports the company's business strategy and investment policy. The debt-to-equity target should never be an objective in isolation; it is merely a convenient mathematical expression of a complex set of financial conditions and underlying assumptions.

FIGURE 3-6

ABC Corporation's Five-Year Plan

	Year 0	Year 1	Year 2	Year 3	Year 4	Year 5	Total
Projected net income		$ 200	$ 230	$ 250	$ 300	$ 330	$1,310
Capital investment		300	400	280	300	200	1,480
Cash needs (income – investment)		(100)	(170)	(30)	0	130	
Total debt	200	300	470	500	500	370	
Shareholders' equity	2,000	2,200	2,430	2,680	2,980	3,310	
Debt-to-equity ratio	0.10:1	0.14:1	0.19:1	0.19:1	0.17:1	0.11:1	
Target debt-to-equity ratio	0.25:1	0.25:1	0.25:1	0.25:1	0.25:1	0.25:1	

Another simplifying assumption is that any incremental debt is free of additional interest cost. In other words, the annual income projections are unaffected by the proportion of earnings paid out as dividends, which must be replaced by debt.

If ABC Corporation's forecast is true, and no dividends are paid, shareholders' equity would be $3,310 after five years and total debt would be $370 if the shortfall of investment in excess of earnings is debt financed. The debt-to-equity ratio will have risen to 0.11:1, still well below the target level. While commendable from the standpoint of rating agencies and creditors, which view dividend outflows as an increased risk to lenders, this lower-than-desired leverage also keeps the company's cost of capital above target. This would presumably cause some otherwise profitable investments to be unattractive when the cost of capital is applied as a hurdle rate. If dividends amounting to $365 are paid to shareholders during the period, with added debt used to fund the extra outflow, the debt-to-equity ratio would be on target at the end of the five-year plan. The dividend amount is a residual of the calculation of the amounts of debt and equity in the total capitalization, given projected earnings, investment, and the target debt-to-equity ratio.

In this example, dividends totaling $365 for five years equal approximately 28 percent of earnings for the period. However, if dividends equal to 28 percent of earnings were paid out in each of the five years, the debt-to-equity ratio would exceed the target in the middle years, perhaps by enough to interfere with management's desired level of financing flexibility. The loss of financing flexibility hinders a company's ability to adapt to unforeseen earnings downturns or unanticipated investment needs without a major dislocation of overall creditworthiness. Perceiving greater financial risk in the resulting higher debt level might convince the rating agencies to downgrade ABC Corporation's bonds in response to some unplanned interim funding need, causing an increase in future financing costs.

While a 28 percent payout may not be excessive for the five years or beyond, if continued profitability is assumed, prudence may dictate a lower payout in the early years with an increase in the later years. Holding the dividend payout to 20 percent of earnings for the first three years of the plan would move the capital structure toward the target but not exceed it. This movement toward the target capital structure would occur if ABC Corporation has the financing flexibility to set 0.25:1 as its target for the debt-to-equity ratio. Such a strategy is also consistent with the observed behavior,

FIGURE 3-7

ABC Corporation's Debt-to-Equity Ratios After Alternative Dividend Payouts

	Year 0	Year 1	Year 2	Year 3	Year 4	Year 5
Projected net income		$ 200	$ 230	$ 250	$ 300	$ 330
Capital investment		(300)	(400)	(280)	(300)	(200)
Residual cash		(100)	(170)	(30)	0	130
Dividend payments						
At 28% of net income		(56)	(64)	(70)	(84)	(92)
At 20% of net income[a]		(40)	(46)	(50)	(84)	(92)
Cash needs (28% payout)		(156)	(234)	(100)	(84)	38
Cash needs (20% payout)		(140)	(216)	(80)	(84)	38
Total debt (28% payout)	200	356	590	690	774	736
Total debt (20% payout)	200	340	556	636	720	682
Shareholders' equity (28% payout)	2,000	2,144	2,310	2,490	2,706	2,944
Shareholders' equity (20% payout)	2,000	2,160	2,344	2,544	2,760	2,998
Debt-to-equity ratio						
With 28% payout		0.17:1	0.26:1	0.28:1	0.29:1	0.25:1
With 20% payout		0.16:1	0.24:1	0.25:1	0.26:1	0.23:1

[a] Dividends are increased to 28 percent of earnings after three years, reflecting improved confidence in forecasts at that time.

namely that corporate management tends to increase dividends at a rate slower than the rate of increase in earnings. As stated earlier, management wants to be certain that the established dividend amount will not have to be reduced. Figure 3-7 shows ABC Corporation's debt-to-equity ratios under the assumption of a 28 percent payout beginning immediately and, alternatively, under the assumption of only a 20 percent payout for the first three years.

[3] Communicating the Dividend Policy

Having set its dividend policy, what should ABC Corporation do next? Whether the dividend policy establishes a dividend payout for the first time or changes the dividend payout, management should fully communicate its intention and expectations to shareholders and to the investment community. Although, according to some studies, the actual dividend amount and its year-to-year change or lack thereof communicate information to investors, management should take advantage of the dividend-setting event to assure that the right message is delivered and understood. Investors generally do not like surprises and will adjust stock prices in response to unexpected news. Although several studies maintain the irrelevance of dividends to stock prices, careful and explicit communication will serve to keep the company's dividend action from being used arbitrarily or incorrectly as a surrogate for information regarding future earnings and returns, all of which have important effects on stock values.

Assume that ABC Corporation's dividend payout had historically been in the range of 25 percent to 30 percent of annual earnings. An unexplained cut in the dividend would leave investors confused and likely to assume that management was trying to conserve cash in the face of anticipated lower earnings or increased capital investment, since internal earnings and investment forecasts are seldom published. Instead, management could use a vehicle such as the annual report to explain that significant future earnings opportunities had been identified, which would require substantial capital investment outlays. If, in management's view, reducing the dividend payout, while expanding leverage within prudent limits, results in the expectation that shareholder wealth would improve, it is likely that investors would have sufficient confidence based on their understanding of management's intentions to support or even bid up the price of the company's shares. Ultimately, however, management will have to earn credibility by consistently delivering the promised returns over time.

Wittebort[21] outlined the experiences of four companies of varying size that combined a cut in the ratio of dividend payout with announcements of increases in investment levels, opportunities for higher returns, and, in one case, a loss from discontinued operations. In each case, share prices were reported to improve. One of the companies, G.D. Searle, also noted a change in its shareholder constituency, as growth-oriented investors replaced income-oriented investors, supporting the clientele effect originally suggested by Miller and Modigliani.

Much has been written about the importance and effectiveness of dividends as a device for communicating management's expectations with respect to investment returns. In the past, this view has been challenged by respected theorists, including Miller,[22] who notes that investors may look for messages in dividends to confirm their own expectations of future earnings, rather than as a communication of the expectations held by management. Stern[23] argues that anything management wants to convey to investors can be communicated clearly and unmistakably (at a far lower cost) by management's careful explanation of financial goals and expectations in vehicles such as the quarterly and annual reports.

3.05 SHARE REPURCHASE AS A CASH DISTRIBUTION ALTERNATIVE

If dividends are irrelevant to investors in determining stock prices, what does that imply about a share repurchase? If dividends do not deliver any information that cannot be communicated effectively through the annual report or announced at the annual meeting, will a share repurchase be viewed differently?

Since a company has the same aggregate income after completing a share repurchase program, earnings per share will increase (the same income would be divided by fewer outstanding shares). If the P/E ratio is unchanged, the size of the share price increase for the remaining shares would be predictable. The relationships between share price, aggregate share value, earnings per share, and the P/E ratio may be used to derive

---

[21] C. Wittebort, "Do Investors Really Care About Dividends?" *Institutional Investor* (Mar. 1981), pp. 213–220.

[22] Merton Miller, "Can Management Use Dividends to Influence the Value of the Firm," *The Revolution in Corporate Finance,* Joel Stern and Donald Chew, eds. (New York: Basil Blackwell, 1987.)

[23] Stern, *op. cit.,* pp. 8–10.

FIGURE 3-8

Effects of Share Repurchase on Share Price

Current earnings per share $= \dfrac{\text{total earnings}}{\text{number of shares}} = \dfrac{\$2,200,000}{550,000 \text{ shares}} = \$4$

P/E $= \dfrac{\$20 \text{ per share}}{\$4 \text{ per share}} = 5$

Earnings per share after repurchase $= \dfrac{\$2,200,000}{500,000 \text{ shares}} = \$4.40$

Expected market price $= (\text{P/E})(\text{earnings per share}) = (5)(\$4.40) = \$22$ per share

the (equilibrium) price the company should offer for the shares to be repurchased. The market price after repurchase should exactly match the repurchase price, other things being equal.

The effects of a share repurchase for ABC Corporation are illustrated in Figure 3-8. ABC Corporation earned $2.2 million in 1990, and 50 percent of this amount was allocated for distribution to common shareholders. There were 550,000 shares outstanding, and the market price was $20 per share. ABC Corporation decided that it could distribute earnings by repurchasing 50,000 of its shares through a tender offer for $22 per share or it could pay a cash dividend of $2 per share. The example assumes transaction costs are equal for both scenarios.

As shown in Figure 3-8, shareholders would receive a benefit of $2 per share in either format, in the form of a $2 dividend or a $2 increase in the stock price. This occurs because it was assumed that the shares could be repurchased at exactly $22 per share and that the P/E ratio would remain constant. If the shares were purchased for less than $22 per share, the remaining shareholders would benefit from the repurchase, but the opposite would occur if the shares were purchased for more than $22 per share. In addition, the P/E ratio might change, depending on how the transaction was received by the investment community.

The example in Figure 3-8 depicts management's point of view. The decision-making process from a shareholder's perspective would be different. If ABC Corporation paid a $2 dividend, shareholders would not need to make a cash receipt decision, and all shareholders would receive cash equal to $2 per share. However, if ABC Corporation elected a share repurchase of 50,000 shares at $22 per share, shareholders have to decide whether to tender their shares at the offering price or hold their shares in anticipation of greater share appreciation. Shareholders that participate in the repurchase will receive $22 per share, while the remaining shareholders will realize a $2-per-share paper gain while retaining ownership of their shares.

In the same way regular dividends tend to become a onetime management event (making the initial decision whether to pay dividends), they later become a fixed disbursement (at least as viewed by management), and are also likely to become a non-event for investors (i.e., only notable when they are changed). However, a stock repurchase program, in conjunction with regular dividends, could serve to catch investors' attention and cause them to analyze management's message more closely than if just a regular dividend had been paid.

[1] Company's Point of View

From management's point of view, there are several major reasons to opt for a share repurchase:

- Because management is generally reluctant to raise dividends if future earnings will not sustain the new dividend, if excess cash is believed to be temporary, management may prefer to make the distribution in the form of a repurchase.

- Shares that have previously been repurchased may be used for acquisitions or released when stock options or warrants are exercised or convertible shares are converted.

- If insiders or directors own large share holdings themselves, they may prefer a repurchase if management is allowed to participate (investors will view a share repurchase more favorably if management is excluded from tendering its shares), rather than dividends, because of the implied lower tax liability on the proceeds of a sale of stock versus dividends.

- Repurchases may be used to handle large-scale changes in capital structure, such as taking on debt to make a repurchase.

- Treasury stock can be resold in the open market if the company needs additional funds.

- Share repurchases may be used as a defensive strategy to thwart the attempts of an unwanted takeover, as was done during the 1980s.

Corporate management must also consider some of the disadvantages of a share repurchase, including the perceptions of outsiders that management cannot locate better investment projects and that companies that repurchase significant amounts of their own stock often produce inferior growth rates and fewer quality investment opportunities.[24] In addition, the IRS could establish that the repurchase was offered in an attempt to avoid the tax liabilities generated by distributing dividends (usually enforced in private companies that complete repurchases on a regular and consistent basis), or the SEC could raise questions if it appears that management may be attempting to manipulate its company's share price.

In an S corporation, a share repurchase is usually only initiated when a shareholder leaves the company. In most instances, the repurchase of the shares is completed with the assistance of a buy-sell agreement. The repurchase price of the shares is determined by a qualified third party or by a formula that should be found within the buy-sell agreement. In many cases, each remaining shareholder will contribute a portion of the needed repurchase funds from its own pocket. Depending on the terms of the buy-sell agreement, the shareholders may allow the repurchase to be completed with corporate funds. In either case, however, the repurchased shares are usually distributed on a prorated basis to the remaining shareholders or as stipulated in the buy-sell agreement.

[2] Investor's Point of View

For shareholders that would be subject to taxes on both capital gains and dividend income, the benefit of a share repurchase is the ability to defer taxation if the investor chooses not to tender shares because the realized gain and therefore the tax are elective. Shareholders that want a distribution can sell some shares (often at better than

---

[24] Eugene F. Brigham, *Financial Management: Theory and Practice,* 4th ed. (New York: The Dryden Press, 1985), pp. 570–574.

market price) and reduce their tax liability because the repurchase effectively substitutes capital gains for dividends. Shareholders that do not need cash or that would have to reinvest it in the same or another company will simply leave their investment alone, and, if the relationship between earnings per share and the P/E ratio holds, they will see an increase in share price.

[3] Tax Effects

As previously noted, individuals are taxed at the same marginal rate under current law, a maximum of 28 percent (or a maximum of 31 percent at certain higher income levels), for both dividends and capital gains. However, while an entire dividend payment is immediately subject to taxation, only the capital gains portion of a payment for stock repurchased by the company is taxed, and only in the year in which the investor decides to sell.

[4] Earnings Effects

If transaction costs of both share repurchase and dividends are ignored, and if neither action affects company investment plans and prospects, the decision whether to distribute a like amount of cash (from equity) to shareholders as a dividend or through the repurchase of company stock has no impact on aggregate earnings. The accounting would differ within the equity section of the balance sheet, but total equity would be the same after either form of distribution. Interest income for the year would be equally lower or interest expense equally higher, depending only on whether the dividend or repurchase was funded from excess cash or new borrowings. However, as previously noted, in the case of repurchase, since the same aggregate earnings would relate to a reduced number of shares outstanding, earnings per share would increase. Shares owned by the company do not figure in the earnings-per-share calculation.

[5] Impact of Share Repurchase on Capital Structure

The level of dividend payment may be used to adjust the company's capital structure, contributing to the need for external financing and affecting the cost of capital. Share repurchases also have an impact on the debt-to-equity ratio, if repurchased shares are not replaced with newly issued ones. Depending on the size of the repurchase program, the effects on the capital structure and cost of capital can be significant. Combining a share repurchase with debt financing has a double impact on the company's financial leverage.

[a] **Share Repurchase With Surplus Funds.** Accounting for a share repurchase is relatively simple and straightforward. Shares purchased and held in the treasury (treasury stock) are still considered issued but not outstanding. The value of shares held in the treasury, computed at the actual purchase cost to the company, is shown as a subtraction in the calculation of shareholders' equity.

In the ABC Corporation dividend illustration, it was noted that without dividends, the company's equity would have grown to $3,310 after five years while debt would have increased to only $370. The debt-to-equity ratio would have been 0.11:1. If ABC Corporation had not paid any dividends and, after successfully completing its five-

FIGURE 3-9

Balance Sheet Effects of Share Repurchase Using Surplus Funds

	Before	After
Cash and marketable securities	$2,000	$ 170
Total debt	$ 370	$ 370
Common stock issued	$ 250	$ 250
Additional paid-in capital	750	750
	$1,000	$1,000
Retained earnings	2,310	2,310
Treasury stock, at cost	—	(1,830)
Shareholders' equity	$3,310	$1,480
Total debt-to-equity ratio	0.11:1	0.25:1

Note: There is no change in the common-stock-issued account, since repurchased shares remain authorized and issued. However, the number of shares issued and outstanding would decline by the number purchased and held in the treasury.

FIGURE 3-10

Balance Sheet Effects of Share Repurchase Using Debt

	Before	After
Total debt	$ 370	$ 735
Common stock issued	$ 250	$ 250
Additional paid-in capital	750	750
	$1,000	$1,000
Retained earnings	2,310	2,310
Treasury stock, at cost	—	(365)
Shareholders' equity	$3,310	$2,945
Total debt-to-equity ratio	0.11:1	0.25:1

year plan, had substantial surplus funds and a desire to reduce its cost of capital by increasing leverage up to the 0.25:1 target, the company could announce an offer to purchase shares with a market value of $1,830. After completion of the repurchase program, equity would equal $1,480, as shown in Figure 3-9, and the debt-to-equity ratio would equal the 0.25:1 target.

[b] Share Repurchase With Debt Financing. The repurchase of shares with debt financing is a quick and simple means of adjusting the capital structure. Because of the leveraging effects of the debt, debt financing requires a much less dramatic purchase program to adjust the capital structure than was previously discussed using surplus funds. As shown in Figure 3-10, only $365 of treasury stock needs to be purchased with debt financing in order to move ABC Corporation's debt-to-equity ratio to the target level, versus $1,830 worth of shares in the example using surplus funds and no debt. Although leverage is the same, total capitalization and financial capacity are very different, depending on the size of the share repurchase program.

[6] Share Repurchase and Shareholder Communication

A share repurchase program should be accompanied by a clear explanation of management's rationale and objectives. It could be pointed out, for example, that while management was pleased that internally generated funds were sufficient to finance all identified profitable investment projects, the cost of capital had increased to a point where otherwise attractive investments could not meet the company's investment criteria. In addition, competitors with lower costs of capital were increasing market share at the company's expense. Management should explain that residual cash flow is being distributed to shareholders at the investors' option without establishing the expectation of a regular dividend. A share repurchase under this scenario also discourages predatory action by unwelcome suitors attracted by the company's cash surplus.

If management's actions are reasonable, it should be able to anticipate a reasonable response from investors. There appears to be no better way to assure that investors accurately perceive and understand management's intentions than to spell out the rationale and objectives for a share repurchase in a clearly written document.

[7] Share Repurchase as a Defensive Strategy

The decade of the 1980s was witness to a significant increase in corporate acquisitions, many of which were unsolicited and/or unfriendly. In a quest to remain independent, corporate management needed to find a defensive weapon to fight off the unwanted suitor. Under these circumstances, the share repurchase became an important management tool for fending off takeover attempts. Two studies, one by Bagwell[25] and the other by Denis,[26] explored the use of a share repurchase as a takeover deterrent.

Bagwell's 1991 study concluded that the takeover cost to the acquiror could be greater if the target company can distribute cash in the form of a repurchase rather than pay a cash dividend or do nothing at all. She states that in a repurchase (prior to the announcement of a takeover attempt, or after the announcement but at a higher price), shareholders that are willing to tender their shares are the shareholders with the lowest share valuations of the company. Therefore, the remaining shareholders are those with higher share valuations, which will require a higher takeover offer, thereby increasing the cost to the acquiror. Bagwell concluded that a share repurchase is more effective as a takeover deterrent when it alters the marginal shareholder, when shareholder diversity is substantial, and when the private benefit of control from a takeover is not too large.

Denis studied the data on 49 companies that used defensive payouts in an attempt

---

[25] L.S. Bagwell, "Share Repurchase and Takeover Deterrence," *Rand Journal of Economics*, Vol. 22 (Spring 1991), pp. 72–88.

[26] David J. Denis, "Defensive Changes in Corporate Payout Policy: Share Repurchase and Special Dividends," *Journal of Finance*, Vol. 45 (Dec. 1990), pp. 1433–1456.

to remain independent during a unwanted takeover. Denis concluded that the announcement of a defensive share repurchase is associated with an average negative impact on the share price of the target company but did not state whether it was effective in maintaining the independence of the target.

3.06 PROS AND CONS OF CASH DISTRIBUTIONS

The relevance of dividend payments to the stock market value of company shares has been debated for several decades, with recent work strongly supporting the theory that investment results, not dividends, critically affect share prices. Dividend payments have been held to be appropriate and useful vehicles for communicating information to investors, although it is also argued that more direct communication is clearer and far less costly. What, then, should financial policy advisers tell their companies?

First, if a company has ample investment opportunities and to date has not established the practice of regular dividend payments, persuasive arguments for beginning to pay dividends do not come to mind. The importance of numerous investment opportunities cannot be overstated. This kind of opportunity implies that the number (and size) of investments yielding returns in excess of the cost of capital is sufficient to keep the company's leverage within its target range without building an increasingly large pool of surplus cash. If such a company were to pay dividends, it would have to obtain replacement funds, with attendant transaction costs, in the capital markets. The company's investment-return record, supplemented by direct communication with investors, should eliminate the reasons for paying out a portion of earnings to shareholders.

Second, for a company with an established policy of paying out a substantial portion of earnings in the form of dividends, it is not a simple matter to end the payments abruptly. If the existence of clientele effect is assumed, a dividend-paying company can be expected to attract a shareholder group that expects and is not opposed to the quarterly distributions. If, even after dividends, the company retains sufficient earnings such that together with modest additional debt financing the cost of capital can be maintained and all attractive investments undertaken, it is probably appropriate to continue the dividend practice. However, if new and larger investment opportunities are discovered or if earnings decline, it is reasonable to reduce or suspend dividend payments. The company's decision to pursue new investment opportunities should be communicated to shareholders, together with management's explanation as to why such action is believed to be in their best interest.

Finally, what about the dividend-paying company with limited investment opportunities and an increasing pool of surplus cash? Certainly, investment opportunities can become limited in a company's traditional line of business, but there are no rules to prevent a company in one industry from making investments in another. Indeed, the company's shareholders are faced with this challenge upon receipt of their dividends, but only after the distributed funds have been reduced by income taxes. Would it not be more in the shareholders' interest for the company to use those funds for new investments, which would generate future capital gains?

These observations also apply in the specialized case of a share repurchase. A share repurchase program has three additional advantages over dividends:

1. There is a potential implied tax advantage relative to dividend payments, together with the ability of shareholders to determine for themselves whether to participate.

2. Since share repurchases are more likely to be viewed by management as onetime events, they are less likely to be considered fixed costs that have to be maintained, even while attractive investments are deferred.

3. Share repurchases provide a relatively quick and simple means of reshaping the capital structure and adjusting the cost of capital.

Early in this chapter, the view was presented that dividend policy must be subordinated to investment policy and remain only one part of overall financial policy. The same is true of share repurchases. In an ideal world, the availability of ample investment opportunities should, over time, be sufficient to enable a company to maintain its desired capital structure and achieve attractive investment returns. The company that has temporarily found its investment opportunities to be limited, to the extent that surplus funds have accumulated or leverage has declined and the cost of capital has increased, may consider a share repurchase a more desirable action than increased dividends.

Much has been written regarding the value of dividends as communicators of management's expectations. It seems likely, when cash builds up or leverage declines in spite of a substantial dividend payout, that the unstated message received by at least the most perceptive investors is that management is unable to identify any acceptable capital projects. In other words, not knowing what else to do, management has transferred the reinvestment decision to the shareholders. If so, those same investors should be expected to look for other investment vehicles with which to increase their wealth.

Finally, the concept of cash distributions and total return to shareholders in an S corporation or partnership was introduced. Although many of the theories and effects discussed throughout this chapter are not applicable to an S corporation, the differences in corporate structures (on a tax basis) are significant, as shown by the effects on total return. It should be remembered that S corporations and partnerships incur only one level of taxation, and cash distributions to shareholders are not treated as dividends by the IRS.

3.07 DIVIDEND POLICY CHECKLIST

Dividend policy should always be one aspect of an overall corporate financial policy. The allocation of earnings between profitable investments and shareholder distributions should be independent events and should not inhibit the wealth objectives of the company. The following checklist contains several questions corporate management should consider before distributing its first dividend or as it reviews its current dividend policy.

☐ What is the company's objective in paying a dividend?

☐ Are management's financial goals consistent with those of its shareholders?

☐ Will paying a dividend cause the company to forgo a profitable investment?

☐ Is the corporate debt-to-equity ratio consistent with management's overall financial policy?

☐ Will the payment of dividends affect management's targeted leverage ratio?

☐ Does the company have the cash, or will it have to borrow to make the payment?

☐ Will the dividend payment convey important information to investors?

☐ Are there other actions management can take that would convey the same information as dividend payments?

☐ Is the dividend payment consistent with management's objective of maximizing shareholder wealth?

The preceding checklist should be used not only by the management of non-dividend-paying companies but also by the management of dividend-paying companies that may want to review the effectiveness of their current dividend policy.

Suggested Reading

Abrutyn, S., and R.W. Turner. "Taxes and Firms' Dividend Policies: Survey Results." *National Tax Journal,* Vol. 43 (Dec. 1990), pp. 491–496.

Bolster, P.J., and V. Janjigian. "Dividend Policy and Valuation Effects of the Tax Reform Act of 1986." *National Tax Journal,* Vol. 44 (Dec. 1991), pp. 511–518.

Brennan, M.J., and A.V. Thakor. "Shareholder Preferences and Dividend Policy." *Journal of Finance,* Vol. 45 (Sept. 1990), pp. 993–1018.

Copeland, Thomas E., and J. Fred Weston. *Financial Theory and Corporate Policy,* 3rd ed. Reading, Mass.: Addison-Wesley, 1988.

DeAngelo, H., and L. DeAngelo. "Dividend Policy and Financial Distress: An Empirical Investigation of Troubled NYSE Firms." *Journal of Finance,* Vol. 45 (Dec. 1990), pp. 1415–1431.

Farrelly, G.E., and K.H. Baker. "Corporate Dividends: Views of Institutional Investors." *Akron Business & Economic Review,* Vol. 20 (Dec. 1989), pp. 89–100.

Ross, Stephen A., and Randolph W. Westerfield. *Corporate Finance.* St. Louis, Mo.: Times Mirror/Mosby College Publishing, 1988.

Weston, J. Fred, and Eugene F. Brigham. *Managerial Finance,* 4th ed. Hinsdale, Ill.: The Dryden Press, 1972.

Chapter 4
Pension Plans

ARTHUR WILLIAMS III

4.01 RATIONALE FOR HAVING RETIREMENT PLANS

Retirement plans can be considered a form of deferred compensation, a reward for long service, or tax-efficient compensation. They can also be used to evade wage controls on employee pay, as they were during World War II. Finally, they can be a means of assuaging the conscience of senior managers or shareholders.

All of these reasons have logic, and corporations can embrace more than one as justification for their retirement plans. However, since all major firms have plans, it is difficult to justify not having one. The issue then becomes what type of plan to have.

4.02 DESIGNING THE PLAN

There are two fundamental questions to be answered in plan design: What benefits are to be provided, and who is to receive them? Retirement plans can be divided into two general types: defined contribution plans and defined benefit plans.

Defined contribution plans are those in which benefits are provided based on the assets accumulated on behalf of the employee. The ultimate benefit will vary depending on the investment results of the fund, with the employee bearing the risk as to the success of these investment results.

Defined benefit plans describe the pension to be received by the employee upon retirement. While the amount of money in the fund at the time of the employee's retirement is related to investment results, as with the defined contribution plan, defined benefit plan benefits are established irrespective of the level of assets in the fund. Thus, in a defined contribution plan, the benefit is based on the assets available for each employee at retirement, whereas in a defined benefit plan the benefit is fixed by the formula prescribed by the plan. It is up to the employer to allocate sufficient funds to pay the promised benefit in defined benefit plans.

An exception to the above structure is the Taft-Hartley or jointly trusteed defined benefit plan established by a number of employers in conjunction with their unions. These plans typically are funded by contributions from the employer based on the number of hours each individual employee works. In this sense, they look like defined contribution plans. However, the benefit is prescribed by an agreement. Unlike corporate or public pension funds, however, there is no employer that is responsible for meeting benefits promised. Rather, the assets in the pension fund must be sufficient in and of themselves to meet pension benefits, or the plan will default on its obligations.

4.03 FUNDING THE PLAN

If the plan is to have defined contributions, funding issues are minimal. Thus, this section is primarily concerned with funding defined benefit plans. While some pension plans, especially public plans, are contributory, most corporate and jointly trusteed plans are not. The following discussion of pension funding assumes that the plan is not contributory.

Why fund a defined benefit plan? In some countries, pension plans are not funded; rather, they are treated as any other liability, reflected on the books of the company but with no specified fund of assets set aside to meet pension benefits. In other words, in some foreign countries, companies can use pay-as-you-go funding. In the United

States, funding of defined benefit plans (putting aside investible funds to provide for future benefits) is considered appropriate because of the following:

- Employees, employers, and regulators feel more confident about the likelihood that benefits will be paid if plans are funded.
- The Employee Retirement Income Security Act of 1974 (ERISA) requires funding for private plans.
- The Internal Revenue Code permits tax deductions for funding of a qualified plan without the employees' concurrently paying taxes on the funds contributed on their behalf.
- Funding establishes the proper allocation of cost, in a cash flow sense, to the employees and periods of service over which benefits were earned.

[1] Determining Eligibility

After the sponsor decides that the plan is to have defined benefits, what the benefits are to be and who should receive them need to be determined. ERISA and the Internal Revenue Service (IRS) impose restrictions on eligibility to ensure that pension plans are not used solely as compensation schemes for managers and key shareholders. As a rule, full-time employees who have reached the age of 21 years and have at least one year of service must be included in the plan.

Other decisions include benefit levels, retirement age, vesting schedule, provisions for early retirement and disability, and any provision for increases in postretirement benefits owing to inflation. Most plans base the benefit on either average salary earned during the career or some form of final average, such as the last five years prior to retirement. A common benefit for salaried employees is one percent of average salary up to a specified "integration level," plus 1.5 percent of average salary in excess of the integration level, all multiplied by the employee's years of service. A 40-year employee might thus receive an annual pension of between 40 percent and 60 percent of his or her average salary.

Vesting is the required period of service to the fund sponsor before benefit rights are earned. Most corporations choose the ERISA option, which provides for vesting only after five years of service and then 100 percent vesting. This is called cliff-vesting.

While inflation has subsided from the high levels of the late 1970s, it nonetheless represents a major threat to the purchasing power of pension benefits. Many companies have addressed inflation by changing to final average rather than career average compensation formulas, where benefits are based on the salary of a period, such as the last five years, rather than of the entire career. However, for most retirees, cost-of-living benefits are at the discretion of the company rather than built directly into the retirement formula. Social Security benefits and benefits to retired federal employees are conspicuous exceptions.

[2] Steps in the Funding Process

Funding is a budgeting process. Although, in common parlance, people speak of actuaries determining the cost of a pension plan, this is not accurate. The ultimate cost of the plan is determined by the benefits provided for in the plan document and the expenses of running the retirement program. The basic formula describing this process is:

Contributions + investment return = benefits + expenses

For a given level of benefits applied to a group of employees, the only way for a company to manage cost is by investing especially successfully or by lowering expenses. The actuary's job is to help management understand the costs associated with the plan and develop methods for allocating these costs to specific years. Although differences in actuarial approaches can change the incidence of costs and funding from earlier to later years or vice versa, the ultimate cost of a plan will not be affected by these decisions.

Funding a plan for retirement at normal retirement age involves five steps:

1. Estimating a benefit at retirement

2. Calculating the value of that benefit, as measured by the value of an annuity purchased at normal retirement age that will pay the annual benefit to the employee for life (and for the spouse's life, if the plan has survivor benefits)

3. Calculating the present value of that annuity, discounted at the assumed rate of return

4. Reducing this amount by the probability that the employee will not be employed at retirement owing to death, disability, termination of employment, or early retirement (the decrement assumptions)

5. Allocating this benefit cost, based on the funding method employed, to past, current, and future years

For example, for a benefit of $20,000 per year, an annuity at age 65 would cost about $8.14244 \times \$20,000$, or $162,849, based on the 1971 group annuity mortality table and an 8 percent interest assumption. For an employee age 30, the present value of this benefit is $162,849 divided by 1.08 to the thirty-fifth power, or $11,014. If the employee has only a 30 percent probability of still being employed by this employer at age 65, the expected cost of this benefit is $0.3 \times \$11,014$, or $3,304. This amount is then allocated to the appropriate periods.

For a group of employees, the process starts with analysis of the benefits under the plan and then of the employee population as to number, age, salary, sex, and years of service. This population could diminish for four reasons (decrements): termination of employment, death, disability, and early retirement. All of these decrements trigger different benefit payouts and, therefore, adjustments to the amount of funds to be accumulated for payment of benefits.

Once the demographics of the plan are understood, the cost of the plan is determined by making assumptions about future salaries, investment returns, and probabilities for the decrements. Consideration must be given to current service and, if benefits are provided for service prior to the formation of the plan, the cost of this past service. Through the choice of a funding method, the costs are allocated to each year, past and present. Finally, the funding process also requires a method of adjusting funding to account for errors made in earlier assumptions.

[3] Assumptions

Because planning for an employee's retirement spans a number of years, assumptions must be made about the future in order to estimate the amount of money that must be contributed to the fund.

The two most important assumptions actuaries and their clients must make are economic assumptions concerning growth in salaries and the rate of return on investments. If the benefit calls for payment based on final salary, projections must be made of salaries over the employee's career in order to estimate benefits. If benefits are based on average salary or on hours worked, the actuary need only estimate future salaries if the funding method spreads costs or benefits over the employee's life, as opposed to recognizing just the current year's benefits. For all funds, the actuary must estimate the return that will be earned on those funds. Other important assumptions relate to the decrements—the timing and number of employees who will terminate employment before retirement, die, become disabled, or retire early.

It is common to view salary increases as having three components—inflation, productivity, and merit—each of which can be estimated and added to determine the expected progression of salaries over the years for the population of employees under consideration. Similarly, an investment return estimate can be made from a projection of future inflation, any real return expected for riskless investments, and a risk premium attributable to the risk category of assets owned.

[4] Corrections for Errors and Changes

With so many assumptions about the future inherent in the funding process, it is inevitable that actual experience will differ from expectations. These differences, which can be either positive or negative, create the need for a formal system of continuing midcourse correction. If, for instance, the plan is funded based on the assumption that invested funds will earn 7 percent, and 10 percent is actually earned, an actuarial or experience gain occurs. If, on the other hand, employees do not terminate (leave voluntarily or involuntarily) to the extent anticipated, then an actuarial or experience loss is realized, since more employees with longer service than was anticipated will receive benefits. These gains and losses are then amortized over a number of years to smooth the impact on any one year.

After a number of years, the annual cost for a plan will consist of the current year's cost, plus past service costs, and each year's amortization of gains and losses.

[5] Funding Methods

The funding method is the procedure used to allocate costs to each year and to measure liabilities for prior years. As such, it is used to calculate the amount of money that should be funded for the current period, but it also can be used to calculate the expense to be charged to the company's books for reporting purposes, the tax expense for calculation of income taxes, or the amount to be credited to the ERISA Funding Standard Account, the monitoring device the government uses to be sure pension plans are being adequately funded. A different funding method, as well as different assumptions, can be used for different purposes, although a consistent method and assumptions must be used to calculate the minimum contribution required by ERISA and the maximum tax-deductible contribution.

The funding method also provides a means of determining progress to date in the accumulation of assets relative to the need for assets.

In general, the funding methods can be classified according to whether benefits or costs are allocated to each year. The unit credit method allocates benefits, while the entry-age normal method allocates costs.

The unit credit method, in its standard form, addresses only the cost of the benefit accrued during the current year. An alternative, the projected unit credit method, projects salaries and benefits to be earned over the employee's career, then allocates the benefits equally to each year. The cost of each year's benefit is then charged to that year. Plans that calculate benefits as a percentage of final average salary are precluded from using the unit credit method; they must use the projected unit credit alternative.

Under the entry-age normal method, the value of the benefit projected at the time the employee enters the plan is determined and is then allocated to each year of the employee's service, usually by expressing cost as a level percentage of payroll or a level annual dollar amount.

The discussion in this chapter so far has related principally to ways of allocating normal costs, the costs for the current period based on current plan benefits when it is assumed that methods and assumptions are appropriate and that assumptions are in fact realized. However, there are additional sources of cost in a pension plan. For instance, when a pension plan is started, or when benefits are improved, it is common to provide benefits retroactively. Since these costs were not considered during previous calculations of cost, it becomes necessary to supplement the nominal cost or provide for these costs for past service.

A need to change the amount being allocated also results from changes in assumptions or methods. If, for example, it is decided that the investment return assumption should be 8 percent rather than 7 percent, an immediate reduction in the present value of liabilities, leading to a reduction in the need for contributions, occurs. To smooth this impact over a number of years and to prevent manipulation of earnings or funding based on changes in assumptions, this gain would be amortized over a period of years. Similarly, if a change in method occurred, any gain or loss from doing so would also be amortized over a number of years. Finally, experience will provide gains and losses from existing assumptions, as actual experience deviates from what was assumed. Gains and losses from these experience factors are also amortized.

As with the normal costs, there are various methods that can be used to allocate supplemental costs. Either a level or declining cost curve typically results from allocation of supplemental costs, because these costs are based on known values to be allocated and do not reflect growth factors, such as salaries, that could lead normal costs to grow each year.

[6] Amortization Period

The period over which the unfunded portion of the actuarial reserve is amortized varies depending on the source of the unfunded amount and when it arose. Until ERISA was enacted, it was not necessary to fund the unfunded portion of the actuarial reserve; a plan sponsor only needed to pay the normal cost plus interest on the unfunded portion of the actuarial reserve at the assumed rate of return. Under ERISA, unfunded actuarial liabilities must be amortized over no more than a certain prescribed number of years.

At the other extreme, the IRS only permits tax deductions for amounts that pay for costs in 10 years or more, to prevent excessive loss of revenue to the Treasury.

It should be noted that the amortization schedule includes interest just as in the case of a mortgage. If a $1.5 million actuarial loss is experienced by a plan because, for instance, salaries increased faster than expected or investment value grew more slowly than expected, an actuarial or experience loss must be recognized. This loss must be funded over a five-year period at most. This does not mean, however, that the fund must charge only $300,000 to the current year's expense. Under the original assumption, the plan would now have an extra $1.5 million liability compared to what it had before the loss. Five years from now, this $1.5 million would have accumulated to an amount as though the fund earned the actuarial investment return each year, compounded on this sum. If a 10 percent rate is used, this amount is $2,415,765. Therefore, the current year's amortization must include not only the $300,000 but sufficient interest such that the total payment for each year would be expected to accumulate to $2,415,765 in five years. This amount is approximately $360,000 per year.

[7] Valuing Assets

Pension fund assets are typically not valued at the current market value for purposes of funding. Although ERISA requires that market value be reflected in some reasonable way, using current market value directly would result in widely varying costs from year to year. Just as actuaries smooth the impact of experience gains and losses, they use a smoothing technique for valuing assets. A common approach is to use a moving average of market value over a period of three to five years. The IRS requires that the actuarial value be at least 80 percent and at most 120 percent of the fund's actual market value.

[8] Ancillary Benefits

Most pension plans have benefits other than pure pensions for the employee. Many plans have disability benefits, which provide payment for workers who are unable to continue working; early retirement benefits, for those who stop working before the normal retirement age; life insurance; surviving spouse benefits; and, in a few cases, cost of living adjustments. The cost of each of these benefits must be added to the pure cost of a pension benefit. Adjustments to the costs accrued to meet these benefits will also be made as experience differs from what was assumed.

[9] Social Security Integration

Many pension plans are integrated with Social Security, meaning that the benefit provided, expressed as a percentage of the employee's pay, is higher at higher pay levels. This is done to offset partially the fact that Social Security benefits are higher, as a percentage of pay, at lower pay levels. Before the Tax Reform Act of 1986, integration was frequently achieved by subtracting a percentage of the employee's Social Security benefit (for example, a typical formula was 1.5 percent of final average salary minus 1.5 percent of the Social Security benefit, multiplied by years of service). Under current law, integration is most frequently achieved by providing different accruals above and below an integration level (for example, one percent of final average salary in excess of $20,000, multiplied by years of service.)

[10] Plan Assets and Unfunded Liabilities

The preceding discussion of funding dealt with the calculation of benefits and how the cost of these benefits can be allocated to each year. Another important use of the funding process is to measure the funded status of a plan, that is, its assets relative to the plan's liabilities or promises to pay future benefits. While the plan's asset valuation is subject to some minor interpretation, considerable confusion can arise from attempts to measure the plan's liabilities. This confusion results from different definitions of liabilities, depending on the use to which the information is put, and different ways of calculating them, depending on the funding method and assumptions employed.

Liabilities can be viewed in terms of present value of benefits to be paid in the future or normal costs accumulated to date. For a given employee at retirement age, these two figures will be the same, but at any point during the employee's career there can be a difference.

Generally, if a plan is terminated, all accrued benefits become vested whether or not an employee has satisfied the plan's vesting requirement (typically five years of service). If the plan is terminated voluntarily by the plan sponsor, the sponsor is generally required to fund all accrued benefits, whether or not they are vested. If the plan termination is the result of the company's bankruptcy, to the extent that plan assets are insufficient to provide accrued benefits the Pension Benefit Guaranty Corporation (PBGC) will guarantee certain benefits. The PBGC will only guarantee benefits up to a legally specified level, so employees with very large benefits will not have their full benefits protected. This level is indexed to the Social Security wage base and for 1993 is roughly $3,000 per month. Further, plan improvements occurring within the five-year period preceding the plan termination will be only partially protected by the PBGC.

All of these calculations assume that the plan will be terminated. The amount of benefit earned by the employee will be fixed at the time of termination, since even if the plan is terminated but the company continues, future service will not be credited toward pension benefits. Thus, the measure of these liabilities is only a function of benefits promised in the plan document and earned to the date of termination and assumptions as to future investment return and mortality. If, on the other hand, the plan continues, the benefits to employees will increase because salaries and years of service will have increased. Even though these years of service have not yet been credited and benefits have not been earned for them, the value of benefits to be paid in the future is calculated under the assumption that additional service will be credited to employees and salaries will be higher in future years. The liability calculated under this approach is called the actuarial reserve.

For all measures of liabilities, a comparison can be made with the market value or actuarial value of assets to determine the funded or unfunded amount or ratio.

[11] Limitations of Actuarial Methodology

The actuary typically looks at a plan with two serious limitations, both of which are caused in part by IRS restrictions on deductibility of contributions. First, no estimate is made for changes in the work force owing to new employees entering the plan. Second, no funding occurs for projected increases in benefits unless they are provided for in the plan document. Companies that wish to avoid sharply higher future costs because of these factors may choose conservative funding methods or assumptions. For instance, if the sponsor would normally assume 8 percent as the expected investment return, it can fund a greater amount by assuming only a 7.5 percent return, thus providing funding for the larger benefits expected in the future. But be careful: The IRS can disqualify corporate tax deductions if the actuarial assumptions are considered overly conservative.

While not overly complicated conceptually, the actual mechanics of actuarial science are complex to the point where very few laymen will find it possible or worthwhile to learn its many intricacies. Nonetheless, those associated with pension plans or investment of pension plans should be at least broadly familiar with actuarial terminology and precepts.

4.04 MANAGING THE ASSETS

The most important issues in managing pension assets are setting goals for the fund, choosing a risk policy, and selecting investment managers.

[1] Setting Goals for the Fund

The goal of a corporation is to maximize the long-term wealth of shareholders. However, it is also necessary to consider two other "constituencies": employees and government. Employees' interests are directly related to the success of the corporation, and retirement plans are directly related to the interests of employees. Government has become greatly involved in retirement plans with the passage of ERISA. It therefore seems appropriate to define the corporation's goal as maximizing the long-term wealth of shareholders while giving full recognition to the needs of employees and the presence of government regulation.

The retirement fund can have an important impact on the corporation's goal of serving the needs of employees. Every employee must consider the economic effects of becoming too old to work. Many employees look forward to a less demanding retirement lifestyle. To the extent that a retirement plan can guarantee income so that employees will have financial security in their later years, the plan is important to the corporation's goal of giving recognition to the needs of employees.

There appears to be a conflict between the goal of keeping employees content by providing them with high-cost fringe benefits and the primary corporate goal, maximizing the wealth of shareholders. This conflict is certainly real in the short run, since a dollar put into a retirement plan is a dollar less (before taxes) for dividends or reinvestment. In the long run, however, an optimal balance is possible, since the welfare of the corporation is intimately related to the productivity of the work force and the welfare of the work force is intimately related to the success of the corporation.

While attempting to operate its retirement funds so as to maximize the wealth of shareholders, the corporation must deal with the growing presence of the federal government. An interesting paradox develops, since ERISA clearly states that retirement funds "must be operated solely for the benefit" of their participants. It also is clear that ERISA was passed partly because some companies pursued the wealth of shareholders at the expense of employee benefits. There are well-known horror stories about employees who worked for many years in the expectation of receiving a pension but then were denied it because of a corporate merger, a plant closing, or some other unexpected event. The conflict between maximizing the wealth of shareholders and operating a plan "solely for the benefit of participants" is real, complex, and unresolved. Yet corporate management must deal with this problem in setting policies concerning plan benefits and investing.

There are numerous ways a corporation can operate a retirement plan so that it gives full recognition to the needs of employees while maximizing the wealth of shareholders. A plan with assets in excess of required levels is a source of comfort to employees. It provides a greater probability that benefits will be paid and possibly even increased. Thus, the corporation and its employees both have a strong interest in seeing the plan's assets enhanced through investment gain.

Each party's attitude toward risk also affects management of the plan's assets. To the corporation, an investment dollar lost is a dollar that must someday be replaced (with interest), and the reverse is true for a dollar gained from investment. To employees, a dollar lost by the fund is a dollar less security and a dollar less potential gain in benefits. However, it is not a dollar in lost benefits. The corporation must still pay the defined benefit, and, presumably, if the corporation does not, the PBGC will (within the limits previously noted). Thus, the employee can be more tolerant of risk than the corporation sponsoring the fund. However, where a fund is extremely underfunded, the corporation may feel that it will probably be required to surrender the statutory maximum 30 percent of its net worth to the PBGC to put its pension liability with the PBGC; hence, it can speculate with what few pension assets it has without regard to loss, in the hopes of making a sufficient "killing" to decrease its PBGC liability to less than 30 percent of its net worth. In this situation, the employee bears no risk and the corporation bears no incremental risk beyond 30 percent of its net worth.

In order to understand how a fund can be operated in such a way as to pursue the goal of maximizing the wealth of shareholders while giving full recognition to government regulation, a summary of the applicable laws is presented in the following section.

[2] Pension Law

Prior to ERISA, trust law was the major body of law that applied to corporate retirement plans (though it is less than clear that national and multinational corporations paid much attention to it). Two types of trust law prevailed: legal lists and prudent man. Under the legal list concept, state legislation listed the criteria for allowable investments in trusts. The prudent man doctrine indicated that a trustee "shall conduct himself faithfully and exercise a sound discretion. He is to observe how men of prudence, discretion, and intelligence manage their own affairs, not in regard to speculation, but in regard to the permanent disposition of their funds, considering the probable income, as well as the probable safety of the capital to be invested."[1]

[a] ERISA. ERISA is now the dominant legislative influence on private retirement plans. Although the act is hopelessly complex in its details, its aim is elegantly simple. A corporation does not need to provide its employees with a retirement plan, but if

[1] From Harvard College v. Amory (1830), the Massachusetts court case that established the prudent man rule. In that case, the court held that all securities have risk and that stocks are not de facto inappropriate trust investments. The quotation is from Harvey E. Bines, *The Law of Investment Management* (Boston: Warren Gorham Lamont, 1978), pp. 1–32.

it does, it must tell the employees in simple terms the whole truth about the plan. It must put aside sufficient money so that the plan can pay the promised benefits, and the plan and its assets must be administered carefully and honestly by competent people with the sole objective of serving the interests of plan beneficiaries.

[b] Williams Amendment. Relevant portions of the Securities and Exchange Commission Act of 1975 (Williams Amendment) describe the conditions under which the investment managers of a fund can also act as brokers for the fund and the conditions under which brokerage commissions can be utilized to pay for services to the fund and to the investment manager.

An appropriate approach to successful operation in a regulated environment is the following:

- Know the relevant law.
- Be alert to the legal impact of significant decisions.
- Conscientiously carry out legal responsibilities.
- See that the necessary legal documents are prepared, and be ready to present a legally acceptable rationale for significant decisions.
- Carefully document key decisions.

[3] Choosing a Risk Policy

The choice of an investment policy (risk policy) for the fund is one of the most important and perplexing problems faced by fund sponsors and fund managers. The question, How much risk can the fund take? can be addressed by looking at the definitions of "risk" and "diversification" and then asking what sources of risk confront the fund, what the historical and theoretical risk-return relationships are, how much risk a particular fund can endure, what specific risk policy decisions must be made, and how those decisions should be made.

[a] Defining Risk. The most widely accepted definition of "risk" is the chance and extent of loss. The most widely used definition of "risk" is variability of rate of return. The more uncertainty there is about the rate of return on an instrument over some future period, the greater the risk. Suppose a sponsor wishes to measure both the return on a portfolio each quarter and after a number of quarters and the risk the portfolio has taken. It can first look at 90-day Treasury bills, which have no risk in a 90-day period. That is to say, if it buys a 3-month Treasury bill, it can tell exactly what its rate of return will be over the next 3 months. If it buys a 5-year Treasury note, the return over the quarter is less certain, since interest rates may move up or down, with a corresponding impact on the security's value. A 20-year Treasury bond has even more uncertainty than a 5-year note because the effect of changes in interest rates will be greater for a 20-year instrument than for a 5-year instrument. A 20-year corporate bond has greater uncertainty than a 20-year government bond because the corporate bond may suffer from changes in its quality (i.e., the ability of the issuer to pay interest and principal on time) as well as changes in the general level of interest rates. Common stocks have even greater risk because they do not have a fixed maturity, and consequently their prices are affected by the full force of changes in economic conditions and specific company factors. Thus, the uncertainty of rate of return is a useful measurement of risk.

The amount of risk a fund has taken can be quantified by calculating the rate of return of the fund or its sectors, finding an average rate of return for the whole period, and measuring the variability of return around the average. The exact methods for doing this include mean absolute deviation, standard deviation, and variance.

The greatest limitation of this measurement is that it can only be made looking backward. That is, until the rate of return is known, the variability of that return cannot be measured. One alternative is to assume that the future will be like the past and to use past variabilities as a measure of future variabilities. Another alternative is to start with a base of past variabilities and then to estimate the changes caused by new factors. For instance, a company that had a certain historical variability might have more variability in the future if the company's capitalization were changed such that the debt-to-equity ratio was greatly increased. A second limitation of the variability approach is that traditionally most investors have not viewed unexpectedly high rates of return as risk. That is, if a stock is expected to rise 10 percent and it actually rises 15 percent, many investors have trouble considering the extra 5 percent as risk. However, under the definition of "risk" as uncertainty of future value, this potential extra profit contributes to risk. A third criticism of the variability notion is that significant risks within a company may cancel each other out, presenting the appearance that very little risk was taken, when in fact the opposite was true. An admittedly exaggerated example might be a situation in which the president of a mining company absconded with $100 million in assets at the same time that a new mine worth $100 million to the company was discovered.

Despite the limitations of variability as a measure of risk, it is hard to find a better one. Most other approaches to risk are intuitive, hence unmeasurable, or they involve measurements that aim at the problem but really do not address it directly. For instance, the quality of management and its impact on stock price are important, but they cannot be measured. The equity/bond ratio is an example of a measurement that aims at the problem but does not address it. If a sponsor does not know the risk level of stocks and bonds, knowing how much of its assets are in stocks as opposed to bonds does not give it a very precise measurement of risk. Consequently, the variability approach has gained considerable acceptance among sponsors, academics, monitoring organizations, and investors.

[b] Diversification. Diversification is the spreading of assets among a variety of securities or among securities in a variety of markets with the goal of reducing risk in a portfolio without reducing expected return. If investments have similar expected returns but earn those returns at different times and under different economic conditions, a portfolio holding more than one of the assets will have the same return as would the investor holding just one asset, but with less volatility from period to period. Not all types of risk can be diversified away. For instance, a stock market investor cannot diversify away the risk inherent in the stock market. It can own stocks that are less risky or more risky, but as long as it owns stocks it will have stock market risk. It can deal with this risk in four ways.

First, it can spread its assets among asset categories, such as stocks, bonds, and real estate. Second, it can purchase less risky investments, such as stocks of well-established companies instead of emerging growth stocks. Third, it can purchase assets in different markets, for instance, buying non-U.S. as well as U.S. stocks. Finally, it can diversify within each market and within the chosen risk level in order to eliminate all nonmarket risk. It is important to understand the difference between the first and second ways and the third and fourth ways to reduce risk, since the former involve a proportional reduction in return, whereas the latter imply no reduction in return for a reduction of risk.

By definition, each marketplace consists of many securities, each of which is affected by at least two sources of risk. The first source is market risk, and the second is nonmarket, or specific, risk. These risks are also sometimes referred to as nondiversifiable and diversifiable risks. In other words, looking at a stock market such as that in the United States, the investor can recognize that the rate of return for a given stock can be affected by factors within the company, such as management, earnings, and new products, and by market factors, such as the general level of the economy, interest rates, and inflation. Further, in any given period unexpectedly favorable or unfavorable things can happen to either the market or the individual stock. The investor in stocks cannot escape the unexpected effects of the economy, but it can minimize unexpected effects on individual stocks by buying many different stocks. Each time it adds another stock to the portfolio, it hopes to maintain the portfolio's expected return while decreasing the chances that a higher or lower return will be earned.

A convenient method for describing the diversification level of an equity portfolio is to measure its correlation with the market. This is done by making a regression analysis of the rate of return of the portfolio relative to the rate of return of the appropriate stock market index. A portfolio that is 100 percent diversified would consist of all the stocks in the marketplace and would be weighted in the same proportion as are the stocks in the marketplace. That is, a security that represents one percent of the value of the entire stock market would have a one percent holding in the portfolio, and so on for each security. With a portfolio constructed in this manner, 100 percent of the fluctuation in the portfolio can be traced to fluctuation in the market and the portfolio would be said to be 100 percent diversified, or to have an R squared (R^2) of 100. (R^2, or coefficient of determination, shows the percentage of a portfolio's fluctuations that are related to movements in the overall market.) At the other extreme, if the portfolio contained only one stock, the market risk would be a much smaller percentage of the total risk and the specific risk would be a much greater percentage. For a typical stock, about 30 percent of the risk in the stock is market related and 70 percent is specific. In other words, 70 percent of the fluctuations in the stock are attributable to company-related matters, whereas only 30 percent are attributable to the market. It is clear that in this case, the investor whose only holding is that stock has a significant exposure to the unexpectedly favorable or unfavorable factors that might affect the stock. If the investor is very confident that it has information regarding the stock that the marketplace does not have, it may wish to put itself in a position of owning only that stock and being 70 percent dependent on its information or judgment.

Most investors, and particularly institutions, find this approach to be unsuitably risky. These investors would be willing to sacrifice the exceptional return that might come from having one excellent stock for the knowledge that they would avoid the possibility of having a disaster from one very unsuccessful stock. They might then add a second stock to the portfolio and find that this increases the percentage of market risk from 30 percent to, e.g., 50 percent. By continuing to increase the number of stocks in the portfolio and by weighting them in the same proportion as they appear in the marketplace, the investor will find that the R^2 quickly rises to the 85 percent to 95 percent level. If the investor feels that the market is essentially efficient or the potential gains from being right are not worth the risk of being wrong, it may establish a diversification policy that aims to have 100 percent of the risk in the portfolio as market risk. In this case, the investor is willing to sacrifice the opportunity to make extra risk-adjusted return for the comfort of knowing that it will never have negative risk-adjusted return. (Further, it also increases its expected return by reducing its transaction costs to practically zero.)

There are thus three ways to look at the issue of the amount of stock market risk in a portfolio: (1) the percentage of equities versus fixed income or cash equivalents; (2) the volatility level of the stocks owned; and (3) the number of stocks owned, particularly stocks in different industries. The remaining issue concerning diversification is that the traditional idea that higher risk leads to higher return refers to market risk and not specific risk. If the investor could diversify away its risk, it would not deserve to be paid for assuming that risk. If anything, it seems as though there should be a penalty for the investor's failure to act in its own best interests, and, in fact, there is, in the sense that the investor has increased its risk without a commensurate increase in the expected return.

There are many cases in which investors do deserve to have a higher rate of return because they are assuming risks that cannot be diversified away. An investor owning long-term bonds will find its total rate of return more variable than that of an investor owning short-term cash equivalents. No matter which bonds are owned and in what proportions, the investor will find that over any reasonable period, the bond portfolio will be more variable in returns than the cash equivalents portfolio. There being no way to avoid or diversify away this risk without also reducing the expected return, the marketplace adjusts the rate of return on the riskier securities such that, in the long run, they provide a higher return than do less risky assets. Another example would be a portfolio invested 60 percent in an index fund and 40 percent in Treasury bills. This portfolio is inherently riskier than a portfolio invested 50 percent in an index fund and 50 percent in Treasury bills. Because stocks are more variable than Treasury bills, the investor in the more aggressive portfolio is virtually certain to have a higher level of risk. For this it can expect, in the long run, a higher rate of return.

[4] Relationship Between Risk and Return

The question of the appropriate investment policy is frequently stated as the question of how much risk the fund can endure. Implicit in this question is the view, first, that the more risk a fund takes, the higher the return that can be expected, and, second, that a fund should seek the highest return by increasing risk to the maximum acceptable point. If return decreased as risk increased, the risk policy question would make no sense, as all funds would seek to have the lowest risk and the highest return. Nonetheless, before blindly following the "high risk equals high return" approach, an investor should explore the risk-return relationship in more detail. Therefore, four questions will be addressed in this section of the chapter:

1. Does return go up as risk goes up?

2. If so, over what period is it reasonably certain that this will occur?

3. What is the relationship between risk and return (that is, as risk doubles, does return go up by 10 percent, 50 percent, 100 percent, and so forth)?

4. How stable are risk and return for each asset type, both absolutely and relatively among assets?

The results in Figure 4-1 for the seven periods from 1926 to 1991 can be used to address these questions. In answer to questions 1 and 2, it does appear that as risk rises, so does return. Within each period, risk rises along the spectrum from short-term governments to small stocks. The exception is the relationship between long-term governments and long-term corporates prior to 1965. While corporate bonds have been less volatile than government bonds at times, this may be because of the higher coupon (and hence shorter duration) of corporates, or just because of anomalies associated with the construction of the indexes, rather than anything fundamental to the risk-return relationship.

However, return does not fall neatly in line with risk. In fact, return does not rise uniformly for any of the periods, although it does for the full 1926–1991 period. An investor might thus conclude that return tends to rise with risk but that this relationship need not hold even for periods as long as 10 years.

Figure 4-1 provides little help in answering question 3 as to the specific relationship between risk and return, at least using annual returns and standard deviations as the measurement. For the 10-year periods shown, it is not possible to discern any such specific relationship.

Regarding question 4, neither risk nor return is stable for any asset type, but the relationship between risk and asset type tends to hold true in every case. That is, for each period, small company stocks are riskier than stocks in general, which are riskier than long-term bonds, which are, in turn, riskier than short-term securities.

This study is rather discouraging for sponsors and investment managers who wish to be precise in controlling their portfolios. Results in the real world appear to be too unstable to permit any degree of precision in portfolio control. However, it is useful to see the results and to recognize how variable they might be. Sponsors should take into consideration when establishing their risk-return policies.

[a] How Much Risk Can a Fund Endure? In order to answer this question, an investor must know the estimated risk-return spectrum available in the marketplace (as shown in Figure 4-2) and the "utility" or risk-return preferences of the fund and of the people responsible for it.

Assume that Figure 4-2 shows the risk-return spectrum available as of a point in time for "efficient" portfolios (meaning that for any given level of risk there is no portfolio with a higher return and for any given level of return there is no portfolio with lower risk). Even for efficient portfolios, it is not possible to say whether an investor should be at any particular point on the line. This is because each investor has a slightly different view of how much risk is tolerable. There is no clear-cut method for measuring the utility of an investor. However, the issues can be discussed and rational, if imprecise, policies can be developed. There are two fundamental considerations in analyzing the fund's utility:

1. How important is the success of the fund to the success of the organization?

2. What are the financial characteristics of the sponsor?

A third consideration has been created by the provision of ERISA that enables the PBGC to attach up to 30 percent of a corporation's net worth. This has the effect of reversing the risk policy wherein a corporation whose fund is in very bad shape would normally take very little risk but now might take the opposite tack because it is already suffering maximum exposure to the 30 percent attachment.

FIGURE 4-1

Return and Risk for Five Asset Types

Source: R.G. Ibbotson Associates, Inc.

10-Year Period	Short-Term Governments		Long-Term Governments		Long-Term Corporates		Common Stocks		Small Companies	
	Return[a]	Standard Deviation	Return	Standard Deviation	Return	Standard Deviation	Return	Standard Deviation	Return	Standard Deviation
1926–1935	2.0	1.7	4.7	6.3	7.1	4.6	5.9	33.5	0.3	57.5
1936–1945	0.2	0.2	4.5	3.3	4.0	1.5	8.4	23.9	19.2	45.5
1946–1955	1.1	0.5	1.3	3.7	1.9	2.7	16.7	18.1	11.3	22.4
1956–1965	2.8	0.7	1.9	6.1	2.6	5.3	11.1	16.5	15.3	25.0
1966–1975	5.6	1.4	3.0	7.3	3.6	8.7	3.3	19.7	4.0	37.8
1976–1985	9.0	2.9	9.0	15.5	9.8	16.2	14.3	14.2	27.8	17.7
1986–1991 (6 years)	6.8	1.1	12.0	9.9	12.1	8.2	15.9	13.7	8.3	27.3
1926–1991 (66 years)	3.7	3.4	4.8	8.6	5.4	8.6	10.4	20.8	18.2	35.5

[a] Returns are geometric (compound) annual returns.

FIGURE 4-2

Efficient Frontier Graph (1977–1991)

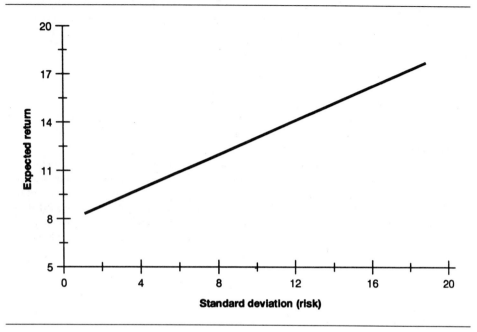

[b] **Importance of the Fund.** The more important the plan is to the organization's success, the less risk that can be tolerated. The greater the consequences of the fund's losing its value, the less risk that the fund should take.

The first consideration in determining the importance of the fund to the organization is to determine what percentage of its employees are covered by the plan and what the characteristics of those employees are (e.g., do they have special skills that would be very difficult to duplicate in the marketplace, as do airline pilots). Obviously, the higher the percentage of employees covered by the plan or the more important the types of employees covered, the more important the plan is to the success of the organization.

A second consideration in determining the fund's importance to the organization is the place of pension benefits in the hierarchy of total compensation. If, as is the case with some public utilities, a good pension is given more weight in relation to current salary than would be the case in, e.g., the advertising industry, the success of the fund is relatively more important to those public utilities.

[5] Financial Characteristics of the Sponsor

The greater the financial strength of the corporation relative to the size of the fund, the greater the fund's ability to bear risk. The most important measurements of the corporation's financial ability to bear risk within the fund are the following:

- *Pretax income relative to the pension fund contribution.* The higher the percentage of the pretax income that flows to pension fund contributions, the more conservative the fund should be, since a risky posture might lead to large losses in the fund that would have to be made up with higher contributions. This would have significant impact on the sponsor.

- *Stability of pretax income.* The more stable the earnings of a company, the greater its ability to bear risk. A highly cyclical company, on the other hand, may find it must increase pension fund contributions when earnings are low, again with a significant impact on the sponsor.

- *Pretax income relative to unfunded vested liability.* The greater the liability relative to income, the more conservative the approach should be, since, again, unfavorable investment results would cause a large percentage of earnings to be diverted to elimination of the liability.

- *Corporate assets relative to unfunded vested liability.* If the liability was eliminated through the liquidation of assets rather than paid off over time through income, the impact on the company could be measured by comparing the assets of the company to the liability of the fund. This possibility has become more significant, since ERISA allows the PBGC to assume 30 percent of corporate net worth in the event of inability to meet pension obligations. If a company's assets are low relative to the fund liability, a conservative posture is implied.

4.05 FUND MANAGEMENT

The focus is generally on the investor sponsoring organization in the viewing of the issue of utility, or the choice of an appropriate place on the risk-return spectrum. However, practical experience and knowledge of human nature dictate that the utility of the people responsible for the fund also be considered. While corporations and pension funds have infinite time horizons, chief executive officers (CEOs) and pension directors do not. Rather, they think in one-to-three-year planning horizons. Further, as with participants in profit-sharing plans, members of management can view the same circumstances and come up with widely different conclusions as to risk policies and methods for implementing goals.

With the recognition of this phenomenon, it is interesting to consider the factors that affect the utility of the various parties to the pension fund. Although the consideration of these utility factors is potentially embarrassing, failure to consider them can be disastrous for the fund, since a supposedly long-term policy may be abandoned at just the wrong time. For instance, suppose a professional analysis suggests that a fund can bear a high level of risk and, therefore, should be invested largely in equities, and the sponsor goes along with this recommendation even though the conservative tendencies of its officers make them very uncomfortable about the plan. If the stock market were to decline precipitously, the board of trustees might liquidate the equity portfolio near the bottom of the market and opt for short-term fixed income investments just when it should be doing the opposite. Conversely, a conservative fund might sell its bonds at the top of the market to move into equities that supported a board of trustee's bias toward more aggressive securities.

A number of decisions must be made in the selection of an investment manager, including whether the fund should be managed internally or externally; how much discretion the investment manager should have; whether the assets should be invested directly in securities or indirectly through pooled or commingled funds; whether the style employed should be active or passive, and, if active, what active style should be employed; and how many managers are needed.

[1] Internal Versus External Investment Management

The principal advantages of internal management are that it gives the sponsor far more control over investment policies and over the individual securities held, the people making investment decisions will be more familiar with the sponsor's needs, and the sponsor can develop a better insight into the problems faced by outside investment managers. The advantages of external management are that the outside manager typically has far more resources, may have special capabilities such as in dealing with private placements or mortgage investments, may be able to demand lower commission costs from brokers and dealers, and, for bond investing, may be able to get better prices by combining smaller blocks of bonds into more marketable larger blocks. Although the outside manager has less time to spend on a particular fund than would an insider, it develops insight and perspective from viewing many sponsors with different needs.

The investment manager working within the organization needs knowledge of the two major decision areas: how to allocate assets among sectors and which securities to buy within sectors. That is, the manager needs to decide what allocations to make among stocks, bonds, liquid assets, and other investments, and also needs to decide which stocks to buy, which bonds to buy, and so on. The importance of the allocation question, and hence the significance of the manager's expertise in this area, rests to a large extent on the sponsor's position with respect to setting an overall risk policy. If the sponsor establishes firm guidelines as to the percentage of the portfolio that should go into each asset sector, the manager's activities can be concentrated in security selection. Conversely, if the sponsor has only general guidelines, the investment manager must choose as well as implement the fund's investment policy. The type of expertise required to make intelligent allocations among investment vehicles is knowledge of economics, particularly monetary economics, and experience with stock and bond market levels over at least two market cycles. (Of course, familiarity with the sponsor and its fund is vital.)

Are the costs of hiring in-house investment managers justifiable? The budgetary considerations are quite straightforward, involving only the cost of using an internal investment staff versus the cost of using outside managers. The cost of outside investment management is typically based on the size of the account and on whether the relationship involves management only or management plus custody and record keeping.

On the basis of these estimates and considering only cost, a fund less than $200 million in size would probably not justify the expense of internal investment management (0.5 percent (estimated outside management fees) of $200 million is $1 million), and a fund of over $400 million probably does justify it. This analysis assumes that the entire portfolio is managed internally. In the more common case, the sponsor decides to manage part of the portfolio internally and to leave the balance to outside managers. If a sponsor decides to manage one third of its assets internally, the fund would have to be about three times as large, or over $1 billion, to justify internal management on a cost basis.

Is the organization willing to manage funds? This can only really be answered by the sponsor. There will certainly be much discussion within the organization before a board of directors or a board of trustees will agree to internal management. This decision relates to the perceived risks and benefits of internal versus external management, including the risk of embarrassment.

Is the organization willing to accept the risk of fund management? In reality, there is probably very little difference in risk to the organization between internal and external management. That is, if the manager does well and the fund prospers, the organization will benefit, regardless of who was responsible for the success. Similarly, if the manager is unsuccessful, the organization will suffer commensurately. The risk to the individuals within the organization is a different matter. Many officials will feel that a mistake made by an outside investment manager is the investment manager's fault, whereas bad results obtained by an internally managed fund might reflect on the personnel who decided to use internal management, a practice contrary to that of most sponsors. Moreover, most sponsors would find it easier to remove an account from an outside manager that is operating unsuccessfully than to disband an equally unsuccessful internal staff. ERISA tends to support the notion that it is less risky for the sponsor to have an outside manager by saying that under certain conditions a sponsor can escape liability for the acts or omissions of its investment manager by choosing outside managers.[2]

In summary, the advantages of internal management to the sponsor are greater control over the policies pursued and the securities purchased, the greater familiarity of the investment manager with the goals and characteristics of the organization, and the greater ability of the investment manager to devote time to the sponsor's portfolio. The disadvantages are a lack of the perspective gained by viewing many different customers and their portfolios and, presumably, a much lower level of resources available to the investment manager. The cost of internal management is normally greater than that of external management for small funds (about $400 million or less) and less than that of external management for large funds.

Sponsors wishing to begin internal management might consider the following approach: Rather than moving a large piece of a diversified portfolio in-house immediately, a sponsor may divert the annual contributions, the income, or the annual contributions plus income on investments to the in-house pool. Further, the sponsor might start with a reasonably passive bond portfolio as the first step toward investing. In this way, relatively small amounts of money will be invested in the less risky assets, and consequently the sponsor can begin an internal operation without taking undue risk.

[2] Investment Manager's Degree of Discretion

It is possible for the sponsor to have an investment manager but to give it only part of the responsibility for investing. The degree of discretion is a function of the organization's willingness to become involved in the investment process and of the extent to which it has defined its investment policies. The degree of discretion ranges from allowing the managers to have the most control (option 1) to allowing them to have the least control (option 5):

---

[2] These conditions are that the outside investment manager must be "qualified" (meaning that it is a bank, an insurance company, or a registered investment adviser, as defined), the manager must acknowledge in writing that it is a fiduciary, the sponsor must have been prudent in hiring the manager, and the sponsor must have been prudent in continuing the use of the manager. See ERISA § 405, Pub. L. No. 93-406, 88 Stat. 829 (codified as amended at 29 USC §§ 1001–1368 (1990) and in scattered sections of 26 USC, as amended).

1. The manager makes all decisions.

2. The sponsor provides either general guidelines as to percentage in equities, such as "Do not exceed 60 percent in equities," or specific guidelines, such as "The equity–fixed income ratio will be maintained as close to 60:40 as possible."

3. The sponsor provides either general or specific guidelines as to the risk level (beta) of the equity portfolio.

4. The sponsor provides either general or specific guidelines as to the quality of stocks or bonds.

5. The sponsor reviews all recommendations prior to their execution.

Because most funds are now managed with separate managers for different asset types, the primary source of risk can be quantified in advance. Thus, it has become common to allow the manager complete investment discretion with its investment style.

Discretionary management enables the manager to implement strategy and take advantage of block purchases and sales as occasions arise. However, the policy of limiting discretion of the investment manager has three advantages. First, the sponsor retains control over what investments are held. Second, there is a greater opportunity for the sponsor to understand the manager and for the manager to get to know the sponsor. And third, the manager is required to think out and articulate its reasons for making a suggestion, rather than potentially "shooting from the hip."

[3] Management Through the Use of Pooled Funds

Sponsors can own securities either directly or through participations in commingled (pooled) funds. Banks, mutual fund management organizations, and insurance companies provide pooled funds in which sponsors can invest.

[a] **Advantages of Commingled Funds.** Commingled funds provide a number of advantages, including ease of administration, diversification, and low cost:

1. *Ease of administration.* From an administrative point of view, the holder of a commingled fund owns only one security and need not be concerned with collecting dividends and maintaining custodial records. Since commingled funds almost never issue certificates, the holder need not worry about custodial problems or the physical transfer of securities. The investor's interest is represented by electronic bookkeeping entries only.

2. *Diversification.* Since a pooled fund combines the assets of many contributors, it can achieve a high degree of diversification by purchasing a large number of securities. Theoretically, a small portfolio could achieve a similar level of diversification, but transactions and administrative and management costs usually discourage the holding of large numbers of securities. Both sound investment practice and ERISA require that portfolios be diversified.

3. *Cost.* Just as it is easier for the fund to own participations in a commingled portfolio, so it is easier for the investment manager to combine the assets of many sponsors into one fund. It need not provide separate management for the sponsor, nor need it provide individual custodial and extensive record-keeping facilities. Consequently, it is able to charge lower fees to the fund sponsors, particularly for small portfolios.

[b] Disadvantages of Commingled Funds. Commingled funds also have disadvantages. The most important disadvantage is that the funds are designed to fill the needs of a number of sponsors and therefore are not adaptable to the requirements of any one sponsor.

1. *Unadaptable to sponsor needs.* Since a pooled fund represents the assets of many sponsors, it is impossible to adapt the portfolio to the needs of each sponsor. Consequently, the sponsor must choose a pooled fund that most appropriately fits its needs and then accept the decisions of the investment manager as to what securities the pooled fund will hold. This limitation can be partly avoided by investing in commingled funds with different objectives, so that the resulting portfolio reflects the sponsor's objectives.

2. *Sponsor unable to control risk.* A sponsor that wishes to achieve a specified risk level must constantly monitor the risk policies of the commingled fund in which it invests. For instance, if a sponsor wishes to be 50 percent in equities and 50 percent in bonds, it may invest in two commingled funds, one equity oriented and the other fixed-income oriented. If the manager of the equity-oriented fund decides that the market is going down, it may cut back the fund's position in equities to 50 percent. The sponsor might then find that it had not invested 50:50 but that it owned 50 percent bonds, 25 percent equities, and 25 percent cash equivalents. Of course, the manager of the equity-oriented fund may be right in its opinion on the market, but the sponsor's asset allocation objective will be frustrated.

[c] Active Management Through Mutual Funds. Typically, fund sponsors hire investment managers and the managers actively manage securities. Some very large funds and aggressive funds frequently add or replace investment management organizations. However, another alternative is available for sponsors that wish to be active yet do not wish to evaluate individual securities. Sponsors can use specialized commingled funds as their primary investment vehicle and allocate money among these funds. For instance, a sponsor might have views as to the relative benefit of stocks versus bonds or of growth stocks relative to value stocks. It could thus pick commingled or mutual funds that reflect these objectives. If stocks became more attractive relative to bonds, money could easily be pulled out of the bond fund and placed in an equity fund. Similarly, if growth stocks became more attractive relative to value stocks, funds could be switched from the growth stock fund to the value stock fund. As pooled funds become even more specialized, emphasizing particular industries as well as investment styles, the sponsor could even control its investments among energy, consumer, or cyclical stocks, or even the oil, computer, or drug industries. The fact that pension, profit-sharing, and endowment funds do not pay taxes facilitates this type of management, whereas taxable portfolios might find it more advantageous to switch securities on an individual basis so that tax consequences of each transaction can be considered.

[4] Active Versus Passive Investment Management

Another decision that the sponsor must make before choosing investment managers is whether to adopt an active or passive management approach. On average, investors that actively manage their accounts will underperform the average passive holders of securities. Active investors, in total, have transactions costs and pay fees. Passive investors do not. Stocks perform the same regardless of who owns them, so the precost return of both is the same. Therefore, active investors, on average, underperform their passive counterparts.

While some investors can outperform others, everyone cannot beat the market. Increasingly, professional investors are well trained. They all go to school and study the same textbooks. They subscribe to the same information services, talk to the same analysts, and read the same newspapers. With the same training and same information received at the same time, it is hard for them to outsmart each other. Further, there is a cost in trying, as well as a risk of failing to one degree or another, to meet the chosen benchmark. With large sums of money moving rapidly as information is discovered, securities prices are efficiently (accurately) priced. These factors have converted a large body of sponsors to passive management.

[5] Passive Investing Versus Indexing

Most investors that think of themselves as investing passively actually index. They attempt to achieve the returns of a benchmark or index by replicating to one degree or another the securities in the index. This means that they change the securities in their portfolio whenever the creator of the index changes the composition of the index. Apparently, this is done with the knowledge that transaction costs will reduce future returns but with the conviction that it is better to track the benchmark than to risk underperforming it.

An index fund is simply a broad, but very specific, portfolio. The returns on that portfolio will, in any single period, be equal to the returns on each asset in the portfolio multiplied by the weight each asset represents of the total portfolio. Further, the index fund has characteristics that can produce varying results in different periods. For instance, an equity index fund has a certain proportion in oil stocks. To the extent that oil stocks perform better than the market as a whole in a certain period, the index fund will tend to outperform portfolios that have less concentration in oil and will tend to underperform portfolios with a greater concentration in oil. Rather than being magical, the results are arithmetical.

In addition, it is not just the factors making up the index that can outperform or underperform the market. Even the index portfolio itself can become a factor, with investors favoring it, as they did in the late 1980s, or disfavoring it, as they did in the late 1970s and early 1980s.

[6] How Many Investment Managers?

If a passive strategy is adopted, it probably makes sense to choose no more than one manager for each asset category (stocks, bonds, and so forth). If active management is preferred, or if only part of the portfolio is to be managed passively, a decision must be made as to the number of managers. The alternatives for this decision can be outlined as follows:

1. Should all of the funds be managed by one manager?

2. If more than one manager is chosen, should the managers be generalists investing in both stocks and bonds, or should they be specialists by asset category?

3. Should more than one manager be chosen for an asset category, and if so, on what basis?

Using more than one manager has these advantages: diversification, the potential ability to achieve the best efforts of a number of specialists, and the increased resources available to the sponsor in the way of investment or other ideas. There are, however, certain problems associated with having more than one manager, including higher cost (since almost all managers charge on a declining fee scale basis), greater administrative burden on the fund sponsor, and, most important, increased responsibility for the sponsor, which must then decide how to allocate money among managers. This burden is greatest when the managers are asset category specialists, since then the decision as to asset allocation falls entirely on the sponsor. That is, if one manager controls equities and the other controls bonds, the sponsor makes the asset allocation decision by establishing the amount that each manager has to invest. Even worse, the sponsor may be reluctant to change the allocation policy because it is cumbersome or embarrassing to move assets from one manager to another. Thus, having a single manager eases the sponsor's administrative burdens, reduces its costs, and enables it to rely more heavily on the manager in making decisions concerning the appropriate asset allocations. Conversely, using multiple managers increases diversification, permits the sponsor to choose specialists, and gives the sponsor greater control over asset allocation.

Within a given asset category, such as equities, it is possible to have more than one manager. The typical reason for doing so is to increase diversification (i.e., to decrease the chances that the fund will be harmed if a manager has particularly bad investment results) and to balance styles (a concept related to diversification). In the former case, the sponsor may decide that it is desirable to have a growth philosophy in the portfolio but that more than one manager of growth stocks will be chosen in order to diversify the results. Conversely, it may be considered desirable to have a portfolio that reflects the market as a whole in terms of proportions of growth stocks, income stocks, and value stocks, and the sponsor may try to achieve high risk-adjusted rates of return by choosing the best growth manager, the best income manager, and the best value manager. There is considerable merit to the idea of having a number of investment managers with different styles. If this method of diversification is to be successful, however, it is critical for the sponsor to choose a manager that excels at the style it wants rather than trying to alter a manager's style to suit the sponsor's need.

[7] Due Diligence in Choosing Managers

In the analysis of prospective managers, efforts should be directed in five areas: investment activity, general diligence, fees, legal issues, and conflicts of interest.

[a] **Investment Activity.** The sponsor should attempt to understand the factors determining the manager's return, such as concentration in companies of a certain capitalization size or industry group; sources of risk, including concentration in a limited number of issues and the risk of the issues owned; who in the organization contributes to the sources of return; depth of management; how risk is controlled; and common factors that could lead to a large number of investments declining at one time.

[b] **General Diligence.** The sponsor should check the amount and trend in assets under management and the number of employees. References from existing clients,

former clients, and others should also be checked. The manager should be visited in its offices to see if its resources are commensurate with its investment process and client base. Sponsors may also want to inquire into policies of equity managers on proxy voting, as proxies are considered part of the asset represented by common stock holdings.

[c] Fee Levels. The level of fees should be reasonable in light of the nature of the activity and any limitation in assets that the manager imposes on itself in order to prevent performance from being diluted by excessive growth in assets under management. Unfortunately, comparison with other managers is the primary method of determining the reasonableness of fees. If incentive fees are proposed, they should be analyzed closely. The sponsor should also learn whether soft dollars (directed commissions) are allocated for research, office expenses, or marketing.

[d] Legal Issues. Investors may want to inquire about any regulatory violations by the manager, any relevant lawsuits, and any side letters between the manager and other investors.

[e] Conflicts of Interest. Potential conflicts include investment by the manager and any commissions or fees that could be earned by the manager other than the advisory fee.

[8] Size of the Management Organization

There is little to indicate that the size of the organization, with respect to either the number of employees or assets under management, should be an important consideration in choosing an investment manager. Large organizations clearly have more resources, yet it is questionable whether they can necessarily bring these resources to bear to the benefit of individual clients. Smaller organizations have few resources yet may be better able to coordinate these resources. They also may have a wider range of investment opportunities, since they can purchase securities of smaller companies and can move in and out of the market more easily. One argument having little merit that is raised against smaller organizations is that the portfolio will be in jeopardy if the key manager dies. Just as a stock does not know who owns it, a portfolio does not know who runs it. In the event of the passing of the key manager, the sponsor can hire a replacement. This may be awkward at the time, but it is a small risk to the fund and one worth taking to have the right manager.

[9] Choosing the Individual Manager Within the Investment Management Firm

Thus far, this chapter has dealt with the organizational and structural aspects of choosing investment managers. It is perhaps equally necessary to recognize the importance of the personal side of the equation. The sponsor should be almost as careful in choosing the individual within the investment management organization as it is in choosing the organization itself. This decision should be based on three factors: the individual's experience, other work load, and intangible personal qualities.

It is to be hoped that the individual who actually manages the sponsor's fund will have had experience in managing portfolios during several market cycles. It is only after seeing several periods of dramatic overvaluation and undervaluation of securities and the passing in and out of favor of a number of investment fads that most people are capable of exercising good investment judgment. Such judgment is a combination of a healthy skepticism, objectivity, humility sufficient to permit changing one's mind when the facts so dictate, the ability to keep one's eye on long-term goals despite the daily contradictions and confusions of the marketplace, and the ability to act independently and decisively when this is warranted by the conditions.

It is important that the sponsor and its portfolio achieve adequate attention. This requires that the portfolio manager not have overly burdensome responsibilities in administration, marketing, or managing other portfolios. In the organizations that manage portfolios most intensively (and charge the highest fees), portfolio managers may have only 5 to 10 clients. In large organizations, which have many clients of moderate size, portfolio managers may be responsible for many times this number of accounts. The sponsor should know in detail the work responsibilities of its portfolio manager before entering into an investment management agreement.

The third factor to be considered in choosing an individual investment manager is not easily measurable. This intangible includes the ability of the individual manager to communicate with the sponsor, personal motivation in learning about the sponsor and attempting to do a good job, and a general willingness to respond to the sponsor's and the fund's needs. This does not mean that the individual should be an errand boy for the sponsor, spending time seeking information unrelated to the fund. However, a certain willingness to put in extra effort on behalf of the client is a most desirable attribute in the individual manager.

[10] Administrative Support for the Investment Manager

Although the investment manager's primary responsibility is to make investment decisions, it is extremely important that the investment manager have adequate accounting and reporting facilities. In addition, the manager should have the ability to create special reports that the sponsor may require from time to time. Finally, the sponsor should inquire about the investment manager's ability to control short-term cash investments, particularly if the manager is not also the custodian of the assets, and about the extent to which the manager's statements are reconciled with those of the custodian, to provide a cross-check on accounting errors.

[11] Using Consultants to Choose Investment Managers

Since the choice of investment managers is so critical, and since the investment management field is both fragmented and specialized, many sponsors consider it desirable to use outside consulting services to assist in the management selection process. A wide variety of such services is available, ranging from those that provide assessments of purely intangible factors to those that have detailed information on the performance of accounts and the qualifications of personnel. In selecting consultants, care must be exercised to ensure that the particular needs of the sponsor are within the consultants' capabilities. It should also be recognized that choosing the manager that will perform best is not much easier than choosing the stocks that will rise the most. Thus, the sponsor should be realistic about what it expects to accomplish through the use of the consultant.

[12] Performance-Based Fees

Although the most common form of payment is a fee based on assets, which typically declines for larger clients' accounts, performance-based incentive fees are becoming increasingly common.

[a] Rationale for Performance-Based Fees.

The two rationales for performance-based fees are to provide an incentive to managers and to align payment with results. Some investors feel that the best people and best effort can be attracted with performance-based fees. The implication is that by providing the opportunity for the manager to make a higher fee, one will attract the best managers and will extract the best effort from those managers, leading to performance worth the higher fees.

The second rationale, aligning payment with results, has much more modest expectations. It does not assume anything about the relationship between fees and performance, but rather focuses on fairness, so that in years with good results the payment is larger than it is in years with poor results.

[b] Types of Performance-Based Fees.

There are two types of performance-based fees: fulcrum fees and percent of profits. The fulcrum fee is based on a performance standard related to the market for the asset being measured. The normal fee is paid for achieving the benchmark, and an incremental fee is added or subtracted for each unit of performance above or below the index. The percent of profits fee, sometimes called the venture capital–type performance-based fee, is literally a percentage of the profits earned. Here, effectively, the benchmark is zero and the manager receives a percentage of any gains above that amount.

[c] Concerns of the Sponsor.

While appealing in many ways, performance-based fees generate concerns of which investors should be aware. The structure should reward excellent performance by the manager but not random market movements. This makes choice of the benchmark important and suggests an extended time frame, preferably with a rolling measurement period, an increment over the benchmark before the performance-based fee starts to accrue, and a cap on the maximum performance-based fee payable. The structure should not induce the manager to take more risk in order to have a higher return. This suggests a longer period for measuring results, a symmetrical fee that takes away as much for bad performance as is given for good performance, and measurement of risk of the manager relative to the benchmark. Further, the risk level of the portfolio should be measured before and after the incentive fee is introduced. Since the fees paid are based on performance, the importance of measurement and measurer are increased. Definitions of the performance period and methodology should be determined prior to the measurement period. And, finally, the sponsor (and the investment manager) should be sure that the fee arrangement is legally permissible.

[d] Effect on the Sponsor's Costs.

If the sponsor structures the fee to achieve a fair sharing of fees based on performance in good and bad times, it may be able to lower fees. Since a standard must be established for determining when a performance fee is payable, the opportunity is provided for setting a benchmark that is above the normal market portfolio. For instance, a U.S. equity manager might be expected to achieve the return of the Standard & Poor's 500 plus the amount of its fees plus 100 basis points. By establishing the bogey in this manner, the sponsor effectively can reduce the average fee, since on average managers cannot be expected to outperform the overall market.

If the sponsor is skillful in choosing managers, the overall level of fees paid may rise with the introduction of performance-based fees. If the managers would have done a good job anyway, there is no benefit to the fund from the higher fee. Further, some managers may want to receive a higher fee level for taking the risk associated with a performance-based fee. A careful analysis should be made of the break-even point between normal and performance-based fees and the cost and benefit of good and bad performance.

Finally, it may be appropriate to consider that if incentive fees really encourage managers to work harder, a manager who receives incentive fees from some clients will work harder for those clients of the firm than for those who do not pay incentives.

4.06 SUMMARY

Pension plans can perform a variety of functions for employees and thus for the sponsors for which they work: deferred compensation, a reward for long service, and tax-efficient compensation. Because of their long life and high cost, pension promises can be extremely expensive contracts. Thus, attention must be given to the level of benefits and to whom they are being promised.

Once the benefit level is established, the primary determinant of cost is the return achieved on invested assets. Prospects for earning a return that is within the range expected by the fund sponsor are enhanced by carefully setting goals for the fund, choosing an appropriate risk policy, and choosing investment managers that responsibly implement the sponsor's policies.

Suggested Reading

Allen, Jr., E.T., J. Melone, J.S. Rosenbloom, and J.L. VanDerhei. "Pensions, Profit-Sharing, and Other Deferred Compensation Plans." *Pension Planning,* 6th ed. Homewood, Ill.: Dow Jones-Irwin, 1988.

Ambachtsheer, Keith P. *Pension Funds and the Bottom Line: Managing the Corporate Pension Fund as a Financial Business.* Homewood, Ill.: Dow Jones-Irwin, 1986.

Arnott, Robert, and Frank J. Fabozzi. *Asset Allocation, A Handbook of Portfolio Policies, Strategies and Tactics.* Chicago: Probus, 1988.

Berkowitz, Stephen A., Louis D. Finney, and Dennis E. Logue. *The Investment Performance of Corporate Pension Plans: Why They Do Not Beat The Market Regularly.* Westport, Conn.: Quorum Books, 1988.

Brealey, Richard A., and Stewart C. Myers. *Principles of Corporate Finance,* 4th ed. New York: McGraw Hill, 1991.

Burk, James E. *Pension Plan Manual: Administration and Investment*. Boston: Warren Gorham Lamont, 1987.

Ellis, Charlie D. *Investment Policy—How to Win the Loser's Game*. Homewood, Ill.: Dow Jones-Irwin, 1985.

Elton, Edwin J., and Martin J. Gruber. *Modern Portfolio Theory and Investment Analysis,* 4th ed. New York: John Wiley & Sons, Inc., 1991.

Ippolito, Richard A. *Pension, Economics and Public Policy*. Pension Research Council, Wharton School, University of Pennsylvania, Dow Jones-Irwin, 1986.

Logue, Dennis E. *Managing Corporate Pension Plans*. New York: Harper & Row, 1991.

Longstreth, Bevis. *Modern Investment Management and the Prudent Man Rule*. New York: Oxford University Press, 1986.

Rosenberg, Claude. *Investing With the Best—What to Look for, What to Look Out for in Your Search for a Superior Investment Manager*. New York: John Wiley & Sons, Inc., 1986.

Williams III, Arthur. *Managing Your Investment Manager,* 3rd ed. Homewood, Ill.: Dow Jones-Irwin, 1992.

Chapter 5

Hedging Financial Risk

JAMES K. SEWARD

5.01   INTRODUCTION

Traditionally, economists have argued that any attempt by corporate management to manage, or hedge, financial risk is simply a waste of shareholder wealth. While practitioners might find this prescription difficult to accept, in fact, corporate hedging policies matter only if they enhance the value of the firm. Because shareholders can hedge against unsystematic risks by holding a well-diversified portfolio of stocks, corporate hedging policies can affect firm value in one of two ways: (1) They can reduce the systematic risk component of security investments, and, thus, reduce the firm's cost of capital or (2) they can increase the stream of cash flows that the corporation expects to receive from its productive investment opportunities. In either case, corporate hedging policies maximize the value of shareholder equity by increasing the net present value of the firm's investment projects.

This chapter explicitly describes and illustrates the conditions under which discount rates and project cash flows can be altered through corporate hedging policies and assesses the financial instruments and techniques that are available to help corporate managers identify and hedge their manageable risk exposures. The chapter considers two broad approaches to the management of financial risk: on-balance sheet techniques and off-balance sheet techniques. Each of the transactions discussed is illustrated in a fairly detailed case study in an effort to provide the corporate manager with a broad but detailed understanding of the most recent advances in the practice of corporate hedging and risk management.

5.02   IDENTIFYING AND MEASURING EXPOSURE TO RISK

Because the market value of most corporations is affected by financial and commodity prices, as the volatility of interest rates, foreign exchange rates, and commodity prices increases, the demand for hedging instruments also becomes greater. Unfortunately for corporations, the last two decades have witnessed an enormous increase in the volatility of these prices. At the extreme, this volatility can be so excessive that otherwise well-run corporations find their financial welfare impaired. Before top managers can effectively deal with these risks, they must be able to identify, measure, and manage such exposures and understand the impact of each of these risks on the firm's financial performance measures. Smith, Smithson, and Wilford[1] use the term "risk profile" to describe the impact of financial risk on the value of the firm. They hypothesize a linear relationship between firm value and financial risk. An example of this measure is contained in Figure 5-1, which illustrates how firm value is affected by changes in a financial or commodity price. For example, what impact does an unexpected change in the price of cocoa have on the market value of Hershey Corporation? To answer this question, it is necessary to understand how to estimate the slope of the risk profile relationship. Identifying a firm's financial risk exposure is complicated by the fact that some price change sensitivities are not apparent from a firm's financial statements. As a result, quantitative techniques that identify the full spectrum of price sensitivities must be used to determine a firm's risk exposure.

---

[1] C. Smith, Jr., C. Smithson, and D. Wilford, *Managing Financial Risk* (New York: Harper & Row, 1990).

FIGURE 5-1

Effect of Price Changes on Firm Value

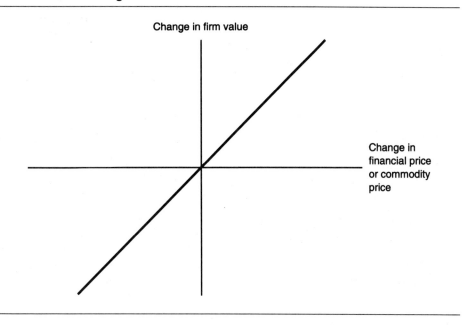

Managers should also note that hedging activities generally will not simultaneously maximize all of the corporation's performance measures. For example, hedging in order to maximize the market value of the firm's common stock will usually not maximize the firm's earnings per share. Thus, determining what should be hedged is a first step that each manager must undertake. Financial economists generally take as a given that the objective of the firm is to maximize the market value of its common equity. This chapter also adopts this view. However, the techniques described here are also applicable to other corporate objectives. Thus, for example, assuming that management's primary objective is to manage the risks associated with earnings per share rather than common equity value, the term "market value of common equity" can be replaced by "earnings per share" throughout the remainder of this chapter without any additional changes.

5.03 THE TECHNIQUE OF HEDGING

In general, the objective of any hedge program is to reduce or minimize the uncertainty of a firm's exposure to certain types of risk. The adoption of a hedge program allows the corporate manager to choose effectively those risks against which the firm will protect itself. Analogously, the decision to leave certain risks unhedged implies (either implicitly or explicitly) that the firm has chosen to bear those risks.

[1] Size of the Hedge Position

The general approach to establishing a hedge depends on the relationship between the firm's risk exposure and the hedge instrument. For example, assume that a firm would like to hedge a liability. In order to determine the size of the hedge position, the firm must estimate the following relationship:

Expected change in value of firm's liability

$$= \alpha + \beta(\text{expected change in value of hedge instrument}) \tag{5.1}$$

In this equation, the coefficient β represents the hedge ratio. Thus, β represents the number of units of the hedge instrument that should be purchased in order to hedge against future value changes in the hedged liability.

In the general case of risk profile analysis, a corporate manager can adapt Equation 5.1 as follows:

$$\text{Change in value of firm} = (a + b)(\text{change in financial price}) \tag{5.2}$$

where b represents the change in firm value per unit change in the financial price. This specification suggests that regression analysis may provide a particularly useful technique for determining the sensitivity of firm value to changes in various financial prices. One immediate complication of this specification, however, is that aggregate firm value is typically not observable. Hence, in order to provide an empirically tractable form of Equation 5.2, a firm's common stock price is often used in lieu of firm value.

Smith, Smithson, and Wilford[2] also describe two other potential problems with this specification. First, since common stock prices follow a random walk, rates of return (rather than prices per se) should be used to estimate financial price sensitivities. Second, financial price risk is only one component of the total risk associated with common stock ownership. Equation 5.2, therefore, must be adjusted to incorporate a measure of market, or nondiversifiable, risk, and corporate managers must estimate the following relationship in order to isolate the true marginal impact of financial price risk on firm value:

$$\text{Rate of return on firm's stock price} = a_1 + a_2(\text{rate of return on market portfolio})$$
$$+ a_3(\text{percentage change in financial price}) \tag{5.3}$$

This expression does not imply that only a single source of financial price risk can be considered. In fact, any number of price sensitivities can be considered, provided that sufficient data is available.

[2] Duration

As an alternative to estimating the historical relationship between the firm's liability and the hedge instrument, the concept of duration can be applied to immunize the firm's risk exposure. The duration of a financial instrument is a measure of the average time to each payment provided by the security. Duration is calculated by the following formula:

---

[2] *Ibid.*

FIGURE 5-2

Calculating Duration of a Bond

Year	Cash Flow	Present Value at 10%	Year × Present Value Total Value
1	$100,000	$ 90,900	0.187
2	100,000	82,600	0.339
3	100,000	75,100	0.463
4	100,000	68,300	0.561
5	100,000	62,100	0.638
6	100,000	56,400	0.695
7	100,000	51,300	0.738
		$486,700	3.621

Note: Duration = 3.621 years.

$$\text{Duration} = \frac{[PV(CF_t) \times 1] + [PV(CF_2) \times 2] + \ldots [PV(CF_n) \times n]}{\text{current market value of security}} \quad (5.4)$$

where $PV(CF_t)$ is the present value of the cash flow to be received at time t. Figure 5-2 illustrates the calculation of duration for a bond.

Duration is a useful measure of the risk associated with an asset or liability that promises a stream of cash flows. Thus, it provides a technique for corporate managers to hedge interest rate exposure by altering the firm's mix of assets and liabilities. When the corporate manager adjusts the asset and liability structure so that the duration of the assets is equal to the duration of the liabilities, the firm is said to be immunized; that is, the firm has neutralized its market value completely against unanticipated changes in the level of interest rates. Stated somewhat differently, the objective of an immunization strategy is to structure the firm's assets to have the same present value and duration as its liabilities.

The usefulness of duration as an interest rate risk management tool increases according to the relative impact of interest rate risk on firm value. For example, duration is used quite regularly by financial institutions to measure their exposure to future interest rate movements. The following example illustrates how duration can be applied to manage interest rate risk. A firm purchases equipment to lease to the ultimate user. The lease company must determine how to fund the purchase in such a way that its market value is unaffected by subsequent changes in interest rates. The lease company manager first calculates the duration of the income stream generated by the promised lease payments. If the equipment is to be leased for seven years at $100,000 per year, the duration of this cash flow stream is 3.621 years (as shown in Figure 5-2).

Next, the lease manager must determine a liability structure that has the same present value ($486,700) and duration as the income stream. There are a number of alternative financing arrangements that can satisfy these conditions, but the most straightforward is for the firm to borrow $486,700 today, with a maturity of 3.621 years, and repay the amount borrowed plus 10 percent interest in one lump sum on the maturity date (i.e., the debt obligation is a zero-coupon bond). If no lender will agree to such specific terms, the least manager might consider a package of $200,000 of one-year debt at 10 percent interest and $286,700 of five-and-one-half-year debt at

10 percent interest (again, a zero-coupon instrument). This package has the same present value and duration as the lease payment stream.

Note that duration has several inherent limitations as a measure of interest rate risk. For example, duration calculations implicitly assume that all interest rate changes occur equally. Hence, if short-term rates and long-term rates do not move together in a parallel shift, matching durations of assets and liabilities will not provide complete protection against future interest rate movements. In addition, as interest rates fluctuate and time passes, duration changes and the corporate manager must continually reassess the net exposure of the firm to interest rate risk. Nevertheless, duration does provide corporate managers with an important tool for managing interest rate risk.

[3] Case Study of Financial Innovation and Security Design

One of the most straightforward ways in which a corporation can manage its risk exposures is through the design of financial securities. This type of on-balance sheet transaction allows the firm to design, for example, a liability stream that offsets an exposure created by the firm's investment decisions. Consider the case of a U.S. company that receives some proportion of its revenue stream in nondollar currencies. This currency exposure potentially can be managed by issuing a liability whose cash flows (and, hence, its market value) also fluctuate with exchange rate movements. Thus, rather than relying on the use of derivative securities in a separate transaction, the firm can embed an option in the design of its primary financial securities. More important, since exchange-traded derivative instruments such as options have specific maturity and exercise prices, the firm may have more flexibility in designing a security that is better-suited for its specific risk exposure.

An example of such an instrument is the foreign currency exchange warrant (FCEW). FCEWs give the holder the continuous right (but not the obligation) to purchase a prespecified number of U.S. dollars at a fixed currency exchange rate at any time before the expiration date. Although the expiration date can be set by the issuer, because FCEWs generally have five-year maturities, they can be viewed as long-term U.S. put options on foreign currencies or call options on the U.S. dollar.

FCEWs have several unique features:

- Unlike equity warrants, they cannot be converted into an ownership claim on the firm's assets.
- Unlike foreign currency options, the respective currencies are not exchanged between the issuer and the warrant holder when the warrant is exercised. Rather, the corporate issuer's obligation is limited to making a U.S. dollar cash settlement.
- They are unsecured obligations of the corporate issuer and are subject to default risk.
- They are usually issued with a note or bond offering, but they are not attached to the notes or bonds, so they trade separately in the secondary market.

FCEWs, despite their name, share many features with an existing market-traded instrument, foreign currency options. Although currency options created by corporations subject purchasers to the risk of default by the issuer, they have advantages over the market-traded options. One is maturity—typically 5 years for FCEWs, compared with 12 months or less for most currency option and futures contracts. (Even over-the-counter currency options offered by broker-dealers rarely have maturities exceeding 2 years.) FCEWs can be viewed as a financial innovation that supplies long-dated options on foreign currencies that might be demanded for hedging or speculative purposes. Corporations complete markets by designing primary securities to satisfy this demand but in the process may create incremental sources of risk (i.e., currency risk) for the firm's shareholders. This suggests that financial innovation at the corporate level is inextricably linked with hedging and risk management. Corporations specialize in risk creation and management at a price that, at the margin, increases shareholder wealth.

Each FCEW entitles the holder to receive from the issuing company the cash value in U.S. dollars of the right to purchase a fixed amount of U.S. dollars (usually $50) at a fixed currency exchange rate. For example, the Student Loan Marketing Association's yen-denominated issue of June 22, 1987 had a strike price of 152.20 yen per U.S. dollar, giving holders the right to purchase $50 at a price of 7,610 yen at any time up to and including the expiration date of July 15, 1992. Hence, FCEWs can be viewed as U.S. (rather than European) long-term options. Generally, however, cash settlement of FCEWs before the expiration date is subject to a minimum exercise of 2,000 warrants. Any FCEWs not exercised by the expiration date are automatically exercised by the issuing company if the cash surrender value of the warrant exceeds zero. Figure 5-3 lists all FCEW public offerings by U.S. corporations during 1987 and 1988. Eleven yen-denominated and five deutsche mark–denominated offerings are issued in this period, with an aggregate market value of $163 million.[3] Each FCEW issue trades on the American Stock Exchange (known as AMEX).

The first yen-denominated FCEW was offered on June 11, 1987, by General Electric Credit Corporation (GECC), which raised $9 million by selling five-year FCEWs. On the issue date, the exchange rate was 142.85 yen per U.S. dollar; the warrant exercise price exceeded this rate by 6.85 yen.

The value of FCEWs on the expiration date is relatively straightforward. As noted, the respective currencies are not exchanged when a FCEW is exercised. Rather, the issuer's obligation is limited to making a U.S. dollar cash settlement, known as the cash settlement value (CSV). The CSV can never be less than zero. Furthermore, if the spot exchange rate (expressed in foreign currency units per U.S. dollar) at the exercise date is at or below the exercise price, the CSV of the warrant is also equal to zero. Hence, FCEWs increase in value as the value of the U.S. dollar increases in relation to the underlying foreign currency. The formula for determining the CSV on exercise is

$$CSV = A - [(A \times E)/S] \qquad (5.5)$$

where:

A = amount of U.S. dollars per warrant

E = exercise price expressed in foreign currency units per U.S. dollar

S = spot exchange rate on the exercise date expressed in foreign currency units per U.S. dollar

At the maturity date, the value of the FCEW is equal to $\max[0, A - ((A \times E)/S)]$.

---

[3] The Student Loan Marketing Association FCEWs that expire on February 11, 1993 have two special features that differentiate them from the issues. First, the exercise price decreases at discrete times during the life of the warrant. The schedule of exercise prices is as follows: 131.75 yen from February 4, 1988 through February 11, 1990; 129.50 yen from February 12, 1990 through February 11, 1991; 127 yen from February 12, 1991 through February 11, 1992; 124.25 yen from February 12, 1992 through the expiration date. The second distinctive feature is a guaranteed minimum cash value on the expiration date. On that date, the value of the warrant is max($9.25, CSV).

FIGURE 5-3

Issues of Foreign Currency Exchange Warrants by U.S. Corporations (1987–1988)

Issuer	Currency	Offering Price per Warrant	Exchange Listing Date	Strike Price	Expiration Date	Issue Size (Millions)
General Electric Credit Corporation	Yen	$4.500	June 11, 1987	¥149.70	June 15, 1992	2
Ford Motor Credit Company	Yen	$4.375	June 19, 1987	¥152.20	July 1, 1992	3
Student Loan Marketing Association	Yen	$4.375	June 22, 1987	¥152.20	July 15, 1992	2
Citicorp	Yen	$4.125	June 24, 1987	¥152.50	July 1, 1992	2
General Electric Credit Corporation	Deutsche marks	$4.750	June 25, 1987	DM1.9120	July 1, 1992	2
Emerson Electric Company	Deutsche marks	$4.625	June 26, 1987	DM1.9180	July 1, 1992	2
Student Loan Marketing Association	Deutsche marks	$4.625	June 26, 1987	DM1.9200	July 15, 1992	2
Xerox Credit Corporation	Yen	$3.875	June 30, 1987	¥154.15	July 1, 1992	2
AT&T Credit Corporation	Yen	$3.500	July 9, 1987	¥158.25	July 1, 1992	3
Citicorp	Deutsche marks	$4.125	July 10, 1987	DM1.9320	July 15, 1992	2.5
Ford Motor Credit Company	Yen	$3.250	Jan. 21, 1988	¥134.00	Feb. 1, 1993	2.5
Student Loan Marketing Association	Yen	$9.250	Feb. 4, 1988	¥131.75	Feb. 11, 1993	4
Student Loan Marketing Association	Yen	$3.375	March 3, 1988	¥135.92	March 1, 1993	2
Citicorp	Yen	$3.375	April 13, 1988	¥132.90	April 15, 1993	2
J.P. Morgan & Company	Deutsche marks	$2.500	June 24, 1988	DM1.9040	July 1, 1991	2.5
Ford Motor Credit Company	Yen	$2.375	July 15, 1988	¥139.78	July 15, 1991	2

FIGURE 5-4

Numerical Example of the Impact of Different Exchange Rates on the Cash Surrender Value of Foreign Currency Exchange Warrants

Exchange Rate (Yen per U.S. Dollar)	Cash Surrender Value
	0
140	0
150	$ 3.125
160	$ 5.882
170	$ 8.333
180	$10.526
190	$12.50
200	

Note: The cash surrender value for a foreign currency exchange warrant equals $A - [(A \times E)/S]$, where A is U.S. dollars per warrant, E is the exercise price expressed in foreign currency units per dollar, and S is the spot exchange rate on the exercise date expressed in foreign currency units per dollar. In this table, $A = \$50$ and $E = ¥150$ per \$1.

Figure 5-4 contains an example showing the impact of different exchange rates on the CSV.

Before the maturity date, the market value of the FCEW exceeds the CSV because of the time value of the settlement. As with foreign currency options, the value of the FCEW before maturity depends on factors such as the volatility of the underlying foreign currency and interest rate differentials. In addition, because FCEWs are unsecured obligations of the issuing company, their value before expiration includes an adjustment for default risk. Johnson and Stulz[4] examine the pricing of options subject to default risk in a Black-Scholes framework.

Rogalski and Seward[5] demonstrate that an innovative security design such as the FCEW can be beneficial to high-credit, quality corporations because they are overpriced by investors. However, a similar security would be useful to a corporation whose revenue stream is dependent on the movement of exchange rates. In particular, since the FCEWs described in Figure 5-4 appreciate in value as the U.S. dollar strengthens against the underlying foreign currency, these instruments would be an effective hedge for a firm whose dollar cash flows increase as the dollar strengthens or decrease as the dollar weakens. Furthermore, since the innovation in this case was overpriced, as illustrated by Rogalski and Seward, the FCEW would represent a cheap source of insurance against adverse exchange rate movements. Finally, since the majority of firms do not have access to long-dated currency options, the FCEW structure allows such firms to design a security that provides long-term hedging protection.

---

[4] Johnson, H. and R. Stulz, "The Pricing of Options With Default Risk, *Journal of Finance*, Vol. 42 (June 1987), pp. 267–280.

[5] R. Rogalski and J. Seward, "Corporate Issues of Foreign Currency Exchange Warrants," *Journal of Financial Economics*, Vol. 30 (December 1991), pp. 347–366.

5.04 DERIVATIVE SECURITIES AS HEDGING TOOLS

[1] Forward and Futures Contracts

A forward contract is a contractual obligation to buy or sell a specific amount of a given commodity or asset on a specified future date, at a price set at the time the contract is entered into. It is important to note that no money is exchanged between the contracting parties when the forward contract is executed. Rather, the forward contract simply establishes the exact terms of a trade that will occur on a known date in the future. Any gain or loss from a forward contract position depends on the difference between the price established in the forward contract and the price of the underlying commodity or asset on the maturity date of the forward contract. A forward contract can serve as a risk management tool by allowing the corporate manager to predetermine, or lock in, the price of the underlying good prior to the actual spot market transaction. The following example provides a brief overview of the primary features of a forward contract. A German exporter agrees to manufacture and sell some customized machine tools to a U.S. company. The agreement specifies that the transaction will occur six months from today at a prespecified price of U.S. $2 million. Since the German exporter's net gain from the transaction depends on the spot exchange rate six months in the future, the exporter may utilize foreign currency forward contracts to eliminate the exchange rate risk. In this case, the exporter would sell $2 million in exchange for a known amount of deutsche marks. This forward transaction eliminates the exporter's currency risk from this sale.

The example illustrates the manner in which the forward contract can mitigate or even eliminate currency risk. By establishing a position in the forward currency market that offsets the firm's exposure in the spot market, any gains or losses on the forward position should be equal to any losses or gains from the sale of the machine tools. Hence, in this case, the forward contract position eliminates the currency price risk by generating a cash flow stream that offsets interim fluctuations in the dollar–deutsche mark exchange rate.

A futures contract is similar to a forward contract in that it represents a contractual obligation to buy or sell a specific amount of a given commodity or asset on a specified future date at a predetermined price. However, futures contracts differ from forward contracts in several important respects. First, futures contracts are standardized contracts that trade on an organized exchange. Thus, futures contracts' sizes and maturity dates are standardized, while these contract features must be negotiated and agreed on in the forward market. Generally, the futures markets provide greater liquidity and lower transactions costs but a more limited range of available contract features. Second, the futures market uses a clearinghouse, which effectively guarantees both sides of any futures contract. The interface between the clearinghouse and each of the contracting parties reduces the risk of nonperformance. Third, any gains or losses on a futures contract position are settled daily, or marked to market. This allows a futures contract to be viewed as a sequence of forward contracts that settle daily. The daily settlement feature of futures contracts reduces their default risk relative to equivalent forward contract agreements.

The role of futures contracts as a corporate hedging tool is best understood by focusing on their unique contractual features and cash flow patterns. First, futures contracts require no initial cash flow exchanges between the contracting parties. Thus, unlike an on-balance sheet hedging transaction through an immediate spot market transaction, futures contracts allow corporate managers to alter their financial risk exposure without the corresponding need to raise large sums of capital. This feature is especially beneficial if the firm's risk exposure is managed by establishing a short position in an asset or liability. Typically, short-positioning a futures contract is much easier and less costly than an equivalent short position established in the spot market. Daily cash flow inflows or outflows, however, must be anticipated as the open futures contract position increases or decreases in value.

Second, futures contracts offer the corporate manager more flexibility to subsequently alter or eliminate the firm's risk exposure, owing to the liquidity of the futures market and the ability to close or eliminate a futures contract position by executing an offsetting trade. The cash settlement feature of futures contracts minimizes the possibility that actual physical delivery of the underlying asset or commodity must be made. Finally, the futures markets offer contracts on a wide range of commodities, currencies, and financial assets. Thus, the variety of price risks that can be hedged and managed through the futures markets is quite broad.

A firm's risk exposure can be directly hedged if a futures contract exactly matches the exposure. For example, a silver mining company can hedge against the possibility of a future decline in the price of silver by selling silver futures contracts today. If the spot price of silver does decrease in the future, the producer's lower revenue in the spot market will be offset by a corresponding gain in the futures contract position. The ability to engage in such matched hedging strategies depends on the correspondence between a firm's risk exposure and the availability of a futures contract.

Sometimes the risks that a firm seeks to manage extend beyond the available futures contracts. In this case, an exact hedge contract will not exist. To gain access to the futures markets for hedging purposes in this event, a firm must enter into a cross-hedge arrangement, which relies on a similar futures contract to hedge the firm's risk exposure. A similar futures contract is one whose price change is highly correlated with the firm's risk exposure. Correlation can be determined by examining the historical relationship between the risk exposure the firm seeks to hedge and the various futures contracts. The statistical technique used for this purpose is regression analysis. The regression coefficient from the estimation indicates the number of futures contracts to buy or sell.

For example, a farmer who grows rye wishes to hedge against future price variability in the commodity. Although no futures contract currently exists for rye, the farmer feels that the spot prices of rye and barley are closely related. By regressing a time series of daily price changes in rye on daily price changes in barley, the regression equation generates an estimated slope coefficient of 0.9, which means that each one percent change in the spot price of rye is accompanied by a 0.9 percent change in the price of barley. If the farmer wishes to hedge his anticipated crop of 100 tons of rye against future price changes, he would sell futures contracts equivalent to 90 tons of barley. Since each barley contract is for 20 tons, the farmer can sell either 4 or 5 contracts.

Although futures contracts can serve as a valuable risk management technique, certain contractual characteristics exist that may affect how well the hedge works and preclude the maintenance of a perfect hedge. However, the ability to neutralize a large percentage of the firm's risk exposure will generally outweigh the costs of imperfect hedging. The two most common sources of imperfect risk management with futures contracts are basis risk and the complex idiosyncracies of certain contractual features.

Basis risk occurs when there is a lack of perfect correlation between the risk that the corporate manager wishes to hedge and the hedge instrument. Therefore, basis risk can reduce the effectiveness of a hedge position. This problem generally arises when a corporate manager establishes a cross-hedge.

The complexity of certain future contracts can be illustrated by considering the case of the U.S. Treasury bond futures contract. On the delivery date, this contract can be satisfied by the delivery of any Treasury bond with a maturity (and call protection) of at least 15 years. Thus, the seller of this particular contract holds a valuable delivery option in that it can choose which security to deliver. As a result, hedge programs that rely on Treasury bonds must be designed to identify and track the bond that is cheapest to deliver. It should also be recognized that the cheapest-to-deliver bond may change during the life of a hedge program. For example, a firm has decided to sell, 6 months from now, $100 million worth of bonds with a 15-year maturity. To protect itself against rising interest rates during the interim 6 months, the firm decides to sell Treasury bond futures. Six months from today, the firm can close its future position in 1 of 2 ways: either buy back the short futures contracts or make delivery of the required number of Treasury bonds. The Treasury bond that represents the cheapest deliverable bond depends on the difference between the price of the bond and the futures price multiplied by a conversion factor.

[2] Options

A call option represents the right (rather than an obligation) to buy a specific quantity of an asset at a specific price. An option that is exercisable only on the contract's maturity date is a European option. If the holder may exercise the option prior to the maturity date, the option is an American option. Currently, options on a broad range of financial assets and commodities trade on organized exchanges. In addition, many financial service firms can synthetically create customized options. Consequently, corporate managers have available a wide variety of option techniques with which to manage financial risk.

One of the distinctive characteristics of an option is that the holder has the right, but not an obligation, to exercise. From a cash flow standpoint, this feature implies that options limit downside risk. Hence, the maximum amount that option buyers can lose on their positions is the initial premium paid to establish the position. This property has been exploited by equity investors through a program known as portfolio insurance. An insured portfolio position can be established by purchasing a stock and buying a put option on that stock. The minimum value of this position under any circumstance is equal to the exercise price of the put contract. Thus, different levels of portfolio insurance protection can be attained by varying the exercise price on the put option contract. However, the cost of portfolio insurance varies accordingly; the option premium increases as the exercise price increases.

The value of an option can be determined through the use of the Black-Scholes valuation model (or one of its many variants):

Call value $= S \times N\{d_1\} - X \times e^{-rt} \times N\{d_2\}$

where:
$$d_1 = \frac{\ln (S/X) + (r + 0.5\sigma^2)t}{\sigma\sqrt{t}}$$

$d_2 = d_1 - \sigma\sqrt{t}$

S = price of underlying asset

$e \approx 2.718$

X = exercise price
t = time until the option expires
r = risk-free rate of interest
σ = standard deviation of the price of the underlying asset
$N(\cdot)$ = cumulative normal distribution function

The term $N\{d_1\}$ also has a useful interpretation in this framework. In particular, it represents the change in the value of the option price relative to a change in the price of the underlying asset. Hence, for risk management purposes, it represents the hedge ratio. As a result, it describes how large the firm's option position must be in order to hedge against adverse changes in the price of the underlying asset. It is important to note that the hedge ratio changes as the option moves closer to the exercise date. Thus, a corporate manager who wishes to utilize options for hedging purposes must recognize that the options position needs to be readjusted periodically. Fortunately, this process is simplified by recalculating the Black-Scholes price and observing the new value of $N\{d_1\}$.

One interesting decision confronting corporate managers today is how to incorporate options into a firm's overall financial policy. For example, many financing arrangements can now be implemented by embedding various options in the design of the firm's securities or borrowing relationships. Suppose a firm wishes to borrow $50 million and investors demand a floating interest rate. This exposes the firm to future changes in interest rates, which can be managed through options in several ways. First, the firm can utilize interest rate options to fine-tune its exposure. Second, the firm may approach a lender that is willing to lend funds and provide interest rate caps (maximums) and collars (minimums). These lending relationships are simply traditional loans combined with the purchase of interest rate options from the lending institution. The lowest cost arrangement depends on the premium that the financial markets and lending institutions charge for these options, but options are so prevalent today that corporate managers must identify and evaluate alternative approaches to using them as a financial price risk management technique.

[3] Swaps

In a swap transaction, there is an exchange of cash flows between two firms. The two primary swap arrangements are interest rate swaps and currency swaps. The typical interest rate swap occurs when one entity exchanges its fixed-rate financing obligations with another entity's floating rate financing obligations. For example, the ABC Corporation seeks 10-year floating-rate financing, while the DEF Corporation seeks 10-year fixed-rate financing. The applicable borrowing rates are as follows:

	Fixed Rate	Floating Rate
ABC	10.0%	LIBOR + 1%
DEF	12.5%	LIBOR + 2%

ABC borrows at the fixed rate of 10 percent, while DEF borrows at the floating rate of the London interbank offered rate (LIBOR) plus 2 percent. The two parties agree to swap payments, as shown in Figure 5-5. In this case, the net cost of borrowing for ABC is now LIBOR plus 0.5 percent, while DEF achieves a net cost of 11.5 percent.

As the example illustrates, the interest rate swap arrangement can reduce the net

FIGURE 5-5

Effect of Payment Swap

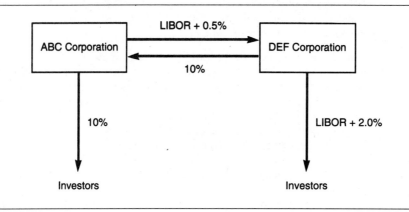

cost of borrowing for both parties in separate financing transactions. ABC reduces its floating-rate financing costs by 50 basis points (from LIBOR plus one percent to LIBOR plus 0.5 percent), while DEF reduces its fixed-rate financing costs by 100 basis points (from 12.5 percent to 11.5 percent). Thus, interest rate swaps can potentially reduce the costs of financial risk exposure for both parties in a transaction.

Why do such mutual advantages arise in swap transactions? As the example illustrates, interest rate differentials for the different creditworthiness of ABC and DEF vary between the fixed-rate and floating-rate market. In particular, the credit spread is 250 basis points in the fixed-rate market but only 100 basis points in the floating-rate market. Interest rate swaps are designed to exploit these differential credit spreads.

In addition to the exchange of interest rate payments, firms may also swap payment streams that are denominated in different currencies. These transactions are known as currency swaps. Typically, a currency swap allows a corporation to manage both foreign exchange risk and interest rate risk. For example, a firm that seeks to borrow U.S. dollars at a fixed rate of interest can do so either directly by issuing in the United States or indirectly by issuing overseas and then swapping the liability into dollars. If a firm borrows in the Japanese market at a floating interest rate, by swapping out of yen into dollars and out of floating interest rates into fixed rates, it has transformed one liability stream into a substantially different obligation. While the efficient markets theory suggests that the net effective costs of borrowing are approximately the same under these two approaches, various market imperfections can be exploited to produce dramatic borrowing cost savings. Thus, the corporate manager could be rewarded for giving attention to a wide variety of financial markets and instruments.

[4] Case Study of Hedging With Derivative Securities

Merck & Company is a large, multinational pharmaceutical company that does business in more than 100 countries. As a result of its business and industry profile, the company faces a significant foreign currency exposure. Merck has approximately 40 percent of its total assets located overseas and generates about 50 percent of its sales outside of the United States. Its sales are generally denominated in local currency, while its costs of finishing, marketing, distribution, research and development, and taxes are a mix of local currency and U.S. dollars.

The first step in the development of Merck's financial hedging program was to identify and measure the extent of the firm's exposure. Foreign currency exchange fluctuations can affect a U.S. company's financial and economic performance in the following ways:

- By changing the dollar value of net assets held overseas in foreign currencies (translation exposure) or by changing the expected results of transactions in nonlocal currencies (transaction exposure)

- By changing the dollar value of future revenues expected to be earned overseas in foreign currencies (future revenue exposure)

- By changing a company's competitive position (competitive exposure)

In the case of Merck, exposure to foreign exchange fluctuations is primarily in the areas of revenue exposure and translation exposure. The company has identified revenue exposure as its most significant source of currency risk. The revenues earned in Merck's overseas product markets are generally converted into dollars through interaffiliate merchandise payments, dividends, and royalty payments. At present, Merck has exposures in approximately 40 different foreign currencies. The company believes that the volatility in earnings and cash flows created by the foreign currency exposure can impair its ability to implement its strategic growth plan.

To identify the firm's exposure to exchange rate movements, Merck constructed a sales index that measures the relative strength of the dollar against a basket of currencies weighted by the size of sales in each country. When the index is above 100 percent, foreign currencies have strengthened against the dollar, which increases the company's dollar revenues and net income. When the index is below 100 percent, the dollar has strengthened against the foreign currencies, which decreases the company's dollar revenues and net income. While this type of index indicates Merck's aggregate exposure to all foreign currencies, it may conceal differential relationships between the dollar and each of the foreign currency exposures. As a result, Merck also examined the impact of each individual foreign currency movement on dollar sales.

Having established that the company's overseas revenue represents a potentially significant exposure to foreign currency fluctuations, Merck then determined the extent to which its sales and costs were matched in foreign currencies. That is, the company's revenue exposure, described previously, need not be problematic if the distribution of the firm's assets and cost structure neutralize, or offset, the firm's revenue exposure. The company determined that concentration of its research, manufacturing, and headquarters operations in the United States meant that it faced a permanent mismatch between costs and revenues. Thus, the firm decided that it could not simply reallocate its worldwide resources in order to currency match its revenues and costs. As a result, the company decided to deal with its exchange exposure through the use of derivative instruments.

In order to implement a financial hedging program to manage its foreign exchange exposure, Merck considered the following five-step process:

1. Project exchange rate volatility.

2. Assess the impact of exchange rate movements on the firm's strategic plan.

3. Determine whether to hedge the exposure.

4. Determine which financial instrument provides the most suitable hedge.

5. Construct the hedge program.

To examine various scenarios for exchange rates during the forecast period, Merck constructed a probability distribution to describe future exchange movements. During this process, Merck relied on four main considerations:

1. Overall assessment of the major factors that are likely to influence exchange rates (e.g., U.S. trade deficit, capital flows, and U.S. budget deficit)

2. Government policies designed to manage exchange rates

3. Development of possible ranges for dollar strength or weakness

4. Survey of outside forecasters

Once Merck calculated the probabilities of various exchange rate movements, the firm entered the second step of its financial hedging program: Merck examined the impact of various future exchange rate movements on its projected earnings and cash flow streams. The firm examined the effect of exchange rate movements on its performance on a year-by-year and a cumulative basis, using the rationale that the latter is a more appropriate measure of currency exposure over a multiyear period. By considering the cumulative impact of adverse exchange rate movements, Merck was better able to assess the potential benefits of hedging multiple-period income and cash flow streams.

Following this analysis, Merck assessed whether hedging the firm's currency exposure was worthwhile. Because Merck believes that the primary impact of foreign exchange rate movements is on the volatility of annual earnings, rather than a permanent source of economic loss, its rationale for hedging was based on its risk tolerance for the firm's earnings and cash flow volatility. The determination of whether to hedge this exposure depended on two sets of considerations, external and internal. The external concerns focused on Merck's assessment of the impact of share price movement on stock prices, investor clientele effects, and dividend policy. While Merck believed that it should consider these issues, the firm's management believed that shareholder value would be maximized by focusing on cash flow maximization. Hence, the benefit of its financial hedging program depended on the manner in which currency risk management assisted the attainment of cash flow maximization. In the case of Merck, the impact of exchange rate volatility on cash flow and earnings uncertainty reduces the amount of resources allocated to research and development activities. Hence, the primary benefit of financial hedging at Merck is that the reduction in cash flow and earnings uncertainty allows the firm to commit the capital necessary to enhance future growth.

Next, Merck had to select the hedge vehicle from the available alternative financial instruments. Merck considered the following alternatives: forward foreign exchange contracts, foreign currency debt, currency swaps, and currency options. Merck determined that its risk preferences could be managed most effectively through the use of currency options. By paying an up-front premium, Merck protects its earnings and cash flow stream against a strengthening dollar while retaining any beneficial effects if the dollar weakens.

The final step in Merck's program was the actual construction and implementation of the financial hedge program. After careful consideration of a number of alternative strategies and outcomes, Merck decided on the following:

- Hedge for a multiyear period by using long-term options to hedge the firm's cash flow and earnings stream against adverse foreign currency exchange rate movements.

- Forgo the use of far-out-of-the-money options as a means of minimizing the initial cost of establishing the hedge.

- Implement the hedge on only a portion of the firm's currency exposure, thereby retaining some degree of sensitivity to exchange rate movements.

The implementation strategy is now monitored continuously through Merck's proprietary hedging simulation model. The computer model has been flexibly designed to allow the company to assess the impact of various exchange rate scenarios, hedging policies, financial instrument choices, and combinations on cash flow. In this way, Merck is able to monitor and adjust its hedging policy continuously to maintain a desired currency risk exposure at a minimum cost.

5.05 SECURITIZATION

Securitization is the process of packaging together a pool of financial assets as a security. Cash flows from the underlying financial assets provide payments for investors and may be either directly passed through or restructured to create securities with tranches of different maturities. Credit enhancement is provided by several parties in order to protect the investor against default risk. The net result of the typical securitized structure is a financial instrument with an AA or AAA credit rating. In fact, a recent securitized issue by a U.S. company in chapter 11 was rated AAA! Clearly, then, the credit enhancement in these transactions can be sufficiently large to transform the financial obligations of a company operating under the protection of the bankruptcy law into the highest credit rating available.

Securitization can create market instruments out of a variety of creditor relationships. As a result, it represents a powerful alternative to the traditional creditor and/or lender relationship. In general, securitization enhances traditional credit relationships in three ways: First, credit securitization effectively isolates the financial assets from the originator's balance sheet, which facilitates the credit transparency of those financial assets. In addition, the pooling and sale of assets creates benefits through improved actuarial analysis and simplification of third-party review. Second, the credit risk associated with these assets is split through the use of tranches and thus can be allocated more efficiently among the economic entities best positioned to absorb it. Therefore, while short-term credit arrangements typically vest credit risk entirely with the originator, securitization spreads it among the originator, credit enhancer or enhancers, and investors. This structure then segments risks in various ways that can be absorbed by entities with distinct risk preferences and profiles. Finally, securitization isolates interest rate risk so that it can be tailored and placed among the most appropriate investor classes. Arguably, the net result of these distinct attributes of the securitization process is that it may produce lower total costs than traditional lending. It is the structuring of the security itself that determines exactly how these unique attributes operate. In particular, the key characteristics of a securitized structure include the characteristics of the underlying collateral (e.g., cash flow periodicity, credit risk, prepayment risk), structural features of the security (e.g., pass-through and versus pay-through and number of distinct tranches), and type and amount of credit enhancement provided.

From a corporation's perspective, there are several incentives for securitizing assets: (1) securitization converts receivables to cash; (2) securitization removes assets from a firm's balance sheet, thereby mitigating corporate exposure to interest rate risk and diversifying credit risk; (3) securitization may provide a cost-effective form of financing; and (4) securitization typically improves a firm's balance sheet and its financial return performance measures.

As a final consideration, the variety of financial assets that can be securitized has expanded dramatically. Credit card receivables, automobile loans, lease receivables, consumer loans, trade receivables, and commercial loans have all been successfully securitized, and the process for securitizing small business loans is under active investigation. The main point is that corporate managers should not limit their thinking about securitization to a preconceived sense of what financial assets are potentially securitizable, because securitization can be done on a public or private placement basis and the denomination of many issues is relatively small, with several having less than $10 million of financial assets.

[1] Case Study in Securitization

Perhaps the largest dollar amount of corporate assets securitized to date is in automobile loan receivables. In general, automobile loans have been securitized through the three basic security structures: pass-through, pay-through, and fixed payment. The primary distinction among these three structures is the way in which the cash flows from the underlying collateral are transformed and partitioned to appeal to financial investors. In order to highlight the range and complexity of the issues involved in the design and distribution of these asset-backed securities, this section will examine a fixed-payment structure utilized by General Motors Acceptance Corporation (GMAC) to securitize $4 billion of auto loans in October 1986.

Figure 5-6 illustrates the structure and Figure 5-7 provides a detailed description and summary of this transaction. A fixed-payment structure pays principal to the asset-backed noteholders according to a schedule that assumes no prepayment. Thus, in contrast to the pay-through or pass-through security structures, investors do not bear the risk of early principal repayment on automobile loans. The underlying loans in this transaction consisted of two pools of low-interest-rate loans: $2.335 billion in 2.9 percent loans with 36-month maturities and $1.914 billion in 4.8 percent loans with 48-month maturities.

As shown in Figure 5-6, GMAC sold these loans to the Asset-Backed Securities Corporation (ABSC), a special-purpose vehicle that was a wholly owned subsidiary of First Boston Securities. The use of a limited-purpose finance corporation subsidiary in these transactions was designed to separate the cash flows and creditworthiness of the securitized assets from the originator's other business operations. This type of structure, in conjunction with other forms of credit enhancement, allows the originator to sell the securitized assets at a higher value than they might otherwise merit. The fact that the limited-purpose finance subsidiary was owned by a security underwriter (First Boston) rather than the loan originator (GMAC) undoubtedly facilitates this delineation.

Although proponents of the structured securitized credit system argue that it is economically more efficient than traditional methods of financing, there are a number of important tax, regulatory, and accounting features that motivate these transactions. First, the limited-purpose finance corporation is subject to federal income taxation.

FIGURE 5-6
ABSC: Structure—Series 1

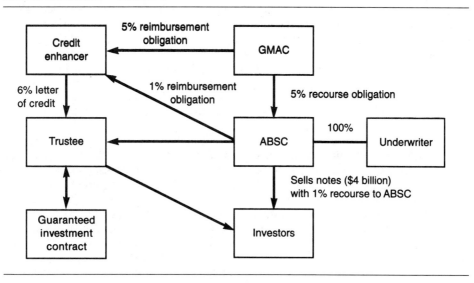

FIGURE 5-7
ABSC: Asset-Backed Obligations—Series 1

Issue	Asset-backed obligations, series 1
	6.25% Class 1-A notes
	6.90% Class 2-B notes
	6.95% Class 1-C notes
Issuer	ABSC
Offering date	October 15, 1986
Rating (S&P, Moody's)	AAA/Aaa
Principal amount	$2,095,000,000 Class 1-A
	585,000,000 Class 1-B
	1,320,000,000 Class 1-C
Collateral	New GM vehicles
Average life (years)	1.05 for Class 1-A
	2.20 for Class 1-B
	3.07 for Class 1-C
Yield to average life (CBE)	6.30% for Class 1-A
	6.96% for Class 1-B
	7.27% for Class 1-C
Payment frequency	Quarterly
Spread to treasuries at offering	69 basis points for Class 1-A
	75 basis points for Class 1-B
	80 basis points for Class 1-C
Recourse (amount/provider)	5% GMAC limited guarantee, 1% ABSC
Credit enhancement	6% letter of credit/Credit Suisse
Managing underwriter	First Boston Corporation

Consequently, the cash flows from the automobile loans received by ABSC are taxable income. In order to minimize ABSC's taxable income, the claims sold by the corporation were treated as debt rather than equity. The Internal Revenue Service (IRS) specifies a number of security characteristics that it examines to determine if a particular claim qualifies as debt for tax purposes. In the case of ABSC, the notes issued to investors to fund the purchase of the automobile loans were deemed to be debt because of a significant equity infusion by First Boston (approximately $40 million) and because the notes issued by ABSC differed from the automobile loan receivables in terms of payment terms and maturity. Clearly, originators and underwriters must carefully consider IRS guidelines in designing these structures in order to obtain favorable tax treatment.

A second concern in this transaction was that the vehicle loans and debt issue of ABSC had to be consolidated by First Boston into its balance sheet for financial reporting purposes. Since First Boston preferred to have this transaction left off its balance sheet, once ABSC sold debt securities to purchase the automobile loans, ABSC would then resell the automobile loan receivables to an owner trust. Because the owner trust would also assume the financial obligation to repay the ABSC notes, the debt obligations and automobile loan receivables would not be reported on First Boston's consolidated balance sheets. Thus, the structure of these transactions can also exert a material impact on a firm's financial statements.

To gain further insights into the structure and economic benefits of securitization, consider these three additional characteristics of the ABSC transaction: payment characteristics, protection against bankruptcy risk, and credit enhancement. The sale of the automobile loans to a special-purpose vehicle allows the maturities of ABSC's notes to be targeted to specific investor clienteles. In the ABSC transaction, the notes were structured into three separate classes, or tranches: a $2.095 billion two-year tranche, a $0.585 billion two-and-one-half-year tranche, and a $1.32 billion four-year tranche. Interest payments to the noteholders in each tranche were fixed and paid quarterly: a 6.25 percent annual rate on the first tranche, a 6.90 percent annual rate on the second tranche, and a 6.95 percent annual rate on the third tranche.

Typically, there is some degree of uncertainty about the principal prepayment of asset-backed securities. Principal payments are normally remitted to noteholders upon receipt. The ABSC transaction was able to offer a fixed-payment maturity structure because of two important characteristics. First, because the automobile receivables were low-interest-rate loans and the underlying loans made monthly payments, early prepayments by the automobile owners could be reinvested at market rates of interest to increase the amount of cash available to repay ABSC noteholders. Second, a guaranteed investment contract was purchased from Morgan Guaranty. As a result, investors that might be drawn to asset-backed securities but would disdain prepayment uncertainty could be attracted by this security structure.

Managing the risk of early prepayment by the automobile loans is facilitated also by the use of the tranche structure. The principal of the highest-tranche (Class I) noteholders must be completely repaid before any principal is returned to the lower-tranche noteholders. As a result, noteholders can invest in whichever tranche most closely meets their maturity preferences without having to be concerned with the risk of early prepayment.

The credit risk inherent in the ABSC security structure is dependent on the underlying cash flows provided by the pool of automobile loans. Generally, default rates on automobile loans are relatively stable. As a result, the pooling of a large number of automobile loans into the ABSC structure allows the expected default rate on the entire pool to be predicted with a fair amount of precision. Still greater precision can be attained by examining eight factors that Pavel identifies as important determinants of automobile loans. These factors, in particular, seem to explain a large proportion of the variability in automobile loan defaults:

1. Term to maturity

2. Seasoning of the loan

3. Loan-to-value ratio

4. Used versus new car

5. Type of automobile

6. Recourse versus nonrecourse loan

7. Geographic concentration

8. Pool selection criteria

The impact of each factor on the creditworthiness of the loan pool is straightforward. For example, loans on used cars, with a high loan-to-value ratio, for longer periods, and without dealer recourse would be expected to all have a higher loss experience.

This situation would seem to present a problem for the typical investor attempting to understand the default risk of a particular security. Fortunately, credit enhancement, either in the form of overcollateralization through an equity base or a third-party guarantee by a counterparty that is deemed creditworthy, eliminates this problem for most investors. As Figure 5-7 indicates, credit enhancement was provided in this case in the form of a 5 percent limited guarantee by GMAC and a 6 percent letter of credit from Credit Suisse. In the latter case, GMAC would reimburse Credit Suisse up to the 5 percent limit. This structure, in conjunction with First Boston's equity infusion, resulted in a security that received an AAA credit rating.

5.06 CONCLUSION

Financial price risk management is becoming an increasingly important and time-consuming component of the corporate finance function. Lack of attentiveness to such risks can, at the extreme, undermine the best operating and competitive strategy. The pace of globalization among product and capital markets, together with the recent volatility among currencies, interest rates, and commodity prices, requires that management understand and control these price risks in order to remain competitive. This chapter has provided a framework for identifying, measuring, and managing these financial price risks. It is vital that corporate managers recognize the breadth of on-balance sheet and off-balance sheet techniques that are increasingly available for achieving desired levels of financial price risk management. This topic will continue to provide a challenge for corporate managers in the years ahead.

Suggested Reading

Acheson, M., and D. Halstead. "Trends in Securitization—Private and Public." *Journal of Applied Corporate Finance*, Vol. 1 (Fall 1988), pp. 52–60.

Brown, K., and D. Smith. "Forward Swaps, Swap Options, and the Management of Callable Debt. *Journal of Applied Corporate Finance*, Vol. 2 (Winter 1990), pp. 59–71.

Bryan, L. "Structured Securitized Credit: A Superior Technology for Lending." *Journal of Applied Corporate Finance*, Vol. 1 (Fall 1988), pp. 6–19.

Einzig, R., and B. Lange. "Swaps at Transamerica: Analysis and Applications." *Journal of Applied Corporate Finance*, Vol. 2 (Winter 1990), pp. 48–58.

Goldberg, C., and K. Rogers. "An Introduction to Asset Backed Securities." *Journal of Applied Corporate Finance*, Vol. 1 (Fall 1988), pp. 20–31.

Goldberg, H., R. Burke, S. Gordon, K. Pinkes, and M. Watson, Jr. "Asset Securitization and Corporate Financial Health." *Journal of Applied Corporate Finance*, Vol. 1 (Fall 1988), pp. 45–51.

Goodman, L. "The Use of Interest Rate Swaps in Managing Corporate Liabilities." *Journal of Applied Corporate Finance*, Vol. 2 (Winter 1990), pp. 35–47.

Lewent, J., and A.J. Kearney. "Identifying, Measuring, and Hedging Currency Risk at Merck." *Journal of Applied Corporate Finance*, Vol. 2 (Winter 1990), pp. 19–28.

Maloney, P. "Managing Currency Exposure: The Case of Western Mining." *Journal of Applied Corporate Finance*, Vol. 2 (Winter 1990), pp. 29–34.

Pavel, Christine. *Securitization*. Chicago: Probus Publishing, 1989.

Rawls, S., and C. Smithson. "Strategic Risk Management." *Journal of Applied Corporate Finance*, Vol. 2 (Winter 1990), pp. 6–18.

Rogalski, R., and J. Seward. "Corporate Issues of Foreign Currency Exchange Warrants." *Journal of Financial Economics*, Vol. 30 (December 1991), pp. 347–366.

Rosenberg, R., and J. Kravitt. "Legal Issues in Securitization." *Journal of Applied Corporate Finance*, Vol. 1 (Fall 1988), pp. 61–68.

Rosenthal, J., and J. Ocampo. "Analyzing the Economic Benefits of Securitized Credit." *Journal of Applied Corporate Finance*, Vol. 1 (Fall 1988), pp. 32–44.

Shapiro, Alan. *Modern Corporate Finance*. New York: MacMillan Publishing Co., 1989.

Smith, Clifford, Jr., Charles Smithson, and D. Sykes Wilford. *Managing Financial Risk*. New York: Harper & Row, 1990.

Zweig, Phillip *The Asset Securitization Handbook*. Homewood, Ill.: Dow Jones-Irwin, 1989.

Chapter 6

Real Estate Finance

STEPHEN E. ROULAC

6.01 INTRODUCTION

Real estate finance embraces such critical corporate finance areas as project finance, capital budgeting, modern portfolio theory and applications, venture capital, and mergers and acquisitions. Each piece of property is properly viewed as a business unto itself, with the concomitant concerns of the managerial, economic, behavioral, and legal disciplines pertinent to that business. Just as finance is fundamental to business, real estate finance is fundamental to real estate.

Title to property is held in many forms, both directly and indirectly, by a multitude of individuals and entities. Ownership can be an equity position or a debt investment with the real property interest being the security for performance on the debt obligation.

Real estate markets, as well as the structure of corporate economics and finance, have changed markedly over the last two decades. Tracking current market conditions and identifying the new concepts that may have an impact on the future performance of real estate markets challenges everyone involved in real estate.

One reflection of the dramatic changes in the real estate markets is provided by the sharp contrast in some 30 key attributes between what prevailed in the environment of the 1960s and 1970s and contemporary circumstances, as shown in Figure 6-1.

Dramatic changes in the structure of the markets combined with current conditions have complicated the market intelligence function for real estate participants. When markets were primarily local, the volume and pace of innovation were modest, the quantity and accessibility of information were very limited, and the research process was reasonably straightforward. However, the information-gathering and planning strategies that worked in the 1960s and 1970s are increasingly invalid in the 1990s. Research is fundamental to comprehending, coping with, and capitalizing on the implications of these dynamic changes and market discontinuities.

6.02 REAL ESTATE INVESTING VERSUS CORPORATE SECURITIES

[1] Valuation of Real Estate Compared With Stock

Because real estate investments are properly viewed in the context of the overall investment universe in which corporate securities are the dominant traditional investment form, it is necessary to consider how real estate investing differs from corporate securities. While a stockholder buys an indirect position removed from involvement in and influence over the business decisions of the company, the owner of real estate and/or the managing agent is in direct control of the asset and all of the business decisions associated with the asset. Securitization of real estate, which allows investors to acquire an indirect interest in real estate through the purchase of shares of an entity holding title to the property in a manner comparable to common stock, places that part of real estate investing on a more parallel basis to corporate securities investing.

Without the opportunity to participate on a securities basis, the real estate investor generally owns 100 percent of a real property asset, compared with the fractional ownership available through the corporate securities investment. This distinction is significant, because securities regulations require that substantial information be made available on an objective and consistent basis to all that are involved with the asset as well as to the overall market. With direct ownership, such information is not readily

FIGURE 6-1

Changing Real Estate Markets

Source: S.E. Roulac, "American Real Estate Society: Cost-Effective Research Resource for Changing Real Estate Markets," Real Estate Finance (Winter 1993)

Attributes	Yesterday	Today
Focus	Transaction	Strategy and policy
Economic environment	Solid growth	Uncertain
Change predictability	Stable	Discontinuous
Change pace	Slow, long lead time	Fast, dynamic
Communications	Slow	Instantaneous
Market structures	Stable	Fragmented, fluid
Business space market condition	Balanced	Extraordinary supply surplus
Business space market demand	Strong, predictable	Declining, uncertain
Tenant orientation	Passive, unsophisticated	Aggressive, strategic, sophisticated
Tenant mobility	Stable, limited	High
Capital access	Residual user	Primary, direct access
Finance source	National	Global
Investor source	Local	Global
Investment form	Direct	Securities
Investor sophistication	Low	High
Investment orientation	Entrepreneurial deal mentality	Fiduciary, institutional
Manager orientation	Opportunistic, value creation	Conservative, survival
Professional service providers	Local	Global
Property market data	Local	National
Analytic tools	Slide rule	Computers
Information sophistication	Low	High
Information availability	Modest	Overwhelming
Capital market data	Nonexistent	National
Data bases	Simple, minimal	Computerized access
Documentation	Short, simple	Lengthy, complex
Financial analysis	Simplistic	Sophisticated
Regulation	Straightforward, predictable	Highly complex, uncertain
Building scale	Small	Large
Building complexity	Simple	High
Academic programs	Modest, narrow	Extensive

available, and consequently evaluating the financial commitments, monitoring the investment, and measuring performance are necessarily compromised.

Little analysis is done of real estate investments compared with what is done for corporate securities investments. This situation contributes to both market inefficiency and pricing variability in real estate and thus makes it even more difficult to measure real estate investment performance.

The implications of a pricing process that applies in a narrow negotiated market, such as the real estate market, are profound. Compared with corporate securities, whose values are based on the latest transaction, the valuation of real property is based on an appraisal, which amounts to an estimate of the value of the asset.

Because the pricing mechanism for corporate securities continually incorporates all known information that influences the future performance prospects of that business, prices change continually and often by dramatic amounts over relatively short periods. Real estate is valued much less frequently, generally on an annual basis, with the result that values may appear to be more stable. In fact, this apparent stability is more attributable to the inherent "smoothing" that results from infrequent appraisals than to the manner in which market forces influence property values. Investors that do not appreciate the implications of appraisal smoothing and reliability considerations may reach the mistaken conclusion that real estate values are inherently subject to a much lesser degree of price fluctuation than corporate securities and therefore that real estate is a less risky investment.

[2] Institutional Investing

The accelerating popularity of real estate as both an institutional and an individual investment during the 1980s was fueled by the perception that real estate delivered at least competitive if not superior performance relative to traditional corporate securities investments. Some of these performance expectations were premised on representations about past as well as probable future performance and employed methodologies whose validity can best be described as dubious.

The performance actually delivered in many instances fell far short of the promise, leading prudent investors to reconsider the rationale for including real estate in their portfolios. In a real estate market characterized by disappointment and discontinuity, investors are challenged to determine whether to diminish or even abandon their commitments to real estate, to stay the course with existing commitments, to alter strategies, or to add additional funds to their real estate allocations. This decision concerning the role of real estate in an investment portfolio, should be made only after reconsidering the issues concerning real estate investment performance measurement.

Measuring real estate investment performance has become a priority for investors, real estate investment managers, investment professionals, the broader real estate community, and the capital market. Standardization and sophistication are less than optimal, and in some cases, idiosyncratic, self-serving, and even naive approaches dominate the measurement of real estate investment performance. These shortcomings have contributed to pension real estate allocations' being stuck in the 5 percent range rather than achieving the long-prophesied 10 percent or greater allocation target.

Persistent barriers to the broad and enthusiastic acceptance of real estate as a legitimate institutional investment have been its dissimilarities from the familiar and accepted patterns of corporate securities investing arrangements, investors' discomfort with the quality, availability, and reliability of real estate investing information.

Unfortunately, many involved in real estate investing have pursued approaches that exacerbated the divergences. If real estate is to be a legitimate individual and institutional investment, it must be subjected to the standards and expectations of the investments with which it seeks to be compared.

The relationship between the broader investment community's views about real estate and the community of real estate investment specialists' approach to the broader investment issues have been characterized by dichotomy, inconsistency, bias, self-serving attitudes, conflicting arguments, unsubstantiated claims, and cautionary admonitions resembling more a discordant cacophony than compatibility, consistency, objectivity, and understanding.

Although they insist on equal treatment by the mainstream investment community and therefore expect an appropriate proportionate allocation of investable assets to real estate, proponents of real estate as an accepted investment class often insist that because real estate is different, its performance cannot be assessed in the same way as corporate securities. Thus, the real estate investment management community advocates the direct comparison of real estate investment performance and corporate securities investment performance only when such comparison serves its purposes.

Investment traditionalists specializing in corporate securities assert that because real estate investing's fundamental attributes differ materially from those of corporate securities, comparisons of the performance of real estate and other asset classes should not be attempted. Since institutional and individual investors committed extraordinary amounts of capital to real estate in reliance on claims of superior investment performance, however, it would be irresponsible not to examine critically the reality of that investment performance.

As difficult, challenging, messy and uncomfortable as real estate investment performance measurement may be, decisions concerning investment policy, manager selection, performance monitoring, financial reporting, performance evaluation, and compensation determination all depend on it. In addition, the need to integrate real estate into overall investing programs for individual and institutional investors requires meaningful and reliable performance measurement information. Therefore, real estate investment performance measurement is not optional but is fundamental to informed investing decisions.

[3] Primary Participants in Real Estate Investing

For corporations concerned with financing their real estate involvements, a clear understanding of the roles and relationships of the various players in the real estate investment process is a must. The real estate sector of the economy has certain distinguishing characteristics:

- The professional standards that apply to other disciplines in parallel fields—financial analysis, accounting, and law—generally are not matched in real estate.

- There is a substantial shortage of participants with training and expertise in the equity investment process, because until the early 1970s the business focused primarily on mortgage financing.

- The real estate market, although in transition, is still largely unorganized and dispersed, with less concentration and regular flow of transaction activity and value information than exists in the corporate securities market.

The real estate financing industry is made of numerous individual decision makers. Among the users are virtually every organization and individual that possesses, temporarily and/or continually, various interests in real property. Some corporations have substantial real estate holdings in connection with their main line of business; every enterprise makes a series of strategic choices concerning the amount and form as well as a series of "make or buy" questions regarding the various real estate services necessary to support their basic business. Owners and investors commit capital to investment positions. They include general partners, individuals, corporations, partnerships, insurance companies, pension funds, real estate investment trusts, commercial banks, savings and loans, foreign capital sources, joint ventures, limited partnerships, and nonprofit institutions.

The development team is involved in creating new investment properties. Those involved in the creation and conversion of the physical asset include developers, which coordinate the overall process; contractors, which manage the direct building effort; and a collection of specialty participants that provide both specialty contracting services and specific products for the building process, such as architects, engineers, and planners.

Professional advisers provide professional services, including legal, accounting, engineering, and design services to all other participants and thereby exert an increasingly influential role in the real estate process. Brokers are specialists involved in facilitating transactions that provide services including the transfer of title through leasing and sale, arranging financing, and creating new capital pools through the underwriting of securities issues for debt and equity investment. Asset managers manage real property investments on behalf of owners and investors in a fiduciary context. Property managers are concerned with management of the property and provide services to users, investors, and property owners.

Property interests are created, administered, adjudicated, and "taken" by the legal process (through condemnation). The role of government and the courts is one of continually expanding influence at the federal, state, regional and local level.

6.03 FINANCIAL FUNDAMENTALS

[1] Debt and Equity Positions

Traditionally, real estate investment positions have been either debt or equity. Mortgage debt was considered to be a relatively secure position with rather predictable cash income. Until the 1980s, most institutions invested in real estate on the lending side. The equity position was viewed as having a less predictable immediate cash income, attractive tax advantages, and the potential of appreciation at sale.

The distinction between debt and equity is not a particularly useful one today. Many possible investment positions, as well as a number of techniques and arrangements, can be utilized to control risk, enhance leverage, and increase yield. Indeed, some equity positions can assume many of the attributes of a mortgage, and many apparent debt positions on closer inspection are seen to have most of the characteristics of equity.

Real estate finance has two primary concerns: costs of using money and returns on invested money. Whether the investor is advancing money on the project as a lender or acquiring an ownership interest, it is very much concerned with how profitable the investment will be. The return to the lender is simultaneously a cost to the owner in the role of the borrower. The cost of borrowed money is of particular importance to the developer or promoter, as it influences how much cash flow will be available to the equity investor. The cash available to the equity investor in turn influences how much it is willing to pay for the project.

Lenders charge interest for the use of their money. Similarly, investors expect a return on the funds they commit to the equity ownership position. Both interest rates and return expectations are influenced by supply and demand forces. Higher rates prevail when the demand for funds is disproportionately high relative to their availability. Thus, the cost of money in the market serves to allocate the available funds to those that can afford them. All parties to a transaction are very much concerned with the yield or rate of return required by the other parties, since it will help determine their own profit.

[2] Mortgage Primer

The majority of real estate investments are financed to some degree by borrowed money. Although in some instances mortgage loans might not involve principal payments prior to the time the note is due, in the majority of circumstances regular payments of interest and principal are required to reduce the outstanding balance of the loan. Although any arbitrary allocation between interest and principal may be made, self-amortizing mortgages are used most often.

Insight into the procedures underlying the analysis for real estate financing decisions can be gained by review of the mechanics of a savings account. With a 5 percent rate and a $100 investment, at the end of a one-year period the balance is $105, the initial $100 plus $5 in interest. At the end of the second year, the balance is $110.25, the initial $100 plus the first year's $5 plus $5.25 interest on the $105 balance at the end of the first year. In the third year, the initial investment has grown to $115.76. But if the initial interest of $5 is multiplied by three, the balance when added to the $100 investment is $115, or 76 cents less. Over time, this difference will increase. The reason for this difference is, of course, compound interest which is interest paid not just on the original investment but also on the interest that was earned in previous years.

In a borrowing relationship, the lender seeks both a return on the investment and a return of the investment over the term of the loan. Amortization consists of a series of level payments that, over the term of the loan, pay down the entire principal amount as well as provide the stated interest return on the effective outstanding balance of the loan. The payment is determined by multiplying the amount of the loan by a factor that is a function of the interest rate and term of the loan. This factor, known as the mortgage constant, provides for both a return on and a return of the investment by the lender.

The relative composition that interest and principal represent in the mortgage constant, which is also known as the debt service constant, changes each year. In early years, interest accounts for a much larger proportion, and in later years this relationship is reversed. This is shown schematically in Figure 6-2.

An appreciation of how the debt service constant works can be gained by considering an illustration of the numerical relationships for a $1,000 mortgage with a five-year term and an 8 percent interest rate, as shown in Figure 6-3. The constant factor is 0.2433, which means that a total of $243.30 per year over five years will pay off the mortgage and provide an 8 percent return on the outstanding balance.

FIGURE 6-2

Composition of Mortgage Constant Over Time

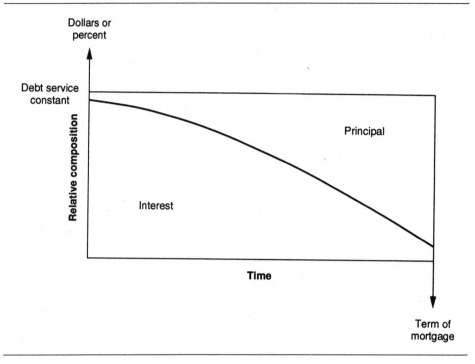

The mathematics used in determining the constant necessary to amortize a loan of a given term and interest rate is the same as that used in compounding of interest. When money is loaned, the lender forgoes the opportunity to invest it and enjoy the gains it would experience if the money were compounding in a savings account. By employing a variation of the compounding techniques, the lender determines how much it should be paid to receive both a return on and return of its investment over time.

Payments on long-term mortgages are generally made monthly so the outstanding principal balance is reduced each month. The monthly table for year 1 is shown in Figure 6-4. The $1,000 balance is not outstanding for the entire first year but only until the first payment is made; each month, the outstanding debt decreases at an increasing rate. With more of the debt service going to principal, the cumulative amount of principal paid grows at an expanding rate.

Certain general relationships prevail concerning the timing of debt amortization and the required mortgage constants for different mortgage terms and interest rates. The amount of principal paid off over time is illustrated by the figures for a 25-year mortgage shown in Figure 6-5. The constant to amortize the loan over its term is highly sensitive to the interest rate and term of the loan, as shown in Figure 6-6; the constants under the 25-year term correspond to the mortgage reduction figures used in Figure 6-5. As illustrated in Figure 6-6, the higher the interest rate and the longer the mortgage term, the closer the constant will be to the interest rate.

FIGURE 6-3

Annual Mortgage Amortization Schedule

Year	Annual Debt Service	Interest at 8% on Balance	Principal	Cumulative Principal Payments	End-Of-Year Principal Balance
1	$243.30	$73.86	$169.44	$ 169.44	$830.56
2	243.30	59.80	183.50	332.94	647.06
3	243.30	44.57	198.73	551.68	448.32
4	243.30	28.07	215.23	766.91	233.09
5	243.30	10.21	233.09	1,000.00	0

FIGURE 6-4

First-Year Monthly Mortgage Amortization Schedule for Five-Year Loan

Month	Beginning Mortgage Balance	One Month's Interest at 8% on Balance	Monthly Principal Payment	Ending Mortgage Balance
1	$1,000.00	$6.67	$13.61	$986.39
2	986.39	6.58	13.70	972.69
3	972.69	6.49	13.79	958.90
4	958.90	6.40	13.88	945.02
5	945.02	6.30	13.98	931.04
6	931.04	6.21	14.07	916.97
7	916.97	6.12	14.16	902.81
8	902.81	6.02	14.26	888.55
9	888.55	5.93	14.35	874.20
10	874.20	5.83	14.45	859.75
11	859.75	5.74	14.54	845.21
12	845.21	5.64	14.64	830.57

FIGURE 6-5

Cumulative Principal Amortization as Percentage of Original Loan for 25-Year Mortgage

Number of Years	Interest Rate			
	6%	7%	8%	9%
5	10.1	8.8	7.7	6.7
10	23.7	21.4	19.2	17.3
15	41.9	39.1	36.4	33.8

FIGURE 6-6

Mortgage Constants

Interest Rate	Mortgage Term (Years)			
	20	25	30	40
6%	8.6%	7.8%	7.2%	6.6%
7	9.3	8.5	8.0	7.5
8	10.0	9.3	8.8	8.3
9	10.8	10.1	9.7	9.3

[3] Leverage

The opportunity to finance properties primarily with borrowed money has long been recognized as one of the major advantages of real estate investments. Through the use of borrowed money, investors can control a larger asset base than they might otherwise. The investor deducts the interest costs while paying off the mortgage debt and realizing the tax advantages of the entire asset and pays back the obligation in the future with cheaper dollars as a result of inflation. "Leverage" is used generally to describe the role of debt, or more popularly, using other people's money, in financing an investment or business.

There are two primary kinds of leverage: financial and operating. Financial leverage occurs when money is borrowed at an interest rate that is lower than the rate of return that would be generated by the proposed investment without debt financing. If a property will generate a 10 percent return on its purchase price, financial leverage exists if debt can be arranged at an interest cost of less than 10 percent. In such a situation, the investor would receive not only the 10 percent return on the equity investment but also the spread between the 10 percent return from the property and the interest rate paid on borrowed funds.

Particularly attractive to investors is the ability to use leverage to benefit from increases in the property's value over time. While the owner may have a relatively small equity investment, it benefits from the increase in value of the entire asset. For example, consider a property costing $100,000 with a $20,000 equity investment and $80,000 mortgage debt. If sold for double the purchase price ($200,000), the value of the equity position after paying off the mortgage is $120,000, a sixfold gain. If this type of investment is repeated again, the equity position becomes $720,000, and another such transaction raises it to $4.32 million. While this illustration ignores tax consequences, it highlights the dramatic multiplying power of favorable leverage. Indeed, most substantial real estate fortunes have been made in this way.

Operating leverage exists when revenues increase while costs stay constant or increase at a lesser rate than revenues. In real estate financing, positive operating leverage can be realized in circumstances where the debt service is fixed. This situation is illustrated in Figure 6-7, where an operating statement for a property is shown at time T and then at time $T + 10$. At $T + 10$, revenues and expenses have increased by 10 percent while debt service, which is the major claim on the revenue stream, has remained constant. Cash flow has increased by 55 percent by virtue of the fact that debt service, which accounts for the major claim on the revenue stream, has not changed because mortgage terms are fixed.

FIGURE 6-7

Simple Example of Positive Operating Leverage

	T	T + 10
Scheduled gross revenue	$100	$110.0
Vacancy	(5)	(5.5)
Effective gross revenue	$ 95	$104.5
Operating expenses	(40)	(44.0)
Net operating income	$ 55	$ 60.5
Debt service	(45)	(45.0)
Cash flow	$ 10	$ 15.5

FIGURE 6-8

Positive Operating Leverage

	1987	1988	1989	1990
Scheduled gross revenue	$100.0	$102.1	$104.1	$106.3
Vacancy	(8.8)	(5.0)	(5.1)	(5.2)
Effective gross revenue	$ 91.2	$ 97.1	$ 99.0	$101.1
Operating expenses	(37.5)	(39.5)	(39.6)	(39.7)
Net operating income	$ 53.7	$ 57.6	$ 59.4	$ 61.4
Debt service	(48.3)	(48.3)	(48.3)	(48.3)
Cash flow	$ 5.4	$ 9.3	$ 11.1	$ 13.1

Note: All items are expressed as an index, with base of 1987 scheduled gross revenue equal to 100.

Discussions of leverage tend to emphasize only the positive aspects. The historical experience of increasing prices and inflation pressures have caused many in the real estate business to approach all projects with considerable optimism. This attitude was reflected in one developer's approach to an apartment project for which the operating statement, recast into an indexed table with the scheduled gross revenue for 1987 set equal to 100, is shown in Figure 6-8. Each item for the projected period, 1987–1990, is expressed in percentage terms of the 1987 scheduled gross revenue figure. As seen, cash flow is projected to more than double from 1987 through 1990; debt service is held constant while other items are increased.

Leverage, however, is a two-edged sword. When it works positively, it can have very favorable consequences, as Figures 6-7 and 6-8 show, but when it works negatively, it can have disastrous consequences. When the actual results of the apartment project did not match projections, the developer found himself in the situation depicted in Figure 6-9. Rather than delivering the expected positive results, the property has operated at a deficit since it opened, and the cash flow hemorrhage is increasing over time.

FIGURE 6-9

Negative Operating Leverage

	1987	1988	1989	1990
Scheduled gross revenue	$100.0	$94.2	$ 89.3	$ 86.4
Vacancy	(14.4)	(14.8)	(4.8)	(15.1)
Effective gross revenue	$ 85.6	$79.4	$ 74.5	$ 71.3
Operating expenses	(38.8)	(38.8)	(44.3)	(45.4)
Net operating income	$ 46.8	$40.6	$ 30.2	$ 25.9
Debt service	(48.4)	(48.4)	(48.4)	(48.4)
Cash flow	$ (1.6)	$ (7.8)	$(18.2)	$(22.5)

Note: All items are expressed as an index, with base of 1987 scheduled gross
revenue equal to 100.

Three problem areas are clearly evident in Figure 6-9:

1. Projected rental increases were not realized.

2. Vacancies were higher than expected.

3. Expenses were higher than projected.

The combined effect of these problems has been to force the break-even point for
1990 to a level above 100 percent of scheduled gross revenues. Like the proverbial
little girl, leverage, when bad, is very bad; but when good, leverage can be very good.

In the consideration of the pros and cons of different financing alternatives, it is
essential that the ultimate decision be based on an after-tax analysis of each alternative.
The fact that the major portion of debt service is interest rather than principal gives
rise to significant tax deductions, which in turn reduce the carrying cost and increase
the after-tax yield. In some situations, what appears to be negative leverage on a
pretax basis is in fact positive leverage on an after-tax basis.

[4] Tax Considerations

Tax considerations play an important role in real estate investment decision making.
The changing structure of the business and evolving transaction arrangements mandate
a careful assessment of the tax implications of each element of the transaction and
management of the property. Real estate taxation is highly complex, with different
rules applying to different property types and each legal form of ownership having a
unique set of tax rules.

While tax factors are of paramount importance, they must not dominate basic economic considerations. Unless the deal has fundamental economic rationality, no
amount of creative tax structuring will by itself make a venture viable. Many of the
problems that have plagued real estate investment in recent years are attributable to
a distortion of priorities, where the quest for a tax shelter overwhelmed the iron law
of business that cash inflows must at least equal cash outflows. The preferred strategy

is to verify the viability of the deal on basic economic grounds and then to investigate tax structuring as a means of enhancing the return to meet the investor's particular needs and objectives.

The basic tax advantages available to the real estate investor involve taking tax deductions today in exchange for tax obligations at a later date and shifting the subsequent obligation to a lower tax bracket than applied to the initial deduction. A deduction taken against ordinary income may subsequently be taxed at capital gains rates. The value of these benefits can be enhanced by the use of borrowed money. Prior to the enactment of the Tax Reform Act of 1986, through aggressive tax structuring, an investor could receive cumulative tax deductions equal to several times the initial equity investment. When tax deductions do not relate to real losses of economic value, they are subsequently recognized as taxable income. Thus, the investor does not avoid income taxes by investing in real estate; rather, the tax obligation may be deferred to a later date and possibly shifted to a lower tax bracket.

Although new tax laws influence investment decisions, they neither impose penalties nor confer benefits on new investors. Those that win or lose as a result of tax changes are those that own assets when a new tax law is passed. It is useful to keep this in mind in considering the potential effects of new tax rules on real estate involvements.

[5] Property Rights

Historically, the legal dimensions of the equity position were defined by rights. A particular investment property is composed of many elements, each of which might be effectively thought of as a separate and distinct right. Ownership of an investment property includes the right to receive cash income, the right to dictate use, the right to benefit from future value (often known as the reversion), the right to use the property, and the right to hypothecate the value as security of a claim.

The right to hypothecate and subordinate certain rights gave rise to the mortgage, which is a priority claim on the property's income and requires transfer of formal title if default on debt service occurs. Over time, certain rights came to be associated with the equity and mortgage positions, but recent developments, both in financing practices and the legal definitions of rights, have rendered the traditional definitions ineffective. The terms "debt" and "equity" now more accurately connote types of rights rather than specific rights.

The property is increasingly being fractionalized into different positions. First, the public sector's claim on income for property taxes precedes all other claims on the property. Second, the expanding police power of local as well as federal government, in the form of land use controls and environmental restrictions, has severely restricted the rights of property owners to make the final decisions on the use of their land and has imposed significant liabilities for environmental contamination, accidents to persons, and illegal acts committed on the property. Third, various rights of property are increasingly being unbundled by the investment community.

Modern real estate financing involves manipulation of the many rights of investment property. The ownership of the property often involves one party's holding title to the land, the building's being owned by another investor, and the leasehold's being held by still a third. It is not unusual for the owner of the leasehold position, which essentially consists of the right to determine the use of a building over a designated period, to assign an operating lease for the property to still another party. The holder of the operating lease then becomes the one that bears the business risks if the property cannot generate adequate income to service its obligations. In turn, the holder of the operating lease may lease space directly to individual tenants for their own purposes and use; such tenants may then sublease excess space to still others.

The folklore of real estate is replete with stories about investors amassing fortunes using other people's money. Indeed, virtually every basic real estate book extols at length the virtues of leverage. Real estate finance textbooks and courses traditionally have concerned themselves only with mortgage lending. The reasons for this traditional emphasis on the debt side of the business to the exclusion of the equity side has been that very often the lender was the only investor with any money in the deal. Developers sought to "mortgage out" by achieving financing in excess of the cost incurred to develop a property. Consequently, little attention was directed to evaluating the equity position. In the last two decades, this state of affairs has reversed itself.

In an environment characterized by universal optimism about real estate's strong performance prospects and limited risks, lenders aggressively seeking real estate deals are willing to provide 100 percent financing. As recognition of market softness and the perception of risks grows, however, lenders may insist on the developer's assigning various elements of the equity rights, asserting more claim on rights that traditionally have been reserved by the equity position. When this occurs, the lender, in addition to a basic interest return on money loaned into the project, will demand some type of equity participation—either in the form of a percentage of the revenues, a percentage of the cash flow, or even a straight percentage ownership of the deal—as consideration for agreeing to make the loan.

The effects of lenders' insisting on terms more favorable to the debt position and the corresponding deterioration of the rights traditionally reserved for the equity position have been far reaching. Where it once may have been possible to achieve positive leverage on cash flow to the equity position by borrowing at a rate less than the overall yield on a free-and-clear basis, now the reverse condition prevails. Often the cost of debt money exceeds the overall yield of a project on a free-and-clear basis, and the little cash available to the equity position is sometimes taken by the lender. Consequently, as the cash flow available to the equity position is being increasingly squeezed, to the point where in some markets there is hardly any cash flow in income properties, investors are buying more and more future appreciation.

An investor that commits money to a venture is buying the prospects of future economic performance. Investors' decisions regarding the prices at which they buy and sell are largely influenced by their different assessments of the relative probability of certain future events. For example, the optimistic investor wants to buy or expects a higher price if selling, while the pessimistic investor wants to sell and will accept a lower price. An investor's behavior reflects an assessment of a risk-return trade-off.

Those that invest in quasi-debt positions (so-called because there are few pure debt positions) are concerned with such things as the security of the investment principal, maximizing the yield on investment, preserving the competitiveness of the yield in light of capital market changes, and preserving the purchasing power of invested capital. The basic security of an investment is affected by the loan-to-value ratio for the particular position and the related break-even point faced by the operator of the property. Also of concern is the relative priority of the claim of the particular investment. Clearly, an investment that has a first claim on the security for the loan (i.e., the property) is more secure than one that has a secondary claim position. Although some lenders traditionally oppose having any secondary financing between them and the fee owner, it can be argued that additional debt investors provide greater security since they may well be motivated to preserve their investment and respond in the event of a default by the equity owner.

Guarantees, which are a means to achieve greater security for an investment, can take a number of forms. They include personal guarantees by the borrower or third parties, various types of lease arrangements, and lease and loan insurance from companies that specialize in providing such insurance. The security of the income stream is highly influenced by the relative certainty of its being received. A property leased to a triple-A credit tenant clearly has more immediate security than a property with no leases at all. In between are properties with leases to multiple tenants or properties secured by sale-leaseback arrangements with the seller, which, in effect, is guaranteeing the loan as is the buyer. Obviously, the relative desirability of the various lease arrangements will depend on the terms of the leases and the strength of the parties on the lease.

Lenders can sometimes achieve higher returns by providing additional increments of debt, thereby increasing the loan-to-value ratio, or by undertaking more risky loans. With less certainty associated with the probable income stream, the borrower must pay a higher price to motivate a lender to place funds at risk. Various specialized financing arrangements are used to achieve higher returns, including land leases, wraparound mortgages, lender participations, and joint venture relationships.

High inflation rates and rapidly fluctuating interest rates pose difficult problems for investors in debt positions. Indeed, the traditional fixed-level interest rate payment schedule is becoming increasingly inappropriate. Instead, the variable-rate mortgage can be used to maintain a competitive yield on the investment. The purchasing power of the invested capital can be preserved by various devices, including an option to purchase the property at a predesignated price, warrants to buy stock in the borrower, if publicly held, and participation in sales proceeds either through various forms of participation arrangements or a convertible mortgage.

The equity investor that uses the lender's funds will be concerned with their availability and cost, and higher loan-to-value borrowing will involve higher costs. Since many equity investors are motivated by a desire to minimize their own cash investment in the deal, they are willing to pay higher rates in exchange for more funds. In some situations, acquiescing to lender participation is a condition for obtaining any loan at all, and on other occasions the equity investor willingly goes along in order to obtain greater total borrowing.

Many equity investors are concerned about risks associated with their position and consequently pay particular attention to the break-even point resulting from the financing in question. An effective means of offsetting a high break-even point and planning for future contingencies is the use of large reserves. Of course, these risks can also be controlled by the various forms of guarantees discussed previously.

The unique risks associated with the development process have given rise to specialized financing arrangements. Among the techniques used to secure the risks associated with construction and development lending are permanent takeout commitments, floor-ceiling loans, and gap financing. On occasion, the land is acquired through specialized transactions such as land purchase salebacks and sale-condobacks.

[6] Secondary Financing

Maximizing leverage allows the equity investor to control a great amount of property; this can have particularly favorable tax advantages. Among the techniques that are used for enhancing leverage are the wraparound mortgage, other forms of secondary financing, and land leases. Leverage can be enhanced by the use of secondary financing. Such debt is in addition to the permanent first mortgage and therefore is subordinated to such first financing. The second mortgage is identical to the first mortgage except that it has a second claim position on the property that is the security. Generally, the second mortgage is of a shorter term at a higher interest rate. Often, the payments are interest only with the unamortized balance due at the end of the loan in a balloon payment. It is possible to have additional secondary financing in the form of third, fourth, fifth mortgages and so on. Second mortgages often originate with the seller lending funds to a buyer to cover the difference between the purchase price and the sum of the property's existing debt financing and the buyer's available cash for a down payment.

Risk can be controlled through various guarantees and insurance arrangements. The investor that uses such arrangements pays a premium to insure against the consequences of adverse operating results. It is critical, though, that the investor verify that the benefit justifies the cost. Too often, the additional security is not worth the cost.

[7] Creative Financing

Because of the dominant role finance plays in real estate, the distinctive nature of the markets that provide capital for real estate ventures, and the entrepreneurial attributes that characterize real estate ventures, so-called creative financing assumes an important role. Simply stated, creative financing involves nontraditional arrangements of timing and priority of cash flows from a venture. Rather than financing a venture with a cash equity investment and a simple self-amortizing mortgage, customized arrangements of different parties and combinations of risk, priority, and participation are employed. In essence, real estate's creative financing was the precursor of financial engineering, popularized in the late 1980s as a means of innovatively designing claims on cash flows from an enterprise to appeal to particular investor objectives.

The application of creative financing is aptly illustrated by the Empire State Building transaction, a classic case of creative real estate financing, presented in Figure 6-10. Involving an initial capital commitment in the 1950s and 1960s of $46 million by Prudential Insurance and $33 million of investor capital and financing, the venture has proven to be a landmark in financial innovation and performance.

6.04 REAL ESTATE CAPITAL MARKETS

[1] Capital Providers

Real estate financing largely occurs in a distinct capital market. While securization is a growing trend and increasingly dominant in the single-family mortgage market, project finance is the predominant commercial real estate financial arrangement. The primary sources of real estate capital are corporations, financial institutions, real estate securities (limited partnerships and real estate investment trusts, which are the real estate equivalent of mutual funds and which combine the funds of individual and institutional investors), pension funds, and offshore investors. For purposes of this chapter, "real estate capital" is defined as pension fund debt and equity, financial institution debt and equity, equity invested by foreign investors (equity investments at least partially funded by debt originated outside of the United States), equity investments by corpora-

FIGURE 6-10

Classic Case Study of Creative Real Estate Financing:
The Empire State Building

Located on a 91,000-square-foot site at Fifth Avenue between 33rd and 34th Streets in midtown New York City, the Empire State Building rises 102 stories above the street, has 2 stories below grade, is 1,472 feet high, and is topped by a 22-story television tower. The Empire State Building has a rentable area of approximately 1,753,000 square feet and, at the time of the joint venture offering in 1961, had 850 tenants and approximately 550 building employees. Even in a city characterized by high-rise buildings, the Empire State Building has long been a dominant landmark in New York's skyline.

The legal relationships governing the Empire State Building involve fee ownership of the building and land, a leasehold interest of 114 years, an operating lease for an equivalent period, and various subleases with different tenants.[a] The significant participants and the relevant terms of their participation include the following:

1. The Prudential Insurance Company of America purchased the land in 1951 for $17 million and subsequently acquired title to the building in 1961 for $29 million. It leases the property to the Empire State Building Associates for an annual return of some 7 percent over the first 30 years and lesser amounts for a subsequent 84 years.

2. The Empire State Building Associates own a leasehold interest with an initial 30-year term that, with renewals, can be extended to 114 years. This entity is a general partnership organized in 1961, consisting of 3,300 units of $10,000 each. Each unit represents a fractionalized general partner interest in one of three partners. The investors receive a 9 percent annual return on their $33 million investment plus "overages" as described below.

3. The Empire State Building Company is an entrepreneurial group that owns a "sandwich" lease, so termed because it stands between the master lease on the leasehold (owned by Empire State Building Associates) and the subleases with tenants that occupy the building. This entity manages and operates the property and pays sufficient rent to the Empire State Building Associates to cover the building and land rent to Prudential Insurance of 7 percent annually, as well as the 9 percent guaranteed return on the initial $33 million investment. The Empire State Building Company receives the first $1 million of income after these obligations are met, and 50 percent of any remaining additional income.

The structuring of this joint venture places Prudential Insurance in the primary position, receiving a relatively low-risk 7 percent return; places the investors in the secondary position to Prudential, receiving 9 percent annually plus the possibility of higher returns; and places the Empire State Building Company in the high-risk position of guaranteeing the Prudential's 7 percent return and the Associates' 9 percent return while enjoying substantial upside potential.

The venture has worked out well. Prudential has regularly received its 7 percent return; the $10,000 unit holders have gotten their 9 percent return plus substantial overage distributions; and the entrepreneurial Empire State Building Company has realized incentive compensation, in addition to its regular fees for services, well in excess of $1 million annually.

Significantly, Prudential recently sold the physical assets, which are subject to the leasehold interest controlled by the Empire State Building Associates, for about $50 million. The leasehold, a paper interest with no tangible attribute but the right to control the property, is now worth many hundreds of millions of dollars.

[a] These relationships are outlined in the prospectus for the Empire State Building Associates, which is reproduced in Stephen E. Roulac, *Syndication Landmarks* (New York: Practising Law Institute, 1974).

tions in real estate, and the aggregate of investment by individuals and institutions in real estate securities. Not included is investment by individuals and debt provided by sources other than those that finance real estate acquisitions.

The pendulum of power for real estate financing and investing has swung sharply from the capital surplus conditions of the 1980s, which favored entrepreneurial developers and deal makers, to the capital shortfall conditions of the 1990s, which favor those that control capital. Whereas through much of the 1980s, capital providers chased deals up what seemed to be an ever-escalating price curve, by the end of the decade economic reality had been reasserted. With growing recognition of space surpluses, soaring vacancies, and declining effective rents, prices have softened and capital flows have slowed. Now the financial institutions that so eagerly shoveled money into real estate are seeking to get it back. However, borrowers, because their ability to pay off existing loans depends on getting a new loan from a new source, are frustrated by most prospective lenders' policies of calling existing loans rather than extending new credit.

In 1990, the dual forces of restraint exercised by investors and constraints imposed by regulators transformed the real estate capital market. The speculative fever that dominated these capital markets through the 1980s was abruptly suppressed in the last months of 1989. The pendulum, which during the 1980s swung toward readily available capital on accommodating terms, has swung abruptly to the opposite extreme, and the real estate markets are now severely constrained. In the early 1990s, some capital sources have been limited by regulatory constraints, some do not have discretionary investable funds available, and still others have funds available but remain unconvinced that real estate is a viable investment for those funds.

The end of the 1980s was the end of an era of excess in terms of real estate capital formation. The amount of capital and the terms and conditions governing access to capital for real estate ventures and real estate related enterprises changed markedly during the latter months of 1989 and the first half of 1990. As the perception of the changed conditions of capital markets became more pervasive, the new conditions of real estate capital access were labeled a crisis by the industry. Although individual market participants and trade groups petitioned regulators to adopt a more accommodating stance toward real estate financing, their efforts were largely ineffective.

The statistics for total real estate capital flows by source from 1980 to 1990 are shown in Figure 6-11. Recent period figures reflect commitments previously made for projects under way, even though the parties involved, if they had to make that decision again in light of subsequent information, might not make the same commitment. The assessment process is further complicated by the fact that projects have long lead times, with significant lags between the date of the commitment and funding. During this period between commitment and funding, market conditions can change dramatically. Consequently, there is an inexorable momentum of real estate capital flows. Still, there is clear evidence of great changes in the composition of real estate capital, both in recent reporting periods and cumulatively. These forces are especially highlighted by consideration of changes within and between components of the different real estate market segments.

Aggregate real estate capital grew by $156 billion in 1990 to more than $4 trillion. Although this represents a 4 percent gain over 1989, the increase in aggregate real estate capital in 1990 was some $37 billion less than the increase in 1989. This 1990 gain was almost one third less than the previous year's gain. The 1991 figures reflected the continuation of a sharp decline in capital committed to real estate ventures. Significantly, 1990 growth in real estate capital of $156 billion was less than one half of the

FIGURE 6-11

Total Real Estate Capital by Source

Source: S.E. Roulac, "Dimensions of the Restructuring in Real Estate Capital Markets," Real Estate Finance Journal (Spring 1992), pp. 5–12

	1980	1981	1982	1983	1984	1985	1986	1987	1988	1989	1990
Pension funds	$ 19.0	$ 30.2	$ 40.1	$ 49.5	$ 56.1	$ 63.7	$ 73.3	$ 87.8	$ 89.8	$ 99.6	$ 118.9
Financial institutions	238.8	262.3	287.7	335.6	402.5	466.8	546.4	652.0	705.5	763.2	774.7
Foreign investors	7.3	10.7	13.5	17.2	20.7	22.8	26.2	32.3	38.4	45.0	56.0
Real estate securities	15.2	19.4	24.9	34.2	49.4	64.3	77.7	90.4	98.4	98.5	93.5
Corporations	1,514.4	1,748.1	1,871.5	2,054.0	2,281.2	2,460.8	2,577.1	2,629.2	2,768.4	2,877.6	3,007.7
Total	$1,794.7	$2,070.7	$2,237.7	$2,490.5	$2,809.9	$3,078.4	$3,280.7	$3,491.7	$3,700.5	$3,893.9	$4,050.8

Note: Dollars in billions.

highest reported growth of $319 billion in 1984, when the figures were inflated by the record high commitments of both real estate securities and corporations. Notably, in 1984 real estate securities capital increased by $15 billion, whereas in 1990 it decreased by $5 billion, a swing of $20 billion. Corporate commitments to real estate capital in 1984 were $227 billion, almost double the $120 billion of commitments in 1990.

In this environment of constrained capital access, capital providers that have both the funds available and the courage to commit them can obtain attractive terms. The financial institutions' imperative to refinance existing loans creates unique opportunities for those motivated to participate in the real estate capital markets. Significantly, certain institutions that were relatively uninvolved in the real estate markets in the 1980s are securing attractive terms in the 1990s.

The statistics for the 1990s' real estate capital flows will reflect substantially lower capital commitments. Corporations will continue to show a dominant position, and pensions will emerge as the clear primary player in the noncorporate segment. The real estate capital markets over the immediate time horizon will likely be dominated by nontraditional institutional investors that, during the 1980s, concentrated on merger and acquisition and leveraged buyout transactions. The capital markets will be characterized by a possible resurgence of foreign capital to exploit the advantageous terms available in the markets and a revitalization of real estate securities designed to be economic in their structures and prudent in their investing strategies.

The real estate markets will continue to be characterized by constant transformation, which will create both opportunities and demand for professional services. Those whose capabilities and vision attract the confidence of capital providers have the potential to do well during the 1990s.

[2] Market Inefficiencies

In contrast to the majority of capital markets, the real estate capital market is relatively inefficient, which has a profound impact on the appropriate strategies for those seeking access to capital and those making capital commitments that depend on the future productivity of real estate assets. A market is termed efficient when it functions so that a given security or investment is fairly priced, reflecting all available information, and therefore purchasers of investments can expect to realize normal returns. A purchaser of an investment in an efficient market has a reasonable expectation of a normal return.

In the efficient market, there are few opportunities to identify undervalued or overvalued investments. Knowledgeable and active participants are continually searching for mispriced investments, buying those they think are undervalued and selling those that are overvalued. Thus, prices of different investments reflect all that market participants know about their future prospects. To the extent that a market is truly efficient, chance can be considered as good a method as any of selecting an investment and an investment portfolio. The efficient market simultaneously provides a reduced payoff for superior knowledge and expertise and a form of protection for the less competent participant. Conversely, payoffs for superior performance and penalties for miscalculation are greater in the inefficient market.

To translate this theory into a workable approach to investing, it is useful to examine the elements of an efficient market: information availability, investment comparability, analytical sophistication, participant knowledge, and liquidity. Significant differences between the attributes of corporate finance and real estate financial markets are highlighted in Figure 6-12. Multiple factors suggest that a real estate transaction is more

FIGURE 6-12

Comparison of Attributes of Corporate Finance and Real Estate Finance

	Corporate Finance	Real Estate Finance
Investment information	Extensive fundamental information available.	Limited, narrow and restricted fundamental information. Few research services.
Press coverage	Comprehensive and varied press coverage of strategies, business operations, and investment prospects.	Press coverage popularized, sketchy.
Pricing information	Extensive and instantaneous. Data on securities transactions widely available at a nominal charge.	Pricing information on real estate transactions is limited and subject to misinterpretation, as key terms are unavailable and/or inaccurately reported.
Financial statements	Independent certified financial statements.	Past performance data is limited. Seller's representations may be unreliable. Verifying past results is expensive, often impossible.
Performance measurement	Many indexes of market performance.	Measures of market performance are limited.
Legal form	Nearly all businesses use corporate form of legal ownership, facilitating comparability.	Legal structure varies significantly. Ownership forms used include partnership, corporate, and trust, complicating investment comparisons.
Analytical sophistication	Shorthand price/earnings (P/E) ratio relatively well understood; supplemented by extensive theoretical and applied literature on investments, especially modern portfolio theory and applications of quantitative methods to measure risk-return characteristics.	Real estate's capitalization rate (inverse of P/E ratio) subject to extreme variances in interpretation; concept of present value only recently accepted by real estate sector; many analytic techniques, especially appraisal applications, extremely primitive.
Performance studies	Extensive historical performance studies.	Limited historical performance studies; insufficient duration and breadth of data to perform historical performance studies comparable to those of corporate securities.
Financial reporting	Reporting of corporate performance independently attested to by certified public accountant, although increasing questions posed as to reliability of historical cost statements and increasing debate over relevance of generally accepted accounting principles.	Reporting of real estate results often based on manager's representation, without independent verification; variations in classification, self-dealing, and tax-motivated interpretations complicate analysis accuracy.

(continued)

FIGURE 6-12   (*continued*)

	Corporate Finance	Real Estate Finance
Educational tradition	Extensive educational programs; many business schools place great emphasis on the stock market and have extensive course offerings.	No major business school approaches a rigorous real estate curriculum. Many educational programs have a brokerage orientation; few take a modern management approach.
Research	Extensive research interest; investments a dominant research topic for academics; existing body of knowledge continues to be extended through numerous journals.	Limited academic research and few publishing opportunities in professional journals; finance and investment journals historically have been reserved for research on corporate finance and investment.
Investment management tradition	Long tradition of investment management; many organizations have extensive experience and track records.	Real estate investment management is a relatively new business. Few organizations have a substantive track record, and few persons have strong training or quallifications in real estate investment analysis and management.
Trading	Usually consistent trading activity on a daily basis for a given security.	Transactions occur infrequently; usually several years or more pass between transfers.
Transaction timing	Transactions are virtually instantaneous. Highly efficient trading mechanism allows impersonal trades based on only two variables; quantity and price.	Buyers and sellers often engage in extensive negotiation of terms other than price. Entire process usually requires a minimum of 30 days.
Investment size	Size of investment may be incrementally adjusted from single share to multi-million-dollar placement.	Investment is often substantial; seldom available in increments. Large increments make diversification difficult.
Transferability	Most shares easily transferable.	Corporate and real estate investment trust shares readily transferable; trust units and majority of partnership interests involve complex, cumbersome transfer. Transfer of ownership a burdensome process; risk of fraud and false transfer necessitate title insurance and independent escrow.

likely to occur at a price divergent from normal value (i.e., a consensus price reached as a result of active negotiation by knowledgeable participants). When this difference occurs, the possibility of superior (and inferior) financial results exists. The inefficiencies of the real estate market pose pitfalls for the unwary, since investors cannot rely on an active trading market of knowledgeable participants as a cushion for their misjudgment. The available means of real estate involvement vary significantly in the degree to which they exploit the best or fall prey to the worst of the attributes of the inefficient market. The performance of some commingled real estate funds may appear impressive when compared with stock market investments, but, if compared with the results of the most effective real estate investment strategy, that performance might seem unimpressive.

[3] Real Estate Assumptions Versus Reality

No one observing the economy over the last number of years can have failed to recognize the extraordinary rise and fall of real estate as an investing option. Two decades ago, undiscriminating bank lending and expanding real estate investment involvement led to the mid-1970s crisis, which was called the worst financial reversal in the real estate markets since the depression of the 1930s. As the market recovered, the combination of the stimulative 1981 tax legislation, inflationary concerns, disappointing corporate securities performance, new pension legislation suggesting that diversified portfolios include real estate, growing offshore investor interest, and economic expansion caused real estate to become a favored investment for both institutions and individuals through the use of real estate securities.

Favored status led to growing investor acceptance, which translated into burgeoning capital flows. Although signs of problems were evident in the middle and late 1980s, financial institutions continued to pour money into real estate deals. The market was sustained not by the demand of tenants to occupy space in buildings but by investors seeking to commit capital to finance and own buildings. Ultimately, when the music stopped, as it inevitably does for any financial market excess, real estate values toppled and extraordinary losses were incurred.

In a period of significant change such as has prevailed in the real estate markets over the last two decades, going long in commitments in markets characterized by short-term volatility, intermediate term transformation, and long-term discontinuity has been at least precarious if not precipitously dangerous. Many in real estate presume that there is an inherent self-correcting cycle of miscalculation leading to surplus space followed by correction, rapid recovery, and a return to a supply-demand equilibrium in the space markets. Because this boom-bust-recovery cycle has occurred before, it is presumed that it will again. This orientation has parallels to the traditional budgeting and control mentality of betting that the future will be a repetition of the past or the strategic long-range planning extrapolation of past trends continuing unabated. This mistaken assumption of the past as a reliable prediction of the future is especially ironic in light of the long-lived nature of real estate decisions made in an environment characterized by discontinuity and the inherent inflexibility of commitments once made.

The divergence between assumptions about the reality of future economic forces and property performance sharply illuminates the linkage of property performance to the economic forces that determine that performance. Significantly, real estate investments are premised upon certain assumptions about economic forces. Although many decision makers intuitively recognize that the purchase of any investment involves the concurrent purchase of the assumptions upon which that investment is premised, seldom is this truism explicitly applied to real estate investing decisions. In practice, most commitments of capital to real estate rely on the general presumption that future economic forces will be a repetition of the recent past.

A primary economic force driving property performance is tax policy, which periodically may feature incentives and/or subsidies to particular real estate activities. Further, certain tax regulations can result in after-tax returns' being higher than pretax returns, an anomalous result that differentiates real estate from most other investing activities. Despite the volatility of tax regulations affecting real estate and the frequency of tax reform in the decade preceding the early 1980s, real estate investors proceeded as if this economic force were a given rather than a dynamic.

The linkages of economic forces to property performance are sharply illustrated by a comparison of the 1990s' reality to the 1980s' assumptions concerning how economic forces would influence property market and capital market conditions and in turn drive property performance. As highlighted in Figure 6-13, the premise of economic continuity included strong absolute demand for space that would not be disproportionate to its supply and led to assumptions of high rents, occupancy, cash flows, and returns on investment, which were enhanced by favorable tax treatment. These high investment return expectations attracted disproportionate quantities of capital, which led to dramatic expansions of the space inventory at the very time when demand was changing, as a result of both a downturn in overall levels of economic activity and, more important, a shift in the basic demand function for business space. Concurrently, real estate's tax treatment changed from very positive to extremely negative.

As seen in Figure 6-13, the combination of a downturn in the economy, confirming that gravity does in fact prevail, and discontinuity in the basic economic structure, leading to the fundamental transformation in the nature and quantity of demand for business space, led to a concurrent extraordinary supply surplus in the face of soft demand and significant investor lack of interest in real estate investments. The resulting property performance was characterized by low rents, occupancy levels, and cash flows, which aggregate low investment returns. Misperception of the implications of economic forces transformed optimistic assumptions into disappointing reality.

Few involved in real estate investing gave sufficient consideration to the impact of information and communications technology advances in transforming how space would be used and therefore how the performance of properties would be affected. While the dramatic surpluses of business space were widely recognized, less appreciated is that while there was an unprecedented explosion of supply additions relative to historic demand patterns, the very nature of demand was being dramatically transformed.

The expectation of strong property performance that motivated capital flows led to substantial space supply additions that dwarfed demand and resulted in disappointing property performance. The initial investor optimism led to a series of events that resulted in investor discouragement, an outcome that was the antithesis of the investor's expectations. Although the logical sequence of steps that resulted in this disappointment can be readily comprehended after the fact, few, if any, investors proceeded in reliance on the anticipation that their optimistic expectations would be frustrated. Frustration and disappointment resulted because the implications of the economic forces on property performance were not explicitly considered.

FIGURE 6-13

Economic Forces and Property Performance: Assumptions and Reality

1980s Assumptions

1990s Reality

ECONOMIC FORCES

MARKETS

Property Performance

MARKETS

ECONOMIC FORCES

PREMISE OF CONTINUITY

Uninterrupted economic expansion

Continued office employment growth

Incremental new construction is consistent with demand

Investors continue to favor property investments

Tax law provides incentives and subsidies to real estate investing

PROPERTY

Strong sustained space demand relative to supply

CAPITAL

Strong sustained investor demand

PERFORMANCE ASSUMPTION	ATTRIBUTES	PERFORMANCE REALITY
High	Rent	Low
High	Occupancy	Low
High	Cash Flow	Low
High	Return on Investment	Low

PROPERTY

Great supply surplus in face of soft demand

CAPITAL

Market investors disinterested; capital flows down

GRAVITY AND DISCONTINUITY PREVAIL

Economy sags in 1990 and downturn persists through 1992

Declining office employment

New construction outpaced demand

Investors perceive property has adverse return-risk characteristics

Tax law treats real estate activities in punitive manner

173

[4] New Financing Environment

In the accommodating financial environment of the 1980s, the real estate lending community forgot about prudence and ignored the textbook guidelines of loan underwriting. In the 1990s, prudence has been rediscovered, risk aversion reinforced, and stringent underwriting reimposed. For those accustomed to the easy times of the 1980s, the change is shocking and inhospitable. For those that are able to deal in the more demanding competitive environment, the change is considered welcome, inasmuch as marginal competitors are eliminated together with their propensity to initiate projects that have the effect of compromising decisions made in reliance on market analysis of presumably rational behavior.

Real estate lending decisions today are more restrictive and less accommodating than in the past. Internal approval processes are more disciplined. Lending decisions consider the borrower's overall financial condition, status of other projects, and past track record, rather than just looking at the perceived prospective future value of the proposed collateral. Increasingly, lenders are insisting the borrowers be legitimately at risk, which means that nonrecourse financing terms are less common and that equity investment must be real and tangible, not hypothetical or represented by the asserted spread between appraised value and the mortgage balance.

In the new real estate financing environment, (1) less money in aggregate is available to finance real estate ventures; (2) the types of real estate projects that were financed in the 1980s cannot and will not be financed in the 1990s; and (3) numerous borrowers that gained access to capital in the 1980s cannot expect, without a major change in their business practices, to gain access to capital for real estate involvements in the 1990s. This new real estate lending environment has profound implications at both the project and enterprise levels for both borrowers and lenders.

The earlier easy money times favored the promotional organization, characterized by flexibility and nimbleness, which fiduciaries presumably lacked, over the substantial institution, perceived as slow and lethargic. Now, in a reversal of the financial climate, substance and prudence prevail over flash and glitz. Specifically, those with capital strength now enjoy disproportionate competitive advantages over those lacking such strength.

The differences between the real estate lending environment that prevailed in the 1980s and the environment that applies for the foreseeable future of the 1990s are summarized in Figure 6-14. This comparison suggests a rediscovery of more disciplined underwriting standards consistent with a textbook approach to real estate financing decisions.

The following will apply to real estate lending decisions of the 1990s:

- They will encompass consideration of more information concerning the property as well as the borrower's other involvements and financial exposure.

- They will require information to be substantiated rather than asserted and confirmed by independent third-party professionals.

- They will presume more disciplined analysis and the application of more rigorous standards by both lenders and borrowers.

- They will apply more explicit criteria concerning what types of projects will be financed on what terms.

- Risk identification and mitigation will be emphasized.

FIGURE 6-14

Capital Access: Then and Now

Attribute	Then	Now
Types of deals	Much flexibility in allowable activities	Emphasis on primary properties and standard deals
Equity requirement	Minimal; equity represented by projected profit from anticipated sale	25–40% real cash investment required
Personal risk	Largely avoided by nonrecourse terms, artful legal structures, and use of minimally capitalized affiliate or subsidiary	Personal guarantees required
Preleasing	Desirable but not emphasized	Absolute condition; required level approaching break-even
Permanent mortgage commitment	Not mandatory	Permanent mortgage commitment required
Loan-to-value ratios	Not necessarily a priority; 100% loan-to-value ratio common	75% maximum; 60% not uncommon
Financing structures	Flexible, creative, accommodating	Emphasis on minimizing lender risk
Financial models	Aggressive rent increases and modest expense changes	No revenue inflation, but expense increases required
Appraisal value	Optimistic; best-case presentation	Conservative; worst-case scenario
Appraisal standards	Flexible, accommodating	More stringent, more discerning
Borrower credit analysis	Casual	Rigorous, extensive
Considerations of borrowers' other involvements	Isolated approach to lending decisions	Mandatory portfolio assessments of multiple projects and contingent exposure
Tenant credit analysis	Minimal	Rigorous, extensive
Required information	Flexible	Extensive; emphasis on third-party professional
Ongoing reporting	Casual	Frequent; comprehensive; emphasis on third-party professional
Real estate as compared to other investments	Not differentiated from other assets	Commercial loans require more capital than securities investments or house mortgages
Capital requirements	Facilitated very high leverage	Stringent risk-based capital guidelines and stringent interpretation limit volume

- Real estate financing decisions will be considered in a portfolio context for purposes of both risk management and regulatory compliance, rather than with the isolated transaction orientation of times past.

- Promotion, speculation, and optimism will be replaced with caution, prudence, and conservatism.

Metaphorically, the financial institution lending decision process of the 1980s was premised upon a view of each project as a glass virtually full. In the early 1990s, the same glass is viewed as almost empty.

Capital for real estate ventures has become a scarce resource. The real estate sector will have to get by with less and do more with what capital is available. Those not previously active in the real estate financing business now enjoy competitive advantages, as do prospective borrowers possessing strong net worth and staying power. Those lacking the attributes favored by current market conditions need to adjust their strategies and restructure their resource base or resign themselves to a less rewarding role.

6.05 PROPERTY ANALYSIS

[1] Sources of Investment Returns

Real estate returns are of two basic types: those that are the result of operations and those that result from a change in the value of the initial equity investment. Operating results are composed of both cash flow and tax effects. Changes in equity value are derived from paying down mortgages and appreciation, with tax effects being an important consideration as well.

Inasmuch as the current return in real estate investing is derived from operating results of the property enterprise, rather than the election by management or the board of the level of dividends to be paid, consideration of the source of investment returns assumes a different priority in real estate than might be the case in corporate securities. Although the realization of investment returns from the investor's perspective is analogous to corporate securities, in that it is largely dependent on a manager's decision whether and what amount of cash to distribute, the practice in real estate investing is to focus on actual results at the property level more than on what amount of cash may actually be distributed. Consequently, understanding the sources of investment returns assumes particular importance.

The investor's tax status has a greater impact on investment returns in real estate than in corporate securities. The tax-paying and tax-exempt investor receive the same form of returns in corporate securities investing but treat the returns differently for purposes of calculating appropriate tax obligations and determining the true after-tax investment return. In real estate, in contrast, the nature of the tax laws causes very different results for the tax-paying investor and for the tax-exempt investor. Depending on the nature of the investment structure, the investment return on an after-tax basis may be higher for the tax-paying investor than the tax-exempt investor; this relationship is the opposite of what would apply in corporate securities.

In real estate investing, the current return consists of both cash flow and tax effects. Depending on the structure of the investment, the nature of the investment property performance, and the investor's characteristics, the tax effect can be a positive or negative number, meaning that it can either increase or reduce cash flow on an after-tax basis. The tax consequences of sale for the tax-paying investor reduce the proceeds available by the amount of tax liability. One notable exception is a specialized exchange transaction, in which the interest in one property is exchanged for another through a transaction that is tax exempt, meaning that no tax liability is created by the transaction.

If an institutional investor that would otherwise be exempt from tax on its investing employs borrowed money to finance its investment activities and thereby creates unrelated business taxable income that is subject to taxation, the tax consequences that apply to the tax-paying investor will also apply to the taxable portion of the institutional investor's involvements. This discussion relates to assessment and tax treatment of returns for an investor that is participating in real estate investing either directly or through a legal entity that achieves flow-through tax treatment, such as a partnership, so taxation consideration is calculated at the investor rather than entity level. Real estate investors that participate by ownership of shares in corporations, where taxes are calculated at the entity level first, treat their investment returns both for measurement and taxation purposes in a manner comparable to their treatment of corporate securities, with current returns being in the form of dividends and the change in equity value being the difference between what was paid to acquire the returns and the value at the measurement date.

Thus, in considering the sources of investment return for both the tax-paying and tax-exempt investor, the three basic components of real estate returns are cash flow, tax effect, and change in equity value.

[a] Cash Flow. "Cash flow" describes distributions from operations. There are usually several claims on the operating income that take precedence over the investors' claims. These include debt service on the mortgage, reserves, and sponsor compensation. The figure remaining after payment of debt service and sponsor compensation, if relevant, is often called the cash available for distribution.

[b] Tax Effect. Tax benefits may result from the fact that the taxable income, because of depreciation deductions, is less than the cash flow. The tax effect is calculated by multiplying the taxable income by the specific effective tax rate. There is a different tax effect for each separate tax rate. Cash flow in excess of the taxable income is tax sheltered. To the extent that the taxable income is negative, as it often is in the early period of the investment cycle, there may be additional tax shelter available to shelter the investor's other income. Of course, once taxable income is positive, the tax effect is negative and thus reduces rather than increases the annual current benefit from operations.

[c] Change in Equity Value. The change in equity value represents the increase in the value of the investment that results from the amortization of the mortgage debt on the property as well as the increase or decrease in the value of the property over time. While many have traditionally viewed principal payments, often termed equity buildup, and appreciation as important components of return, they are returns only when realized. They should be thought of as tax-contingent, deferred, and conditional returns. Perhaps most significant, changes in equity value are realized only after the associated tax liabilities are paid. Funds obtained by mortgage refinancing would not give rise to a taxable event, but a sale or foreclosure would cause taxes to be due if a gain had been realized. Investment benefits from operations could be significantly reduced by a tax liability in excess of cash proceeds at sale. Such changes in equity value are deferred in the sense that they are available only when the property is sold or refinanced, and they may be even further delayed if, in the event of a sale, secondary debt is involved or, in the event of refinancing, the funds generated are used for reinvestment in the property. They are conditional because they are available only if the value of the property is maintained. Given the risks associated with any investment in a dynamic and uncertain business environment, there is no guarantee that values will not change dramatically.

It is important to distinguish the timing of the various returns. Cash flow and tax effect are current returns, since they are immediately available. Changes in equity value are deferred, conditional and tax-contingent returns, since their realization is delayed, uncertain, and quite possibly nominal, if not negative. The sum of the cash flow and the tax effect is called the total current benefit and represents the total benefits, consisting of cash flow plus tax shelter or minus tax liability, that are available in the current period.

[2] Measuring Investment Returns

There are a number of approaches used to measure the return on real estate investment. Most are simplistic and can result in misleading information and undesirable decisions. Among the measures of investment return employed are the following:

- Free-and-clear return
- Broker's equity return
- Payback period
- Accounting return
- Profitability index
- Internal rate of return (IRR)
- Adjusted rate of return

Most of these so-called return measures are simply indicators of financial relationships and are therefore more properly classified as financial ratios than rate of return measures.

Six considerations should be incorporated in an accurate and reliable measure of return:

1. The amount, timing, and full tax consequences of the initial investment.

2. All cash flows from operations over the entire life of the investment.

3. All tax effects, both from tax shelter and tax liability, if any, over the entire life of the investment.

4. The cash proceeds (or obligations) from sale after all tax considerations, including capital gains tax, the ordinary income tax liability on the recapture of the excess of accelerated depreciation over straight-line depreciation, and the refund of any unused prepaid expenses or reserves where appropriate.

5. Recognition of the time value of money.

6. Expression of the return as an index figure that permits comparison of different projects. Projects involving different amounts of invested capital, different tax consequences, and different termination dates should be readily comparable.

Consideration of the degree to which various profitability measures meet these criteria yields insights about their efficiency, representativeness, and reliability. As profitability measures, free-and-clear return, payback period, and accounting return all leave much to be desired. Their chief shortcomings include recognition of equity buildup and appreciation prior to the time they are actually realized in cash, use of average figures, failure to consider all flows of both cash and tax effects over the entire investment cycle, and disregard of the time value of money.

Although many in the real estate business still rely on these somewhat unsophisticated profitability measures, there is evidence of considerable progress toward higher standards. The involvement of more sophisticated investors, accustomed to advanced capital budgeting and securities analysis techniques, has been an important influence, as has the concern of securities regulators. With increasing attention to the communication of the expected and achieved results of real estate ventures, more emphasis has been directed to the appropriate measure of invested results. Indeed, an often reliable indicator of a real estate company's competence in modern institutional real estate is its attitude toward and familiarity with the more sophisticated profitability measures, such as the IRR and the adjusted rate of return.

[a] **Free-And-Clear Return.** "Broker's equity return" is defined as the annual cash flow available to the investor divided by the equity investment. This definition is frequently used in broker's setups to describe a particular property. Two critical factors are involved. First, does the investment's return include any of the following:

- Cash flow?
- Cash flow plus tax effect?
- Cash flow plus tax effect plus equity buildup?
- Cash flow plus tax effect plus equity buildup plus appreciation?

Second, how is equity investment defined?

- As original cash down payment only
- As original total cash payment including principal down payment plus such other items as prepaid expenses, underwriting commissions, and legal fees
- As original total cash payment plus such other items as prepaid expenses, underwriting commissions, and legal fees, adjusted for the tax effect of the deductible items?

For both "return" and "equity investment," there are a number of additional possible definitions. The impact of alternative definitions or components of return may be seen in the following example. For an apartment building requiring a $100,000 equity investment, there was a $7,000 cash flow, $4,000 of tax effect (resulting from a taxable loss of $10,000 for an investor in the 40 percent tax bracket), $3,500 of equity buildup, and $4,000 of appreciation (reflecting a 1% increase in value on the $400,000 initial purchase price). The impact of alternative definitions of "return" is highlighted in

FIGURE 6-15

Impact of Alternative Definitions of Return

	Dollar Return	Return on $100,000 Equity Investment
Cash flow	7,000	7.0%
Cash flow plus tax effect	7,000 + 4,000	11.0
Cash flow plus tax effect plus equity buildup	7,000 + 4,000 + 3,500	14.0
Cash flow plus tax effect plus equity buildup plus appreciation	7,000 + 4,000 + 3,500 + 4,000	18.5

Figure 6-15. Clearly, the components of return have a marked impact on what the return on investment turns out to be.

[b] Payback Period. "Payback period" is defined as the amount of time required to recover the investment. For example, a project requiring $10,000 in equity with annual distributions of $2,500 per year would have a four-year payback period. While the payback method usefully identifies the period over which the invested funds are at risk, investors are interested in receiving a return beyond mere recovery of the investment. With this method, it is possible to select mistakenly an investment that achieves a rapid payback of invested funds but no more while rejecting an investment that has a slower payback but generates substantial total payments over and above the initial investment.

[c] Accounting Return. "Accounting return" is defined as an average return over the entire holding period. It is derived by determining the sum of all returns less the initial investment, dividing that figure by the term of the investment expressed in years, and then dividing this amount by the initial investment amount. If the project described previously returned $2,500 per year for five years, the accounting return would be calculated as follows:

$$\text{Return} = \frac{[5(\$2,500) - \$10,000]/5}{\$10,000}$$

$$= \frac{(\$12,500 - \$10,000)/5}{\$10,000}$$

$$= \frac{\$2,500/5}{\$10,000}$$

$$= \frac{\$500}{\$10,000} = 5\%$$

The advantage of the accounting return over the payback method is that the accounting return considers all flows over the entire term of the investment.

[d] PI. The profitability index (PI) is defined as the ratio of the present value of all positive flows to the present value of all negative flows at a given interest rate.

For example, an investment has cash flows over four years of $100, $400, $900, and $1,200, with an initial investment cost of $1,300 in year zero, and the investor must pay out $500 in year 5. The calculation of present value at a 10 percent discount rate of the positive cash flows is as follows:

Year	Cash Flow	Discount Factor	Present Value
1	$ 100	0.909	$ 91
2	400	0.826	330
3	900	0.751	676
4	1,200	0.683	820
Total	$2,600		$1,917

The present value of the payouts (negative flows) is calculated as follows:

Period	Flow	Discount Factor	Present Value
0	$1,300	1.000	$1,300
5	500	0.621	310
Total	$1,800		$1,610

The PI can be readily calculated:

$$PI = \frac{\text{present value of positive payments}}{\text{present value of negative payments}}$$

$$= \frac{\$1,917}{\$1,610} = 1.2$$

Since the PI at a 10 percent interest rate is greater than one, the investment has a rate of return in excess of 10 percent. If a 10 percent return was the criteria for selection, this particular investment would be acceptable, since it provides more than a 10 percent return.

[e] **IRR.** While the PI facilitates comparison of different investment opportunities, many investors want to know what rate of return they are earning on their investment. The IRR, which is an extension of the PI, provides this information. "IRR" is defined as the interest rate that equates the present value of all positive inflows to the present value of all negative outflows. All of the considerations identified as basic for an accurate and reliable measure of investment performance are incorporated in the IRR. Calculation of the IRR requires information for the full investment cycle. The numbers that are used in the calculation should be expressed on an after-tax basis. The IRR adjusts all flows to their present values and expresses the returns as an index figure that facilitates comparison of one project to another.

Computer technology advances have vastly simplified financial calculations, especially the IRR. The procedure is virtually automatic, although some making and interpreting such calculations, lacking a true understanding of the process, would be hard put to explain the methodology, let alone implement it. To compute the IRR, the PI (i.e., the ratio of the present value of positive inflows to the present value of negative outflows) is fixed at 1.0, and the unknown is the interest rate that is required to make the present values of these two flows equal to each other. Thus, the IRR is the interest rate that makes the present value of the positive inflows equal to the present value of the negative outflows.

FIGURE 6-16

Calculation of IRR

| | | 18% IRR | |
Period	Amount	Discount Factor	Present Value
0	$(1,300)	1.000	$(1,300)
1	100	0.847	85
2	400	0.718	287
3	900	0.609	548
4	1,200	0.516	619
5	(500)	0.437	(219)
			$ (20)

| | | 19% IRR | |
Period	Amount	Discount Factor	Present Value
0	$(1,300)	1.000	$(1,300)
1	100	0.840	84
2	400	0.706	282
3	900	0.593	534
4	1,200	0.499	599
5	(500)	0.419	(210)
			$ (11)

While the computational process of determining the PI is relatively straightforward, the calculation of the IRR is cumbersome, because a series of repetitious calculations must be undertaken. The process is one of trial and error, and the numerous calculations can be very time consuming unless a computer is used.

In the previous calculations, since the PI at a 10 percent interest rate exceeded 1.0, the IRR for the illustration exceeded 10 percent. "IRR" is defined as the interest rate where the PI is equal to 1.0; therefore, to calculate the IRR, one must first select a trial interest rate of return. An interest rate is selected and used to calculate the present values. If the sum of all discounted flows exceeds zero, the interest rate selected is too low and a higher rate is needed. If the sum of the discounted flows is negative, the interest rate selected is too high.

This process of selecting an interest rate and calculating the present value of all flows continues until a rate is chosen where the sum is zero. That rate, by definition, is the IRR. For this example, start with a rate of 19 percent. The calculation is shown in Figure 6-16. Since the sum of the present values of the separate flows is negative ($11), the rate selected is somewhat higher than the IRR for this particular investment. Therefore, a somewhat lower rate, 18 percent, is chosen; the calculation is also shown in Figure 6-16. As can be seen, the sum of the present values is $20, indicating that the IRR is between 18 percent and 19 percent.

Although discount factors are presented in financial tables for several places to the right of the decimal point, such tables are of questionable validity and utility. First, they tend to imply more accuracy in measuring returns than is found in most circumstances. Second, they are extremely cumbersome. Where it has been determined that the IRR is between two numbers, the actual number corresponding to the IRR can be found by the process of interpolation.

From Figure 6-16 it can be seen that the absolute difference between the present values at 18 percent and 19 percent interest rates is 31. The IRR by straight-line interpolation is equal to 18 percent plus 20/31 or, expressed in a different way, 19 percent minus 11/31. Straight-line interpolation is used here for simplicity, but the relationship between one discount rate and another is not linear. Consequently, the IRR for the illustrative investment is approximately 18.64 percent, derived by subtracting 0.36(11/31) from 19 percent or adding 0.64(20/31) to 18 percent.

As suggested earlier, calculation of the IRR by hand can be a cumbersome process. Since multiple calculations are required, it can be quite time consuming if one wishes to test a variety of different assumptions. The use of a computer can result in significant time savings and allow the analyst to consider a much broader range of operations.

[f] Adjusted Rate of Return. The IRR has the disadvantage that for nonsimple investments whose flows have multiple changes of sign there are no unique solutions. Thus, multiple returns are indicated for some investments. Further, with the IRR, it is implicit that all flows during the investment period are invested and reinvested at the same internal rate earned by the project. Where returns are particularly high or low, the reinvestment rate to be used for the released cash must be close to the IRR; otherwise, there will be a distortive effect, and good projects will look better and poor projects will look worse than they really are. This overstating effect can be particularly pronounced where the initial contributions are staged over time. To overcome the deficiencies of the IRR, a modified approach, known as the adjusted rate of return, can be used. Several variations are possible.

[3] Appraisals

Traditional appraisals have long played a key role in real estate financing. Most lenders rely on an appraisal, prepared by their own staff or a third party, to verify that the subject property represents adequate security for a proposed loan. Appraisals are generally required by government regulators to support the fairness of public securities financings. Investors often look to appraisals in making investment decisions. Appraisals can be of particular importance to institutional investors when used to set values for financial reporting purposes. If outside investors want to redeem their interests, the appraisal will determine how much they receive as well as the value of the remaining interests.

An appraisal is an estimate of value as of a specific date based on the judgment of the expert who has prepared it. Most appraisals seek to determine the fair market value of the property. Other appraisals may define more specialized values. The results of the appraisal may be communicated in a letter opinion of value or a narrative report. The latter documents the results of the appraiser's research and shows how the conclusions were reached.

The three traditional appraisal methods are reproduction cost, market comparison, and income capitalization. Traditional theory holds that where possible, the appraiser should use all three methods. The final judgment of value is reached by correlation, a means of adjusting for differences between the different appraisal methods.

The purpose of an appraisal is to provide an indication of the market value of a specific property. The term "value" can assume many meanings. Indeed, appraisal theoreticians go to great lengths in tracing the origins of various concepts of value and in debating which definition of "value" is most appropriate. Though some traditionalists steadfastly insist that there is only one value for a particular property at any point in time, a more realistic view holds that a preferred concept is a range of values. Since so many factors influence values, the more modern viewpoint holds that it is better to consider the relevant range than a single figure.

It is appropriate to consider why all appraisers are not in unanimous agreement as to a value for a given income property. One reason is that the appraisal process, although using logical techniques, is an art that involves combining careful judgment with scientific methods. Reasonable professionals can and do disagree as to the interpretive and subjective aspects of the appraisal process.

The most widely used definition of "market value" or "fair market value" is that defined by the courts:

> [t]he highest price estimated in terms of money which a property will bring if exposed for sale in the open market allowing a reasonable time to find a purchaser who buys with knowledge of all the uses to which it is adapted and for which it is capable of being used.

Other definitions extend this by stipulating that (1) the seller must also have full knowledge of current and potential uses; (2) neither party be acting under duress; and (3) the seller receives all cash. Essentially, these various definitions seek to postulate a normal transaction free of special circumstances.

While these approaches to the definition of "value" indicate how it is derived, they do not precisely address what value is. Value is the present worth of future benefits to typical users and investors arising out of ownership. Thus, market value reflects the combined judgments of the marketplace as to the value today of benefits that will be realized in the future. Another way of expressing this point is to state that the purchaser of an income property is buying a stream of future benefits consisting of income over time plus the residual value of the property at the time the investment is terminated.

The value derivation process, although difficult and complex in application, is simple in concept. It consists of three steps:

1. The future economic benefits of the subject property are forecast.

2. A valuation method is selected to translate the predicted benefits in the future to a value today.

3. A capitalization rate (equivalent to the rate of return the investor seeks on his money) is selected to be used with the particular valuation method.

Different analysts and investors will have different expectations of the level and timing of the economic benefits that can be expected from a property. There are a number of different valuation methods and techniques from which the valuation analyst can choose. Different appraisers will interpret the market for capitalization rates differently. And it is a fact of investor behavior that expectations as to what a reasonable or satisfactory return is vary markedly. There is a wide range of actual investment performance and little agreement on a norm. All of these factors suggest that it is not at all surprising that there will be different values for the same property. Value, like beauty, is in the eye of the beholder.

Given the different value indicators that can result, it is helpful to know the basic assumptions behind these alternative outcomes. The more precisely one can evaluate a set of assumptions and compare them to those of another appraisal, the better the investment decision will be. In practice, however, traditional appraisal methods are often more implicit than explicit in their approach. Because the key assumptions are often hidden, rather than being out in the open, it is frequently difficult to evaluate the reasoning the appraiser used in reaching the ultimate valuation decision.

The cost approach requires the appraiser to estimate the cost of replacing the improvements on the subject property in terms of today's costs of building materials and supplies. The appropriate input for the land is derived by a market comparison process to determine what similar sites are selling for in that particular area. If the physical improvements suffer from obsolescence or depreciation, an appropriate downward adjustment is made to the cost estimate.

Although many early appraisal theoreticians, reasoning that no buyer would pay more than the cost of replacing a particular building, argued that the cost of replacement set the upper boundary on value, this viewpoint has essentially been rejected by the appraisal profession. On its face, the cost method is a contradiction of the basic objective of the development business: the creation of an asset whose value in the marketplace exceeds the cost of producing that asset. The importance of the entrepreneurial and creative functions is not readily susceptible to a cost estimate.

The market comparison approach to value involves identifying comparable properties and then expressing the value of the subject property in terms of those comparable properties. The appraiser makes adjustments for the characteristics that distinguish the subject property from the comparables properties. Some appraisers argue that where good comparables exist, this approach to the appraisal process is the most reliable. The difficulty with the market comparison method, however, is that it can be extremely hard to find good comparable properties for appraisal purposes. If such comparable properties are available, the question remains of the appropriate model to be used in the comparison process. Although several appraisal theoreticians have argued forcefully for the merits of the market comparison method, none has advanced an effective model that has consistently been used in practice. An effective model would require an accurate identification of the crucial variables that influence value backed up with sufficient data to be statistically reliable.

The income approach involves estimating the probable income that will be generated by the property and then translating this income stream into value by capitalization. Usually the income used is premised upon a free-and-clear basis with no debt. The appraiser divides the indicated income figure by the capitalization rate that is deemed appropriate for the particular circumstances at hand.

Because of the deficiencies noted in the other two traditional appraisal methods and the fact that the capitalization approach most closely approximates the manner in which investors evaluate investment property, many appraisers prefer to use the income approach. Where the purpose of the appraisal is related to an investment decision, the income approach is clearly the most appropriate. Indeed, the definition of "value" as the present worth of rights to the future benefits arising from ownership argues for use of the income approach.

A number of different approaches reflecting varying degrees of sophistication can be elected for income capitalization. One can choose to capitalize either the gross income or the net income. While traditional net income capitalization values the property on a free-and-clear basis, the several interests—mortgage and equity or land and building for example—can be valued separately. In certain situations, residual techniques are used to derive the values of particular interests. The capitalization rate used can assume income to perpetuity, or losses in the property's value over time can be reflected by various recapture methods.

Over the last decade, the income approach has increasingly been presented as a discounted present value analysis. Because the valuation analysis involves a forecast of the property's probable future performance over the full holding period and includes expected proceeds from sale of the property at the end of the holding period, it increasingly parallels investment analysis. The crucial difference is that the investment analyst works with a given purchase price, forecasts future performance, and calculates the return on investment, while the appraiser specifies the return on investment and calculates the indicated purchase price.

Despite the importance of a property's value to all involved in real estate investment activity, standardized "generally accepted valuation principles" are lacking. Part of this deficiency is attributable to the diversity of approaches to valuation and part is attributable to the fact that there has not been a consensus regarding need for such uniformity. It is clear, however, that the new institutional investors are increasingly demanding and that the appraiser's task is to improve disclosure while upgrading the quality of presently used techniques.

6.06 CORPORATE REAL ESTATE

[1] Strategic Priority

The rapid technological changes, international competition, changing product and market cycles, and greater scrutiny by investors, analysts, and regulators that have stimulated the restructuring of U.S. businesses have parallel real estate implications. While corporations, in their drive to maintain their competitive postures, strengthen balance sheets, and protect themselves against the prospects of hostile takeovers, have begun to reevaluate their strategies for using and managing real estate assets, this reevaluative process and its direct effect on shareholders' value has yet to be fully recognized.

Shortfalls in the management of corporate real estate assets have been highlighted by several studies. Corporations that have not yet begun to focus more closely on real estate assets are being forced to do so for a number of reasons, including the following:

- Real estate is a major component of the asset base and cost of operations of a business, constituting an average of 25 percent of all assets, as well as 10 percent of operating costs. This means that space use expense is second only to payroll. Corporate real estate can be a significant source of improved financial strength and shareholders' value, whether through cash from the sale of property or reduction in operating costs through restructured patterns of usage, lease renegotiation, or debt reduction.

- Financial Accounting Standard Board (FASB) Rules 13 and 33 show the trend toward the requirement for more accurate and complete reporting of the current value of real estate assets, changing the past practice of carrying property or capital leases on the books at original cost.

- Firms with undervalued assets, such as real estate or raw material reserves, are being targeted for corporate takeover. Chevron paid $13 billion for Gulf Oil, primarily for its vast oil reserves. However, the purchase price was reduced by $1.5 billion when Gulf Canada was resold to a group that was interested primarily in its real estate assets. It is in the company's and the shareholders' interest that these real estate assets not be raided and that productive and profitable use be achieved by the existing enterprise.

- Overbuilding in many markets and increased competition for tenants give corporations new opportunities to improve their control over the economics of occupying space through renegotiated lease or equity positions in buildings.

Corporate real estate has long suffered from a passive, facilities management approach. Real estate has received very little attention from most organizations. Consequently, a focus on real estate can offer the prospect of higher returns than could be achieved by many other managerial studies and analyses. Moreover, real estate is of such significance to the financial performance and value of a company that the tendency toward limited professionalism and lack of strategic commitment is no longer acceptable. Although, real estate decisions are simultaneously complex, specialized, and nonrecurring, all attributes that favor a managerial approach, most businesses lack the requisite economics of scale and power to achieve the systematization and specialization necessary for superior results. In many cases, deficiencies in real estate decisions are directly attributable not only to the nature and context of those decisions but also to management's disregard of the potential payoffs. Any corporation of substantial scale and continuity probably possesses several unrecognized opportunities to realize value from real estate.

How can management measure the effect of real estate policies on shareholders' value? Corporate executives must first understand how their companies' assets are valued in the real estate market. The tendency of corporate managers is to assume that the value of real estate is not earnings-driven. "Value" in real estate markets is commonly defined as the expectation of future cash flows and prospective capital gains. Earnings per share and other accounting ratios have significant limitations as measures of the impact on value of various business and real estate strategies compared with a cash flow approach.

Corporate real estate today is the focus of tremendous attention, in stark contrast to an historically indifferent attitude. Real estate professionals are devoting more attention to corporate real estate, and real estate investment banking is now a primary business line on Wall Street. Corporate management, however, still lags in viewing real estate issues in a strategic rather than a transaction context and in exploiting opportunities to unlock the value of real estate. This passivity regarding real estate decisions can leave a firm more vulnerable to a threat of hostile takeover.

Many takeover transactions and leveraged buyout (LBO) arrangements have been motivated by the perception that corporations control substantial real estate assets whose value is not sufficiently reflected in share prices. In an effort to unlock this hidden equity, the corporate finance function and the Wall Street investment banking community has used the value of corporate real estate to secure the capital to fund takeovers or to pay off debt assumed at the time of the LBO. Thus, corporate real estate is both the motive for and the means to finance LBO transactions.

Conventional accounting does a poor job of communicating the true story of the economics of corporate real property investment. Much of the value of corporate real estate is attributable to acquisitions made in past years, but in many markets appreciation and inflation have pushed current market values to much higher levels than original cost. Especially misleading is the depreciation entry that suggests a steady erosion of the value of corporate property, when in fact many such holdings have appreciated greatly or even dramatically.

The real estate values of corporations will, inexorably and unavoidably, be unlocked; the only question is by whom and for whose benefit. Corporations holding significant real estate that is undermanaged and/or whose value is underrecognized by the financial community are extremely vulnerable as takeover targets. Unfortunately, the very circumstances that create the potential for an extraordinary gain from unlocking corporate real estate values suggest that the present management may be an unlikely candidate first to identify the potential windfall and then to design and implement a strategy that preserves control for the management's continuing stewardship of the enterprise. Most corporations lack an appreciation of the significance of real estate to their business strategy, its financial impact on current performance, and its contribution to overall corporate value. The inherent custodial orientation to real estate results in a commodity attitude rather than a value-enhancing attitude. Instead, management needs to take a hard look at the corporation's real estate to determine how its values can best be identified and realized for current shareholders.

[2] Implications of Corporate Real Estate Mission

The particular corporate real estate mission pursued influences real estate financing strategies and decisions. Corporate real estate missions can range from a passive custodial approach to active service support to proactive strategic impact. Among the corporate real estate missions are the following:

- Supporting operations
- Cost control
- Promoting the marketing message (i.e., a visible advertising statement of certain values, such as Transamerica Corporation's pyramid building)
- Promoting sales objectives (i.e., emphasis on high traffic and/or prestige locations)
- Facilitating service delivery through an orientation to suppliers' and/or customers' convenience
- Capturing real estate value creation, by virtue of the enterprise's demand-generating activities that lead to real estate value creation

Various means can be used to implement these corporate real estate missions.

[3] Corporate Real Estate Opportunities

The environment in which real estate decisions are made is changing. In the early 1990s, many space markets are in disarray. The regulatory guidelines covering business have been realigned with changing tax regulations, financial reporting requirements, and related developments. In addition, the structure of the markets in which the real estate service firms operate is being realigned and is exerting parallel challenges and pressure on organizations that use real estate services. Nonetheless, certain trends in the real estate markets present significant opportunities for the successful and profitable restructuring of corporate real estate assets:

- Overbuilding in many geographic markets has increased competition for tenants, lowering rents and increasing the tenant's economic power. Anticipating further rent increases over the already high levels prevalent in the early 1980s and planning for expansion, many companies leased more space than they needed for their prevailing level of business. This resulted in lease expenses that are inflated beyond market levels and no assurance that the vacant space can be subleased to others. Consequently, owners have shown themselves willing to renegotiate lease terms, particularly with major tenants. This reduces the tenant's current expenses and usually minimizes rent increases at the expiration of the current lease.

• Corporate tenants are cultivating new relationships with development firms. In some cases, corporate tenants are facilitating the financing of new construction projects at a time when lenders are wary of speculative risks. The surfeit of commercial construction in recent years has been fueled by the availability of capital rather than by demand generated by space users, and developers and lenders have been forced to retreat from aggressive speculative building. Credit tenants are now able to negotiate favorable lease terms. These leases can then be used as collateral in securing financing either from traditional sources or through mortgage-backed securities. The rent in such cases is usually set by the level of the debt service. Since a lease with a strong tenant can lead to lower interest rates on the financing for the building, the tenant can control its cost of occupancy and, in many cases, participate in the property's appreciation through a share of the equity.

• Many firms have established subsidiaries to control and manage their real estate, while others are using the emerging master limited partnerships (MLPs) for the same purpose. While an MLP can consist of either shareholders in common or shareholders other than those of the corporation, management can still control the decisions as the general partner. By putting the tangible property into a single tax entity, which is traded on the basis of cash flow without the dilution of taxation that occurs in the corporate form, real estate value can be enhanced. In addition, since the structure of the business is more effectively positioned along the risk-reward spectrum, a higher multiple may be attached to the basic business of the company, as it is not dragged down by a drain resulting from its real estate investing activities.

• Certain office and production functions have moved closer to the homes of employees for cost savings and for labor supply reasons. Employers recognize the value of locating near a high-quality labor pool, both to secure a continuous supply of skills and to reduce employee turnover, which can cause significant business losses if new employees must be trained. Back office operations are relocating out of the central business districts, as firms compare the higher costs of central locations with the resulting contribution to revenues. In response to this trend, new office space has been built in suburban locations, where rents are lower.

[4] Multiple-Entity Financing

Traditionally, business organizations have operated as corporations and have financed their ongoing and expansion capital needs by issuing debt and equity securities and arranging loans secured either by the corporation's general credit or specific assets.

Corporate financing patterns involving multiple entities, particularly partnerships and trusts, are now providing new flexibility and new access to financial resources. Through multiple-entity financing, the corporation's shareholders hold interests in multiple securities, with the composition of the shareholders often varying among legal entities. Real estate financing is an ideal application for multiple-entity financing arrangements. Physical assets that are highly capital intensive can often be better financed off the corporation's balance sheet. Particularly in the instances of real property and major equipment, substantial gains in after-tax results and improved financial reporting can be achieved.

A particular attraction of multiple-entity financing arrangements is that they allow project-specific financing while the sponsoring management organization retains overall control of its enterprise. In direct participation financing, unlike traditional corporate financing, the investor participates in only one specific project or business and not in the balance of the sponsoring corporation's activities. The direct participation arrangement permits substantial expansion in one aspect of a business while the new entity remains separate and distinct—legally, financially, organizationally, and tax-wise—from the firm's other activities.

Various ownership forms may be used, and each has a unique combination of tax consequences, liability exposure, limits on investment activity, securities law disclosure requirements, transferability of interests, management relationships, and terms. Clearly, the participants' objectives and the particular business plan largely influence the choice of ownership form. Important characteristics to consider include the following:

- *Taxation status*. Is the entity eligible for single taxation, with the income tax results of the business flowing directly to the investors, or is there double taxation with taxes being paid twice, both by the entity and by the individual participants?

- *Investors' liability*. What is the amount of investor risk? Is it limited to the amount of the investment, or can the participant be liable for losses and claims in excess of the investment?

- *Management*. What restrictions are there on how management decisions are made? Can all investors participate? Can the decision making be centralized?

- *Transferability of interests*. Can participants freely transfer their interests? Are there restrictions on transferability?

- *Allowed activities*. Are there limitations on the types of activities in which the entity can engage?

While many considerations are involved in selecting the appropriate legal entity, the partnership form is preferred for investments with more aggressive objectives because it is the most flexible legal entity and consequently offers certain advantages in investment situations that feature active, rather than supervisory, management. Generally, the limited partnership form is used because it allows limited liability to the investor.

Employing syndication financing as a corporate financing vehicle is a more sophisticated variant of asset redeployment arrangements, in which a company sells a part of its interest in an enterprise while retaining an equity position and exerting effective control over the direction of that business. Such financing allows investors to participate specifically and directly in the fortunes of the particular business enterprise. Some investors find this concentrated arrangement more appealing than the inevitable dilution that occurs through the broad diversification of business activity that occurs when a mix of businesses is owned by many large corporations.

[5] Feasibility and Financing Plan

The following financing plan and feasibility analysis program is appropriate for corporations that wish to employ multiple-entity financing arrangements:

- Integration of the corporate financing strategy with the contemplated syndication financing program

- Determination of what business activity and/or specific assets should be devoted to a syndication program and over what time frame, with consideration to both present business activity and contemplated future business plans
- Economic analysis of the appeal of investment in this identified business activity and specific assets versus other forms of investment
- Formulation of financing structures that merit detailed consideration, with an emphasis on considering the following:
  —Appropriate legal form
  —Investment emphasis in terms of cash distribution versus capital appreciation
  —Tax orientation, including both front-end deductions and ordinary income versus capital gain considerations
  —Accounting consequences of alternative arrangements as well as the tax implications of a transaction to the corporation
  —Appropriateness of specialized arrangements involving disproportionate allocation of investment benefits
  —Desirability and degree of involvement of existing shareholders in ownership
  —Appropriate management relationships and controls
- Competitive analysis of other investment offerings, with a particular emphasis on offerings with parallels to the contemplated business syndication
- Detailed analysis of financing options in terms of the following:
  —Cost to capital, accounting, and tax consequences to the corporation
  —Competitiveness of investor return in contrast to competing investment opportunities and marketability of investment product
  —Compatibility with the corporation's financing strategy
  —Compatibility of syndication financing with operations of the basic business or businesses
- Formulation of a recommended program design and financial structure, in concert with securities and tax counsel, as well as economic analysis of the recommended program from the perspective of investors and the corporation
- Implementation guidelines for taking the proposed financing to market

In the implementation of multiple-entity financing arrangements, the following issues merit particular consideration:

- Ensuring a reasonable balance among fiduciary concerns of the multiple entities, whose objectives may be in conflict, by protecting against abuses associated with self-dealing and by verifying that equitable pricing and sharing arrangements are employed
- Complying with relevant securities regulatory requirements regarding disclosure, documentation, registration, distribution, and ongoing reporting
- Verifying that the legal form selected and the tax treatments elected are appropriate and consistent for the business in question and the corporation overall
- Recognizing that the money raised and financing coordination processes are inherently different for direct investment financing arrangements in that new channels and new requirements are involved

This program provides a managerial means to address the challenge to maximize the corporation's real estate involvements. By pursuing a logical approach to financing its real estate involvements, the corporation can enhance its communicaitons to the financial community, garner support for its securities, minimize its exposure to take-over initiatives motivated by the perception of undervalued real estate, and clearly provide a responsible answer to the "We're not in the real estate business" issue.

Suggested Reading

Anania, J.J., and D.S. Frankel. "Troubled Loan Restructurings: Workouts May Trigger Severe Tax Consequences." *Real Estate Accounting and Taxation* (Summer 1990), pp. 5–16.

Books, R.P. "Commercial Real Estate as a Capital Market." *Real Estate Finance,* Vol. 5 (Fall 1988), pp. 17–20.

Brueggemann, William B., and Jeffrey D. Fisher. *Real Estate Finance and Investment,* 9th ed. Homewood, Ill.: Richard D. Irwin, Inc., 1989.

Carter, J.R. "Understanding a Borrower's Strategic Thinking and Minimizing Lender Liability." *The Journal of Commercial Bank Lending,* Vol. 70 (February 1988), pp. 9–18.

Chrystie, Thomas L., and Frank J. Fabozzi, *Left Hand Financing—An Emerging Field of Corporate Finance.* Homewood, Ill.: Dow Jones-Irwin, 1983.

Clapp, J.M., and S.M. Miller, "Underwriting Income Property Mortgages." *National Association of Review Appraisers and Mortgage Underwriters* (Fall 1987), pp. 1–30.

Clauretie, Terence M., and James R. Webb, *The Theory and Practice of Real Estate Finance.* Fort Worth, Tex.: The Dryden Press, 1993.

Corgel, J.B., and G.D. Gay, "Local Economic Base, Geographic Diversification, and Risk Management of Mortgage Portfolios." *AREUEA Journal,* Vol. 15 (Fall 1980), pp. 256–267.

Crockett, J.H. "Workouts, Deep Pockets, and Fire Sales: An Analysis of Distressed Real Estate." *AREUEA Journal,* Vol. 18 (1990), pp. 76–90.

Downs, Anthony. "Banks and Real Estate: How to Resolve the Dilemma." Working Paper, The Urban Land Institute, 1991, pp. 1–33.

———. *The Revolution in Real Estate Finance.* Washington, D.C.: The Brookings Institution, 1985.

Friedman, J. "Return to Old Tyme Religion." *Real Estate Finance* (Summer 1992).

Graff, R.A., and J. Tung, "Default Risk and Required Return in the Commercial Mortgage Market." *Journal of Real Estate Research,* Vol. 7 (Winter 1991), pp. 13–31.

Grieves, R. "Tools for Tough Decisions: Which Loans Should You 'Workout'?" *Secondary Mortgage Markets,* Vol. 6 (Summer 1989), pp. 16–20.

Kau, James B., Donald C. Keenan, and Walter J. Muller, III. "Designing Commercial Mortgages and Their Mortgage-Backed Securities." Working Paper, University of Georgia, 1992, pp. 1–19.

Kau, J.B., D.C. Keenan, W.J. Muller, III, and J.F. Epperson, "The Valuation and Securitization of Commercial and Multifamily Mortgages." *Journal of Banking and Finance,* Vol. 11 (September 1987), pp. 525–546.

Maisel, Sherman J. *Real Estate Finance,* 2nd ed. Fort Worth, Tex.: The Dryden Press, 1992.

Marks, E.M. "Rating Process for Commercial Mortgage Debt Accelerates Securitization Trends in Real Estate." *Real Estate Finance Journal,* Vol. 2 (Fall 1986), pp. 22–29.

McCoy, B.H. "The New Financial Markets and Securitized Commercial Real Estate Financing." *Real Estate Issues,* Vol. 13 (Spring/Summer 1988), pp. 5–9.

McKinley, Conway, Laura Jones-Kelley, and Linda L. Liston, *Sight World—The Book of Corporate Global Strategies.* Atlanta: Conway Data, 1991.

Muldavin, S. ''New Approaches to Risk Analysis.'' *Real Estate Finance Journal,* Vol. 4 (Winter 1989), pp. 89–92.

Nourse, Hugh O. *Managerial Real Estate—Corporate Real Estate Asset Management.* Englewood Cliffs, N.J.: Prentice-Hall, Inc., 1990.

Phyrr, Stephen A., James R. Cooper, Mary E. Wofford, Stephen D. Kapplin, and Paul Lapidis, *Real Estate Investment Strategy, Analysis, Decisions,* 2nd ed. New York: John Wiley, Inc., 1989.

Ross, S.A., and R.C. Zisler, ''Risk and Return in Real Estate.'' *The Journal of Real Estate Finance and Economics,* Vol. 4 (June 1991), pp. 175–190.

Roulac, Stephen E. ''Dimensions of the Restructuring in Real Estate Capital Markets.'' *Real Estate Finance Journal* (Spring 1992), pp. 5–12.

———. ''The Evolution of Real Estate Decisions.'' *Appraisal, Market Analysis and Public Policy in Real Estate: Essays in Honor of James A. Graaskamp.* Kleimer Academic Publishers, 1993.

———. ''How to Value Real Estate Securities: Harder Than It Looks.'' *The Journal of Portfolio Management* (Spring 1988), pp. 35–39.

———. ''Implementing Due Diligence Priority.'' *National Real Estate Investor* (Nov. 1991), pp. 32, 34.

———. *Modern Real Estate Investment: An Institutional Approach.* San Francisco: Property Press, 1976.

———. ''Planning, Financing and Developing Pioneering Projects.'' *Urban Land* (Oct. 1984), pp. 7–11.

———. ''Profit From the Past: A Quarter Century Perspective on Evolving Real Estate Markets.'' *Urban Land* (May 1993).

Roulac, S.E., L. Lynford, and G. Castle, ''Real Estate Decision Making in an Information Era.'' *Real Estate Finance Journal* (Summer 1990).

Seldin, Maury Y., and James H. Boykin, eds. *The Real Estate Handbook,* 2nd ed. Homewood, Ill.: Dow Jones-Irwin, 1990.

Shilton, L.G. ''Commercial Mortgage Loans: Sleuthing the Loan-to-Value Ratio Mystery.'' *Real Estate Accounting and Taxation,* Vol. 5 (Winter 1991), pp. 40–47.

Sirmans, C.F., *Real Estate Finance,* 2nd ed. New York: McGraw-Hill, 1989.

M. Snyderman, ''Choosing Between Bonds and Mortgages.'' *Real Estate Review,* Vol. 21 (Spring 1991), pp. 55–64.

———. ''Commercial Mortgages: Default Occurrence and Estimated Yield Impact.'' *Journal of Portfolio Management,* Vol. 17 (Fall 1991), pp. 82–87.

Titman, S., and W. Torous, ''Valuing Commercial Mortgages: An Empirical Investigation of the Contingent-Claims Approach to Pricing Risky Debt.'' *The Journal of Finance,* Vol. 44 (June 1990), pp. 345–373.

Vandell, Kerry D., Walter Barnes, David Hartzell, Dennis Kraft, and William Wendt, ''Commercial Mortgage Defaults: Proportional Hazards Estimation Using Disaggregate Pooled Data.'' Working Paper, University of Wisconsin—Madison, pp. 1–38.

Chapter 7

Bankruptcy, Liquidation, and Reorganization

MICHELLE J. WHITE

7.01 INTRODUCTION

A central tenet in economics is that competition drives markets toward a state of long-term equilibrium in which surviving firms produce at minimum average costs. In the process of transition to long-term equilibrium, inefficient firms, firms using obsolete technologies and those producing products that are in excess supply are eliminated. Consumers benefit because, in the long run, goods and services are produced and sold at the lowest possible price. The mechanism through which inefficient firms leave the market is frequently bankruptcy, the legal process applied to firms unable to pay their debts. In 1991, 87,500 businesses filed for bankruptcy. Over half of them filed to liquidate in bankruptcy, and the rest filed to reorganize in bankruptcy. The total liabilities of firms that filed for bankruptcy in 1991 came to $111 billion, up from $59 billion the previous year.

Economic theory suggests that bankruptcy should serve as a screening device to eliminate only firms that are economically inefficient and whose resources could be better used in some other activity. However, a number of problems make it difficult to design a bankruptcy law that serves as an efficient screening device. One problem is that firms that are insolvent may still be economically efficient, in the sense that the value of their assets is greatest in their current use. But insolvent firms cannot pay all their debts, and so particular creditors have an incentive to insure that their claims are repaid by levying on assets of the firm in a way that disrupts its operation and reduces its going-concern value. An important historical example of this was the threat by creditors of failing U.S. railroads to take possession of rails and ties, even though the rails and ties were more valuable in place than removed and sold piecemeal.[1] More generally, as in a bank run, creditors of a failing firm have an incentive to race to be first to sue the firm, since they are paid in full in the order in which they win their suits. Thus, the creditor that hesitates and sues late is likely not to be paid at all, since the firm's assets will have been exhausted in paying creditors that sued earlier. The problem of premature shutdown of failing firms and loss of going-concern value is an issue in U.K. bankruptcy (insolvency) law. In the United States, this problem has largely been eliminated by giving managers of failing firms the right to file for bankruptcy and, within limits, the choice of when to do so. Filing for bankruptcy invokes a collective procedure that settles all creditors' claims simultaneously. This reduces the incentive for creditors to race to be first to sue failing firms. But it introduces a countervailing problem, that of excessive delay in filing for bankruptcy, which often benefits managers and shareholders of failing firms but harms creditors and wastes assets by delaying the shutdown of insolvent firms that are inefficient. Thus, in structuring bankruptcy laws, there is a difficult trade-off between protecting creditors at the cost of shutting down firms that may be economically efficient and protecting the going-concern value of failing firms, sometimes at the cost of wastefully delaying an inevitable shutdown.

While firms usually exit from markets by way of the bankruptcy route, there is no necessary connection between bankruptcies and firms that are economically inefficient. Firms end up in bankruptcy normally because they cannot meet financial obligations that are currently due. This usually means that the value of their liabilities is equal to or greater than that of their assets, since otherwise they could borrow to pay current obligations. But a firm developing a new product might be unable to pay its

---

[1] See Baird and Jackson (1985), pp. 20–30, for discussion of the historical development of bankruptcy law.

196

bills and unable to borrow, even though its new product would be extremely profitable if the development process were completed. On the other hand, some firms should shut down from an economic efficiency standpoint, even though they are not losing money. For example, last year's Mexican restaurant might be breaking even but is nonetheless inefficient since its assets could be used more profitably if they were converted to this year's food fad, the Creole restaurant. In this case, the owners of the Mexican restaurant have an incentive to shut it down, since they should be able to earn more by selling or leasing their assets to a Creole restaurant operator.

There is also no necessary connection between business shutdowns and bankruptcies. For example, if a parent firm shuts down its factory in the North but opens a factory in the South, where costs are lower, the shutdown is unlikely to involve a bankruptcy, since the parent firm will meet all of the obligations of the Northern factory. But suppose the parent is a conglomerate that owns an unprofitable subsidiary that is separately incorporated. Then the parent firm has an incentive to use the bankruptcy process in order to avoid paying the subsidiary's debts. This strategy, however, will not work if the parent firm has guaranteed the subsidiary's debts.

Once a firm files for bankruptcy, there are two alternative procedures. The first is bankruptcy liquidation, under which the firm is shut down, its assets sold, and the proceeds distributed to creditors according to a predetermined procedure. The second is bankruptcy reorganization, under which the firm continues to operate after the bankruptcy filing and an agreement is made to compensate creditors partially for their claims. Reorganization in bankruptcy is a curious procedure from an economic standpoint, since it has the effect of prolonging the operation of firms that are financially shaky and likely, but not certain, to be economically inefficient as well. The two bankruptcy procedures are discussed in the following sections. The discussion of legal procedures and the economic issues they raise is followed by a discussion of bankruptcy trends for the United States and the treatment of creditors in bankruptcy. The final section deals with current policy issues and proposed reforms of bankruptcy procedures.

7.02 LIQUIDATION

As a previously profitable firm slides further and further into financial distress, its managers would normally consider first whether to file to reorganize in bankruptcy or to remain out of bankruptcy. They would probably not consider filing for bankruptcy liquidation unless the firm had already exhausted all other possibilities. However, liquidation is the basic bankruptcy procedure. Even for firms that file to reorganize rather than liquidate in bankruptcy, the liquidation procedure sets the framework for bargaining over a reorganization plan. Therefore, liquidation is considered first.

When a firm files either to liquidate or to reorganize in bankruptcy, a collective legal procedure is initiated by which all claims against the firm are settled. As part of the procedure, individual creditors are prevented (stayed) from initiating or continuing with lawsuits against the debtor. Thus, bankruptcy law is substituted for the normal commercial and tax law that governs firms outside of bankruptcy. Without a collective procedure, individual creditors would engage in a costly and unproductive race to be first to sue the firm for repayment of their own claims. Creditors that sued first would receive payment in full until the firm's assets were exhausted, after which other creditors would receive nothing. Resources would be consumed both by creditors' duplicative monitoring expenses and by the costs of the lawsuits themselves. The effect of bankruptcy is to eliminate the benefit of being first, since all claims against the firm are settled simultaneously and all creditors having the same type of claim against the firm receive the same payoff. Even under bankruptcy, there is still an incentive for creditors to race to sue the firm first, but the incentive is muted, since any appreciable volume of suits will cause the firm's manager to enter bankruptcy.

[1] Law of Bankruptcy Liquidation

When the liquidation procedure under chapter 7 of the U.S. Bankruptcy Code (Code) is initiated, the bankruptcy court appoints a trustee who shuts down the firm, makes a search for its assets and either sells or abandons them, and turns the proceeds over to the court for payment to creditors. The firm receives a discharge from its liabilities. (Since corporations have limited liability, the discharge aspect of bankruptcy is much less important for them than for unincorporated firms.) There are no creditors' committees appointed in liquidations. Creditors do not get actual ownership of the firm, as is often assumed. Instead, they get the proceeds from selling the firm's assets.

  [a] Voluntary Versus Involuntary Bankruptcy. Firms may enter bankruptcy either voluntarily or involuntarily. Voluntary bankruptcies occur when the manager of the firm files for bankruptcy, while involuntary bankruptcies occur when creditors force the firm into bankruptcy. Involuntary bankruptcies, which require that three or more creditors of a firm petition the Bankruptcy Court to initiate proceedings, are quite rare in the United States.[2] This may be because creditors that initiate involuntary bankruptcy proceedings that later turn out to be unjustified are liable for damages to the firm. More likely, it is because an individual creditor that forces a firm into bankruptcy mainly benefits other creditors, since it initiates the collective procedure that settles all their claims. Many creditors can do better for themselves by bargaining individually with the firm's managers for better treatment of their claims in return for not initiating bankruptcy. This means that managers generally choose when to file for bankruptcy, although they may do it one step ahead of creditors that have chosen to sue the firm for repayment (perhaps because they were unable to negotiate successfully with managers).

  [b] APR. Once the firm's assets are found and liquidated, the bankruptcy priority rule determines in what order individual creditors are paid and how much each receives. The priority rule in bankruptcy liquidations is called the absolute priority rule (APR). The APR specifies that claims are paid in full in a particular order: first, administrative expenses of the bankruptcy process itself, including court costs, attorney fees, the trustee's expenses, and any loans incurred by the firm after the bankruptcy filing (with the court's permission); second, claims taking priority by statute, including tax claims,[3] rent claims, consumer deposits, and unpaid wages and benefits that accrued

---

  [2] The three creditors must hold at least $5,000 each in claims. If the firm has 12 or fewer creditors, only 1 creditor holding $5,000 or more in claims is necessary.

  [3] Tax claims include payroll taxes, property taxes, and sales taxes. Some tax claims, such as income or payroll taxes withheld from employees' pay, legally belong to the government even while in the possession of the firm and are not dischargeable in bankruptcy. Managers face criminal penalties if these taxes are not paid in full.

before the bankruptcy filing (wages and benefits are each subject to a $2,000 limit); and third, unsecured (or general) creditors' claims, including those of trade creditors, utility company creditors, and holders of damage claims against the firm (such as claims by users injured by the firm's defective products or claims against the firm for breach of contract),[4] claims for wages and benefits beyond the $2,000 limits, and claims of long-term bondholders. Unsecured creditors' claims rank equally in priority, unless there are subordination agreements between particular creditors and the firm specifying priority orderings within the class. Such agreements sometimes occur in long-term bond contracts (subordinated debentures), which might specify that the bondholders' claims rank below the claims of other unsecured creditors. These agreements are followed in bankruptcy by the creation of subclasses within the class of unsecured creditors. Finally, equity holders come last.

Debt claims are for the face value of the amount owed plus interest accrued before the bankruptcy filing. Accrual of interest stops at the time of the bankruptcy filing. This means that some debt holders may benefit from firms filing for bankruptcy, if their claims had market value below face value owing to interest rate increases since the loans were made.

The APR provides for secured creditors to be outside of the priority ordering. Secured creditors are those that have bargained with the firm for the right to claim a particular asset (or its value) if the firm liquidates in bankruptcy. The asset might be a piece of machinery, such as a computer, or could take the form of a general lien on the firm's inventory and accounts receivable. In the latter case, when the firm sells finished goods from inventory, the lien floats from the inventory to the accounts receivable and from there to the new inventory of unfinished inputs purchased by the firm. Liens must be recorded in public records, a process referred to as perfecting the lien. In bankruptcy liquidations, secured creditors are allowed to claim their lien assets directly if the value of the asset is less than the amount of the claim. In these cases, the remainder becomes an unsecured claim. If the value of the asset exceeds the claim, the trustee sells the asset and pays the secured claim from the proceeds, retaining the remainder. In this case, the secured creditor is entitled to interest after the bankruptcy filing. When a firm has a mixture of secured and unsecured claims against it, secured creditors may receive a payoff in bankruptcy even when all other creditors receive nothing.

[c] **Administration of Liquidation Cases.** Trustees in a bankruptcy liquidation have the responsibility to act on behalf of the unsecured creditors. They locate and evaluate any assets of the firm not subject to secured creditors' liens and decide whether to take possession of and liquidate or to abandon each of the assets. The trustee is also empowered to examine all transactions of the firm for six months prior to the bankruptcy filing and to challenge any that are fraudulent or that benefited insiders at creditors' expense. This is known as the avoiding power of the trustee. Trustees also have the power to examine secured creditors' liens and challenge any that are not properly recorded. If successful, this benefits unsecured creditors by increasing the amount available for distribution to them.

---

[4] Pennzoil's claim against Texaco and claims by victims of asbestos disease against the Johns Manville Company fit into this category. Also included are the claims of state governments against toxic waste–dumping firms that attempt to elude state clean-up orders by liquidating in bankruptcy and abandoning their dump sites.

Trustee's fees and expenses must be covered by the proceeds of assets liquidated; no funds are provided by the court. Trustees receive a fee equal to a declining proportion of the value of the assets they liquidate.[5] Under this system, trustees have an incentive to spend time and incur expenses in searching for assets only to the point where the extra expenditure of time brings in enough extra assets so that the fee as a proportion of the value of the extra assets compensates trustees for their time. If the fee is a low proportion of assets, trustees have little incentive to spend time on search. But more effort by trustees in general could generate a higher payoff to unsecured creditors in liquidation cases, which in turn would increase the expected return to future creditors of similarly situated firms. Thus, a system that encourages too little search by trustees raises borrowing costs for firms in general. Trustees also sometimes hire themselves as the attorneys representing creditors in suits to avoid prebankruptcy transactions by the firm. This increases the trustee's compensation but leads to the filing of many fruitless lawsuits, which delays completion of the bankruptcy process and payment of creditors.

Abuses of the trustee system were common before adoption of the new Code. Since bankruptcy judges both appointed trustees and decided disputes to which the trustees were parties, opportunities for conflicts of interest were common. This led to the administrative reforms of the new Code, one of which transferred the power to appoint and supervise trustees to a new office of the U.S. Trustee, which is separate from the bankruptcy court. This reform had the effect of limiting bankruptcy judges to deciding disputes. Also, the status of bankruptcy judges was upgraded.

[2] Economic Efficiency Considerations of the Liquidation Process

Economic efficiency issues relating to bankruptcy have been analyzed using two different approaches. One is the collective negotiations approach, proposed by Posner (1972) and used extensively by Jackson (1986), in which bankruptcy law provisions are analyzed by considering whether in a hypothetical meeting of all the firm's creditors and equity holders particular provisions of bankruptcy law would have been adopted unanimously. The second approach is the coalition behavior approach, first proposed by Bulow and Shoven (1978) and developed by White (1980) and Gertner and Scharfstein (1991), which involves assuming that the firm is run by a coalition of managers, who represent the interests of equity, and a subset of creditors. The two approaches are considered separately.

[a] **Collective Negotiations Approach.** The collective negotiations approach involves determining what agreement the firm's creditors and equity holders would have negotiated concerning procedures to be followed in the event of bankruptcy had they all gotten together to reach such an agreement before entering into their own transactions with the firm. (Such an agreement could never actually have taken place, both because it would be too costly and because the identity of the firm's creditors and shareholders can change frequently and is unknown in advance.) It is assumed that if all parties having a stake in the firm were at such a meeting, no procedure would be adopted if it benefited one party at the expense of another, unless the harmed

---

[5] The compensation schedule for trustees under the Code is 15 percent of the first $1,000 of liquidated assets and 6 percent of the next $2,000; it thereafter declines in successive steps to 3 percent, 2 percent and 1 percent of additional amounts liquidated.

party was compensated. Since this is the definition of economic efficiency (Pareto efficiency), bankruptcy procedures that followed the terms of this theoretical agreement would be economically efficient.

It would be in the joint interest of all parties having a stake in the firm to maximize the value of the firm, defined as the value of debt plus equity, or equivalently as the present value of the firm's future revenues minus all costs other than the costs of debt service. Transactions costs, defined as the costs of making and enforcing agreements, are important components of costs. It is in the interests of all parties to reduce but not minimize transactions costs, since this increases the value of the firm. If creditors and equity holders are risk averse, it is also in their joint interest to reduce the variance of revenues minus costs.

Transactions costs occur both before and after the bankruptcy filing. After the filing, they include the administrative costs of bankruptcy: court costs, attorney and other professionals' fees incurred by both the debtor and creditors, and costs of the court-appointed trustee who sells the debtor's assets. Before the bankruptcy, transactions costs include the costs of making agreements with the firm and the costs to creditors of monitoring the debtor's behavior to insure that the agreements are not breached. It is in the joint interest of creditors and equity holders to reduce these costs, since they reduce the value of assets available to meet creditors' claims. (Creditors' transactions costs are paid by creditors themselves, while in bankruptcy the debtor's transactions costs are also paid by creditors.) However, creditors do not want to minimize the transactions costs, since unmonitored managers might make economically inefficient decisions that benefit equity holders at the creditors' expense.

Adopting a collective bankruptcy procedure is in the joint interest of all creditors for several reasons. First, as indicated previously, without a bankruptcy procedure, individual creditors have an incentive to race to be first to sue the firm for repayment of their debts, and this can lead to premature liquidation of the firm and losses to all but the first creditor. This is a form of the well-known prisoner's dilemma. (See Webb (1987).) To illustrate, suppose a firm has two creditors, C and D. Each is owed $100 in principal next period and $10 in interest immediately. The firm is in financial difficulty and must either borrow the $20 to make the interest payments or default on the loans. If the firm's assets were liquidated immediately, it is assumed that they would be worth $110. If the firm continued to operate, it would have a 50 percent chance of earning $250 next period and a 50 percent chance of earning $50 next period, for an expected value of $150. From an economic efficiency standpoint, it is better for the firm to continue operating, since its expected value as a going concern ($150) exceeds the liquidated value of its assets ($110). It is also in the joint interest of the two creditors for it to continue. But individually, each creditor has an incentive to sue the firm for immediate repayment. Suppose the first creditor to sue (actually the first to succeed in its suit) is C. C's suit forces the firm to sell off its assets to pay C's claims. C therefore receives $110, or full repayment. D receives nothing. But if the firm had continued to operate, both C and D would have received $75 (in expected value) the next period. Thus, liquidation of the firm causes C to gain $35 at the cost of a loss to D of $75. Since the incentive to sue the firm applies to both creditors, in the absence of an agreement, both would be expected to sue the firm, with the result that the firm liquidates immediately. But this is inefficient. It would be in creditors' joint interest for them to agree on a collective procedure, such as bankruptcy. The bankruptcy procedure would settle all claims simultaneously, so as to eliminate the race to be first, and would shut down the firm or sell it as a going concern, depending on which alternative has the highest value.

Thus, creditors generally would agree that bankruptcy should be a collective procedure that settles the claims of all creditors at once. However, creditors would probably want to permit bankruptcy filings to be either voluntary, initiated by the firm's managers, or involuntary, initiated by creditors. Involuntary bankruptcy filings are in the interests of creditors generally, since they force the firm into bankruptcy as soon as any creditor has determined that the firm is failing. This benefits all creditors by preventing managers from delaying the firm's bankruptcy filing and wasting its assets in the process. European countries encourage involuntary bankruptcy filings by creditors, but such involuntary filings are rare in the United States.

The basic shift under bankruptcy law from paying creditors in full in the order in which they pursue their claims to one in which creditors' claims are settled simultaneously is also a sensible procedure from the viewpoint of reducing transactions costs. This is because the race to be first gives all creditors an incentive to monitor the firm's financial situation closely, to make sure that they acquire adverse information early and act on it. But duplicative monitoring by creditors and multiple lawsuits are expensive. These transactions costs are reduced under the bankruptcy procedure.

The collective bankruptcy procedure also has the effect of protecting the interests of creditors that make long-term rather than short-term loans to the debtor. Long-term loans are riskier than short-term loans because there is more time for adverse events to occur. Also, since long-term loans are not renegotiated and rolled over frequently, long-term creditors do not have access to the same up-to-date information concerning the firm's financial status as do short-term creditors. Therefore, if the debtor's situation becomes precarious, short-term creditors such as banks can demand immediate payment of their outstanding balances and can immediately sue the debtor if payment is not forthcoming. Thus, long-term creditors are at a disadvantage relative to short-term creditors outside of bankruptcy. In bankruptcy, however, the long-term creditor is protected, since the effect of the bankruptcy filing is to accelerate all debts, present and future, to the present and settle them all at the same time. This puts long-term and short-term unsecured creditors on equal footing. It also benefits the firm and equity holders by making creditors more willing to lend on a long-term basis.

Transactions cost considerations can also explain some aspects of the APR, which determines the order by which individual creditors' claims are paid in bankruptcy. In the example just discussed, creditors C and D were assumed to have equal priority in bankruptcy. However, the APR allows some creditors' claims to be paid before others' in bankruptcy. For example, suppose a firm borrows from many different creditors and incurs and pays off some loans each period. If it is assumed the value of the firm's assets remains constant, then if all loans took equal priority, each time the firm incurred a new loan the value of all its existing loans would be lowered. This is because if the firm filed for bankruptcy, its assets after liquidation would be divided proportionately among a higher number of claims. Conversely, each time the firm paid off an old loan, existing claims would increase in value. This implies that creditors would want to adjust the interest rate they charged on their loans each time their claims changed in value because the firm incurred or paid off a loan. Thus, all creditors would have an incentive to monitor the firm's financial condition in order to adjust the interest charged on their loans.

Alternatively, some loans take higher priority than others. For example, the firm might offer C highest priority in bankruptcy in return for a lower interest rate on C's loan. In this case, C's claim would not change in value as the firm incurs and pays off other loans, as long as the value of the firm's assets in bankruptcy exceeds the amount of C's claim, since all other loans would only be paid in bankruptcy after C's claim had been repaid in full. As a result, C would not have an incentive to monitor the firm's financial condition, and transactions costs would be saved. Giving highest priority to C's claim would make other loans to the firm more risky. But concentrating risk and monitoring costs on a few claims instead of spreading this risk across all claims can reduce total monitoring costs, particularly if some creditors specialize in low-priority loans and if expertise in monitoring is subject to economies of scale. Also, if the firm had both high-priority and low-priority claims, some risk-averse lenders might be willing to lend to the firm on a high-priority basis that would not be willing to lend at all under an equal-priority regime.

Finance models usually assume that creditors in a bankruptcy proceeding are paid in order of the well-known me-first rule associated with Fama and Miller (1972). Here, the claims of creditors are assumed to be ranked in order chronologically, with creditors that made earlier loans to the firm taking priority over creditors that made later loans to the firm. In the example just discussed, C would have priority over other creditors under the me-first rule if C made the earliest still-outstanding loan to the firm. The me-first rule is attractive from the viewpoint of reducing monitoring costs, since, in a dynamic setting, it frees creditors from the need to monitor loans to the firm made subsequent to their own loans. For example, D's loan, made just after C's, will rank below C's claim and those of any earlier creditors. The value of D's loan depends on all of the loans to the firm made earlier, but it is fairly easy for D to determine and evaluate the earlier loans at the time D makes its loan to the firm. Loans made after D's rank below it, so these later loans do not affect D's priority and thus do not affect the value of D's claim. This means that D needs to monitor the firm only at the time D's loan is made and not afterwards. If, instead, all creditors had equal priority, D would have an incentive to monitor the firm continually, which would be much more expensive. However, even under the me-first rule, D still has an incentive to continue monitoring the firm if the value of its assets varies over time, since the firm's liquidation value might decline so much that D is not repaid in full in bankruptcy even with me-first priority relative to later loans. (This consideration is discussed in the next section.)

Secured loans can also be viewed in the collective negotiations framework as a means of reducing monitoring and transactions costs. Suppose creditor E lends a firm the amount needed to buy a computer and receives a security interest in the computer. If the firm defaults on the loan, E has the right to reclaim the computer immediately. This reduces E's monitoring cost because only the computer, not the firm's entire operation, needs to be monitored. As a result, E may be willing to lend to the firm on a longer-term basis or at a lower interest rate than it would otherwise. The secured loan has transactions costs that are initially high, since a more complicated agreement must be negotiated between the firm and the creditor and because the lien must be registered. But transactions costs are low thereafter. Also, if all creditors were secured, no new lender could take a lien on an asset already subject to a lien (unless the new lien were subordinate to the old). This would make it impossible for later lenders to improve their position in the priority ordering at the expense of earlier creditors in bankruptcy.

However, when the firm has a mixture of secured and unsecured loans outstanding, the existence of secured loans makes unsecured loans more risky, since assets subject to liens are not available for payment to unsecured creditors if the firm files for bankruptcy. Also, secured loans can be used to circumvent the me-first rule. In a different example, suppose creditor F lends money to a firm on an unsecured basis but has me-first priority as the firm's earliest lender. The money is used to purchase inventory.

Later, creditor G lends to the firm on condition that G receive a "floating" security interest in the firm's inventory and accounts receivable, which are assumed to be its only assets. Then if the firm files for bankruptcy, G will receive the inventory and accounts receivable (if these are worth less than G's claim) and F will receive nothing, despite F's me-first priority. This undermines the advantage of the me-first priority rule, since it forces F to monitor the firm's behavior vis-à-vis its subsequent creditors.

It might be argued that unsecured creditors anticipate this and will either demand to be secured themselves or lend on an unsecured basis but raise the interest rate they charge to compensate for the added risk. While unsecured lenders may demand higher interest rates to cover extra risk, once their loans are made, the higher interest rate becomes merely a negative income effect to the firm. Afterwards, managers have an incentive to arrange new loans to the firm that rank high in the priority ordering, since the new loans will carry a lower interest rate owing to their high priority.

These examples illustrate that, in general, there is a tension between the ex ante collective incentive of creditors and equity holders to adopt a rule that insulates prior creditors' claims from changes in value when the firm incurs subsequent claims and the ex post incentive of managers and equity holders to make arrangements with later creditors that protect them at the cost of reducing the value of earlier creditors' claims. The benefit to managers of doing so is that later creditors will be willing to lend to the firm on more favorable terms, since their loans are less risky.

Viewed in this light, it is not surprising that only the largest firms have unsecured long-term debt (subordinated debentures). Unsecured claims in general have the least protection from reductions in the value of the firm, and long-term claims are more risky than short-term claims, since short-term debt must frequently be rolled over, giving the short-term creditor frequent opportunities to change the terms of its loans as the firm's financial condition changes. Lenders are willing to lend on a long-term unsecured basis to very large firms, both because their large size makes them less risky and because they are less costly to monitor, since, if they are publicly held, they must make public disclosures concerning their financial status in reports to shareholders and filings with the Securities and Exchange Commission. Other types of unsecured claims, such as trade creditors' claims, are usually too small or too short term to make bargaining for a secured interest worthwhile, or they are involuntarily unsecured, as with damage claims or claims for unpaid taxes.

In addition to conversion of loans from unsecured to secured status, there are many other ways in which unsecured creditors can improve their positions in the priority ordering. One involves the practice of setoff. Here, at the time of the bankruptcy filing, a bank having an unsecured loan outstanding can claim the firm's account balance with the bank in partial payment of the loan. This allows the bank to be paid before other unsecured and statutory creditors. Another involves one firm's buying another as a subsidiary and guaranteeing its loans. This in effect allows the subsidiary's creditors to jump ahead of the parent's in the priority ordering. A third possibility is that an unsecured creditor might force the firm to file for bankruptcy as a condition of the creditor's renewing its loan. Then the new loan is considered an administrative expense of the bankruptcy proceeding (regardless of whether the firm later liquidates or reorganizes) and is placed in the highest-priority class.

[b] Coalition Behavior Approach. The major economic issue raised by the existence of bankruptcy is whether firms have an incentive to choose bankruptcy when doing so would be economically efficient and not otherwise. This question in turn focuses attention on the incentives of firms' managers, who are assumed to make the decision to file for bankruptcy, under different bankruptcy priority rules. Since bankruptcy implies that all creditors cannot be paid in full, the bankruptcy priority rule is central to the inquiry because it determines who gets what.

Consider three possible priority rules: the me-first rule, the last-lender-first rule, and the equal-priority rule. Under the me-first rule, all creditors of the firm are assumed to be unsecured (and no claims have statutory priority). Creditors are ranked in order of the date on which they made their loans to the firm, with the earliest claims ranking highest. In bankruptcy, the proceeds of liquidating the firm's assets are used to pay off claims in full in order of their ranking. If anything remains, it goes to equity holders, which would otherwise receive nothing. The last-lender-first rule is identical to the me-first rule except that creditors are ranked in reverse chronological order. Thus, the most recent lender ranks first and the earliest lender ranks last. Finally, under the equal-priority rule, all creditors have the same ranking in bankruptcy and are paid the same fraction of the face value of their claims.

The APR contains some elements of all three of these rules. The me-first rule is followed among long-term bondholders if the firm has several bond issues outstanding and later bond issues are subordinated to earlier issues. The equal-priority rule applies to unsecured creditors not covered by subordination agreements. The last-lender-first rule frequently prevails among groups of creditors, because creditors that make late loans to the firm bargain for high priority or secured status. They then may be paid in bankruptcy, while unsecured creditors that made their loans to the firm earlier receive nothing.

To analyze the effects of these priority rules on economic efficiency, it is useful to examine a coalition model of how the decision to declare bankruptcy is made and under what circumstances. Assume either that managers, representing equity, make decisions so as to maximize the value of equity or that decisions are made by a coalition of equity holders and a lender referred to as the bank. The coalition assumption is used when a firm is failing, i.e., when the firm has insufficient assets to pay obligations that are due in the current period. To avoid bankruptcy, the firm must obtain new financing that is assumed to take the form of a loan from a bank. In this case, the decision concerning whether the firm files for bankruptcy is made to maximize the total value of the coalition's holdings. The bank is a short-term lender that monitors the firm's behavior closely and has bargaining power since it is willing under some circumstances to make new loans to the firm. For simplicity, the bank is assumed to have no prior loans outstanding to the firm. Other creditors, referred to here as debt, do not have such bargaining power and are unwilling to make new loans to the firm.

The failing firm's bankruptcy decision is made in the first period of a two-period model. The firm has $100 of outstanding debt due in period 1 and $200 of outstanding debt due in period 2. If it filed for bankruptcy and liquidated in period 1, its assets (sold piecemeal) would be worth $250 after subtracting the transactions costs of liquidating. Its value would be less than the sum of its liabilities, so equity holders would receive nothing. Alternatively, the firm might continue operating outside of bankruptcy for another period. Since it is assumed to have no cash on hand, in order to avoid bankruptcy in period 1 it must obtain a new loan equal to the debt owed in period 1, which is $100. (Interest and discount rates are assumed to be zero for simplicity.) The new loan must come from the bank. Since the coalition chooses whichever alternative maximizes the total value of equity plus the bank's claim, the equity holders would be willing to give the bank up to the entire value of equity in order to induce it to make a new loan, so that the firm can avoid bankruptcy in the first period. Equity holders would be willing to do this, since equity would be wiped out if the firm filed for bankruptcy in period 1.

The bankruptcy decision when the firm's future earnings are certain. First, the coalition model is applied to a case where a firm must decide whether to continue operating or file for bankruptcy and its future earnings are assumed to be known with certainty (perhaps because it is in a mature industry with stable earnings). If the firm gets a loan and continues operating, its earnings in period 2 after nondebt expenses will be E. From an economic efficiency viewpoint, it is efficient for the firm to continue operating if E is greater than $250, the amount that would have been received by liquidating the firm's assets in period 1, and to file for bankruptcy if E is less than $250.

The coalition's decision is affected by each of the three priority rules. Under the me-first rule, if the coalition chooses bankruptcy in period 1, it will receive nothing. If the coalition chooses continuation, it will receive $E,$ but it must pay off both the $200 debt owed in period 2 and the $100 loan taken out in period 1. Thus, the coalition will choose continuation if E exceeds $300 (which also exceeds the $250 required for economic efficiency). Therefore, continuation will only be chosen when future earnings exceed the firm's liquidation value, that is, if continuation is economically efficient. However, suppose E is less than $300. In this situation, both liquidation and continuation lose money, so the bank refuses to make the loan that allows the business to continue to period 2. Nevertheless, either alternative might be more economically efficient, since if E is less than $300 but greater than $250, a loan would allow the business to lose less money than if it liquidated immediately. Thus, when both alternatives lose money but continuation loses less, debt holders would be better off by the difference between E and $250 if continuation were chosen.

Under the me-first rule, therefore, the coalition chooses continuation only when that alternative is economically efficient, but it may sometimes choose to liquidate even when continuation is more efficient. For this reason, some firms end up in bankruptcy when they should continue to operate from an economic efficiency standpoint. This occurs because whenever the coalition chooses continuation, it must share the efficiency gain with debt holders (the inframarginal creditors) by paying them in full. The coalition only chooses continuation when the efficiency gain is great enough to pay debt holders their share and still have something left over.

Under the rule of last-lender-first, the coalition's return under liquidation is the same as in the previous example. The coalition's net return under continuation remains equal to E minus 300, if this amount is positive. In this situation, continuation is economically efficient and is preferred by the coalition, since it is profitable. Suppose, however, that E is between the amount owed in period 1, $100, and the total amount owed, $300. Then the coalition's net return is 0, since the bank must be paid first in full and there is nothing left for equity after the debt due in period 2 is paid. In this case, the coalition is indifferent regarding the 2 alternatives and has no incentive to make the choice that would pay more to debt holders. But while the coalition is indifferent, economic efficiency would require that it choose the more efficient alternative, which is continuation if E exceeds $250 and liquidation if not.

Finally, under the equal-priority rule the repayment of the bank loan is neither first nor last. Therefore, if continuation is chosen, the return to the coalition will fall between the returns under the other two rules. Thus, the coalition also has an incentive under this rule to choose continuation only when it is efficient, but sometimes it will choose liquidation when continuation is more efficient.

In this simple case, all three bankruptcy priority rules have similar results. All have a one-sided efficiency property in that they give the coalition an incentive to choose continuation only when it is efficient, but sometimes give the coalition an incentive to choose liquidation when continuation would be the most efficient outcome. None of the three bankruptcy priority rules always gives the bank-equity coalition an incentive to make economically efficient bankruptcy decisions. The reason is that when continuation is more efficient but the coalition chooses liquidation, a cost that is ignored by the coalition is imposed on holders of debt, since they are not repaid in full. Therefore, coalitions tend to choose liquidation too often. The bias toward choosing liquidation is worse under the me-first rule than under the last-lender-first rule, since debt holders rank higher under the me-first rule and therefore would have received more of the gains from the coalition making an efficient choice.

In this discussion, interest rates have been assumed to be zero. However, if positive interest rates are introduced and if they have risen in the market since the firm's long-term debt was issued, an offsetting effect is introduced that may give the coalition an incentive to choose continuation under any of the three priority rules. This is because choosing liquidation could cause debt holders to receive a windfall gain, since their claim in liquidation is for the face value of the debt, whereas if they sold the debt, it would be worth less than its face value even without default risk. If, instead, interest rates have fallen since the firm's long-term debt was issued, this effect is reversed and it provides an additional incentive for the coalition to choose liquidation under any of the three priority rules. Another consideration is whether the bank has previous loans outstanding against the firm. These may influence the coalition's decision in either direction. If the bank's previous claim is unsecured, it may be more willing to lend to the firm as a means of obtaining me-first priority or secured status for its prior claim. But if the bank's prior claim is already secured, perhaps because of an earlier rescue of the firm, the bank may prefer that the firm file for bankruptcy.

The bankruptcy decision when the firm's future earnings are uncertain. Most firms' future earnings are uncertain rather than certain, so it is important to apply the coalition model to a case in which the firm's earnings under continuation are uncertain. Assume that if the firm continues, it will earn either $380 (the good outcome) or $50 (the bad outcome) in period 2. The good outcome is assumed to occur with 60 percent probability and the bad outcome with 40 percent probability. The firm's debts are still assumed to be $100 due in period 1 and $200 due in period 2. The firm still has no cash on hand, so the new bank loan necessary to rescue it is $100. In this example, if the firm continues to operate in period 2 and the good outcome occurs, it will be able to pay all its debts. If the bad outcome occurs in period 2, the firm will not be able to pay all of its debts and will file for bankruptcy at that time.

From an efficiency standpoint, the firm should continue to operate if the expected value of its future earnings exceeds the liquidation value of its assets. The expected value of the firm's earnings if it continues is $0.6(380) + 0.4(50) = \$248$. The value of its assets in liquidation is $250. Thus, it is economically efficient for the firm to shut down.

Suppose the me-first rule is in effect. If continuation is chosen and the good outcome occurs, the firm earns $380 and pays $200 to debt holders, so that the coalition receives $180. If the bad outcome occurs, the coalition receives nothing, since all of the firm's earnings must go to debt holders, which have higher priority. The coalition's expected return is $0.6(180) = 108$, minus the bank's loan of $100, or $8. If the coalition is risk neutral, it will choose continuation. But continuation is economically inefficient.

The result of introducing uncertainty is that continuation becomes more attractive to the coalition, even in situations when liquidation is more efficient. Continuation becomes increasingly attractive to the coalition as the variation in earnings and/or the probability of the good outcome's occurring gets larger, since the coalition receives all of the profits after debt holders are paid in the good outcome and loses only the amount of the first period bank loan (debt holders lose the rest) in the bad outcome. Continuation is also more attractive if the firm has more debt due in period 2 and less in period 1, since the new bank loan required to finance continuation is smaller.

Introducing uncertainty into the coalition model thus has the effect of reversing the bias in the liquidation/continuation decision from the coalition's choosing liquidation too often to the coalition's choosing continuation too often. In the certainty case, the coalition must repay period 2 debt in full if it chooses continuation. In contrast, in the uncertainty case, choosing continuation forces period 2 debt holders to participate in a risky activity with uncertain returns: the continued operation of the firm itself. The coalition gets the upside benefit, while debt holders disproportionately bear the downside costs. Thus, the well-known tension between debt and equity regarding risk taking—debt holders prefer safer investments while equity holders prefer riskier investments—also emerges in the bankruptcy decision. When the firm's earnings are risky, continuation itself is a risky investment. Then the coalition prefers continuation even though liquidation may be more economically efficient.[6] In both situations, the coalition has an incentive to choose the alternative in which it benefits from redistribution away from creditors. When uncertainty is introduced, the redistribution possibilities shift from favoring liquidation to favoring continuation.

The results are similar but even stronger under the last-lender-first rule. In this case, the coalition's gain from choosing continuation is even larger than under the me-first rule, because repaying the bank loan now has priority over repaying previously owed period 2 debt, and therefore the coalition receives more when the bad outcome occurs. In this case, the coalition would receive $380 − $200 = $180 in the good outcome and would receive $50 in the bad outcome, since the bank's claim has priority over the claims of debtholders. The coalition's expected return is 0.6(180) + 0.4(50) = $128, minus the bank's loan of $100, or $28. The coalition chooses continuation in this case, since its return in liquidation would be zero. But continuation is still inefficient, since the firm's expected earnings of $248 are less than its liquidation value of $250.

The coalition's incentive to choose continuation is stronger under the last-lender-first rule than under the me-first rule. In some cases, the coalition may have an incentive to choose liquidation when the me-first rule is in effect, when it would choose continuation under the last-lender-first rule. For example, assume the firm has earnings of $400 in the good outcome and zero in the bad outcome, with probabilities of 60 percent and 40 percent respectively, and all other figures remain the same. In this case, liquidation is economically efficient and the coalition chooses liquidation under the me-first rule but chooses continuation under the last-lender-first rule. Thus, when liquidation is economically efficient, the last-lender-first rule has less efficient results than the me-first rule, since it more strongly encourages firms to choose continuation. Under both rules, the incentive to choose continuation over liquidation becomes stronger as the firm's future earnings become riskier. This is because the coalition's

---

[6] Stiglitz (1972) was the first to make the point that managers of firms have incentives to engage in risky investment projects when there is a possibility that the firm might go bankrupt.

decision depends mainly on the firm's earnings in the good outcome, while efficiency would require that it consider the firm's earnings in both the good and the bad outcomes.

It is a common assumption in finance literature that failing firms file for bankruptcy as soon as their liabilities rise to the point that they equal the value of the firm's assets. But if the last-lender-first rule is followed, firms observed in bankruptcy are likely to have liability-to-asset ratios well in excess of 1. The reason is that a bank may be willing to lend money, even if liabilities exceed assets, when it is assured of being repaid first. Many failing firms end up following the last-lender-first rule because banks that are willing to lend demand a lien on some asset of the firm and thus are paid first in bankruptcy. In the previous example, if the firm filed for bankruptcy in period 1, its ratio of total liabilities to assets would be 300:250, or 1.2. But suppose it continued to operate and the bad outcome occurred in period 2, forcing it to file for bankruptcy then. In that case, suppose its only assets were its earnings. Then its ratio of total liabilities to assets at the time of the bankruptcy filing would be 300:50, or 6. The data presented later in the chapter on the characteristics of firms that file to liquidate in bankruptcy support the prediction of the last-lender-first rule that firms observed in liquidation have high ratios of total liabilities to assets.

Finally, under the equal-priority rule, the bank loan is neither first nor last in being repaid, so the coalition's return falls between its returns in the other two cases.

Analysis of the coalition model indicates that no single priority rule in bankruptcy gives the bank-equity coalition an incentive to choose continuation or liquidation only when that alternative is economically efficient. When the firm's future earnings are certain, all three priority rules sometimes discourage continuation decisions even when they are economically efficient, with the me-first rule having the strongest bias. Moreover, as the firm's future earnings become increasingly uncertain, all three rules begin to encourage too many firms to continue operating, even when the most efficient outcome would be liquidation. The me-first rule works best at discouraging inefficient continuation decisions, but none of the rules always works. Thus, not only do none of the priority rules lead to economically efficient results in all situations, but none of the three rules seems to dominate the others. Inefficient bankruptcy decisions and inefficient investment incentives appear to be the price society pays for limiting the liability of equity owners. From the standpoint of economic efficiency, no simple bankruptcy priority rule works as well as unlimited liability of the firm's owners.

It should be noted that inefficient outcomes might be reversed under any of the priority rules by debt holders offering a side payment to the coalition to induce it to choose the efficient outcome. But transactions costs are likely to be high in bargaining over bankruptcy. Severe free rider problems arise when attempts are made to collect money from debt holders to pay the transactions costs of bargaining with the coalition and the costs of the side payment itself. Debt holders' interests thus do not tend to be actively represented in ex post bargaining between creditors and the firm.

7.03 REORGANIZATION

Firms filing for bankruptcy have a choice between liquidation under chapter 7 of the Code and reorganization under chapter 11 of the Code. Managers of a firm make the initial choice. The reorganization procedure in bankruptcy is designed to allow failing firms that are in temporary financial difficulty but are worth saving to continue operating while the claims of creditors are settled using a collective procedure. A drawback of this procedure is that managers of the firm and not an outside party make the decision to file under chapter 11. Thus, managers have an incentive to choose the bankruptcy procedure that is best for themselves and for equity holders, which implies that sometimes firms that are not worth saving from an economic efficiency standpoint may be reorganized. Thus, a dilemma of reorganization is that while it may allow some efficient firms to continue operating that would otherwise liquidate, it is likely to facilitate the rescue of some economically inefficient firms.

[1] Law of Bankruptcy Reorganization

When a firm files to reorganize in bankruptcy under chapter 11 of the Code, its existing management normally remains in control. Creditors can petition the bankruptcy court to appoint a trustee to replace management, but incompetence by the old management, which is strongly suggested by the very fact that the firm is in bankruptcy, is not considered to be a sufficient reason for replacing management. Usually creditors must show grounds for suspecting that the management is stealing the firm's assets or making preferential transfers to favored creditors. One or more creditors' committees are appointed to represent the interests of creditors.

Firms that file under chapter 11 must adopt a reorganization plan. There are two separate procedures for formulating such a plan: the unanimous consent procedure and the cramdown procedure.

[a] Unanimous Consent Procedure. Under the unanimous consent procedure (UCP), classes of creditors and equity must consent unanimously to the reorganization plan, although not all members of each class are required to consent. The assumption behind the UCP is that the firm's assets will have a higher value if it reorganizes and continues operating than if it liquidates. This value differential, which under the APR would go entirely to high-priority creditors, must be divided up among all classes of creditors and equity by means of a negotiating process, with all parties sharing the gain. Firms must be solvent in order to use the UCP, in that the value of creditors' claims must be less than the value of the firm as a going concern. This implies that the firm's old equity has value and so can remain in effect. Otherwise, the firm is considered insolvent, old equity is worthless, and the UCP cannot be used, since equity holders cannot consent to a reorganization plan that eliminates their interest. To support the fiction of solvency, reorganization plans often incorporate inflated valuations of the firm's assets, making them appear to be worth more than the liabilities under the plan.

UCP reorganization plans must be approved by all classes of creditors and by equity as a class. Each class of unsecured creditors must vote in favor of the plan by a two-thirds margin, weighing claims by value, and also by a simple majority, weighing all claims equally. Secured creditors are each a class and must each vote for the plan if their claims are impaired. (If their claims are not impaired, secured creditors' consent to the plan is not needed.) Equity must vote for the plan by a two-thirds margin. (If old equity is eliminated because of the firm's insolvency, equity is deemed to have voted against the reorganization plan and the UCP cannot be used.)

Thus, reorganization plans under the UCP provide for a different division of the firm's assets than would occur under the APR liquidation rules. Under the UCP, every class must receive something. Under the APR, equity and low-priority creditors often receive nothing at all.

Management is in a strong bargaining position in negotiations over the reorganization plan under the UCP. During the first four months after the bankruptcy filing (and lengthy extensions are often granted), managers have the exclusive right to propose a plan. Then an extra two months are allowed for voting on management's plan. Only after this time has elapsed and only if no further extensions have been granted can other parties propose plans. Managers can also threaten to transfer the firm's bankruptcy filing from chapter 11 to chapter 7 if creditors do not agree to a plan, a threat that is often effective in prodding unsecured creditors to accept the plan, since they anticipate receiving little or nothing if liquidation occurs. Managers also run the firm during the negotiating process, so secured creditors often fear that the value of their lien assets will decline. Finally, even after the exclusive period elapses, managers remain in a strong bargaining position. Individual creditors are often unrepresented except in the largest cases, and severe free rider problems arise when creditors attempt to form groups and raise funds to take an active part in bargaining.

[b] Cramdown Procedure. The aptly named cramdown procedure comes into play when a reorganization plan fails to meet the standard for approval by all classes under the UCP or when the firm is clearly insolvent and old equity must be eliminated. In a cramdown case, if at least one class of creditors has voted in favor of a plan, the bankruptcy court can confirm the plan nonetheless, as long as each dissenting class is treated fairly and equitably. The fair and equitable standard closely reflects the APR in that it requires that all unsecured creditors either receive full payment of the face value of their claims over the period of the plan (usually six years) or that all lower-ranking classes receive nothing. It also requires that secured creditors retain their prebankruptcy liens on assets (or the indubitable equivalent) and that they receive periodic cash payments equal to the value of their claims. Cramdown plans usually involve higher transactions costs than UCP plans, since the bankruptcy judge is likely to require appraisals by outside experts and more court hearings before approving the plan.

[c] Establishing Classes of Creditors. There is often intense bargaining and litigation over construction of classes of creditors in a reorganization. Creditors that are in substantially the same position vis-à-vis the firm are placed in the same class to assure that they receive the same treatment under the reorganization plan. Creditors in different positions are placed in different classes. However, managers sometimes wish to prevent particular creditors from defeating a reorganization plan, and to do so they argue that the particular creditor should be part of a larger class in which the creditor's opposition will be outvoted. Moreover, individual creditors sometimes prefer to be part of a larger class. For example, one explanation given for Pennzoil's willingness to accept a $3 billion settlement for its $10.5 billion damage claim against Texaco was its fear that Texaco would successfully persuade the bankruptcy judge that Pennzoil's claim was different from those of other unsecured creditors and should be made a separate class. If this tactic were successful and if the value of Texaco's assets turned out to be less than its liabilities, including the $10.5 billion in damages, Texaco's management could have proposed to pay Pennzoil less than its other unsecured creditors. This would have prevented the plan from being adopted under the UCP, but the cramdown procedure could have been used.

If no reorganization plan is adopted under either the UCP or cramdown, managers sometimes voluntarily sell the firm as a going concern on the open market. (Such sales can be made to existing shareholders if they are willing to put up new funds.) In that case, the proceeds of the sale are paid to creditors according to the APR. This liquidating reorganization is similar to a chapter 7 liquidation, except that the firm is sold as a going concern and is not shut down. (However, since most firms probably go through extended bargaining and months of disruption before such a sale occurs, their value when sold is likely to be less than if the firms were offered for sale immediately after the bankruptcy filing.) Finally, if no progress is being made toward completion of the chapter 11 reorganization, then normally some creditor petitions the bankruptcy judge to order a shift of the firm's bankruptcy filing to a chapter 7 liquidation. Thus, all of the alternatives to adopting a reorganization plan under the UCP involve compensating creditors more or less according to the APR.

[2] Economic Efficiency Considerations of the Reorganization Process

Economic efficiency considerations of reorganization are examined separately using the collective negotiations approach and the coalition behavior approach. Some policy issues are also considered, including subsidies to firms in reorganization and proposed reforms of the bankruptcy reorganization procedure.

[a] **Collective Negotiations Approach.** Suppose all creditors and equity holders could meet ex ante to consider a procedure for bankruptcy reorganization. They would need to agree on (1) the circumstances under which the firm would reorganize rather than liquidate if bankruptcy occurs and (2) how much, if anything, creditors and equity holders would receive in a reorganization.

One obvious point of agreement for all parties might be that reorganization rather than liquidation of the firm should occur if and only if the going-concern value of the firm's assets, net of transactions costs, is greater than the liquidated value of its assets. Since firms that liquidate in bankruptcy always shut down, a bankruptcy reorganization procedure that allows failing firms to continue operating can potentially improve efficiency by saving their going-concern value. Thus, having two bankruptcy procedures—one involving liquidation of the firm and piecemeal sale of its assets and one involving reorganizing the firm so that its operations continue—is something that all parties would find in their interest to agree on. The firm should shut down or continue operating in bankruptcy, depending on which alternative has the highest value. Note that if continued operation is the more efficient outcome but some creditor is made worse off by this choice, it must be possible for other parties to compensate the harmed party and still remain better off than if shutdown occurred.

Thus, creditors have an incentive to adopt some sort of reorganization procedure that allows the firm to continue operating in bankruptcy. Doing so eliminates the problem discussed in the previous section of failing firms' liquidating when their going-concern value exceeds their liquidation value. However, adopting a reorganization procedure does not logically imply adopting a procedure such as the UCP, in which claims by all creditors are cut back. Instead, creditors might agree in advance that all firms in bankruptcy reorganization would be sold as going concerns to the highest bidder and the proceeds paid to creditors according to the APR. The new buyer would then have the choice of whether to continue operating the firm or to liquidate its assets piecemeal. The buyer's incentive would be to choose whichever alternative had the highest value. The new buyer could also decide whether to retain the existing management or not. Therefore, if the buyer had good information about the firm in advance, it would be willing to pay an amount equal to the maximum of the firm's liquidated value and the value of its future earnings if it continued to operate. This would insure that creditors receive the highest possible payoff. Such a market-based reorganization procedure has been advocated by a number of writers, as discussed in the later section on proposed reforms of the reorganization procedure.

However, when a firm is in bankruptcy, managers' incentive to act in their own interest, rather than that of the creditors or equity, is particularly strong. Suppose creditors agreed in advance to adopt a reorganization procedure based on the sale of all firms in bankruptcy on the open market. Managers are likely to fear losing their jobs in this situation, and equity holders also want to avoid reorganization, since they anticipate receiving nothing under the APR. Managers can finance new investments by arranging new loans that jump over existing creditors' claims and rank at the top of the priority ordering. Only when a firm's assets are exhausted are managers willing to file for bankruptcy, and then there is little left for creditors. Thus, for managers and equity holders, a market-based reorganization procedure is similar to a liquidation in bankruptcy and hence an alternative they wish to avoid at all costs. As discussed in the previous section, when liquidation is the only bankruptcy alternative, managers and equity holders have a strong incentive to delay filing for bankruptcy as long as possible and to use the firm's assets for risky investments designed to avoid bankruptcy. The market-based reorganization procedure would in theory allow firms in bankruptcy to continue operating. But if managers and equity holders view the procedure as eliminating their interests, they avoid it. Then, the only firms that would use such a procedure are those whose assets have already been exhausted in risky ventures designed to avoid it.

The UCP reorganization can then be viewed as a compromise designed to make bankruptcy more attractive to managers and equity holders than a liquidation procedure would be and therefore encourage managers to use it while the firm still has some chance of being saved. In effect, retaining old management and equity interest intact is a bribe by creditors to induce managers to choose bankruptcy earlier. Since managers are also often equity holders, treating equity favorably under the UCP is a way of increasing the attractiveness of the procedure to management and equity. The UCP procedure also makes sense if managers have valuable firm-specific skills that would be difficult to replace. While making the UCP attractive to managers may be sensible as a means of increasing the use of chapter 11, the cost of doing so may be to reduce creditors' return on their claims and to save many failing firms that, from an efficiency standpoint, should be shut down.

Creditors would probably also want to agree in advance that an independent appraisal of the firm's assets will be made, both to verify that the firm is worth more if it reorganizes and to determine how much the firm can pay to old creditors. In a liquidation, the firm's assets would be sold on the open market, so their value would be known. In a reorganization, the assets are not sold, so it is more difficult to determine their value. Creditors might decide to require limits on how much or what types of new investment a reorganized firm is permitted. Extensive new investment in new lines of business would suggest the existence of assets that could be sold and the proceeds used instead to pay old creditors a higher return. Unsecured creditors are also likely to agree on some sort of less-than-unanimous voting procedure to approve a firm's reorganization plan. Such a procedure would prevent small groups of creditors from holding out for greater compensation than others with the same priority. In contrast, secured creditors are likely to demand payments or claims equal to the market value of their lien assets in return for allowing an individual lien on some capital asset, and they are not likely to agree on a majority voting rule. Instead, each one will favor negotiating individually with the firm.

Finally, creditors and equity holders might also agree ex ante that the transactions costs of reorganizing could be reduced by avoiding a formal bankruptcy filing altogether. If the firm appears to be failing, the parties could get together outside of bankruptcy and renegotiate their claims. The type of plan they would agree on would probably be similar to what would be arrived at in a formal bankruptcy reorganization proceeding. This is because all creditors would realize that if the informal negotiations failed, the firm would file for a formal reorganization. To reduce transactions costs, creditors would probably be willing to bind themselves to vote in favor of any formal reorganization plan that was substantively the same as an informal reorganization plan negotiated before the bankruptcy filing. Many firms have succeeded in reorganizing without ever filing in a bankruptcy court, but recent research shows that they are in relatively good financial condition. See Gilson, John, and Lang (1990).

A further problem with selling reorganizing firms on the open market is determining who will manage the sale. Ideally, the last class of creditors that receive payment should manage the sale, since this group has an incentive to sell for the highest price. Higher-ranking creditors are entitled to payment in full under the APR and therefore have no incentive to look for a buyer that will pay more than the face value of their own claims. Lower-ranking creditors are not entitled to any payment and therefore should not have a voice in managing the sale. However, it may be difficult to determine which class of creditors is the correct one, since the firm's actual value is uncertain. Lower-ranking creditors (or equity holders) have an incentive to argue that the firm's value is high so as to obtain a voice in the sale of the firm. If they are successful, they may try to delay the sale of the firm, hoping for an unreasonably high price. Furthermore, if the firm's value is uncertain, lower-ranking creditors have an incentive to decide the sale in a way that may reduce the return to higher-ranking creditors. For example, suppose the firm can either be sold for $200 immediately or be held on the market for one more period, in which case its value would be either $100 or $300, each with a 50 percent probability. Higher-ranking creditors have claims of $200. They prefer to sell the firm immediately to receive full compensation. Lower-ranking creditors prefer to delay the sale in case the good outcome occurs and they receive $100. If they are successful in delaying the sale, higher-ranking creditors will receive a return of only $100 in expected value, rather than full compensation of $200.

[b] **Coalition Behavior Approach.** In deciding whether to file for bankruptcy, the firm's managers have a choice between liquidation, reorganization, and continuation outside of bankruptcy. This decision can be approached using an extension of the bank-equity coalition model analyzed in the earlier section. Assume that a firm has both unsecured and secured debt that may be due in period 1 or period 2. Managers propose a reorganization plan under which all unsecured claims will receive a payoff rate in period 2 equal to a fixed proportion of face value and all secured claims will receive a payoff rate equal to a higher fixed proportion of face value. The amount not paid to creditors under the plan is referred to as debt forgiveness. The firm also incurs a fixed transactions cost of reorganizing, T, which must be paid in full in period 1. T includes court costs, attorney fees, and the cost of lost management time. If the firm's earnings fall in reorganization as a result of disruption, this also can be considered

part of the fixed cost of reorganization. Again, for simplicity, interest and discount rates are assumed to be zero.

The bank-equity coalition makes the decision between the firm's reorganizing and liquidating in bankruptcy. Assume that equity will receive nothing if liquidation is chosen. In order for the firm to reorganize, the coalition bank must be willing to extend a new loan to the firm that covers the fixed costs of reorganization, T, plus any payment that must be made to creditors during the first period. Assume that the new loan will be available if giving it last-lender-first priority (i.e., highest priority) makes it certain to be repaid. An advantage of reorganizing (as opposed to continuing outside of bankruptcy) from the coalition's standpoint is that the new loan from the coalition bank is likely to be smaller and easier to obtain if the firm reorganizes in bankruptcy. This is due to both debt forgiveness under the reorganization plan and payments to creditors under the reorganization plan being spread out over several years (six years is the most common), making the amount that must be paid in the earlier periods smaller.[7]

As in the example of the previous section, suppose that the firm has debt due in period 1 of $100 and debt due in period 2 of $200. Assume the period 1 debt is secured and the period 2 debt is unsecured. The liquidation value of the firm's assets is $250, and its future earnings if it reorganizes are $248 with certainty. The transactions costs of reorganization are $50. It is economically efficient for the firm to liquidate rather than to continue operating outside of bankruptcy, since its liquidation value of $250 exceeds its going-concern value of $248. It is also economically efficient for the firm to liquidate rather than to continue operating in bankruptcy reorganization, since its value in reorganization, which is $248 minus the $50 transactions costs of reorganization, or $198, is less than its liquidation value of $250.

Assume that under the reorganization plan, the payoff rate to unsecured creditors under the plan is 25 percent and the payoff rate to secured creditors is 60 percent. The amount that must be paid to secured creditors is 0.6($100), or $60, and the amount that must be paid to unsecured creditors is 0.25($200), or $50. The coalition will choose reorganization if the firm's future earnings of $248 minus the total amount of secured and unsecured debt not forgiven under the plan, which is $110, exceed the fixed cost of reorganizing, which is $50. Since this condition is satisfied, the firm prefers reorganization. Note that if payments to creditors are deferred until period 2, to finance continuation the firm only needs to borrow the transactions cost of reorganization, or $50, since only that amount must be paid in period 1. Even if the reorganization plan requires that some amount be paid to creditors in period 1, the new bank loan will still be smaller than if the firm remains out of bankruptcy, as long as the amount paid to creditors in period 1 is less than $50.

The economic efficiency gain from a firm's reorganizing is the difference between the value of its future earnings and the liquidation value of its assets (if this difference is negative, there is no gain and it is economically inefficient to reorganize). Reorganization is economically worthwhile if the efficiency gain exceeds the fixed transactions cost, T. Nevertheless, a coalition will choose reorganization if the value of its future earnings minus the amount of debt not forgiven under the plan exceeds T. Therefore, a coalition may choose reorganization even when liquidation is more economically efficient or may choose liquidation even when reorganization is more economically

---

[7] Actually, when a firm files under chapter 11, all of its debts are accelerated and become due immediately except where acceleration is prevented by curing any default on the debt and retaining the debt contract intact.

efficient, depending on whether the firm's liquidation value is larger or smaller than the amount of unforgiven debt owed to creditors.

In the previous discussion of the liquidation/continuation decision under certainty, the coalition had an incentive to choose liquidation too often, since it ignored the gain to creditors from the continuation choice, unless the coalition also profited from continuation's being chosen. Here, exactly the same effect occurs, with an additional factor affecting the coalition's choice. When the alternative to liquidation is reorganization (instead of continuation), there is a transfer of benefits from noncoalition creditors to equity in the form of debt forgiveness on secured and unsecured debt. This subsidy makes reorganization even more attractive. As a result, while the coalition may choose either reorganization or liquidation when the other outcome is more efficient, it is more likely that inefficient decisions will favor continuing the firm's operations under reorganization.

Since the amount of debt forgiveness affects the coalition's choice between liquidating and reorganizing, there is a level of debt forgiveness under which the coalition has an incentive to make the economically efficient choice. This occurs when the amount of debt not forgiven under the plan equals the liquidation value of the firm's assets. The average payoff rate to all creditors under the reorganization plan then must equal the liquidation value of the firm divided by the total face value of noncoalition debt. Thus, an economic efficiency justification for using the APR as a default standard in reorganization when bargaining over a plan under the UCP breaks down is that paying creditors in total an amount equal to the firm's value in liquidation gives the coalition an incentive to make the economically efficient choice between liquidation and reorganization. (However, this result does not hold when the firm's earnings are uncertain.)

In the more likely case where a firm's future earnings under reorganization are uncertain rather than certain, reorganizing becomes much more attractive to the coalition than liquidating. The reason is similar to that of continuation versus liquidation discussed in the previous section: By reorganizing, the coalition forces creditors to invest their remaining claims in a risky activity, the continued operation of the reorganized firm. Again, equity receives the upside benefit and creditors disproportionately bear the downside risk. Suppose that the firm's future earnings are $380 with 60 percent probability and $50 with 40 percent probability, for an expected value of $248. The coalition's return in reorganization if the good outcome occurs is $380 − $110 = $270, and its return if the bad outcome occurs is zero. After the bank's loan of $50 is subtracted, the coalition's net return in reorganization if the good outcome occurs is 0.6($270) − $50 = $112. Since the coalition previously was assumed to receive zero if liquidation occurred and only $8 to $28 under the various priority rules if continuation outside of bankruptcy occurred, reorganization is very attractive to the coalition. (However, in circumstances such as these, creditors might demand higher payoff rates as a condition for agreeing to a UCP reorganization plan.)

In general, a coalition chooses reorganization whenever the expected value of its earnings in the good outcome is positive. The coalition thus bases its choice only on earnings in the good outcome, when economic efficiency would require that the decision be based on both the good and the bad outcomes. The attractiveness of reorganizing also increases as the variance of the firm's future earnings increases and as the payoff rates to secured and unsecured creditors fall.

How are the payoff rates to secured and unsecured creditors determined? Without a more complete model of the bargaining process in reorganization, the actual payoff rates in reorganization cannot be predicted. However, the bankruptcy rules discussed previously suggest that the strength of bargaining power varies among different creditors' groups. If negotiations over a reorganization plan fail and a firm is liquidated, secured creditors can reclaim their lien assets. Each of these assets has an individual liquidation value. Each secured creditor is likely to demand a payoff rate equal to the liquidation value of its assets divided by the face value of its claim. Since individual secured creditors usually each form a separate creditors' class, they can individually block a UCP reorganization plan by voting against it. Therefore, they are in a relatively strong bargaining position. However, they may settle for a lower payoff rate to avoid prolonged bargaining over a UCP reorganization plan, if disruption to the firm during the bargaining process would cause their lien assets to decline rapidly in value.[8] This discussion implies that regardless of the exact decision rule applied to secured creditors in reorganizations, firms having more secured debt in their capital structures are more likely to liquidate and those having more unsecured debt are likely to reorganize. This is both because secured creditors are more likely to oppose reorganization and because they are in the best position to block a proposed reorganization plan. Unsecured creditors as a group also have the power to block a reorganization plan under the UCP, but if they do and the firm liquidates or goes through a liquidating reorganization, their returns will tend to be quite low. Their payoff rate will be at least equal to what unsecured creditors expect to receive if the firm is liquidated.

Since earnings uncertainty increases the attractiveness to the coalition of reorganization as opposed to liquidation, giving noncoalition creditors a total payoff in reorganization equal to the firm's liquidation value would still leave the coalition with an incentive to choose reorganization too often. Using the APR as a default standard in reorganization when voluntary bargaining does not succeed leaves the coalition with an incentive to choose reorganization more often than is economically efficient. In order to give the coalition economically efficient incentives when future earnings are risky, the default standard in reorganization would have to give creditors more in total than the firm's liquidation value.

The arguments concerning a firm's decision to reorganize in bankruptcy suggest that as long as a firm's future earnings are risky, too many firms will reorganize in bankruptcy. They are motivated to file for bankruptcy reorganization both by the transfer from noncoalition creditors in the form of debt forgiveness under the plan and by the incentive to gamble with creditors' remaining claims by investing them in the firm's continuing operation.

[3] Subsidies to Firms That Reorganize

The U.S. Congress has tended to view the role of reorganization as that of providing breathing space to viable firms that are in temporary financial distress in order to save jobs, reduce the burden on the unemployment compensation and welfare systems, and avoid disruption to local communities. In contrast, liquidation is viewed as the process of winding up the operation of firms that are not viable. (The fact that the wrong firms might choose to reorganize in bankruptcy has not been an important public policy issue.) Therefore, in order to make reorganization attractive to managers and equity holders, Congress has provided a number of subsidies to firms in reorganiza-

---

[8] See Gordon and Malkiel (1981) for discussion of bargaining strategies of high-priority creditors in reorganization, suggesting that they are willing to give up 20 percent to 30 percent of their claims to facilitate quick adoption of a plan. For models of the bargaining process in reorganization, see Brown (1989); Bebchuk and Chang (1992); and Baird and Picker (1991).

tion. These subsidies come either from the government or from creditors. They give firms in reorganization advantages relative to firms that continue operating outside of bankruptcy and firms that liquidate. The six major subsidies are as follows:

1. Firms that reorganize retain most of their accrued tax loss carryforwards, which would be lost if they liquidated. These loss carryforwards shelter the firm from paying corporate profits taxes for a period in the future if their operations start to be profitable. They also make reorganized firms attractive merger partners for profitable firms, since the profitable firm can use the tax loss carryforward immediately. This subsidy makes reorganization more attractive than liquidation for a failing firm but has no effect on the choice between reorganization and remaining out of bankruptcy.

   The tax loss carryforward provision in itself is purely a transfer from the government to firms that have reorganized in bankruptcy. However, in order to qualify for the subsidy, firms must meet certain continuity requirements that have economic efficiency implications. A firm that merges with a profitable partner after going through bankruptcy reorganization must transfer to the partner either an active business or substantially all of its assets in order to qualify for favorable tax treatment. Thus, while some assets may be sold, firms going through bankruptcy reorganization are inhibited from closing down inefficient businesses or selling obsolete assets. These requirements have the effect of delaying the movement of resources to more profitable uses.

2. When reorganizing firms settle liabilities for less than their face value, the amount of debt forgiveness is deducted as a loss by the creditor but is not immediately treated as taxable income to the reorganizing firm. The debt forgiveness amount becomes taxable (often after a long time lag) when the reorganized firm becomes profitable, by reducing either its tax loss carryforward or its depreciation allowances.

3. Firms reorganizing under chapter 11 have the right to terminate underfunded pension plans, and the U.S. government picks up the uncovered pension costs. For example, three large firms that filed for bankruptcy in the 1980s, LTV, Wheeling-Pittsburgh Steel, and Allis-Chalmers, terminated their pension funds and together transferred almost $3 billion of uncovered pension liabilities to the government. Several years before its bankruptcy filing, Allis-Chalmers made an agreement with its union simultaneously to raise pension levels (which were insured by the government) and lower pension funding. When it filed for bankruptcy, the assets in its pension plan equaled only 3 percent of its guaranteed benefits. The Pension Benefit Guaranty Corporation has become more active in chapter 11 bankruptcy proceedings in recent years and may block a reorganization plan from being adopted unless it agrees with the firm on a settlement of pension claims.

4. The Code provides that when firms file for bankruptcy, their obligation to pay interest to prebankruptcy creditors, both secured and unsecured, ceases. They do not have to start paying interest again until a reorganization plan is approved, and the unpaid interest does not become a claim against the firm. This subsidy clearly gives managers of failing firms an incentive to file for bankruptcy earlier and to delay proposing a reorganization plan.

5. Firms in reorganization can reject any of their contracts that are not substantially completed. Thus, they can get out of any unprofitable contracts. While firms are still liable for damages to other parties to rejected contracts, such damage claims are unsecured and likely to receive a low payoff rate. Thus, the cost to the firm of shedding unprofitable contracts is small. The firm's ability to selectively "decontract" makes reorganization more attractive relative to continuing outside of bankruptcy (where firms must perform on all their contracts) and liquidating (where all contracts are canceled). Firms not in

bankruptcy also have the right to avoid performing their contracts by paying damages, but the damage payments are so much higher that it is not worthwhile except in very unusual cases. Substantially uncompleted contracts that firms in reorganization can reject also include any loan agreements that carry higher interest rates than the firm could obtain on a new loan. This allows firms to retain only loans that carry low interest rates.

6. Firms in reorganization can reject their collective bargaining labor agreements. Since 1984, however, this step has required the approval of the bankruptcy judge. This has particularly benefited unionized firms in industries that have a mixture of unionized and nonunionized establishments by enabling them to cut all wages to nonunionized levels. A prominent example is Continental Airlines, which, under airline deregulation, filed to reorganize in bankruptcy in 1983. Continental was allowed to cut wages by 50 percent and cut its work force by 65 percent. Other examples are Wheeling-Pittsburgh, UNR Industries, and the Manville Corporation. Only firms that file under chapter 11 can reject their collective bargaining agreements, since, outside of bankruptcy, the National Labor Relations Act prevents employers from modifying collective bargaining agreements without the consent of the union. When a collective bargaining agreement is terminated, workers have a claim for the reduction in wages over the remaining term of the collective bargaining agreement, but the claim is unsecured.

These subsidies increase the attractiveness to the coalition of reorganizing rather than liquidating or continuing outside of bankruptcy by increasing the total amount of debt forgiveness in reorganization. However, the subsidies also cause the firm's earnings to become less risky. Therefore, the coalition will find reorganization more attractive, but the effect will be smaller than if the subsidies increased rather than reduced the riskiness of the firm's earnings. Finally, the subsidies have no effect on the economic efficiency of reorganization relative to liquidation or continuation. Thus, if too many firms were already choosing reorganization, to the extent that the subsidies cause failing firms to choose reorganization more often they worsen the problem.

In practice, the subsidies are also likely to change the nature of the bargain made between creditors and the coalition in reorganization. Under the UCP, all creditors' classes and equity must consent to the plan, so that the subsidies strengthen the bargaining position of creditors generally and probably cause all payoff rates to rise. The subsidies are in effect divided among creditors' groups and equity, with the firm itself retaining equity's share. Alternatively, if a liquidating reorganization occurs and the firm is sold on the open market, the subsidies will cause the firm's sale price to rise, although probably by less than the full amount of the subsidies (since the new owners will also focus primarily on equity's earnings in the good outcome in deciding how much to bid for the firm). In this case, since the sale proceeds must be distributed according to the APR and will be exhausted before paying off all creditors' claims in full, creditors get the entire increase in the sale price. The new owners of the reorganized firm get the benefit of whatever proportion of the subsidies was not capitalized into its sale price. In either case, creditors are likely to demand and receive a substantial proportion of the value of the subsidies.

If the intent of Congress in providing the subsidies was to improve the viability of firms that reorganize and save their jobs, to the extent that the subsidies leave the firm in the form of increased payments to creditors they fail to accomplish their purpose and are wasted. The subsidies could theoretically accomplish their purpose at lower cost if the reorganization procedure were changed to prevent this effect, but it is difficult to see how this could be done. Eliminating at least some of the subsidies, for example by requiring that all firms fully fund their pension plans, would seem desirable from an efficiency standpoint.

Subsidies vary in importance for different industries. But they potentially enable unprofitable firms to substantially reduce their costs by filing for bankruptcy under chapter 11. For example, the Chrysler Corporation, which benefited both from its tax loss carryforward and from explicit government aid in the form of loan guarantees,[9] has recovered from its financial problems. It is unlikely that jobs were saved, however. Following its bailout, Chrysler cut its employment level by 45 percent from 1978 to 1980, compared to decreases of 15 percent to 18 percent during the same period by General Motors and Ford. Another industry affected by bankruptcy subsidies is the steel industry, where there is overcapacity and a need for overall contraction. Analysts have estimated that LTV, one of the largest steel companies, was able to reduce its steel-making costs from $460 to $380 per ton as a result of filing to reorganize in bankruptcy. LTV's costs were estimated to be $60 per ton below average steel industry costs.[10] Similarly, the subsidies to LTV have affected the entire steel industry, both by enabling LTV and other reorganized steel firms to continue to produce steel and by putting pressure on their competitors to file for bankruptcy (and receive the subsidies) as well. This has also occurred in the airline industry, where the bankruptcy filings of some airlines caused their competitors to incur losses and, in some cases, also to file for bankruptcy. One viewpoint is that the subsidies may enable inefficient firms to remain in operation and slow the contraction of the industry and the movement of assets to more valuable uses. Another viewpoint is that the subsidies may put previously uncompetitive steel firms on a more even footing with competitive steel firms in other countries. In either case, the subsidies probably save some jobs that would otherwise have been lost, but at a very high cost.

[4] Proposed Reforms of the Reorganization Procedure

The discussion in the previous section suggests that substantial inefficiencies result from the existence of two separate bankruptcy procedures. In liquidation, equity interests rank last, while in reorganization under the UCP, equity is maintained intact, although it may be diluted. This means that managers, representing equity, always prefer reorganization over liquidation, because by reorganizing they can transfer income from creditors to equity. (Managers may not always succeed in attracting a bank lender that will finance reorganization, but they always prefer reorganization over liquidation.) In addition, managers' personal interests also strongly favor reorganization because in reorganization, existing management is usually retained, while in liquidation managers' jobs are eliminated. This preference for reorganization over liquidation causes too few firms to liquidate and generates inefficiency by delaying the movement of assets from less productive to more productive uses.

Several writers in the law and economics area have proposed changes in the role of reorganization that would drastically change or even eliminate it. Their motivation for suggesting changes seems to be concern that equity gets too much and high-priority

---

[9] Actually, Chrysler never explicitly filed for bankruptcy; it negotiated a settlement with creditors similar to a bankruptcy reorganization plan, aided by the creditors' knowledge that it could file under chapter 11 if the bargaining broke down.

[10] See C.F. Mitchell and J.E. Beazley, "LTV is Healthier Under Chapter 11, but Not Cured," *The Wall Street Journal* (July 24, 1987), p. 5, col. 1.

creditors too little in reorganization under the UCP. Nevertheless, equity and efficiency are related in the bankruptcy context: The larger the transfers between classes of creditors and equity owing to the bankruptcy decision, the larger the deadweight costs of an inefficient bankruptcy decision may be. Thus, by reducing the transfers, the deadweight costs can potentially be reduced.

One proposed change to bankruptcy reorganization (Roe (1983)) is that all firms reorganizing be required to have an all-equity capital structure after reorganization and that the value of the assets of all firms reorganizing be set by an actual sale of equity on the market. For large firms, Roe proposed that 10 percent of the new shares be sold on the market. For firms too small to justify selling a new equity issue publicly, he suggested that the firm itself might be offered for sale on the market. The resulting market valuation in either case then would be used to determine whether the firm is solvent and therefore whether old equity interests can participate in the reorganization. Creditors would be compensated according to the APR but with a mix of cash and new equity in the firm. Roe's proposal would in effect force all reorganizations to use the cramdown procedure described previously.

Bebchuk (1988) proposed a variation on Roe's idea that would also require that the reorganized firm have an all-equity capital structure, but would involve creditors and old equity holders receiving options on the firm's new equity. For example, suppose the firm has high-priority creditors with claims of $100, low-priority creditors with claims of $200, and 100 shares of old equity. The value of the firm is uncertain. The reorganized firm also has 100 new shares. The high-priority creditors receive a share in the reorganized firm for each dollar of their claims, but their rights are subject to a call option given to low-priority creditors for each $2 of claims to purchase the shares from high-priority creditors for $1 each. The low-priority creditors, in addition to having the option to purchase the shares of high-priority creditors, are subject to a call option held by old equity holders to purchase the new shares from low-priority creditors for $3 each. Whether the options are exercised depends on the value of the reorganized firm, but the overall effect is that high-priority creditors either receive $100 in total, which is full payment of their claims, or own the shares in the reorganized firm. Low-priority creditors either receive $200 in total, which is full payment of their claims, or own the shares in the reorganized firm. Old equity holders either receive nothing or, if they compensate both high-priority and low-priority creditors in full by exercising their options, own the shares in the reorganized firm. The idea can be extended to any number of priority classes.

Bebchuk's options proposal is interesting in that it avoids the problem of who will run the sale of the reorganizing firm. Under his proposal, the sale of the firm can proceed even if its value is unknown. However, all creditors must know in advance the priority of their claims, but issues of relative priority are often in dispute in bankruptcy.

Another advantage of both the Roe and the Bebchuk proposals is that they increase the reorganized firm's future viability by eliminating its old debt. Having no debt, the new firm can easily attract working capital from a new lender, even if the old bank lender refused to make a new loan. Also, reducing old debt makes creditors' return in bankruptcy more predictable, which should make senior debt less risky and therefore available at lower interest rates. But its main advantage from an economic standpoint is that it would reduce the number of failing firms that are saved by reorganization and therefore continue in the same line of business with the same ineffective management.[11]

---

[11] See Bradley and Rosenzweig (1992); Aghion, Hart, and Moore (1992) for recent reform proposals along the lines of Bebchuk's. See Warren (1992) for a defense of chapter 11.

A more drastic proposal was made by Baird (1986) that would eliminate bankruptcy reorganization completely. (Jackson (1986) made a similar point.) Baird proposed that all bankruptcies take place under chapter 7 but that the old managers continue to run the firm temporarily, rather than shutting it down immediately. The firm would then be sold as a going concern if such a sale seemed likely to bring in more than the value of the firm's assets sold piecemeal. The proceeds of sale would be paid to creditors according to the APR. Clearly, from an economic efficiency standpoint, as long as all firms in reorganization were automatically offered for sale on the open market as going concerns, it would not matter whether the procedure involved using chapter 7, chapter 11, or both. Changes in current bankruptcy law and bankruptcy tax law would be needed to implement any of these proposed changes.

These proposals require that all bankrupt firms be sold on the open market as going concerns rather than as piecemeal assets after shutdown and that the proceeds be paid to creditors and old equity holders according to the APR. The new owners of the firm would choose whether to shut it down or continue its operations. Since the new owners would have an incentive to choose whichever alternative has greater value, the shut-down/continuation decision would be made efficiently. The new owners would also decide whether to keep the old managers on or replace them and would have an incentive to make the efficient choice. The amount that the firm would sell for is the maximum of what the new owners would pay for its piecemeal assets versus its price as a going concern. This would guarantee the maximum total compensation to prebankruptcy creditors and equity holders. Requiring that all bankrupt firms be sold on the open market would thus eliminate the deadweight cost that arises when firms whose resources would be more valuable elsewhere continue to operate or when bad managers remain in control. It would also increase efficiency by speeding up the bankruptcy procedure, since there would be no need for creditors and managers to bargain over a reorganization plan that specifies how each group is compensated. Assuming that length of time in bankruptcy is positively related to indirect bankruptcy costs, any reform that eliminates the need for bargained agreements is likely to reduce deadweight costs.

Despite these advantages, a unified procedure involving market valuation or sale of all bankrupt firms would not be a panacea for bankruptcy ills. The efficiency of the bankruptcy process itself would probably improve if reforms along these lines were adopted. But improving the bankruptcy procedure itself would be likely to exacerbate the problem of inefficient decision making outside of bankruptcy. Managers have an extremely strong incentive (except when future earnings are certain) to avoid bankruptcy if the bankruptcy procedure follows the APR and puts equity last. Therefore, if the unified bankruptcy procedure used the APR, only firms in the worst possible financial shape would file for bankruptcy. Managers would have an incentive to choose the riskiest investment projects, to waste the firm's assets, and to do anything possible for as long as possible to avoid walking into bankruptcy court. A unified APR-based bankruptcy procedure would probably dramatically increase the deadweight costs of inefficient bankruptcy decisions. Only when the worst outcomes occurred and the firm's assets were exhausted would managers consider filing for bankruptcy.

The current two-pronged bankruptcy procedure has the effect of reducing the deadweight costs of inefficient bankruptcy decisions by allowing firms to reorganize in bankruptcy under rules that are more favorable both to equity interests and to managers themselves. In reorganization under the UCP, equity interests are maintained intact even when creditors' claims are cut back. Managers remain in control during the reorganization process. Managers of firms in financial difficulty thus have less incentive to take extreme steps to avoid bankruptcy when reorganization is an option.[12] Firms filing for bankruptcy reorganization tend to be in better financial condition on average than firms filing to liquidate in bankruptcy. Bankruptcy reorganization, which makes the bankruptcy procedure itself more complicated and costly than if all firms were liquidated, has an offsetting advantage of reducing deadweight costs outside of bankruptcy. A further advantage is that once the firm has filed under chapter 11, there is some supervision of managers' decisions by the bankruptcy court, which probably prevents at least the worst abuses.

There is a trade-off between improving the bankruptcy procedure itself and improving the efficiency of decision making outside of bankruptcy. As long as streamlining the bankruptcy procedure involves compensating creditors according to the APR, managers will have an incentive to gamble with creditors' assets as they try desperately to avoid bankruptcy's draconian treatment of equity under the APR. Ironically, while bankruptcy is meant to be the procedure by which the economy moves toward long-term efficiency, the bankruptcy liquidation procedure in fact gives managers of failing firms incentives to engage in inefficient behavior in trying to avoid it.

Are there any possible solutions to this dilemma? One, not very practical on other grounds, would be to eliminate limited liability completely and make equity holders responsible for the firm's losses. This would take away managers' ability to make transfers from creditors to equity, the source of their incentive to make economically inefficient decisions. Another possibility is to unify and streamline the bankruptcy procedure along the lines of the reforms previously discussed but with old equity and management treated somewhat more favorably. All bankrupt firms could be sold as going concerns on the open market, existing management could be kept in place during the sale, and the sale proceeds could be divided among various creditors' classes and equity in a way that would provide partial compensation to all groups. Reform along these lines would in effect try to strike a balance between conflicting efficiency objectives. But the basic problems of bankruptcy are not caused by design flaws in the bankruptcy system, so tinkering with the design of bankruptcy procedures will not solve them. As with any trade-off, the best that can be done is to strike the right balance.

7.04 BANKRUPTCY TRENDS FOR THE U.S. ECONOMY

There are two main data sources concerning aggregate bankruptcy levels. The first is provided by the Dun & Bradstreet Corporation (D&B), which publishes the number of firms that failed, their liabilities, and other characteristics. The data include as failures all firms that ceased operations with loss to creditors, were involved in a bankruptcy proceeding, or reduced creditors' claims in a voluntary agreement without actually filing for bankruptcy. However, the data exclude many small firms, a number of service industries, and all agricultural firms. Coverage of the banking, insurance, real estate, railroad, shipping, and several other sectors was added in 1984, so that

---

[12] The notion of rewarding bankrupts as a means of encouraging them to cooperate with the bankruptcy process is not new. An English bankruptcy law of 1705 rewarded cooperative bankrupts by allowing them to keep 5 percent of the estate. However, it also provided for the death penalty for uncooperative bankrupts. 4 Anne, ch. 17 (1705). See Baird (1986) for further discussion.

figures prior to 1984 are not directly comparable to figures for 1984 and after. Also, by definition, "liabilities" excludes long-term, publicly held debt.

Figure 7-1 lists historical failure trends for the United States since the 1930s. During the period 1950–1980, the number of failures was essentially trendless, fluctuating between about 9,000 and 11,000 per year. It began to rise steadily in the 1980s, however, and increased from 12,000 in 1980 to 61,000 in 1987, although part of the rise reflects the increase in D&B's coverage. The number of failures fell in 1988 and 1989 but has been rising very quickly since then. The 1991 figure of 87,600 represents an increase of 45 percent over the 1990 figure of 60,500. Between the 1930s and the early 1980s, the failure rate was always below 1 percent (or 100 per 10,000 firms) per year and usually below 0.5 percent per year. Thus, business bankruptcies are rare events. However, the failure rate rose above 100 from 1983 through 1987 and fell below 100 again from 1988 through 1990 but rose to just under 100 (98) in 1991. The recession of the 1980s thus appeared to have a much more serious effect on business failures than any of the previous post–World War II recessions. The average level of liabilities per failure increased steadily in nominal terms over the entire period covered but in real terms has tended to fluctuate without strong trends since the early 1970s. However, the 1991 figure represented the highest on record, an increase in the real value of liabilities per failed firm of 24 percent from 1990.

The second important data source concerning bankruptcy is collected by the Administrative Office of the U.S. Courts. A statistical report on its operations, *Federal Judicial Workload Statistics,* is published each year. Figure 7-2 gives the number of bankruptcy filings by type each year since 1970.

The 1970–1978 data refer to the period before the adoption of the current U.S. bankruptcy law, which is known as the (new) Bankruptcy Code. The Code abolished old chapters X, XI, and XII and replaced them with new chapter 11 and replaced old chapter XIII with new chapter 13. Chapter 13 is used mainly by individuals who have regular income and agree on a plan to repay part of their debts, but it is also used by small unincorporated businesses to reorganize.

Since 1970, the total number of bankruptcy filings has increased dramatically, from 194,000 in 1970 to 569,000 in 1987 to 942,000 in 1991. This includes both business and personal bankruptcies. Starting in 1980, business bankruptcy filings are reported separately from nonbusiness bankruptcy filings. There were about 44,000 business bankruptcies in 1980; this figure jumped to 64,000 in 1982 and then remained fairly constant until 1986, when it rose again to 81,000. Since then, the number of business bankruptcies has fallen: There were 62,000 in 1988 and 70,000 in 1991. Thus, in recent years the large increase in the number of bankruptcy filings has been due to increases in the number of personal bankruptcies, not business bankruptcies. The data also highlight the difference in coverage between the D&B data and the comprehensive U.S. courts data; in 1981, for example, the D&B data indicate that there were 16,800 business failures, but Figure 7-2 reports that there were 48,000 business bankruptcy filings. In 1991, the two sets of figures were 87,000 and 70,000 respectively.

Figure 7-2 breaks down the number of bankruptcy filings by chapter. Bankruptcy liquidations are given in the third column. They are referred to as straight bankruptcies under the old Bankruptcy Act and as chapter 7 filings under the new Bankruptcy Code. The proportion of all business bankruptcies filed as liquidations fell from 0.77 in 1980 to 0.62 in 1986. However, many firms that file to reorganize in bankruptcy later shift their filing to liquidations.

There were always very few chapter X cases, an average of 122 per year from 1970 to 1979, compared to 2,413 per year under chapter XI during the same period. Use

FIGURE 7-1

Failure Trends for the U.S. Economy (1933–1991)

Source: The Business Failure Record *(New York: Dun & Bradstreet Corporation, 1983, 1988);* Economic Report of the President *(Washington, D.C.: U.S. Government Printing Office, 1988), p. 313*

Year	Number of Failures	Failure Rate per 10,000 Listed Concerns	Average Liability per Failure	Average Real Liability per Failure	Percentage of Failures in Business 5 Years or Less
1933	19,859	100	$ 23	NA	NA
1940	13,619	63	12	NA	NA
1945	809	4	37	NA	NA
1950	9,162	34	27	37	68
1955	10,969	42	41	51	57
1960	15,445	57	61	69	59
1965	13,514	53	98	104	57
1966	13,061	52	106	109	57
1967	12,364	49	102	102	55
1968	9,636	39	98	94	54
1969	9,154	37	125	114	53
1970	10,748	44	176	151	55
1971	10,326	42	186	160	54
1972	9,566	38	209	167	56
1973	9,345	36	246	185	57
1974	9,915	38	308	209	60
1975	11,432	43	383	238	57
1976	9,628	35	313	184	55
1977	7,919	28	391	215	53
1978	6,619	24	402	206	53
1979	7,564	28	353	162	55
1980	11,742	42	395	160	54
1981	16,794	61	414	152	49
1982	24,908	88	627	217	46
1983	31,334	110	513	172	47
1984[a]	52,078	107	562	181	57
1985	57,253	115	645	200	56
1986	61,616	120	726	221	55
1987	61,622	102	590	175	51
1988	57,097	98	693	204	NA
1989	50,361	65	841	237	NA
1990	60,608	75	989	268	NA
1991[b]	87,592	98	1,266	331	NA

Note: Dollars in thousands. For gross national product price deflator used to construct average real liability per failure data, 1967 = 100.

[a] Coverage increased in 1984, so data prior to 1984 is not directly comparable to the data for 1984 and thereafter.

[b] Preliminary.

FIGURE 7-2

Bankruptcy Filings by Chapter of the Old Bankruptcy Act and the New Bankruptcy Code

Source: Federal Judicial Workload Statistics, *A.O.C. Statistical Analysis and Reports Division (Washington, D.C.: various years)*

Year and Type	Total Filings	Straight Bankruptcy or Chapter 7	Chapter X	Chapter XI or 11	Chapter XII	Chapter XIII or 13
1970	194,399	162,451	115	1,262	58	30,510
1971	201,352	168,364	179	1,782	120	30,904
1972	182,869	153,934	105	1,361	92	27,373
1973	173,197	145,914	101	1,458	92	25,632
1974	189,513	157,967	163	2,171	172	29,023
1975	254,484	209,350	189	3,506	280	41,176
1976	246,549	209,067	141	3,235	525	33,579
1977	214,399	181,194	96	3,046	640	29,422
1978	202,951	168,771	75	3,266	650	30,185
1979	226,476	183,259	63	3,042	669	39,442
1980	331,098	249,157		6,353	—	75,584
Business	43,269	33,698		5,878		4,052
Nonbusiness	287,463	215,460		471		71,532
1981	363,847	260,664		10,041	—	93,139
Business	48,014	34,062		8,928		5,022
Nonbusiness	315,832	226,602		1,113		88,117
1982	373,837	255,798		16,613		101,418
Business	63,595	41,924		14,704		6,959
Nonbusiness	310,242	213,874		1,909		94,459
1983	362,059	242,672		20,833		98,544
Business	65,937	40,853		17,813		7,261
Nonbusiness	296,122	201,819		3,020		91,283
1984	346,500	235,190		19,960		91,338
Business	62,882	38,649		17,396		6,825
Nonbusiness	283,618	196,541		2,564		84,513
1985	383,510	257,928		22,602		102,967
Business	69,132	41,838		19,864		7,417
Nonbusiness	314,378	216,090		2,738		95,550
1986	530,008	374,452		24,740		130,200
Business	81,019	50,626		21,370		8,491
Nonbusiness	448,989	323,826		3,370		121,709
1987	568,727	406,761		19,901		142,065
Business	75,881	46,683		17,142		12,056
Nonbusiness	492,844	360,076		2,759		130,009
1988	611,541	437,882		17,690		155,969
Business	61,711	38,590		15,541		7,580
Nonbusiness	549,830	399,292		2,149		148,389
1989	678,502	476,993		18,281		183,228
Business	61,749	37,357		16,303		8,089
Nonbusiness	616,753	439,636		1,978		175,139
1990	781,585	543,334		20,783		217,468
Business	63,478	36,394		18,282		8,802
Nonbusiness	718,101	506,940		2,501		208,660
1991	942,455	656,460		23,989		262,006
Business	70,018	39,101		20,794		10,123
Nonbusiness	872,437	617,359		3,195		251,883

of chapter X declined in the late 1970s from 189 cases in 1975 to 63 in 1979. However, since chapter X cases always involved large firms, their relative importance was greater than the numbers alone suggest. Use of chapter XII, which applied to firms holding mainly real estate, increased rapidly during the 1970s, from 58 in 1970 to 669 in 1979. Chapter 11 business bankruptcies have increased rapidly since the adoption of the new Code, from around 6,000 in 1980 to 21,000 in 1991.

Chapter 13 provides a simplified bankruptcy reorganization procedure for individuals, allowing them to pay off a portion of their debts from future earnings rather than by giving up their assets. Use of chapter 13 increased rapidly during the years after the adoption of the new Code; there were around 40,000 filings in 1979, 93,000 in 1981, 130,000 in 1986, and 262,000 in 1991.[13]

Unfortunately, the bankruptcy court statistics do not provide any kind of breakdown on characteristics of firms going through bankruptcy proceedings. To pose and answer questions concerning characteristics of firms filing for bankruptcy or treatment of creditors in bankruptcy, survey data must be used.

[1] Survey Evidence of Business Bankruptcies

There have been two basic types of surveys of firms that have filed for bankruptcy since the adoption of the Code. The first involves examining the records of firms that file for bankruptcy under chapter 7 or chapter 11 in a particular bankruptcy court. Since most firms that file for bankruptcy are relatively small, these surveys provide evidence concerning the characteristics of small firms in bankruptcy. The other type of survey involves large firms with publicly traded debt or equity that have filed for bankruptcy, almost always under chapter 11. A variety of data sources are used to obtain information concerning large firm bankruptcies, including bankruptcy court records, annual reports, Form 10K filings, trading data, information from articles in *The Wall Street Journal* and other financial publications, and interviews with lawyers and managers.

Figure 7-3 summarizes much of the information. Since large firms virtually never file under chapter 7, there is no column for large firms filing under chapter 7. The reason for separating large and small firms is that their experiences in bankruptcy are generally quite different.

[a] **Small Firms in Bankruptcy.** Much of the information concerning small firms in bankruptcy comes from White's (1984) survey of approximately 120 firms that filed for bankruptcy under chapter 7 or chapter 11 in the Bankruptcy Court of the Southern District of New York (New York City) and LoPucki's (1983) survey of 48 firms that filed for bankruptcy under chapter 11 in the Western District of Missouri (Kansas City). A larger but less detailed source of information is Ames's (1983) survey of 500 firms that filed for bankruptcy under chapter 7 and 500 firms that filed under chapter 11. All of these surveys took place in the early 1980s, just after the Code went into effect.[14]

Consider first the characteristics of small firms at the time they file for bankruptcy

---

[13] For an economic analysis of personal bankruptcy, see M.J. White (1987).

[14] Dollar values in Figure 7-3 are not adjusted for inflation, so for small firms they represent dollars of the early 1980s.

FIGURE 7-3

Characteristics of Firms in Bankruptcy

	Small Firms Under Chapter 7	Small Firms Under Chapter 11	Large Firms Under Chapter 11
Assets	$ 10,000[a] $437,000[c]	$ 257,000[a] $1,400,000[c] $1,100,000[d]	$222,000,000[b]
Liabilities	$ 72,000[a] $710,000[c]	$ 357,000[a] $1,900,000[c] $1,000,000[d]	$313,000,000[e]
Secured liabilities	$ 10,000[a] $182,000[c]	$ 154,000[a] $ 893,000[c]	
Ratio of liabilities to assets	1.6[c] 7.2[a]	1.4[c] 1.4[a] 0.93[d]	0.77[b]
Ratio of secured liabilities to assets	0.42[c] 1.0[a]	0.64[c] 0.60[a]	
Time in bankruptcy		10 months[d]	2.5 years[b] 3.7 years[f] 2.1 years[e]
Probability of adoption of a plan		0.41–0.47[c] 0.26[d]	0.86[b]
Payoff rate to unsecured creditors	0.04[c]	0.16 + 0.18[c] 0.14 + 0.22[d]	0.49[g] 0.53[b] 0.69[e]
Direct costs of bankruptcy			0.031 of assets[b]
Probability of deviation from APR			0.37[g] 0.23[e] 0.79[b] 0.78[f]

[a] Ames.
[b] Weiss.
[c] White.
[d] LoPucki.
[e] Eberhard, Moore, and Roenfeldt.
[f] Franks and Torous.
[g] LoPucki and Whitford.

under chapter 7. The ratio of liabilities to assets at the time of filing is well above 1.0 in all three studies, providing support for the hypothesis that managers are able to delay filing for bankruptcy until well after the point where their firms become insolvent. The ratio of secured liabilities to assets is of interest, since managers attempting to avoid filing for bankruptcy have an incentive to convert unsecured claims to secured claims as a means of inducing creditors to renew their loans. If the ratio of secured liabilities to assets equaled 1.0, all of the firm's assets would be subject to some creditor's claim. Thus, a ratio of secured liabilities to assets of 1.0 represents an outer limit for delay in filing for bankruptcy, although measurement of assets at book rather than market value distorts the comparison. It is nonetheless interesting that the Ames study finds a ratio of exactly 1.0.

Given the delay in filing for bankruptcy, it is not surprising that unsecured and priority creditors receive little in bankruptcy liquidations. By the time firms file under chapter 7, most of their assets have either been claimed by secured creditors already or are subject to secured creditors' liens. There are few remaining assets available to unsecured creditors, and these have a tendency to disappear before the bankruptcy trustee can find them. Thus, unsecured creditors receive very little. White finds an average payoff rate to unsecured creditors of 4 percent. This represents an average for many firms in which creditors received nothing and an occasional firm in which creditors received a substantial payoff.

Turn now to small firms that file under chapter 11. All of the surveys suggest that firms filing under chapter 11 are larger than firms filing under chapter 7. This is not surprising, since reorganizing under chapter 11 involves reasonably high legal and accountants' costs, so that it is presumably not feasible for the smallest firms. Both the Ames and the White surveys also show that firms filing under chapter 11 are in better financial condition than firms filing under chapter 7, as measured by lower ratios of total liabilities to assets. (However, White's survey finds a higher ratio of secured liabilities to assets for firms filing under chapter 11.) This suggests that if managers intend to attempt a reorganization, they should file for bankruptcy when the firm is in better financial condition than if they intend merely to liquidate in bankruptcy. On the other hand, LoPucki provides evidence that suggests otherwise. He examines the events that precipitate firms' chapter 11 bankruptcy filings and finds that 73 percent of the firms filed at the time they did because they would otherwise have been forced to close down within several days by creditors claiming assets necessary for the firm's operation. Thus, managers may prefer to delay filing for bankruptcy as long as possible, and those that file under chapter 11 may be firms whose creditors happened to be unusually quick in taking legal action against the firm.

Both LoPucki's and White's evidence suggests that creditors play a relatively small role in the reorganization process. Trustees are virtually never appointed to replace managers of the firm, creditors' committees are often not appointed because creditors are unwilling to serve, and creditors almost never propose reorganization plans. Thus, in a typical chapter 11 case, managers continue to run the firm, eventually proposing a reorganization plan that creditors vote to accept or reject. Creditors' lack of participation in the bankruptcy process is not surprising, since their claims are invariably too small to justify spending time or hiring a lawyer to represent them. In LoPucki's sample, creditors' committees were appointed in 40 percent of cases and a trustee or examiner was appointed in 19 percent of cases. However, in several of the cases where a trustee or examiner was appointed, the firm had already closed down. In LoPucki's sample, reorganization plans calling for continuation of the firm's operations were proposed 40 percent of the time and plans were adopted 26 percent of the time. Thus, the probability of small firms' being saved in chapter 11 was not particularly high. However, LoPucki found that for the largest firms, particularly large manufacturing firms, the probability of the firm's being saved was much higher than for the smallest firms. (The fact that large manufacturing firms are most likely to be saved is not surprising, since their capital is likely to be specialized and therefore to have no higher value use.) Firms that did not eventually adopt a reorganization plan shut down. The payoff rates to unsecured creditors under the plans ranged from 10 percent to 100 percent; however, most of the plans included no interest and proposed repayment periods of 2.5 to 14 years. Thus, unsecured creditors tend to do better when firms reorganize than when they liquidate, although the comparison is biased by the fact that firms that reorganize are in better financial condition on average than firms that liquidate.

In White's sample of 64 firms that filed under chapter 11, 41 percent adopted reorganization plans and another 6 percent had reorganization plans that were pending at the time of the study and may or may not have been adopted. Thus, between 41 percent and 47 percent adopted reorganization plans. In another 23 percent of cases, creditors and management were not able to agree on a plan, but the firm continued operating and was sold as a going concern under chapter 11. Under this "liquidation reorganization" procedure, creditors were paid according to the APR. Thus, as many as 70 percent of the firms may have continued to operate in some form. The average payoff rate to unsecured creditors under the confirmed reorganization plans was 16 percent to be paid at the time of adoption of the plan plus 18 percent to be paid in future installments. (The installment figures are undiscounted and do not take account of the delay in payment to creditors.) Finally, the remaining 30 percent of firms converted from chapter 11 to chapter 7, shut down, and were liquidated piecemeal. Firms that had confirmed reorganization plans were in better financial condition than the entire group of firms filing under chapter 11: They had twice as many assets and only 50 percent more liabilities. However, they were not larger on average. The group of firms that underwent liquidation reorganizations were larger on average but had more secured claims: They had $3 million in liabilities compared to $2 million for all firms filing under chapter 11, but their ratio of secured liabilities to assets was 1.1, compared to 0.64 for all firms filing under chapter 11. Thus, secured creditors may have blocked the adoption of reorganization plans in these cases.

[b] Large Firms in Bankruptcy. Turn now to the experience of large, publicly traded firms in chapter 11 bankruptcy. Most of the information concerning large firms in bankruptcy comes from four studies: Weiss (1991); LoPucki and Whitford (1990); Eberhard, Moore, and Roenfeldt (1990); and Franks and Torous (1991). These studies all examine the experience of firms with publicly traded debt or equity that filed for bankruptcy during the 1980s. Because relatively few large firms filed for bankruptcy, the four samples of firms overlap substantially.

Weiss examines 37 firms listed on the New York Stock Exchange or the American Stock Exchange that filed for bankruptcy between 1980 and 1986. The average value of assets at the time of the filing was $222 million, and the average ratio of debts to assets was 0.77. Thus, these firms were much larger than the firms just discussed and were in better financial condition at the time they filed for bankruptcy. Presumably, this is because large firms' creditors have larger claims, so it is worthwhile for creditors to monitor the firms more carefully and initiate legal action against it more quickly.[15] These firms remained in bankruptcy for an average of 2.5 years (the standard deviation was 1.4 years).

Of the 37 firms in Weiss's study, 35, or 95 percent, filed under chapter 11 and 2 filed under chapter 7. Of the 35 firms that filed under chapter 11, 30 adopted reorganization plans that provided for the firm to continue operating and 5 were liquidated in chapter 11. Thus, the probability of firms' adopting a reorganization plan, conditional

---

[15] Weiss notes that the average ratio of debt to assets for all publicly traded firms is 0.51. Thus, the ratio for firms that filed for bankruptcy was only 50 percent higher.

on filing under chapter 11, is 86 percent. The payoff rates to unsecured creditors in Weiss's sample were 0.53 if the firm reorganized and 0.61 if the firm liquidated in chapter 11. (These figures ignore payment in stock in the reorganized firm.) It is interesting that creditors received more if the firm was liquidated in chapter 11 than if it reorganized. The direct costs of bankruptcy reorganization (legal costs plus other professional fees associated with the bankruptcy filing) were 3.1 percent of the value of the firm (market value of equity plus book value of debt). Of the 2 firms that filed under chapter 7, one paid nothing to unsecured creditors and the other paid a positive amount that was not specified. Thus, the small amount of available evidence for large firms in liquidation suggests that unsecured creditors receive little.

Weiss's study and a number of the others had the goal of documenting that the APR is violated in most reorganization plans. This means that equity receives some positive amount under the plan, even though creditors receive less than full payoff.[16] The fact that the APR is violated should be no surprise, since chapter 11 requires that equity holders vote in favor of the plan for it to be adopted by the uniform consent procedure and equity holders are unlikely to vote for a plan that eliminates them entirely. Weiss found that the APR was violated in 27 of 34 plans, or 79 percent of the time.

The samples examined by Eberhard, Moore, and Roenfeldt and Franks and Torous are similar. Eberhard, Moore, and Roenfeldt examined 30 firms that adopted reorganization plans under chapter 11, and Franks and Torous examined 41 firms that adopted reorganization plans under chapter 11.[17] Eberhard, Moore, and Roenfeldt found that firms took an average of 2.1 years from bankruptcy filing to confirmation of a reorganization plan, with a range from 10 months to over 6 years. They found that the APR was violated in 7 of 30 cases, or 23 percent. Franks and Torous found that firms took an average of 3.7 years from bankruptcy filing to confirmation of a reorganization plan. In their survey, the probability that the APR was violated was 78 percent.

LoPucki and Whitford examined 43 firms that filed under chapter 11. All had assets of at least $100 million, had some form of publicly traded security, and adopted reorganization plans by 1988. An interesting aspect of the study is that in most cases, the bankruptcy judge extended managers' exclusive period to propose a reorganization plan until a plan was adopted. Thus, creditors never had an opportunity to present a plan. A surprising number of these plans, 21, or 49 percent, were adopted using cramdown because at least one class did not vote in favor of the plan. However, only in 3 cases did any of the classes that voted against the plan contest its adoption. Thus, LoPucki and Whitford's evidence suggests that creditors' involvement in the reorganization process, whether through the proposal of their own plans or active opposition to the adoption of management-initiated plans, is rare.

LoPucki and Whitford distinguish between insolvent and solvent firms in calculating characteristics of reorganization plans, where insolvent firms paid less to unsecured creditors and equity together than the amount of unsecured creditors' claims. Of 30 insolvent firms, the average payoff rate to unsecured creditors was 30 percent, with a range from 0.5 percent to 81 percent. Nine of the 30 plans, or 30 percent, violated

---

[16] Note that the APR is not violated if unsecured creditors receive a positive payoff when secured creditors receive less than full payment. This is because secured creditors receive payment equal to the value of the assets on which they hold liens, and these assets may be worth less than the amount of the claim.

[17] Franks and Torous compare these firms to an additional sample of firms that underwent out-of-bankruptcy workouts.

FIGURE 7-4

Relationship Between Equity and Creditors' Claims

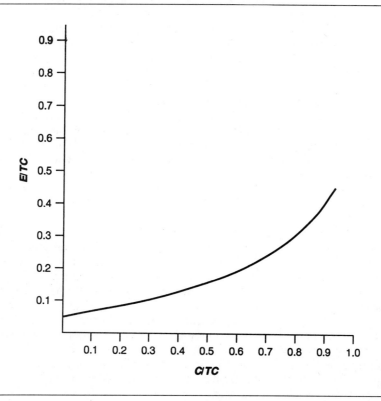

the APR by making a distribution to equity when unsecured creditors were not paid in full. Of 11 solvent firms in their sample, 6 firms, or 55 percent, adopted plans that violated the APR. The average payoff rate to unsecured creditors for the insolvent firms was 102 percent. Thus, the overall average payoff rate to unsecured creditors in LoPucki and Whitford's sample was 49 percent.

Data from these four studies can be used to investigate the nature of deviations from the APR and to predict how equity holders fare in chapter 11 reorganizations relative to unsecured creditors. Suppose that the amount paid to equity as a fraction of a creditors' total claims is E/TC and the amount paid to creditors as a fraction of creditors' total claims is C/TC. If the APR held precisely, a graph of the relationship between E/TC and C/TC would run along the horizontal axis as long as C/TC is less than 1 and would shift to being vertical where C/TC is equal to 1. Alternatively, if equity holders received a constant share of the firm regardless of the amount paid to creditors, the relationship would be linear and positive regardless of the level of C/TC. To establish the nature of the relationship, the author regressed E/TC on C/TC, using several different functional forms. The best-fitting regression was log-linear and is shown in Figure 7-4. The results suggest that equity holders always receive a low return in chapter 11 reorganizations, about 5 percent of creditors' claims, regardless of the firm's financial condition. But their return rises only slowly as the firm's financial condition improves, until the reorganization plan approaches full repayment of creditors' claims. When creditors are paid 80 percent of their claims, equity holders' expected payment is about 40 percent of creditors' claims.

7.05 BANKRUPTCY COSTS

Bankruptcy costs are the deadweight economic efficiency costs of the bankruptcy process, i.e., the resources consumed by the bankruptcy process itself. The previous discussion suggests that these costs play an important role in a firm's choice between liquidation, reorganization, and continuation outside of bankruptcy. Thus, it is of interest to know how high these costs actually are. Unfortunately, there is disagreement concerning the definition of "bankruptcy costs," with different writers focusing on different costs. A broad definition would include three types of bankruptcy costs: (1) costs incurred by all firms as a result of the bankruptcy system; (2) costs incurred when firms are failing but do not necessarily file for bankruptcy; and (3) costs incurred only when firms actually file for bankruptcy.

The first general category of bankruptcy costs, those incurred by all firms regardless of whether they are failing or not, is the broadest. Aghion, Hart, and Moore (1992) assert that because chapter 11 treats managers of failing firms gently, managers have an incentive to slack off in their efforts to maximize the firm's profits. They know that even if the firm makes losses and eventually enters chapter 11, they will retain their jobs and equity will remain intact at least temporarily. In contrast, under a bankruptcy system that provided for more drastic punishment of managers (such as one that would require all bankrupt firms to be sold on the open market), profits would be higher because managers would not slack off. According to this argument, the costs of bankruptcy are equal to the difference between firms' higher profits under an all-liquidation bankruptcy system and their lower profits under a bankruptcy system such as chapter 11. Conversely, it can be argued that if managers are risk averse, they may react to a harsh bankruptcy system by acting too conservatively and passing up efficient but risky investment opportunities because such investments endanger the firm.

Another bankruptcy cost in this category results from the fact that lenders ration funds and/or raise interest rates to all firms, since they anticipate that managers will engage in excessively risky investments if the firm begins to fail. The resulting shortage of capital leads firms to invest less in general and to pass up some economically efficient investment opportunities.

The second general category of bankruptcy costs consists of costs incurred when firms are actually failing. As discussed previously, managers of failing firms have an incentive to undertake excessively risky investments, because if the investments succeed, they will save the firm and the managers' jobs, while if they fail the losses will be borne by creditors. Bankruptcy costs result if managers undertake investments that are attractive because they are risky but are economically inefficient.

The last general category of bankruptcy costs consists of costs incurred when firms actually file for bankruptcy. Here, a major source of inefficiency results from misclassification of failing firms between the two U.S. bankruptcy procedures of chapter 7 liquidation and chapter 11 reorganization. Some firms entering bankruptcy are economically efficient, while others are economically inefficient. Correct classification occurs when inefficient firms liquidate under chapter 7 and efficient (although temporarily distressed) firms reorganize under chapter 11. However, since it is difficult to identify which failing firms are of which type, misclassification in bankruptcy is likely to be a common occurrence. One type of misclassification occurs when economically efficient firms liquidate, resulting in bankruptcy costs equal to the going-concern value of the firms, which is lost. The other type of misclassification occurs when inefficient firms reorganize under chapter 11 and are saved, at least temporarily. Then bankruptcy costs are incurred because reorganization delays the movement of resources from less-efficient to more-efficient uses. An interesting aspect of these two types of bankruptcy costs is that the former is quite obvious while the latter is hidden. When a firm shuts down, the resulting job losses and increases in unemployment and welfare claims make an important impression on policymakers. However, when firms that should shut down do not, the resulting bankruptcy cost is economic stagnation, which only becomes obvious when slow economic growth persists for many years.

[1] Empirical Estimates of Bankruptcy Costs

These bankruptcy cost components are difficult to quantify and a number of them have never been measured. Much of the research on bankruptcy costs has focused instead on a very narrow component of bankruptcy costs: the administrative costs of the bankruptcy procedure itself. Evidence on these costs is usually taken from bankruptcy court records, and most studies have shown them to be around 3 percent of the value of the firm.[18]

One way of measuring bankruptcy costs more generally involves using the risk premium on corporate bonds. The spread between interest rates on high-risk and low-risk corporate bonds with the same term measures investors' expectations of loss, converted to an even level over the terms of the bond. Actually, this amount should exceed creditors' expected losses by the amount of the costs investors expect to incur if a default occurs (such as costs for participating in bankruptcy negotiations), plus a premium for idiosyncratic risk. Figure 7-5 shows the spread between Moody's Baa and Aaa corporate bond rates, which are highest-quality and medium-quality corporate bonds, during the period 1970–1985. The spread averaged 0.013 during the period. The average total level of current liabilities of U.S. nonfinancial corporations over the same period, as reported by the *Federal Reserve Bulletin*, was $698 billion. These figures imply that investors expected to lose around $10 billion per year over the period. D&B data on actual losses, however, averaged $8.5 billion per year over the same period.[19] Thus, investors predicted that losses would be higher than they actually were. However, the figures fluctuate over the period. Failed liabilities have been increasing more quickly than investors' expectations. For 1985, failed liabilities equaled 3 percent of total liabilities, but the interest rate spread was only 0.013.

Another approach to measuring total bankruptcy costs makes use of the trade-off between the firm's tax incentive to replace equity with debt and the increase in expected bankruptcy costs that results from adding more debt and thereby making the

---

[18] See Haugen and Senbet (1978); Ang, Chua, and McConnell (1982); Altman (1984); Wruck (1990). See White (1983) for an attempt to measure the bankruptcy cost incurred when inefficient firms reorganize under chapter 11.

[19] Current liabilities rather than total liabilities of U.S. corporations are used, since the D&B data on failed liabilities exclude long-term subordinate debt. The two data series are still not completely comparable, however, since the D&B data include financial corporations.

FIGURE 7-5

Investors' Expectations of Business Failures Compared With Actual Failures

Source: Economic Report of the President *(Washington, D.C.: U.S. Government Printing Office) (interest rates and failed liabilities);* Federal Reserve Bulletin *(various issues), p. A36 (total liabilities).*

	Failed Liabilities	Total Liabilities	Ratio of Failed to Total Liabilities	Spread Between Moody's Baa and Aaa Bond Rates
1970	$ 1,888	$ 304,990	0.00619	0.0107
1971	1,917	326,000	0.00588	0.0117
1972	2,000	375,600	0.00532	0.0095
1973	2,299	450,900	0.00510	0.0080
1974	3,053	453,400	0.00673	0.0093
1975	4,380	451,600	0.00970	0.0178
1976	3,011	495,100	0.00608	0.0132
1977	3,095	557,100	0.00555	0.0095
1978	2,656	669,300	0.00397	0.0076
1979	2,667	807,800	0.00330	0.0106
1980	4,635	890,900	0.00520	0.0173
1981	6,955	971,000	0.00716	0.0187
1982	15,611	986,000	0.01583	0.0232
1983	16,073	1,059,000	0.01518	0.0151
1984	29,269	1,163,000	0.02517	0.0148
1985	36,809	1,200,750	0.03066	0.0135
Average	8,520	697,647	0.00981	0.0132

Note: Dollars in millions.

firm more risky. Gordon and Malkiel (1981) assumed that the first dollar of debt contracted by the firm causes zero bankruptcy costs and the last dollar of debt contracted by the firm causes bankruptcy costs equal to the tax advantage per dollar of debt over equity. (They also assumed that the firm has chosen the amount of debt in its capital structure that will minimize taxes plus bankruptcy costs.) The range between the first and last dollars of debt causes linearly increasing bankruptcy costs to be incurred, starting with zero and ending at the cutoff point implied by the equality. The firm's total capitalization is assumed to remain fixed; only its debt-to-equity ratio changes.

Then total bankruptcy costs can be estimated by the area under the bankruptcy cost function, which in this case is a triangle. Gordon and Malkiel calculate the size of the triangle for the entire U.S. economy. The height of the triangle is the tax incentive per year of replacing a dollar of equity with a dollar of debt, assumed to be $0.014 in 1975 dollars. The base is the total amount of corporate debt, which was $440 billion in 1975. The resulting estimate of total bankruptcy costs is $3.1 billion per year in 1975 dollars. Since U.S. corporate profits taxes were around $44 billion in 1975, this means that total bankruptcy costs were 7 percent of the value of corporate tax payments.

While none of these studies are definitive, they suggest that total bankruptcy costs are high and constitute quite a sizable drain on the economy. The Tax Reform Act of

1986 reduced these costs by lowering corporate tax rates, which reduced corporate firms' incentive to raise their debt-to-equity ratios. Another way to reduce bankruptcy costs is to improve the actual U.S. bankruptcy procedure. But as the previous discussion of proposals to streamline bankruptcy procedures suggested, doing so has ambiguous effects, since improvements to the bankruptcy procedure itself tend to give managers of failing firms an incentive to avoid bankruptcy. This in turn increases the deadweight costs of delay and inefficient use of assets, as managers turn to excessively risky investments in their attempts to avoid bankruptcy.

Suggested Reading

Aghion, P., O. Hart, and J. Moore. "The Economics of Bankruptcy Reform." *Journal of Law, Economics and Organization,* Vol. 8 (Oct. 1992), pp. 523–546.

Altman, E.I. "A Further Empirical Investigation of the Bankruptcy Cost Question." *Journal of Finance,* Vol. XXXIX (Sept. 1984), pp. 1067–1089.

Ames, Nancy, et al. *An Evaluation of the U.S. Trustee Pilot Program for Bankruptcy Administration: Findings and Recommendations.* U.S. Department of Justice, Consultants' Study. Cambridge, Mass.: Abt Associates, 1983.

Ang, J.S., J.H. Chua, and J.J. McConnell. "The Administrative Costs of Corporate Bankruptcy: A Note." *Journal of Finance,* Vol. XXXVII (Mar. 1982), pp. 219–226.

Baird, D.G. "The Uneasy Case for Corporate Reorganizations." *Journal of Legal Studies,* Vol. XV (Jan. 1986), pp. 127–147.

Baird, Douglas G., and Thomas Jackson. *Cases, Problems and Materials on Bankruptcy.* Boston: Little, Brown & Co., 1985.

Baird, D., and R. Picker. "A Simple Noncooperative Bargaining Model of Corporate Reorganization." *Journal of Legal Studies,* Vol. 20 (1991), pp. 311–350.

Bebchuk, L.A. "A New Method for Corporate Reorganization." *Harvard Law Review,* Vol. 101 (1986), pp. 775–803.

Bebchuk, L.A., and H. Chang. "Bargaining and the Division of Value in Corporate Reorganization." *Journal of Law, Economics and Organization,* Vol. 8 (1992), pp. 253–279.

Bradley, M., and M. Rosenzweig. "The Untenable Case for Chapter 11." *Yale Law Journal,* Vol. 101 (1992), p. 1043.

Brown, D. "Claimholder Incentive Conflicts in Reorganization: The Role of Bankruptcy Law." *Review of Financial Studies,* Vol. 2 (1989), pp. 109–123.

Bulow, J., and J. Shoven. "The Bankruptcy Decision." *Bell Journal of Economics,* Vol. 9 (Autumn 1978), pp. 437–456.

Easterbrook, F. "Is Corporate Bankruptcy Efficient?" *Journal of Financial Economics,* Vol. 27, 411–417.

Eberhard, A., W. Moore, and R. Roenfeldt. "Security Pricing and Deviations From the Absolute Priority Rule in Bankruptcy Proceedings." *Journal of Finance,* Vol. XLV (1990), pp. 1457–1469.

Fama, Eugene F., and Merton H. Miller. *The Theory of Finance.* New York: Holt, Rinehart and Winston, 1972.

Franks, J., and W. Torous. "An Empirical Investigation of U.S. Firms in Reorganization." *Journal of Finance,* Vol. XLIV (1989), pp. 747–769.

Gertner, R., and D. Scharfstein. "A Theory of Workouts and the Effects of Reorganization Law." *Journal of Finance,* Vol. XLVI (1991), pp. 1189–1222.

Gilson, S.C., K. John, and L.H.P. Lang. "Troubled Debt Restructurings: An Empirical Study of Private Reorganization of Firms in Default." *Journal of Financial Economics,* Vol. 27 (1990), pp. 315–353.

Gordon, Roger H., and Burton G. Malkiel. "Taxation and Corporate Finance," *How Taxes Affect Economic Behavior,* H. Aaron and J. Pechman, eds. Washington, D.C.: The Brookings Institute, 1981.

Haugen, R.A., and L.W. Senbet. "The Insignificance of Bankruptcy Costs to the Theory of Optimal Capital Structure." *Journal of Finance* (May 1978), pp. 383–393.

Jackson, Thomas H. *The Logic and Limits of Bankruptcy Law.* Cambridge, Mass.: Harvard University Press, 1986.

LoPucki, L.M. "The Debtor in Full Control—Systems Failure under Chapter 11 of the Bankruptcy Code?" *American Bankruptcy Law Journal,* Vol. 57 (1983), pp. 99–126 (first installment), pp. 247–273 (second installment).

LoPucki, L., and W. Whitford. "Bargaining Over Equity's Share in the Bankruptcy Reorganization of Large, Publicly Held Companies." *University of Pennsylvania Law Review,* Vol. 139 (1990), p. 125.

Nelson, Phillip B. *Corporations in Crisis: Behavioral Observations for Bankruptcy Policy.* New York: Praeger, 1981.

Posner, Richard. *Economic Analysis of Law,* 1st ed. Boston: Little, Brown & Co., 1972.

Roe, M. "Bankruptcy and Debt: A New Model for Corporate Reorganization." *Columbia Law Review,* Vol. 83 (Apr. 1983), pp. 527–602.

Stiglitz, J. "Some Aspects of the Pure Theory of Corporate Finance: Bankruptcies and Take-Overs." *Bell Journal of Economics,* Vol. 3 (Autumn 1972), pp. 458–482.

Warner, J.B. "Bankruptcy Costs: Some Evidence." *Journal of Finance* (May 1977), pp. 337–348.

Warren, Elizabeth, "The Untenable Case for Repeal of Chapter 11." *Yale Law Journal,* Vol. 102 (1992), pp. 437–479.

Webb, D.C. "The Importance of Incomplete Information in Explaining the Existence of Costly Bankruptcy." *Economica,* Vol. 54 (Aug. 1987), pp. 279–288.

Weiss, L. "Bankruptcy Resolution: Direct Costs and Violation of Priority of Claims." *Journal of Financial Economics,* Vol. 27 (1990), pp. 285–314.

———. "Restructuring Complications in Bankruptcy: The Eastern Airlines Bankruptcy Case." Working Paper, Freeman School of Business, Tulane University, 1991.

White, M.J. "Bankruptcy Costs and the New Bankruptcy Code." *Journal of Finance* (May 1983), pp. 477–488.

———. "Bankruptcy Liquidation and Reorganization." *Handbook of Modern Finance,* 1st ed. Dennis Logue, ed. Boston: Warren Gorham Lamont, 1984, ch. 35.

———. "The Corporate Bankruptcy Decision." *Journal of Economic Perspectives,* Vol. 3 (1989).

———. "Personal Bankruptcy Under the 1978 Bankruptcy Code: An Economic Analysis." *Indiana Law Journal.* Vol. 63 (1987), pp. 1–53.

———. "Public Policy Toward Bankruptcy: Me-First and Other Priority Rules." *Bell Journal of Economics* (Autumn 1980), pp. 550–564.

Wruck, K.H. "Financial Distress, Reorganization and Organizational Efficiency." *Journal of Financial Economics,* Vol. 27 (1990), pp. 419–440.

Chapter 8
Corporate Restructuring and Reorganization

James K. Seward

8.01 INTRODUCTION

Although a large number and diversity of decisions and activities confront modern corporate managers, the field of finance generally focuses on the relationships between firm value and three particular aspects of managerial behavior: investment, financing, and distribution of cash to shareholders. As economic, regulatory, competitive, and financial conditions change, however, the ability of corporate managers to implement value-maximizing decisions may be constrained by a firm's existing organizational structure. The various techniques of corporate restructuring and reorganization provide methods by which corporate management may implement changes in asset structure, financial structure, ownership, and corporate governance that facilitate the adoption of value-maximizing decisions. The purpose of this chapter is to review the current methods of corporate restructuring and reorganization, examine the causes and benefits of this activity, and discuss its relationship to merger and acquisition activity. The primary argument is that the activity of restructuring and reorganizing corporations serves as an important and useful means to enhance economic efficiency and therefore firm value. This objective is accomplished by creating organizational structures and managerial incentives that facilitate the adoption of value-enhancing investment, financing, and cash distribution decisions.

The modern corporation is often characterized as a "nexus of contracts," many of which are necessary to mitigate the conflicts of interest that arise as a consequence of the separation of ownership and control. Within a given organization, it is the responsibility of the board of directors to monitor the decisions of top management. The board of directors has two means available to control and direct the actions of management: the design of managerial incentive contracts and managerial turnover or dismissal decisions. But, as corporate asset and financial structures change, it may not be possible to use the threat of dismissal or changes in management compensation contracts to motivate efficient decisions within a given organizational structure. For example, as the operations of a firm evolve and become increasingly complex and diversified, it may not be possible to design a single compensation and incentive structure that motivates top management to utilize the firm's assets as efficiently as possible. In this case, as corporate performance deteriorates, incumbent management may face a challenge for control by other firms. In this view, corporate restructuring and reorganization represent an opportunity to realign the interests of shareholders and management. It should be noted, however, that corporate restructuring and reorganization activities do not necessarily guarantee improved performance. What matters is that the process of restructuring and reorganization creates the organizational change necessary to then facilitate the implementation of more efficient managerial decision making.

Although many types of firms can potentially benefit from some form of restructuring or reorganization, diversified conglomerates are often cited as a classic example of an entity that is likely to benefit from this activity. By design, the process of corporate diversification moves the firm in the direction of new and often unrelated lines of business. While these new operations can be started and developed within an organization, corporate diversification often takes the form of acquisition of other entities. Corporate restructuring and reorganization provides a means to divest some (or, in the extreme case, all) of the assets acquired in these transactions.

Restructuring and reorganization techniques allow firms to sell assets, create new and independent organizations for some portion of a firm's existing assets and liabilities, alter a firm's financial structure, write new management compensation contracts,

FIGURE 8-1

Classification of Corporate Restructuring and Reorganization Techniques

Reallocating assets
  Sell-offs
  Voluntary liquidations
Reallocating debt and equity
  ESOPs
  Dual-class recaps
  Leveraged recaps
  Exchange offers
  Share repurchase programs
Creating new private ownership organizations
  Going-private transactions (LBOs and MBOs)
  Joint ventures
Creating new public ownership organizations
  Spin-offs
  Equity carve-outs

create new board structures, or temporarily separate certain corporate assets and capital. With regard to the latter case, some of the benefits of corporate restructuring and reorganization can be achieved without necessarily implementing permanent, irreversible changes in a firm's organizational structure. Restructuring and reorganization techniques represent a dynamic opportunity that requires continuous attention and monitoring by corporate managers. Perhaps one of the most important lessons of the 1980s is that if current management is not alert and attentive, there are other outside forces that may benefit by identifying such opportunities, perhaps even replacing the existing management in the process.

8.02 TECHNIQUES FOR CORPORATE REORGANIZATION AND RESTRUCTURING

The decision to restructure and/or reorganize a corporation depends not only on the costs and benefits of a particular activity but also on an analysis of alternative techniques. The decision involves a determination of the objectives sought through a formal restructuring, and then the selection of the methods appropriate to those objectives. It is important to emphasize that these activities can create valuable strategic and financial benefits even in the case of a corporation that appears to be operating successfully. Corporations need not be financially distressed in order to reap the benefits of this activity.

Figure 8-1 contains a general classification scheme for the most common forms of corporate restructuring and reorganization. The organization of Figure 8-1 provides one way to think about the linkage between the corporation's objectives and the use of various restructuring techniques. Although these categories are not mutually exclusive (e.g., going-private transactions often involve a substantial reallocation of a firm's capital from equity to debt), they provide a classification scheme based on the most salient feature of each technique. Broadly speaking, the classification scheme is based on two general objectives: restructuring an organization's existing balance sheet (i.e., reallocating assets and financial claims) and creating new organizational structures (i.e., publicly owned and privately owned entities). In order to gain a better understanding of each technique, we now examine each in detail.

[1] Reallocating Assets

[a] **Sell-Offs.** A sell-off, or divestiture, is the sale of some portion of a company to a third-party buyer. In this transaction, the seller transfers control of subsidiaries, divisions, or some other set of operating assets to the buyer in exchange for cash, securities, or even perhaps some segment of the purchaser's assets. Thus, sell-offs represent a way in which the selling corporation can transfer part of its current asset base to an acquiror that, for various reasons, is able to employ those assets more efficiently. The seller effectively transforms the asset side of its balance sheet by exchanging one set of assets (e.g., plant and equipment) for another (usually cash). To the extent that this activity facilitates the transfer of some portion of an organization's assets to another organization that can utilize and manage the assets more efficiently, aggregate economic activity and performance improves. From the seller's viewpoint, however, the sale is desirable if and only if the net sale proceeds exceed the present value of the net future cash flows generated by continued ownership. These observations suggest that the benefits of selling assets depend on what alternative uses (including value added from the new management) exist for the assets and the competition among potential acquirors for those assets. The existence of higher-value alternative uses will determine the magnitude of the total incremental value generated by the divestiture, and the competition among potential acquirors is likely to determine the allocation of these benefits between the buyer and the seller. As an example, suppose that the present value of the net future cash flows from a particular set of existing assets is $100. Suppose that the present value of these same assets is equal to $150 under the ownership of another firm. The difference in these flows, $50, represents the aggregate benefit from the asset sale. The bargaining process between buyer and seller will then determine how this benefit of $50 is to be divided. The higher the sale price, the greater the benefit that is allocated to the selling firm.

This example also suggests two important observations. First, although the aggregate economic benefit created by this activity depends on the ability of the buyer to put those assets to more efficient use, at least some of the improvement is paid to the shareholders of the selling firm. The higher the sale price, the greater the proportion of the benefit that is earned by the shareholders of the selling firm. If the buying firm offers to pay $150 for the assets, the entire improvement from the divestiture goes to the selling firm's shareholders. Even though the assets in this example are more valuable to the potential acquiror, they should not be transferred at a price higher than $150. If the acquiring firm offers to pay a higher price, the transaction will actually decrease the wealth of the acquiring firm's shareholders. In this case, while divestiture is still desirable from an aggregate economic standpoint, the net benefit to the acquiring firm is actually negative.

Management may, however, be reluctant to divest corporate assets. This situation can arise even if the sale of assets would enhance the firm's market value. Boot (1992), for example, argues that managers may avoid divestitures if such decisions are perceived as adversely affecting outside perceptions of managerial ability. Thus, managers who care about their own reputation may elect to maintain ownership of an ongoing project in order to avoid the appearance that they are not skilled enough to manage those assets. It is important to recognize, however, that the reluctance to sell assets by incumbent management may represent an opportunity for an outside acquiror to buy the firm and then implement the value-maximizing divestment decision. Many of the acquisitions that occurred during the 1980s that were then sold piecemeal to new owners illustrate the feasibility of this approach. Baker (1992) provides a detailed study of the potential profitability of this strategy in his examination of Beatrice Companies. Thus, the desire to maintain ownership of unprofitable divisions or assets by incumbent management must be balanced by the awareness that this decision may increase the likelihood of a takeover attempt.

[b] Liquidations. Although liquidations are often associated with formal bankruptcy proceedings (i.e., chapter 7 of the U.S. Bankruptcy Code), corporations may occasionally elect to liquidate voluntarily. The focus here is on the latter case. The outcome of voluntary corporate liquidations is the cessation of the activities of a corporation. A firm sells all of its assets, generally to several buyers. Thus, a voluntary liquidation may be viewed as an extreme case of a sell-off. Once the assets have been sold, the proceeds are used to retire the firm's existing debt. Any remaining funds are then distributed to the firm's shareholders as a liquidating dividend. The decision rule for adopting a voluntary corporate liquidation is similar to that in the case of divestiture: When a firm's entire set of assets can be sold for an amount that exceeds the present value of future net cash flows from continued operation, liquidation may be in the best interest of shareholders.

Although liquidations share many characteristics in common with sell-offs, at least two important distinctions need to be considered. In a liquidation, a firm's existing creditors must be paid completely before shareholders receive any distribution. Thus, if the market value of a firm's debt is less than its face value, some of the proceeds from the asset sales will accrue to the bondholders. Liquidation effectively accelerates the principal repayment. For firms that are performing poorly or have a large amount of debt outstanding, this distinction may represent a dominant concern. The second distinguishing feature of a voluntary liquidation is that the firm's assets are often sold in pieces to several different buyers. Hence, the liquidating firm is engaged in bargaining over asset sales and prices with several acquirors. Since the selling firm always has the alternative of seeking a single acquiror for all of the organization's assets, the sales to separate buyers presumably allocate the assets to the entity that values them the highest. Thus, voluntary liquidation may be a better alternative than selling the entire firm to a single buyer because in the former case, the liquidating firm's shareholders keep all of the excess sales proceeds while in the latter case, the acquiring firm's shareholders may obtain some of these benefits. This would happen if the acquiring firm purchases all of the assets of the selling firm and then sells the acquired assets to separate buyers at an aggregate price that exceeds its own acquisition cost.

In summary then, sell-offs and voluntary liquidations represent restructuring techniques that facilitate the transfer of assets from one organizational management group to another. This activity is beneficial if the management of the acquiring organization is able to employ those assets more efficiently. Figure 8-2 provides a summary of corporate sell-off activity for the years 1982–1991. The intensity of corporate divestiture activity increased substantially throughout the 1980s, both in terms of the number and the dollar value of transactions. However, the dollar value of the average corporate divestiture has declined dramatically since the 1988 peak of $156.4 million. This trend

FIGURE 8-2

Corporate Divestitures (1982–1991)

Source: Mergerstat Review (Chicago, Ill.: W.T. Grimm & Co.)

Year	Divestitures	Number of Divestitures Disclosing Price	Total Value Paid (Millions)	Average Purchase Price (Millions)
1982	875	317	$16,050.3	$ 50.6
1983	932	376	24,173.9	63.3
1984	900	401	29,379.0	73.3
1985	1,218	525	45,825.6	87.3
1986	1,259	543	59,926.9	110.4
1987	807	388	58,290.6	150.2
1988	894	445	69,614.9	156.4
1989	1,055	508	70,843.7	139.5
1990	940	409	42,179.8	103.1
1991	849	332	29,256.1	88.1

toward smaller price transactions is similar to recent events throughout the entire corporate control arena, including mergers and acquisitions. Nevertheless, the information contained in Figure 8-2 suggests that many corporate managers use divestitures to reallocate assets and that this process involves a substantial restructuring of assets in market value terms.

[2] Reallocating Debt and Equity

[a] **Exchange Offers.** An exchange offer is a transaction in which corporate management offers current holders of certain classes of a firm's financial securities the opportunity to exchange some fraction of their claims for a different class of the firm's securities. Exchange offers are generally made to all of the holders of the class of securities sought by the firm, but the firm usually sets a maximum limit on the total number of securities that it will accept for exchange. In the event that more securities are offered by the holders than are sought by the firm, each participating holder's offer is rationed. Figure 8-3 provides a summary of various exchange offers that have been used by corporations.

Recently, the incidence of exchange offers has increased as the number of firms experiencing financial distress has increased. For such firms, common-stock-for-debt exchanges provide a method by which highly leveraged firms can reduce their debt burden. But firms that are not financially distressed also utilize exchange offers to implement changes in capital structure and ownership allocation. For example, consider a firm that has a stable cash flow, moderate capital expenditure requirements, and a high marginal corporate tax rate. If the firm was currently financed primarily by equity, a debt-for-common-stock exchange offer would provide a way to increase leverage and enhance firm value by increasing corporate tax shields. Generally, exchange offers do not alter a firm's asset base, nor do they provide new financial claimants. They represent a simple shifting of the type of claim held by a portion of the

FIGURE 8-3

Examples of Different Classes of Exchange Offers

Source: J. Fred Weston, Kai Chung, and Susan Hoag, *Mergers, Restructuring and Corporate Control* (Englewood Cliffs, N.J.: Prentice-Hall, Inc., 1990), pp. 452–453

Debt for common stock
Preferred for common stock
Debt for preferred stock
Income bonds for preferred stock
Common stock for debt
Private swaps of common stock for debt
Preferred stock for debt
Common for preferred stock

existing providers of capital. In order to induce some of the existing claimants to exchange one type of claim for another class, the firm will have to offer favorable terms in the exchange. That is, the market value of the new securities offered by the firm must exceed the value forgone by exchanging the existing securities. Otherwise, none of the current holders would participate in the exchange offer. But this suggests that there must be some offsetting benefit that is obtained by completing the exchange offer and that this benefit must exceed the premium offered by the firm in the exchange offer. In the absence of such benefits, the cost of the premium is borne by the firm's nonparticipating financial claimants. In this case, exchange offers would represent an undesirable transfer of existing wealth rather than a method to implement a value-enhancing alteration of the firm's financial structure.

Exchange offers grant claimants the *right* but not the *obligation* to participate. As a result, some holders may elect to hold out in the expectation that the postexchange offer value of their existing claim will exceed the value of participation in the exchange. Since all existing claimants face similar incentives, there is some probability that any exchange offer will fail. In practice, some corporations have relied on coercive techniques in order to successfully complete exchange offers. In the case of public debt, this is accomplished by modifying the bond covenants through a technique known as consent solicitations or exit consents. The combination of exit consents and exchange (or tender) offers works as follows. A firm announces an exchange offer, but conditions the offer on a bondholder vote to change or eliminate the issue's covenant or covenants. The issuer also conditions its acceptance of the exchanged debt on approval of the consent solicitation by the requisite majority. The loss in value for bondholders that elect to retain their original, stripped debt claim generally outweighs the benefits of electing not to participate. As a result, firms can design financial restructuring programs that simultaneously strip the protection of existing bond indentures and coerce participation in tender or exchange offers. The important point is that the firm may ultimately find that the costs of resolving the holdout problem in exchange offers can be sufficiently large so as to eliminate all of the economic benefit created by a successful debt restructuring.

[b] Share Repurchase Programs. In a common stock repurchase, a firm acquires a fraction of its own outstanding stock in exchange for the distribution of cash to the tendering shareholders. Share repurchases that are financed by corporate borrowing are thus somewhat similar to a debt-for-common-stock exchange offer. However, there are at least two important differences. First, cash is distributed to the participating equity claimants in the share repurchase, while debt securities are distributed to the exchange offer participants. Second, the equity participants in the share repurchase often cease to hold any financial claim against the firm upon completion of the transaction. The equity participants in the exchange offer continue as claimants against the firm, but now as creditors rather than owners. Since, as is the case with exchange offers, participants must be induced to participate, premiums are often paid in share repurchase programs. The actual premium paid depends on the number of shares that the firm seeks and the method by which the repurchase is to be completed. There are three general methods by which a firm may elect to repurchase shares: tender offer, open-market repurchase, and targeted share repurchase. There are two types of tender offer share repurchase methods: fixed-price and Dutch auction.

In a fixed-price tender offer, the company will normally specify (1) the (maximum) number of shares the firm is offering to repurchase; (2) the (fixed) price at which the firm will repurchase the shares; and (3) the offer's expiration date. Usually, if the actual number of shares tendered exceeds the number specified in the offer, either all shares tendered can be purchased or the shares can be acquired on a pro rata basis. If shareholders tender less than a prespecified minimum number of shares that the firm seeks to repurchase, the firm may (1) withdraw the offer; (2) only repurchase shares that were tendered, even though the offer is undersubscribed; or (3) extend the offer's expiration date.

The distinguishing feature of the Dutch auction method is that instead of announcing a single, fixed repurchase price, the firm announces a range of prices (including a minimum and maximum) at which the firm is willing to buy shares. Shareholders then decide whether to tender their shares and on a price within the range that they would accept for their shares. The actual repurchase price is established as the minimum price sufficient to buy the specified number of shares. All of the successful tendering shareholders receive this same price. One distinction then is that in the case of the Dutch auction, shareholders tell the firm the price at which they are willing to sell shares. In the fixed-price method, the firm announces one price, and shareholders decide whether that price is acceptable or not.

In an open-market repurchase, the firm seeks to periodically buy shares (anonymously) in the secondary market rather than through a formal tender offer. Compared to the tender offer method, open-market share repurchases are more frequent, generally represent a smaller fraction of the firm's shares, and take longer to complete. Targeted share repurchases are discriminatory in the sense that the firm seeks to buy back the ownership stake of a particular shareholder or group of shareholders. Thus, in these programs, it is not at the discretion of each shareholder to determine whether to participate. It is the firm that makes this decision. Common examples of targeted share repurchases include greenmail (which prevents the possibility of a hostile takeover) and odd-lot share ownership (which economizes on shareholder servicing costs). Generally, share repurchases are more complex transactions than exchange offers because they change the composition of a firm's assets, alter the firm's financial structure, and revise the ownership proportion of each shareholder. Share repurchases represent just one way to distribute cash to shareholders. Figure 8-4 presents some general information on other methods of cash distribution and also provides some indication of the increasing importance of share repurchases.

FIGURE 8-4

Annual Cash Distributions to Shareholders (1977–1987)

Source: L. Bagwell and J. Shoven, "Cash Distributions to Shareholders," *Journal of Economic Perspectives,* Vol. 3 (1989), p. 131

Year	Cash via Acquisitions	Dividends	Share Repurchases
1977	$ 4,274	$29,450	$ 3,361
1978	7,228	32,830	3,520
1979	16,888	38,324	4,507
1980	13,081	42,619	4,961
1981	29,319	46,832	3,973
1982	26,247	50,916	8,080
1983	21,248	54,896	7,709
1984	64,244	60,266	27,444
1985	69,971	67,564	41,303
1986	74,522	77,122	41,521
1987	62,240	83,051	54,336

Note: Current dollars in millions.

   [c] Leveraged Recapitalizations. A leveraged recapitalization (often called a leveraged recap) is a transaction in which a firm replaces the majority (but not all) of its equity with debt. Thus, although leveraged recaps involve a substantial increase in financial leverage and a concurrent reduction in equity, the public shareholders retain some ongoing ownership claim in the company. Typically, a company involved in a leveraged recap uses new debt to pay its current shareholders a large onetime dividend. Since management usually holds some ownership in the firm and does not participate in the dividend distribution, leveraged recaps substantially increase management's proportional ownership of the recapitalized firm. Thus, in the process of changing from an equity-denominated to a debt-denominated financial structure, management concentrates its ownership position without any additional personal investment. The firm's existing asset base is used as collateral to borrow large sums, which are used in turn to decrease the outside ownership of the firm. An example might help to clarify these points.

   On February 24, 1986, the FMC Corporation announced that it would borrow approximately $1.5 billion in order to implement the following recapitalization plan. Each public shareholder would receive $70 plus one share of new FMC stock for each share held prior to the restructuring. The company thrift plan participants would receive $25 plus 4 new shares. Finally, management and the company stock ownership plan participants would receive no cash but 5⅔ new shares. This allocation of shares increased the ownership of corporate insiders from 19 percent to 40 percent. Note also that by fixing the allocation of shares in the newly recapitalized firm in advance, the postrecapitalization value of the holdings of each of these three shareholder groups could differ, depending on the actual share price of the new shares. (Subsequently, the Colt Industries leveraged recap introduced the concept of a "floating" share exchange ratio based on the initial market price of the postrecapitalization equity). Thus, FMC's shares continue to be publicly traded so that the public shareholders receive the special dividend payment and have the opportunity to share in future share price appreciation. Corporate insiders obtain a substantially larger ownership position in the recapitalized firm but at the cost of not participating in the cash dividend payment.

[d] **Dual-Class Recapitalizations.** The most common form of equity ownership in U.S. corporations involves a single class of common stock with each share conveying the same proportional rights to residual cash flows and voting rights. However, some companies have multiple classes of common stock outstanding. These classes differ with regard to their respective rights to future cash flows and/or their voting power. Thus, dual-class recapitalizations (often called dual-class recaps) represent a technique in which proportional ownership of cash flow rights can be differentiated from proportional ownership of voting rights. There are three distinct methods by which firms can implement their dual-class recaps.

The first, known as the dividend method, begins with a stock split or dividend that is distributed to existing equity claimants. The new stock is generally designated as the low-vote stock, in that it has fewer votes per share than the high-vote class or it is entitled to elect only a minority of the board of directors. The firm then allows shareholders to exchange their high-vote shares for low-vote shares and generally offers a higher dividend to induce conversion. As long as some conversion by public shareholders occurs, corporate insider ownership will increase accordingly. As in the case of the leveraged recap, this larger voting control right can come about with no incremental personal investment. However, unlike leveraged recaps, dual-class recaps generally confer future voting power and control at the expense of ownership of future residual cash flows. This occurs because the low-vote class generally receives higher dividend and/or liquidation rights. Thus, management must derive some benefit independent of its residual cash flow rights in order for this transaction to make economic sense.

The second form of dual-class recap is known as the exchange method, in which the firm offers to directly exchange low-vote, high-cash flow shares for existing high-vote, low-cash flow shares.

The final method of implementation is known as the length-of-time method, in which the voting rights of existing common stock are based on the length of time that shares are held. At the recapitalization date, all shares become high-vote shares (e.g., 10 votes per share). Subsequently, as soon as shares are traded, they lose the excess voting power.

A dual-class recap involves no change in asset structure or the composition of senior financial claims. It merely represents one way to separate the ownership of residual cash flow rights and the ownership of voting rights. Here, concentration of voting power in the hands of insiders can occur without adversely affecting the personal wealth positions of management. Ownership concentration may also be financed through a leveraging of corporate assets. Often, the insider ownership position of management increases by an amount large enough to guarantee majority voting power. While such a position may protect insiders from a hostile takeover, it may also effectively insulate management from the operation of the market for corporate control. Thus, given these conflicting impacts, it is not clear whether these transactions are beneficial or harmful to current public shareholders.

[e] **ESOPs.** An employee stock ownership plan (ESOP) is a defined contribution employee benefit pension plan that invests primarily in the common equity of the

FIGURE 8-5

Participants and Assets of ESOPs

Source: J. Weston, K. Chung, and S. Hoag, *Mergers, Restructuring and Corporate Control* (Englewood Cliffs, N.J.: Prentice-Hall, Inc., 1990), p. 376

Type	Participants		Assets		
	Number (Thousands)	Percent	Total (Millions)	Percent	Median/ Participant
Tax credit	6,931	90	$14,800	79	$2,952
Leveraged	158	2	1,450	8	8,660
Leverageable	293	4	1,445	8	7,149
Nonleveraged	238	3	961	5	5,098
Other	2	0	1	0	0
Total[a]	7,083	100	$18,660	100	$5,226

[a] Sums may not add owing to rounding.

employer. Thus, an ESOP is a method that enables employees to gain a tax-free owner-ship stake in their employer firms. There are four different types of ESOPs: leveraged, leverageable, nonleveraged, and tax credit. In a leveraged ESOP, the plan borrows funds from a financial institution to purchase the securities of the employer firm. In turn, the employer firm makes contributions to an ESOP trust (which holds the securi-ties) in order to meet the plan's interest and principal payments. Employee ownership of the shares accrues according to the rate at which the principal on the loan is repaid. In a leverageable ESOP, the plan is authorized but not required to borrow funds to purchase the employer firm's securities. Under this plan, cash or securities may be contributed to the plan according to a defined formula. A nonleverageable ESOP makes no provision for the use of borrowed funds by the plan. This form of ESOP is similar to a stock bonus plan and must invest primarily in the securities of the employer firm. Finally, a tax credit ESOP is funded by company tax credits earned on plant and equipment (in which case it is called a TRASOP) or on payroll (in which case it is called a PAYSOP). Figure 8-5 provides some indication of the number of participants in and the assets controlled by each type of plan. The data pertain to 1983, the last year for which such detailed data are available (as of spring 1991).

Although tax credit ESOPs are the dominant method, this type of ESOP was termi-nated as of December 1986. However, since the remaining types also provide some degree of tax advantage, they will likely continue to be an important source of equity ownership in the future. ESOPs have been used as vehicles for a variety of activities, such as buying private companies, acquisition of divested subsidiaries or divisions, takeover defense, and attempting to save failed companies. The purpose of this form of restructuring seems to be that it allows employees to participate in the ownership of their employer firms. In principle, this linkage between firm performance and employee ownership allows the employees of the firm to benefit financially from their efforts. Since ESOPs also have favorable tax consequences associated with them, they can provide a technique to improve employee incentives and performance while reducing taxes.

[3] Creating New Ownership Organizations

[a] **Spin-Offs.** A spin-off separates a firm into two or more independent entities. In a spin-off, the firm may distribute all (or part) of some subset of its existing assets and liabilities to its current shareholders as a dividend in kind. Management usually distributes the new shares pro rata, so that the transaction does not alter the shareholders' proportional ownership of the parent company and the newly spun-off entity. Thus, spin-offs per se involve no cash flow changes; they merely represent a stock distribution to existing shareholders of a newly created, independent entity. Whereas before the spin-off the shareholder held a single claim against the assets of the firm, after the spin-off the shareholder owns separate equity claims against two different organizations. As a result of the separation of the firm into two parts, investors now have the opportunity to invest in whichever part (or both) they desire.

For example, when Dart & Kraft wanted to separate its food products operations from its consumer products division, the parent company organized the division into a company called Premark, which was spun off to the firm's shareholders. The parent company retained the food products operations and renamed the company Kraft. Before the spin-off, any investor that wanted to own equity in Dart & Kraft's food operations would also have to own equity in its consumer products operations. As a result of the spin-off of the latter, Dart & Kraft shareholders now owned separate equity claims and could trade each independently of the other. From an organizational standpoint, since there were now two separate companies, each would have its own chief executive officer and board of directors. Both Kraft and Premark would now provide financial information and statements on their own operations, and the separated equity would permit executive incentive compensation contracts tied only to food operations or only to consumer products. Before the spin-off, with only a single equity claim traded, this degree of refinement would not be possible.

Although no new equity or debt capital is raised in a spin-off, it is interesting to note that these transactions can be structured so as to transfer substantial amounts of wealth between corporate claimants. An example of such a structure is the spin-off proposed by the Marriott Corporation, in which Marriott decided to spin off a portion of the firm's assets (primarily its extensive real estate operations) but all of the firm's preexisting debt. This effectively strips away a substantial portion of the firm's assets and cash flows from the protection afforded to the bondholders. When Marriott announced this transaction, the market value of the firm's public debt dropped by approximately 30 percent. Thus, in spite of the fact that Marriott was not adding any new debt, the value of the firm's existing debt decreased substantially as a consequence of the proposed spin-off. This example also highlights the important role of bond covenants in constraining the actions that corporate management may undertake.

[b] **Equity Carve-Outs.** An equity carve-out is the initial public offering of a partial equity stake in a wholly owned subsidiary. Since these transactions involve the sale of new equity by a publicly traded firm, they are somewhat similar to a public offering of seasoned equity. Among the differences, though, is that the equity carve-out initiates public trading of an equity claim on the assets of the subsidiary alone. Thus, as is the case with a spin-off, this transaction creates a distinct equity claim in the subsidiary that trades separately from the common stock of the parent organization. However, there are two important distinctions between these two transactions. In an equity carve-out, equity in the subsidiary is sold in the public market for cash. The cash may go to the subsidiary or the parent, depending on which entity offers the shares. Generally, then, the owners of the subsidiary equity will be different from the owners

of the parent equity. In a spin-off, the subsidiary's shares are distributed pro rata as a dividend to the current stockholders. Thus, there are no cash payments involved and the subsidiary stockholders are the same proportional owners of the parent's equity (at least initially). Equity carve-outs raise new investment capital, but spin-offs do not. The second distinction is related to the posttransaction control that the parent can exert over the subsidiary.

In general, a spin-off involves the distribution of the parent firm's entire ownership position in the subsidiary. As a result, the parent relinquishes its entire control over the assets of the subsidiary. In an equity carve-out, the parent normally sells only a minority interest in the equity of the subsidiary. Thus, the parent usually retains control over the assets of the subsidiary. Interestingly, recent research has found that an equity carve-out is usually the first stage of a two-stage process that eventually leads either to (1) disposition of the parent's entire ownership interest in the subsidiary or (2) reacquisition of the subsidiary's publicly traded shares. The latter is accomplished by the parent's tendering for the outstanding shares, and the former by finding a buyer or selling (or spinning off) the remainder to the public. Finally, it may also be noted that both equity carve-outs and divestitures raise capital for the parent in exchange for relinquishing some degree of control over the subsidiary assets. However, in a sell-off, the subsidiary is completely sold to another company, while in a carve-out, the subsidiary is partially sold to new shareholders. The carve-out initiates a new equity claim on the carved-out assets, while in a sell-off the subsidiary is acquired by the buyer, and hence does not create a distinct equity claim against the divested assets.

[c] Joint Ventures. A joint venture is an organization that is formed when two or more companies contribute separate resources in order to accomplish some particular objective. These ventures are generally organized as a partnership or a corporation, with the ownership and management shared by the parent organizations. A recent example is the formation of a new company called Coca-Cola Nestle Refreshment Company, a joint venture of Coca-Cola Company and Nestle, S.A. Under the terms of the agreement, concentrates and beverage bases will be manufactured and marketed for the production of ready-to-drink coffee, tea, and chocolate beverages under the Nescafe, Nestea, and Nestle brand names. The new company has its own board of directors (in this case, each company makes an equal number of appointments) and a top manager. However, the equity is owned entirely by Coca-Cola and Nestle and, hence, in this sense can be considered a "private" new organization. Figure 8-6 describes other examples of and stated motivations for intercorporate joint ventures.

Since joint ventures involve some combination of resources of two or more parent corporations, they have some similarity to corporate mergers. The primary distinction between a corporate merger and a corporate joint venture is that the latter represents only a partial combination of resources under new management. However, the original management of the parent firms remains unaltered by the joint venture. Furthermore, joint ventures are limited-duration corporate combinations. They generally last for a limited time and are subject to an extremely high failure rate. In fact, up to 70 percent of announced joint ventures fail for a variety of reasons. However, many joint ventures are successful and make business sense for a variety of reasons, such as the following: (1) to augment insufficient financial or technical ability to enter a particular line of business; (2) to achieve economies of scale; (3) to enable the sharing of technology or management skills; (4) to provide tax advantages; and (5) to reduce the risk involved in expanding into new or foreign markets.

FIGURE 8-6

Examples of Intercorporate Joint Ventures

Source: "Corporate Odd Couples," *Business Week* (July 21, 1986), p. 101

Companies	Product	Managerial Motivation
AT&T/Olivetti	Computers	Foreign market
Boeing/Mitsubishi/Fuji/ Kawasaki	Small aircraft	Cut costs, share technology
Corning/Ciba-Geigy	Lab instruments	New market
Ford/Measurex	Factory automation	Cut costs
GM/Toyota	Automobiles	Cut costs
GTE/Fujitsu	Communications equipment	Cut costs, better marketing
Kodak/Cetus	Biotechnology diagnostics	New market, better distribution
3M/Harris	Copiers	Better marketing
U.S. Steel/Pohang Iron & Steel	Steel	Raise capital, expand market
Westinghouse/General Electric	Power semiconductors	Cut costs, better marketing

[d] Going-Private Transactions. A going-private transaction involves the transformation of a publicly held firm into a privately owned organization. There are three general types of going-private transactions: leveraged buyouts (LBOs), management buyouts (MBOs), and unit, or divisional, management buyouts. The most widely known of these transactions is the LBO.

In this transaction, an outside equity investor group, usually in conjunction with some members of the target firm's management group, acquires all of the assets, or stock, of a public company. The acquisition price is financed primarily through the use of debt, so that the post-LBO firm is highly leveraged. Hence, LBOs have some of the same characteristics as leveraged recaps. Both of these types of transactions finance large cash payments to shareholders through borrowed funds and tend to concentrate ownership in the hands of management. An important distinction, however, is that the post–leveraged recap firm retains publicly traded equity and ownership by its outside shareholders whereas in an LBO, the firm is taken private through the acquisition of all of the target corporation's equity. Outside shareholders retain no equity ownership, and the shares are not publicly traded. An MBO has many of the same characteristics as an LBO with the following exceptions: The pretransaction ownership position of management is higher in MBOs, less debt is used in MBOs, and MBOs are typically accomplished without the participation of an outside equity group. However, as is the case in an LBO, the assets of the target corporation are fully acquired by the buyout group. Figure 8-7 provides some summary information on the recent history of going-private transactions.

A variation on the MBO is a divisional buyout by management. In this transaction, members of the management of either the parent firm or the subunit being divested acquire a division, subsidiary, or some operating unit of the parent firm. In this sense, divisional management buyouts are similar to interfirm asset sales, except that the purchaser of the unit is a corporate insider. Figure 8-8 provides a recent history of

252

FIGURE 8-7

Going-Private Transactions

Source: Mergerstat Review (Chicago, Ill.: W.T. Grimm & Co.)

Year	Total Going-Private Transactions	Total Dollar Value Paid (Millions)	Average Purchase Price (Millions)	Median Purchase Price (Millions)
1980	13	$ 967.4	$ 74.4	$ 25.3
1981	17	2,338.5	137.6	41.1
1982	31	2,836.7	91.5	29.6
1983	36	7,145.4	198.5	77.8
1984	57	10,805.9	415.6	66.9
1985	76	24,139.8	317.6	72.6
1986	76	20,232.4	281.0	84.5
1987	47	22,057.1	469.3	123.3
1988	125	60,920.6	487.4	79.8
1989	80	18,515.4	231.4	52.8
1990	20	3,539.2	177.0	36.9
1991	9	334.2	37.1	28.2

FIGURE 8-8

Management Buyouts of Divisions (1980–1991)

Source: Mergerstat Review (Chicago, Ill.: W.T. Grimm & Co.)

Year	Divestitures	Divisional Management Buyouts	Percent of Total Divestitures	Number of MBOs Disclosing Price	Total Price (Millions)	Average Price (Millions)
1980	666	47	7	15	$ 363.3	$ 24.2
1981	830	83	10	30	484.1	16.1
1982	875	115	13	41	1,361.1	33.2
1983	932	139	15	51	2,499.4	49.0
1984	900	122	14	42	3,833.4	91.3
1985	1,218	132	11	50	5,005.4	100.1
1986	1,259	144	11	57	9,541.9	167.4
1987	807	90	11	43	5,957.2	138.5
1988	894	89	10	47	8,521.6	181.3
1989	1,055	91	9	38	4,049.5	106.6
1990	940	63	7	26	2,115.6	81.4
1991	849	35	4	16	855.7	53.5

the relationship between divisional management buyouts and aggregate corporate divestiture activity. The table indicates a sharp decrease in the number of divisional management buyouts as a percentage of total divestiture activity. In 1991, the total price paid in these transactions declined 60 percent from the 1990 level, while the average price reported for disclosed transactions fell by 34 percent.

Perhaps more than any other form of corporate restructuring and reorganization activity, going-private transactions are subject to seemingly endless debate and scrutiny. The primary reason is the conflicting positions occupied by management in these transactions. On the one hand, management is hired to maximize the value of the firm's ownership claims—the common equity. In this capacity, management should negotiate the highest possible price for any portion of the firm's assets sold to a purchaser. However, since management often participates in the buyout group, its interests are best served by its acquiring the target assets at a price that is as low as possible. These dual objectives clearly can create a conflict of interest that raises the possibility of managerial self-dealing at the expense of the firm's outside equity investors.

[e] Reverse LBOs. A company that is taken private through an LBO or a divisional management buyout may eventually seek to establish public ownership. A reverse LBO describes the process in which these privately held organizations go public through an initial public offering. Figure 8-9 provides a fairly comprehensive listing of firms that emerged as public companies through a reverse LBO during 1991 and provides some information on the subsequent share price performance of these companies. The market performance of reverse LBOs is of interest because the return to public ownership seems to reverse many of the value-enhancing aspects of highly leveraged going-private transactions, in particular, the creation of value and efficiency through high financial leverage, concentrated equity ownership, close board monitoring, and enhanced managerial incentives. A reverse LBO reduces financial leverage, disperses equity ownership, returns the firm to public ownership, and reduces the ownership stake of the LBO sponsor. Because a reverse LBO alters the firm's organizational ownership and financial structure, future firm performance might be expected to approximate the firm's performance prior to the going-private transaction. At an extreme, a reverse LBO might even completely dissipate the organizational and operational benefits and efficiencies generated in the going-private transaction.

8.03 POTENTIAL CAUSES AND BENEFITS OF CORPORATE RESTRUCTURING AND REORGANIZATION

This section discusses alternative motivations for corporate restructuring and reorganization. Many of the explanations advanced to explain this activity have also been examined in merger and acquisition activity. This is perhaps to be expected because many of the factors that create the opportunity to enhance value through restructuring and reorganization would also be valuable to an outside acquiror. Consequently, the level of corporate restructuring and reorganization activity is likely to be related to the level of merger and acquisition activity for at least two reasons. First, the probability exists that an outside acquiror may make an offer for a firm that will motivate management to restructure, if such activity will enhance shareholder value. In this sense, the market for corporate control serves as a disciplinary device for the behavior and decisions of incumbent managements. Second, if an acquiror successfully com-

FIGURE 8-9

1991's Reverse LBOs: A Mixed Bag

Source: IDD Information Services

Offer Date	Issuer	Dollar Amount (Millions)	Percent Price Change to Dec. 31, 1991	Percent Change Relative to S&P 500[a]	Percent Change Relative to NASDAQ[b]
1/22/91	Alta Health Strategies	14.3	+30.26	+3.22	−24.43
2/5/91	Health Management Associates	40.8	+138.28	+119.54	+102.62
2/27/91	Zilog	22.0	+84.09	+70.67	+54.03
2/28/91	Sonic	46.3	+150.00	+136.37	+120.58
3/7/91	Community Health Systems	33.6	+35.94	+24.99	+12.69
3/19/91	Maverick Tube	21.6	−56.48	−70.26	−83.17
3/20/91	Take Care	47.5	+2.63	−10.73	−23.17
3/26/91	Amsco International	81.9	+64.29	+53.45	+41.77
4/1/91	AutoZone	59.8	+191.85	+179.52	+169.91
4/24/91	Caldor	86.5	−14.29	−23.26	−31.92
4/30/91	Filene's Basement	56.6	+106.90	+95.78	+85.94
5/1/91	Duracell International	365.6	+130.00	+120.32	+109.81
5/2/91	Homedco Group	55.5	+66.67	+57.06	+47.28
5/9/91	Haemonetics	105.6	+72.16	+63.33	+54.38
5/9/91	Hi-Lo Automotive	41.6	+4.81	−4.02	−12.97
5/15/91	Carlisle Plastics	74.3	−10.23	−23.39	−32.87
5/16/91	Ann Taylor Stores	127.4	−41.83	−53.89	−63.54
5/21/91	Wisconsin Cent Transportation	34.7	+21.21	+10.09	−0.03
5/23/91	BWIP Holding	92.8	+53.45	+42.22	+33.69
5/31/91	Wheatley TXT	36.0	+2.50	−4.49	−13.35
6/5/91	Cherokee	14.3	−48.08	−56.39	−64.14
6/6/91	Au Bon Pain	22.5	+83.33	+74.61	+66.75
6/21/91	DeVry	21.2	+37.50	+27.09	+16.81
6/21/91	Regis	44.4	−30.77	−41.18	−51.46
6/24/91	International Specialty Products	217.0	+0.81	−11.63	−22.57
6/28/91	Fruehauf Trailer	35.2	+3.41	−8.96	−19.79
7/10/91	Revell-Monogram	17.1	0	−11.00	−20.36
7/11/91	Kaiser Aluminum	81.2	−24.11	−34.75	−44.17
7/12/91	IHOP	49.6	+45.00	+35.31	+26.00
7/15/91	Marvel Entertainment Group	69.3	+177.27	+168.20	+150.03
7/19/91	Enquirer/Star Group	151.2	+50.00	+41.45	+32.15
7/24/91	Catherines Stores	24.0	+20.31	+10.16	+0.02
7/24/91 *	Interstate Bakeries	200.0	+13.28	+3.13	−7.01
8/1/91	Singer	163.8	+26.79	+19.05	+10.49
8/6/91	MGIC Investment	206.1	+73.96	+67.18	+57.90
8/29/91	Foxmeyer	108.8	−20.69	−25.89	−32.08
9/12/91	Treadco	40.0	−3.13	−10.81	−15.64
9/19/91	Maxum Health	18.8	−6.00	−13.62	−18.18

[a] Standard & Poor's 500 index.
[b] National Association of Securities Dealers Automated Quotation system.

(continued)

FIGURE 8-9   *(continued)*

Offer Date	Issuer	Dollar Amount (Millions)	Percent Price Change to Dec. 31, 1991	Percent Change Relative to S&P 500[a]	Percent Change Relative to NASDAQ[b]
9/23/91	Super Rite	32.6	−22.58	−30.66	−34.33
10/1/91	York International	184.0	+12.50	+5.33	+1.56
10/4/91	Sunbelt Nursery Group	27.2	−32.35	−41.75	−45.02
10/8/91	ShopKo Stores	198.0	−14.17	−23.74	−27.53
10/10/91	Presley	56.0	+5.00	−4.60	−8.64
10/11/91	RP Scherer	140.4	+70.83	+61.49	+57.87
10/11/91	Wamaco Group	96.0	+24.37	+15.03	+11.41
10/17/91	Health Care & Retirement	263.1	+30.15	+23.73	+20.81
11/8/91	Amphenol	127.7	−2.70	−8.86	−9.68
11/13/91	Guaranty National	72.5	0	−4.95	−5.42
11/15/91	Horace Mann Educators	214.2	+23.61	+14.60	+13.25
11/15/91	Joy Technologies	122.4	−11.76	−20.77	−22.12
11/22/91	Stop & Shop	170.0	+11.00	−0.11	−0.37
12/6/91	Jimbo's Jumbos	9.0	−4.17	−14.19	−13.50
12/11/91	Owens-Illinois	528.0	+9.09	−1.34	−1.20
12/12/91	Healthtrust—The Hospital Company	511.0	+8.93	−0.38	−0.46
12/16/91	Perrigo	128.0	+85.94	+77.45	+78.10
	Total	5,266.7	+28.69	+18.36	+10.56

[a] Standard & Poor's 500 index.
[b] National Association of Securities Dealers Automated Quotation system.

pletes a takeover of a target, there is no reason why the acquiror would necessarily benefit by keeping all of the assets of the target. In this case, the acquiror may keep a portion of the target's assets and restructure the remainder. Again, this activity reinforces the notion that if incumbent management does not continually seek opportunities to allocate assets to their most productive use, an outside group may find it advantageous to acquire the firm and implement that policy. It is in this sense that one can view the market for corporate control as a competition among alternative management groups for the right to manage a particular set of assets.

[1] General Motivations for Corporate Restructuring and Reorganization

There is no single explanation that can account for every restructuring and reorganization. It is likely that several of the explanations that follow may be important in some transactions. The goals of this section are to present the alternative explanations that have been suggested and to discuss the reasons why each might plausibly motivate a restructuring or a reorganization. The theories considered include the following:

- The impact of tax and/or regulatory factors
- The existence of asymmetric information

- The desire to eliminate managerial inefficiencies
- The strengthening of managerial incentives
- The expropriation of wealth from other corporate stakeholders
- The facilitation of a merger
- The creation of synergies
- The creation of a defense against a hostile takeover

[a] **Tax and/or Regulatory Factors.** Tax factors may influence corporate restructuring and reorganization activity in a number of different ways. First, the use of debt financing creates corporate tax savings because interest payments are deductible for income tax purposes. These tax benefits are limited only by an organization's ability to generate sufficient revenue to earn the tax deduction. Federal income tax laws also provide some special provisions for certain restructuring transactions. One example is the use of debt financing in a leveraged ESOP. In this case, both the interest and principal payments made by the parent to the ESOP are deductible for income tax purposes. In addition, a portion of the payments received by the financial institution that provides the loan to establish the ESOP are nontaxable. As a result, the financial institution would presumably accept a lower rate of interest on an ESOP-related loan than on other loans of equivalent risk. Another example of a favored tax position relates to the spin-off of assets into a natural resource royalty trust or a real estate investment trust. As long as these organizational entities pay at least 90 percent of shareholders' income, they pay no income tax. Thus, certain spin-offs may allow shareholders to escape one level of the normal double taxation on cash distributions.

A related aspect of the personal income tax laws is the differential tax treatment accorded to distributions to shareholders. For example, prior to 1986, the capital gains tax rate was below the ordinary income tax rate. Thus, all else being equal, the after-tax value of a $1 distribution to shareholders subject to capital gains tax exceeded that subject to ordinary income tax. Cash dividend payments are ordinary income, while share repurchases are treated as capital gains. Thus, share repurchases would seem to present a preferred method to distribute cash to shareholders.

Even though capital gains and ordinary income tax rates were equalized in 1986, share repurchases have the advantage of allowing shareholders to elect whether to receive the distribution or not. With dividend payments, shareholders have no such discretion. Hence, share repurchases provide shareholders with a valuable tax timing (deferral) option. Shareholder distributions from other forms of corporate restructuring can be taxable or tax-free, depending on how they are implemented. For example, spin-offs can be structured as taxable or tax-free distributions, depending on the size of the share distribution in the transaction.

A final tax factor to consider is that certain restructuring activities allow asset values to be revised upward for the purpose of determining the depreciation expense. Since depreciation is deductible for income tax purposes but does not involve an outlay of cash, it provides a valuable tax shield. As in the case with interest expense, the tax shield from depreciation depends upon the firm having a revenue stream sufficiently large to utilize the deduction.

Regulatory factors depend on a number of considerations, many of which may change through time. For example, antitrust enforcement became looser in the 1980s than in previous decades, thereby permitting some corporate combinations that might not have otherwise been permitted. Corporations with regulated and unregulated operations may also consider the merits of a restructuring or reorganization. To the extent that regulators include benefits from the unregulated activities in their decisions, the unregulated operations may provide a partial subsidy for the regulated activity. Through the separation of these different lines of business, the ability of regulators to assess the regulated activities alone would increase. Finally, multinational corporations are subject to the laws and regulations of many different countries. Some forms of restructuring and reorganization may facilitate entry into these markets (e.g., joint ventures), while others may be used to circumvent confiscatory laws and regulations (e.g., a spin-off of a foreign subsidiary). Thus, the impact of tax and regulatory factors on corporate restructuring and reorganization activity is quite complex, depending on factors such as corporate and personal tax rates, financing methods, and national and international rules and regulations.

[b] Asymmetric Information. The problem of asymmetric information arises because corporate managers have better information about the activities, operations, and policies of their firms than do outside investors. This creates the possibility of a difference between the stock market's valuation of a firm and the actual, or true, value of a firm. The discrepancy arises because outside investors value a firm on the basis of their understanding of the firm, and this information is not fully accurate. There are many potential explanations for why this informational discrepancy can arise and continue to exist. The separation of ownership and control vests decision-making authority in professional managers. Management's knowledge of a firm's operations cannot always be credibly conveyed to investors, so that the wedge between market value and true value may persist. This problem is likely to be most problematic when a firm is undervalued. In this case, the firm is vulnerable to acquisition by an informed hostile bidder (e.g., a competitor firm), or by the informed inside management group (e.g., through an LBO). The true value of a firm's assets is especially likely to be obscured when a firm has a complex organizational structure and operates in a number of different lines of business. Corporate restructuring and reorganization activities might be used to serve a number of useful purposes here.

First, since restructuring can lead to the establishment of a new, separate organization, the incentives and opportunity for outside investors and analysts to gather and analyze information are enhanced. Second, some formal theories of the problem of the asymmetric information show how financial policies and shareholder cash distribution policies can be used directly to credibly convey information to outside investors. For example, heavier reliance on debt financing may indicate that the firm believes future cash flows will be sufficiently high to cover these fixed obligations. Dividend payment increases and share repurchases may accomplish much of the same, because both implicitly increase a firm's financial leverage as well. Thus, corporate restructuring and reorganization techniques may ameliorate asymmetric information by facilitating evaluation of the firm by outside investors, either through enhanced availability of information or credible changes in corporate operating and/or financial policies.

[c] Managerial Inefficiencies and Incentives. Complex organizational activities not only inhibit the flow of information but also make it difficult for management to manage operations. That is, as organizations grow in size, diversity, and complexity, management may simply lack the ability or capacity to manage the firm effectively. This "negative synergy," if severe enough, may interfere with the efficient operation of those assets for which management is well-suited. Management inefficiencies can arise for a number of reasons, so that the solution to this problem depends on the cause. For example, management may be inefficient owing to a lack of ability. In this case, the best action would likely be dismissal. However, in other cases, management may appear to be inefficient because of inappropriate incentives or because it has more diverse activities than it can attend to. Here, the appropriate solution would be to alter the organizational structure and incentive compensation schemes in order to facilitate efficient decision making. For example, consider the management of the subsidiary of a firm. Suppose that the subsidiary is a relatively small component of the overall firm but is highly profitable and growing rapidly. The use of incentive compensation plans that tie subsidiary performance to stock options on the parent company may not be effective. The link between subsidiary management compensation and performance is weak because the parent company's stock performance may not be closely related to a subsidiary's opportunities. By creating separate equity claims in the subsidiary (e.g., through a carve-out or a spin-off), incentive schemes tied directly to the market performance of the subsidiary become feasible.

Management incentives can also be improved by increasing management's ownership stake. Restructuring and reorganization techniques such as leveraged recaps, dual-class recaps, MBOs, and LBOs would all seem to be methods that facilitate this objective. Interestingly, these techniques increase management ownership initially, and then management reaps the benefits of the anticipated improvement in performance. Incentive compensation schemes increase the ownership position of management as performance improvements occur. Thus, increased ownership occurs if performance improves, rather than preceding it. As discussed previously, different restructuring techniques can be useful to facilitate achievement of either objective.

[d] Wealth Transfers. Economic efficiency is served best when activities are organized in such a way that corporate managers make decisions that increase aggregate wealth. Shareholders benefit financially from these wealth-enhancing activities. However, there are many stakeholders in the modern corporation—creditors, preferred stockholders, customers, employees, localities and the federal government. In general, since each of these stakeholders holds a different type of claim against the firm, decisions that benefit one group may harm the interests of another group. Thus, management can make decisions that benefit shareholders not because they increase wealth but because they simply transfer wealth away from other stakeholders. For example, when RJR Nabisco went through a $25 billion LBO, the value of the firm's preexisting bonds dropped by approximately 25 percent. Although RJR's stockholders received a substantial premium in the buyout, the new debt taken on to finance the transaction greatly diminished the wealth of the old bondholders.

While the distinction between wealth-increasing and wealth-transfer decisions is clearly important, the ability to actually detect differences in practice is quite difficult. To a large extent, this is due to the fact that some of the claims held by the nonshareholder stakeholders do not trade in secondary markets and hence do not have observable market prices. Much of the empirical evidence on the impact of corporate control, restructuring, and reorganization activities is based on share price reactions to these events. The point to bear in mind is that the possibility of wealth transfers requires that some caution be exercised in the use of share price reactions to make general inferences about how stakeholders as a whole benefit from these activities.

[e] Takeover Activity. The role of corporate restructuring and reorganization activities is somewhat ambiguous in the case of takeovers. On the one hand, takeovers can be facilitated by the use of preacquisition restructuring or reorganization techniques. For example, when Celeron Corporation spun off its Trans Louisiana Gas Corporation subsidiary, the remaining assets of the parent corporation were acquired by Goodyear Tire and Rubber Company. The purpose of the spin-off was to facilitate the acquisition of Celeron's remaining assets by Goodyear. In theory, Goodyear could have acquired the entire firm and then spun off (or perhaps sold) Trans Louisiana itself. One potential benefit of restructuring Celeron before the acquisition is that it reduced the amount of capital that Goodyear needed to raise in order to acquire Celeron. In addition, it was Celeron's shareholders rather than Goodyear's shareholders that retained the ownership of Trans Louisiana. To the extent that the spin-off increased the value of Trans Louisiana, the benefit would be retained by Celeron's shareholders. Furthermore, since this part of the transaction was tax-free, Celeron shareholders were able to defer capital gains taxation on this portion of the firm's restructuring. Thus, in addition to facilitating the acquisition of a portion of a firm's existing assets, corporate restructuring and reorganization techniques may convey other valuable benefits to target firm shareholders.

Corporate restructuring and reorganization activities can also be employed as a defense against a hostile takeover attempt. For example, dual-class recaps have been used to provide management with majority ownership of voting rights. One of the interesting aspects of this type of transaction is that management can gain this position without necessarily expending any incremental wealth to increase its ownership. Other defensive restructuring techniques that have been used include the sale of a firm's "crown jewels" or the use of a leveraged recap. Thus, while these restructuring techniques can be valuable if they are used to increase shareholder wealth, they can also be used to block some transactions that would be in the interest of shareholders. In this case, restructuring and reorganization techniques can entrench corporate management, generally at the expense of the firm's shareholders. Unfortunately, while it could be beneficial to restrict these harmful activities, it may not be feasible to fully preclude them without also eliminating productive uses of these techniques.

[f] Creating Synergies. Broadly speaking, synergy arises in any transaction where the value of two entities combined into one exceeds the aggregate value of the two separate entities. This difference may occur because of revenue enhancements and/or cost reductions that can be achieved by more efficient operation. Since, by definition, synergy requires the combination of separate entities, some corporate restructuring and reorganization activities create no synergistic benefits. For example, the benefits of ESOPs, LBOs, or share repurchases cannot be explained as arising from the synergies that they create. However, activities such as asset sales and joint ventures combine separate entities and hence create the opportunity for synergies. In the case of asset sales, synergy can arise because the assets involved are worth more when combined with the buyer's existing assets than if they remained as part of the seller's organization. The synergy created in the case of joint ventures arises because a portion of the existing asset bases of two separate organizations can be temporarily combined to achieve some specific objective. Hence, joint ventures can provide synergistic benefits by bringing together complementary resources of firms that already exist.

Corporate assets can also be combined and organized in such a way that a negative synergy, or anergy, exists within a firm. In this case, a portion of the firm's current passet base may interfere with the remaining, profitable operations of the firm. Corporate restructuring and reorganization activities can also serve to enhance firm value in this situation by diminishing these negative valuation effects. For example, consider a subsidiary that becomes involved in a protracted legal dispute (e.g., a product liability suit). In this case, management is likely to spend a disproportionate amount of time attending to the operation of this subsidiary. The value of the firm's other remaining assets may diminish as time and effort are diverted to the subsidiary. Other possibilities include inefficient production decisions, lack of complementarity in product distribution channels, and inappropriate organizational structure and design.

[g] **Summary.** Financial economists suggest that there are several potential explanations of the incidence and wealth effects of corporate restructuring and reorganization activity. Although corporate managers often provide statements regarding their purpose in implementing a restructuring or reorganization of the firm's current operations, these claims do not always necessarily convey the full picture. First, management may not fully disclose its purpose and intentions if it believes that such information would convey valuable insights to competitors. Second, statements made by corporate managers are often subject to ambiguities and are difficult to calibrate. Thus, in order to quantify the expected impact of a restructuring or reorganization, it is necessary to link the actual event with an analysis of the principles of firm valuation. Finally, management may elect to engage in activities that are in its own interest but not necessarily in the best interests of the firm's shareholders. In this case, it is important to be able to disentangle management statements about the perceived benefits of a restructuring and reorganization from their actual economic and financial impact. This can best be accomplished by application of the principles of firm valuation (see Chapter D6).

The theories described in this section provide an important link between corporate restructuring and reorganization activity and the value of the firm. However, while theories provide important insights regarding potential advantages and disadvantages of corporate restructuring and reorganization, they do not tell definitively which activities are beneficial and which are harmful.

8.04 EMPIRICAL EVIDENCE ON THE VALUE OF CORPORATE RESTRUCTURING AND REORGANIZATION

Although researchers use a variety of accounting and financial information to study corporate transactions, financial economists focus on stock price reactions to the announcement of an event in order to infer its impact. In well-functioning markets, prices react quickly and efficiently to the arrival of new information. Since the market for common stock is widely regarded as efficient, much of the empirical research on corporate restructuring and reorganization uses share price reactions as a measure of the wealth impact of these activities.

[1] Event Study Methodology

The use of stock market information to evaluate the economic consequences of corporate restructuring and reorganization activity is predicated on the notion that the stock price efficiently incorporates all available information about a firm's prospects. The application of the event study methodology is based on the idea that to the extent that restructuring and reorganization events are not anticipated by the market, share price reactions observed at the announcement of these events reflect the market's unbiased estimate of their true economic effect.

However, in order to isolate the impact of a particular event, it is necessary to adjust observed returns around the announcement date for risk and general market movements. For example, the inference about a 5 percent share price increase at the announcement of a spin-off depends on whether the stock market was increasing or decreasing during this period and how risky the stock was relative to the stock market. The difference between the observed pattern of stock price returns and risk-adjusted market rates of return around the announcement date is referred to as the abnormal share price reaction. Financial economists equate this abnormal return with the market's aggregate, unbiased assessment of the expected economic effect of a particular transaction. In the absence of any unanticipated events or if the market attaches no economic significance to an event, this abnormal return should equal zero. Thus, if positive abnormal returns are observed around the announcement of an event, the inference is that the transaction provides economic benefit. Alternatively, a pattern of negative abnormal returns indicates that the event has diminished shareholder wealth, and hence the transaction is not consistent with the managerial objective of maximizing shareholder value.

In order to improve the statistical properties of the inferences that can be drawn from these event studies, portfolios of common stocks are created for firms that undertake the same type of transaction. Thus, rather than reporting abnormal returns for a single firm, studies in the financial economics literature report average results for a large number of firms engaged in the same type of transaction. Users of this portfolio approach can have greater confidence that the results observed are a common outcome, rather than a single, isolated event.

One potential difficulty with this methodology is that the event under consideration occurs at different calendar dates for different firms. This problem is resolved by using an event time (rather than a calendar time) approach to forming the portfolio. For example, each announcement date of a particular transaction for the firms in the portfolio is arbitrarily designated as time zero, or $t = 0$. Thus, regardless of the actual calendar date for a transaction, the announcement date is taken to be the focal point around which abnormal returns are measured. The event study methodology averages abnormal returns across all firms in the sample for a particular date and then cumulates these average returns through event time. Statistical tests can then be applied to determine the significance of these abnormal returns.

Another difficulty that arises in applying this methodology is the determination of the appropriate length of the event period. Generally, one would expect new information to arrive in the market fairly often. Thus, in order to be sure that the abnormal return observed is directly related to the event under consideration, one would suspect that the event period should be quite short. The difficulty with this is that it may convey an unrepresentative view of the complete effect of a transaction because the period is too short. Thus, the length of the event period varies across studies, in part a reflection of the somewhat arbitrary trade-offs that researchers must make.

[2] Empirical Evidence on Corporate Restructuring and Reorganization Activity

Figure 8-10 provides a general summary of the average abnormal share price reaction at the announcement of various forms of corporate restructuring and reorganization activity.

FIGURE 8-10

Summary of Share Price Reactions to Announcements of Various Restructuring and Reorganization Events

Event	Abnormal Share Price Reaction
Sell-offs	Positive
Spin-offs	Positive
Equity carve-outs	Positive
Going-private transactions	Positive
Voluntary liquidations	Positive
ESOPs	Positive
Dual-class recaps	Negative
Leveraged recaps	Positive
Joint ventures	Positive
Share repurchases	Positive
Exchange offers	
Leverage increasing	Positive
Leverage decreasing	Negative

The shareholders of firms that undertake corporate restructuring and reorganization activities benefit if the value created by the transaction exceeds the value of the firm under its existing financial and operating policies. The evidence on the incremental valuation effects of corporate asset sales suggests that selling firm shareholders earn small but statistically significant positive abnormal returns. Klein (1986) examines these transactions in detail and finds that the size of the return earned by selling firm shareholders depends on (1) whether the final sale price is announced and (2) the percentage of the firm's asset base sold in the transaction. The abnormal return earned by the selling firm shareholders is higher when the sale price is announced and as the percentage of assets sold increases. Furthermore, all empirical studies in this area suggest that the share price of the acquiring firm has virtually no abnormal reaction to these events. Since selling firm equity value increases and acquiring firm equity value exhibits no abnormal effect, the evidence is consistent with the hypotheses that on average, sell-offs increase aggregate shareholder wealth by reallocating some corporate assets to higher-valued uses, and virtually all of the wealth gains generated by this form of corporate restructuring are captured by the shareholders of the selling firm. These results are fairly consistent with the empirical evidence on merger and acquisition activity, where it is also the selling firm shareholders that earn the largest portion of the abnormal positive return created by corporate combinations.

Corporate spin-offs represent a unique form of corporate restructuring and reorganization because they simply create two or more separate organizations from what formerly operated as a single entity. Thus, they do not normally affect shareholder ownership stakes, nor do they directly alter asset and financial structures. However, early studies by Schipper and Smith (1983) and by Hite and Owers (1983) document that these transactions on average increase aggregate shareholder wealth. Thus, there is something in the process of creating separate and independent organizational structures from a formerly unified organization that enhances value. Seward and Walsh (1990) investigate the conjecture that these gains are related to changes made in management compensation policies and the structure of the board of directors. In their study, they confirm that these transactions generate positive abnormal share price reactions on average and that the size of the reaction is related to the size of the assets spun off. A spin-off creates separate equity claims and separate top management and board structures. Seward and Walsh document the increased reliance on equity-based incentive compensation (e.g., executive stock options) as well as substantial board turnover that occurs in spin-offs. They interpret their findings as supportive of the conjecture that corporate performance can be enhanced by creating organizational structures that facilitate the use of market performance–related compensation policies and improved board monitoring services. The performance of the board may be improved by the selection of members that may be better able to provide guidance for each of the separated organizations. This occurs, for example, if board members differ in their ability to provide a particular organization with guidance, judgment, and direction.

Schipper and Smith (1986) studied the performance of 81 companies that carved out a portion of the equity ownership of a subsidiary. In the majority of these cases, the parent firm maintains a majority ownership position in the subsidiary's equity. Schipper and Smith document a positive abnormal share price reaction upon the announcement of an equity carve-out and also note that this is the only form of public sale of seasoned common equity that generates a positive stock price response (for example, when parent companies announce equity offerings of additional shares, the share price generally decreases). Schipper and Smith also note that most of these carve-outs represent only a temporary public market for the shares of the subsidiary. Within a period of several years after the initial sale of shares, the parent firm repurchases all of the outstanding shares of the subsidiary or the subsidiary is sold to an acquiror. In either case, the majority equity ownership position held by the parent facilitates the completion of these subsequent transactions.

The positive market reaction upon the announcement of an equity carve-out is especially noteworthy because the market reacts adversely to all other forms of selling common equity (e.g., seasoned equity offers). This suggests that the sale of new equity claims on a portion of a firm's assets is perceived differently from the sale of new equity claims on all of the firm's assets. Nanda (1991) argues that these different market reactions can be explained by the fact that a carve-out may reveal favorable information about the value of the firm's assets. This argument is based on the presumption that management possesses better information about the value of the firm's assets than do outside investors. Under these conditions, Nanda shows that the firms that elect to sell common stock in an equity carve-out are generally undervalued by the market. Conversely, firms that issue equity in the parent corporation are generally overvalued by the market. However, Nanda provides no empirical evidence that formally supports his theoretical analysis.

McConnell and Nantell (1985) studied 210 firms that engaged in 136 joint ventures during the period 1972–1979. They document that, on average, joint ventures increase shareholder wealth, as abnormal share price reactions are positive for this type of activity. Their study also examines the dollar magnitude of the gain that arises in these transactions, as well as the relationship between firm size and shareholder wealth. Their results show that the average value of the gains created in these transactions is generally evenly divided among the participants but that the abnormal returns are larger for smaller firms. These results can be explained by the fact that larger firms are spreading the same dollar returns as the smaller firms over a larger equity base; hence, the calculated return is smaller. The authors interpret their results as supportive of the synergy hypothesis as the source of gains in these transactions. Some care is required in interpreting these results, however, because McConnell and Nantell report results only for successful, ongoing joint ventures. Their study does not explicitly incorporate the fact that a relatively large number of joint ventures fail. Thus, the results reported in McConnell and Nantell pertain only to successful joint ventures, and hence may be an upwardly biased estimate of the aggregate value of this activity.

As noted previously, shareholders benefit from the liquidation of an ongoing entity only if its liquidation value exceeds its continuation value. Hite, Owers, and Rogers (1987) examine a sample of 49 voluntary liquidations during the period 1963–1983. They find that (1) the average abnormal share price reaction exceeds 10 percent at the announcement date and (2) approximately half of the firms in their sample had previously been targets of other corporate control contests (e.g., mergers and tender offers). Their findings suggest that shareholders benefit substantially from voluntary corporate liquidations and argue that these gains arise because the firm's assets are sold piecemeal to higher-valued uses. These results have been confirmed in a separate study by Kim and Schatzberg (1987). They find positive abnormal share price reactions that are comparable to but slightly larger than the results described in the Hite, Owers, and Rogers study. Kim and Schatzberg also examine the tax ramifications associated with voluntary corporate liquidations. Their analysis compares tax effects with those in a nontaxable merger and find that from a purely tax perspective, the latter is more desirable. However, voluntary liquidations may still be preferable if the gains obtained by the piecemeal sale of the firm exceed the gains received in a merger with a single company.

As discussed previously, firms can repurchase their own shares in several different ways: tender offer, open market, and targeted repurchase. Here, the focus is primarily on the evidence related to the self–tender offer method. Dann (1981) and Vermaelan (1981) examine the impact of fixed-price self–tender offers on the value of firms. Independently, Dann and Vermaelan document positive abnormal share price reactions of approximately 15 percent upon announcement of this form of share repurchases. In their samples, the firms on average sought to repurchase approximately 15 percent to 20 percent of their outstanding shares and offered premiums of about 23 percent over their preannouncement share price. Vermaelen also examines the impact of the source of funds utilized in the share repurchase on the magnitude of the share price reaction. In his sample, he finds that (1) existing cash balances are used to repurchase shares about four times as often as new debt financing; (2) shareholder wealth effects are higher for debt-financed repurchase offers; and (3) the percentage of outstanding shares sought by the firm is higher in debt-financed than in cash-financed share repurchases.

Kamma, Kanatas, and Raymar (1990) provide a comparative analysis of fixed-price and Dutch auction self-tender offers. Their recent evidence suggests that firms are more likely to use the Dutch auction method today, perhaps in part because that technique is more efficient as a defensive technique. They also document that the share price reaction to the announcement of a Dutch auction is positive and is of approximately the same order of magnitude as that described previously in the case of fixed-price offers. Finally, Barclay and Smith (1988) examine open-market share repurchases in detail. They document that firms that announce this type of program also experience positive abnormal share price reactions, although of a lower order of magnitude than tender offer programs. This difference may be due to the smaller average size of the typical open-market repurchase program or the lack of a premium offered by firms in the open-market repurchase program.

The use of exchange offers facilitates the process of altering a firm's existing capital structure. Since this type of transaction affects only the right-hand side of a firm's balance sheet, exchange offers per se do not affect investment decisions. The empirical evidence on exchange offers suggests that the expected average abnormal share price reaction depends on whether the transaction increases or decreases corporate leverage. Exchange offers that increase leverage tend to result in positive abnormal share price reactions, while leverage-decreasing transactions result in negative abnormal share price reactions. Masulis (1983) found positive share price reactions in the following exchange offers: debt for common stock, debt for preferred stock, and preferred stock for common stock. He also demonstrates that the following exchanges lead to negative share price reactions: common stock for debt, preferred stock for debt, and common stock for preferred stock. In general, then, the market's inference about the valuation effects of exchange offers depends on their impact on the firm's leverage position.

Kleiman (1988) examines the shareholder wealth effects of a leveraged recap. He documents that average excess shareholder returns in these transactions are positive but that the magnitude of the gain depends on whether the firm is a takeover target. The gains are larger in the case of a "voluntary" recapitalization than in a "defensive" recapitalization. Since these transactions generally transform conservatively leveraged firms to predominantly leveraged firms, some of the value increase occurs because of the benefits of debt financing.

Closely related to the leveraged recap is the decision to go private. Typically, both leveraged recaps and going-private transactions concentrate management ownership of the firm's equity and make extensive use of debt financing. One of the primary differences, though, is that the common equity of a firm that undertakes a leveraged recap remains publicly traded and the original equity holders retain a stake in the firm. DeAngelo, DeAngelo, and Rice (1984) examine the share price reactions for 75 firms at the announcement date for going-private proposals. They find abnormal positive share price reactions in excess of 20 percent and suggest that shareholders benefit substantially from these transactions. Furthermore, since this abnormal return is not substantially different from those observed in interfirm tender offers and mergers, the premium received by shareholders in these transactions is close to that received in more arm's-length transactions. In a subsequent study, Lehn and Poulsen (1988) find that the size of the firms undertaking these transactions has increased through time and that the premiums offered in the buyout have increased. Finally, Hite and Vetsuypens (1989) find that the share price response at the announcement of divisional management buyouts is positive but substantially smaller than is the case where the entire firm is taken private.

Muscarella and Vetsuypens (1990) examine the performance of 72 firms that returned to public ownership through a reverse LBO. They find that the companies in their sample implemented a variety of changes in order to enhance the efficiency of the firm's operations. Among the most important changes were increased management and director equity ownership, adoption of incentive compensation plans, and higher levels of financial leverage. Improved profitability occurred but was attributable primarily to cost reductions rather than revenue enhancement or improved asset turnover. While capital expenditures were reduced on average, reductions in labor employment were not evident. Thus, valuation enhancements in reverse LBOs seem to be attributable to improved capital efficiency rather than labor efficiency. The authors interpret their findings as evidence that going-private transactions improve asset utilization and redirect resources towards high-valued uses. In addition, the return to public ownership does not appear to dissipate the efficiencies created in the going-private process. Thus, it appears that the organizational changes necessary to enhance firm performance can be implemented and retained even though private ownership is a temporary organizational form.

Dual-class recapitalization appears to stand out as the primary form of corporate restructuring and reorganization that decreases shareholder wealth. Jarrell and Poulsen (1988) examine the shareholder wealth effects at the announcement date for firms that recapitalize with dual classes of common stock. Their sample consists of 94 firms making announcements in the time period 1976 through 1986. They note that approximately two thirds of the firms in their sample recapitalized after the New York Stock Exchange (NYSE) declared a moratorium on its policy of delisting firms with dual classes of common stock. Jarrell and Poulsen argue that corporate managers use this form of recapitalization in order to entrench themselves. Their results differ from an earlier study by Partch (1987), who concluded that dual-class recaps do not diminish shareholder wealth. One explanation for these different results is that Partch examines firms only in the premoratorium period; the NYSE moratorium created an opportunity for managers to use this technique in order to entrench themselves. However, the results described in the Jarrell and Poulsen research suggest that some managers are utilizing this technique to consolidate their control of the corporation, thereby reducing or eliminating the possibility of a takeover in the event that the firm is poorly managed.

Finally, a comprehensive study of the firms engaged in ESOPs has not yet been published. As a result, no definitive evidence on the shareholder wealth effects of the formation of ESOPs is presented. However, Chen and Kessinger (1988) provide a useful general analysis of ESOPs. They note that the substantial tax benefits associated with these transactions can lead to a misallocation of resources. This result occurs because the tax subsidies may encourage participants to continue operating, perhaps in an unviable company. They also note that ESOPs do not necessarily create a better-motivated work force, especially if management (rather than the employees) controls the firm after the ESOP is created. These observations await rigorous analysis through a comprehensive empirical study.

[3] Assessment of the Evidence

The empirical evidence summarized in the previous section suggests that most forms of corporate restructuring and reorganization described in this chapter enhance shareholder value. But it is not necessarily the case that all managerial decisions that increase share prices also enhance firm value. This divergence can arise because managerial decisions merely transfer wealth to shareholders from other claimant classes (e.g., bondholders, employees, and suppliers), rather than create new wealth. Since the event study methodology can be used to assess wealth impacts only if reliable market prices exist, most studies of corporate restructuring and reorganization focus only on share price reactions. Thus, the ability to identify whether a particular transaction increases or merely transfers wealth is hindered by the absence of market prices for all of the firm's contractual claims.

Explicit applications of the event study methodology to the wealth transfer problem have largely been limited to the case of bondholder expropriation. Many publicly traded corporations also have public issues of debt outstanding. To the extent that valid market prices for these securities, can be observed, the hypothesis that shareholder gains arise because some transactions merely diminish the value of a firm's debt can be examined. Any transaction that substantially increases the amount of debt outstanding or increases the riskiness of a firm's operating strategy could decrease the value of the firm's outstanding bonds. At an extreme, a transaction may benefit shareholders solely because it increases the firm's risk, rather than enhancing aggregate firm value. Despite these opportunities to benefit shareholders at the expense of some other claimant class, most of the empirical evidence suggests that on average, expropriation of bondholder wealth is not a pervasive source of shareholder wealth in corporate restructurings and reorganizations. The most notable exception to this general consensus is the findings of Asquith and Wizman (1990), who document that certain types of corporate debt lose substantial value in highly leveraged transactions.

A second caveat is that while the event study methodology is a useful technique to document wealth effects of various transactions, it may not provide direct evidence on the source of these effects. In other words, it is an empirical technique that is most useful in assessing the likely valuation effects of an event rather than identifying the actual, underlying economic cause of the change in investor perception. As a result, event studies have proven to be more useful in eliminating possible explanations of the observed wealth effects of a transaction rather than providing a definitive explanation for why a particular reaction is observed. While documentation of reliable, systematic empirical evidence on a particular event is certainly useful information, the ultimate concern is identifying the change within a firm's decision-making process that leads to those outcomes.

A related concern is that the event study methodology is designed to test for the existence of a common explanation for an observed event. For example, early studies of the possibility of bondholder wealth transfers in highly leveraged transactions found that expropriation was not a consistent, systematic explanation for the observed share price reactions. But as the study by Asquith and Wizman demonstrates, it is sometimes necessary to consider specific characteristics of financial contracts in order to identify actual effects. Asquith and Wizman showed that it is only certain types of corporate debt, not all bonds, that are substantially impaired by the highly leveraged transactions. This suggests that a common explanation may be difficult to identify for a particular type of restructuring and reorganization. However, the effect may be important in explaining the results for at least some of the restructuring and reorganization activities under consideration.

These caveats notwithstanding, the existing empirical evidence on corporate restructuring and reorganization activity provided by the event study methodology indicates that these transactions generally enhance aggregate economic efficiency. The evidence documents that on average, shareholders benefit from these activities, sometimes quite substantially. As a result, these techniques represent important and useful methods that corporate managers can and should use to enhance the market value of their firms.

Firms can also elect to restructure their existing operations in response to performance declines without resorting to the rather large-scale ownership and organizational changes on which this chapter focuses. For example, rather than the event study methodology, John, Lang, and Netter (1992) examine actual changes in the operational and financial policies of 46 large firms that experienced large negative earnings between 1980 and 1987. They find that in general, management acted decisively and quickly to cut costs and decrease firm size. In particular, firms implemented significant reductions in labor costs and production costs. In addition, while research and development costs were cut, overall investment increased. However, these capital expenditures were allocated over a reduced number of business segments in which the firm operates. On the financial side, both debt and dividends were reduced on average. Thus, the evidence provided by John, Lang, and Netter demonstrates how quickly and broadly managers respond in their policy decisions as corporate performance declines.

8.05 IMPACT OF CORPORATE CONTROL ACTIVITY ON RESTRUCTURING AND REORGANIZATION

The material contained in this chapter thus far illustrates a number of useful observations about corporate restructuring and reorganization. First, the sheer diversity of restructuring and reorganization techniques has increased within the last decade. Important innovations such as leveraged recaps, LBOs, and Dutch auction share repurchases have become viable restructuring mechanisms within this period. Second, the level of corporate activity has also increased. Corporate management seems to be more proactive in the adoption of these techniques, clearly providing some recognition that shareholder wealth maximization is an important corporate objective. However, many of the techniques described can also serve as effective defensive mechanisms for corporate managers who seek to entrench themselves at the expense of shareholders.

Consider the role of corporate restructuring and reorganization in the larger context of how competition for the rights to manage a firm's assets and resources contributes to overall economic efficiency. In order to gain some useful insights into this broad issue, one must examine the following questions: (1) What is the empirical evidence on the relationship between merger and acquisition activity and corporate restructuring and reorganization and (2) how does the existence of an active market for corporate control influence the incentives of corporate managers to adopt value-enhancing restructuring and reorganization decisions?

The main point is that corporate restructuring and reorganization are natural consequences of merger and acquisition activity for several reasons. First, an active market for corporate control serves as an external disciplinary mechanism for the opportunistic behavior of corporate managers. If the incumbent management does not make value-maximizing decisions, outsiders can acquire the firm and implement these decisions. Thus, corporate restructuring and reorganization increase as merger and acquisition activity increases because managers assess the likelihood of a hostile offer as being greater. Second, as competition within an industry changes owing to mergers and acquisitions, other industry members may elect to use corporate restructuring and reorganization techniques in order to preserve or enhance their own competitive positions. This may involve increasing their own presence in an industry or leaving an unprofitable line of business. Third, corporate restructuring and reorganization activity increases when merger and acquisition activity increases because acquirors may be interested in acquiring and managing only a subset of the target's assets. The remainder can be disposed of through whichever corporate restructuring and reorganization technique maximizes firm value.

Kaplan and Weisbach (1990) try to assess the success of corporate acquisitions by examining subsequent divestiture activity. They examine the sale of assets by 271 firms that made large acquisitions between 1971 and 1982. By December 1989, they found that the initial acquirors had sold 44 percent of the acquired firm's assets. Thus, during this period, almost half of the assets acquired by the firms in their sample were subsequently sold. Although their primary purpose is to characterize acquisitions as successes or failures, their evidence provides important information about the relationship between merger and acquisition activity and subsequent restructurings. This evidence is consistent with well-known aggregate activity relationships between acquisitions and divestitures: Their levels of activity are highly correlated, but divestiture rates generally lag behind merger rates by a period of several years.

Denis (1990) examines defensive changes in corporate payout policies (i.e., share repurchases and dividends) by managers. The use of changes in payout policies as a defensive mechanism against hostile takeover attempts is due to the fact that they alter voting rights within the target firm. Hence, these policy changes represent restructuring or reorganization techniques that inhibit certain merger and acquisition activities. Denis's evidence suggests that the adoption of these defensive policies, especially share repurchases, may diminish shareholder wealth. Thus, the papers by Denis and by Kaplan and Weisbach provide useful empirical evidence on the concurrent or subsequent adoption of corporate restructuring and reorganization techniques relative to the onset of a corporate control contest.

By its very nature, there is little evidence on the adoption of corporate restructuring and reorganization techniques in anticipation of an outside offer for the firm. If restructuring serves to enhance the value of a potential target, it will be less likely that an outside firm would find it profitable to make an acquisition. Thus, potential target firms in this category are difficult to examine empirically because they involve transactions that never occur. This view does not suggest, however, that firms that restructure cannot subsequently become targets. For example, Dart & Kraft spun off its nonfood operations into an entity called Premark in 1986. Within three years, however, the parent company, Kraft, became the target of a hostile takeover attempt by Philip Morris. Indeed, the Seward and Walsh investigation of corporate spin-offs found that over one third of the spun-off entities were subsequently acquired within five years. Beranek, Klein, and Rosenfeld (1990) document that the majority of subsidiaries separated in an equity carve-out are either subsequently acquired by another firm or reacquired by the parent. Thus, corporate restructuring and reorganization do not necessarily preclude subsequent acquisition activity.

In summary, then, the empirical evidence suggests that the level of corporate restructuring and reorganization activity and the level of merger and acquisition activity are related. Restructuring and reorganization activity may be useful as a means to facilitate subsequent mergers, defend against hostile acquisition offers, or divest certain target firm assets after an acquisition.

Walsh and Seward (1990) provide a useful framework that explains how and why to expect these results. They argue that corporate restructuring and reorganization techniques represent an intermediate stage between the breakdown of a firm's internal corporate control mechanisms and the initiation of an external corporate control contest. As time passes and the environment within which a corporation operates changes, it may be that new corporate structures or organizations become efficient. That is, it may not be possible to alter an existing organization's methods of creating incentives or governance structures in meaningful ways. In this case, a firm will not function properly. The existence of an active, external market for corporate control ensures that alternative entities capable of correcting these inefficiencies exist. It is the threat of these external forces that encourages incumbent managers to seek alternative forms of corporate structure or organization that enhance firm value. In the absence of these outside forces, corporate managers (especially in firms with dispersed ownership structures) may not necessarily continuously pursue policies that maximize shareholder value.

FIGURE 8-11

Active Divestitures (1980–1989)

Source: Mergerstat Review (Chicago, Ill.: W.T. Grimm & Co.)

Selling Parent Company	1980	1981	1982	1983	1984	1985	1986	1987	1988	1989	Ten-Year Total
Beatrice Companies	1	7	3	9	12	10	10	2	1	0	55
General Electric Company	0	1	4	12	3	3	7	6	7	2	45
Allied-Signal, Inc.	2	3	5	8	5	2	0	9	7	2	43
Allegheny International, Inc.	2	1	7	4	2	6	6	9	1	1	39
ITT Corp.	8	6	2	2	5	7	4	1	0	1	36
Textron	0	4	0	0	0	10	3	8	3	1	29
Westinghouse Electric, Inc.	0	3	4	4	5	2	3	0	2	5	28
WCI Holding Corporation	1	3	4	4	2	1	5	5	3	0	28
Armco, Inc.	2	3	0	3	2	6	8	1	1	0	26
Control Data Corporation	0	0	0	3	1	7	7	1	0	6	25
Sequa Corporation	2	0	3	7	2	5	1	1	2	2	25
RJR Nabisco, Inc.	2	1	0	2	1	2	9	5	3	0	25
Sara Lee Corporation	3	2	0	3	1	8	2	2	1	2	24
Whitman Corporation	1	2	3	2	0	7	4	3	1	1	24
Union Carbide Corporation	5	3	0	1	4	5	5	0	0	1	24
CBS, Inc.	3	0	2	2	0	9	5	2	1	0	24
DuPont Company	0	0	8	6	3	0	4	2	0	0	23
Whittaker Corporation	1	0	0	5	1	1	4	5	0	5	22
Litton Industries, Inc.	0	1	0	3	5	8	1	0	2	1	21
Metromedia, Inc.	2	2	5	2	2	2	5	0	0	1	21
Monsanto Company	0	2	0	3	0	5	5	0	3	2	20
Atlantic Richfield Company	2	1	0	3	2	5	4	2	0	1	20
Times Mirror Company	2	2	1	1	2	5	5	1	1	0	20
Tenneco, Inc.	0	3	2	4	0	2	1	0	5	2	19
Xerox Corporation	0	2	0	4	1	6	3	1	1	1	19
Allis Chalmers Corporation	0	0	1	3	1	2	3	2	5	1	18
United Technologies Corp.	1	1	3	1	0	5	2	1	4	0	18
Ashland Oil Company	1	3	1	2	2	6	0	0	1	1	17
Amfac, Inc.	0	0	1	0	4	2	2	0	7	0	16
Reichhold Chemicals, Inc.	0	1	0	2	0	10	3	0	0	0	16
Texaco, Inc.	0	1	0	0	8	6	0	0	1	0	16
Total	41	58	59	105	76	155	121	69	63	39	786

However, this process is a dynamic one. Conditions change continually, and corporate managers must be prepared to continuously evaluate their businesses. As Figure 8-11 shows, active companies during the past decade divested what are perhaps a surprisingly large number of units. This activism is at least partially due to the fact that many of these companies were involved in merger and acquisition activities during the same period.

In conclusion, there are important reasons that explain the close relationship between merger and acquisition activity on the one hand and corporate reorganization and restructuring on the other. Each is an important component of the other. Corporate management needs to be aware of these relationships because inattention to the objective of maximizing firm value creates the opportunity for outsiders to acquire firms and implement appropriate changes. Much of the corporate control activity during the preceding decade is due to the fact that the environment had changed but the majority of firms had not. Therefore, the recent lull in merger and acquisition activity, especially hostile transactions, should not be construed as an opportunity for corporate managers to pursue agendas that do not enhance firm value. Rather, corporate management should remain aware of changes in their operating environments, making use of the broad range of corporate restructuring and reorganization techniques that are available to maximize the value of their firms.

8.06 SUMMARY

This chapter describes a number of corporate restructuring and reorganization techniques that when properly designed and implemented can enhance firm value. Since the opportunity to increase the value of the firm is likely to vary between corporations, it is important to understand how each of these techniques works in order to select the appropriate method. The techniques described in this chapter can be used to alter corporate balance sheets, change the form of corporate ownership, and create new organizations. Corporate managers need to understand the value creation aspects of these techniques in order to ensure that their firm's performance reflects efficient utilization of resources. As many corporate managers discovered during the 1980s, inattention to these aspects of corporate performance can ultimately lead to a loss of control. Furthermore, as was discussed, corporate managers should not equate corporate restructuring and reorganization with financial distress. The economic performance of many corporations that can meet their periodic liability payments can still be improved by implementing these techniques.

Suggested Reading

Asquith, P., and T. Wizman. "Event Risk, Covenants, and Bondholder Returns in Leveraged Buyouts." *Journal of Financial Economics,* Vol. 27 (Sept. 1990), pp. 195–214.

Bagwell, L., and J. Shoven. "Cash Distributions to Shareholders." *Journal of Economic Perspectives,* Vol. 3 (Summer 1989), pp. 129–140.

Baker, G. "Beatrice: A Study in the Creation and Destruction of Value." *Journal of Finance,* Vol. 47 (July 1992), pp. 1081–1119.

Barclay, M., and C. Smith. "Corporate Payout Policy: Cash Dividends Versus Open Market Share Repurchases." *Journal of Financial Economics*, Vol. 22 (Oct. 1988), pp. 61–82.

Beranek, W., A. Klein, and J. Rosenfeld. "The Two Stages of an Equity Carve-Out and the Price Response of Parent and Subsidiary Stock." Unpublished manuscript, New York University, 1991.

Boot, A. "Why Hang On to Losers? Divestitures and Takeovers." *Journal of Finance*, Vol. 47 (Sept. 1992), pp. 1401–1423.

Brickley, J., and L. Van Drunen. "Internal Corporate Restructuring: An Empirical Analysis." *Journal of Accounting and Economics*, Vol. 12 (Jan. 1990), pp. 251–280.

Chen, A., and J. Kessinger. "Beyond the Tax Effects of ESOP Financing." *Journal of Applied Corporate Finance*, Vol. 1 (Spring 1988), pp. 67–75.

Dann, L., "Common Stock Repurchases: An Analysis of Returns to Bondholders and Stockholders." *Journal of Financial Economics*, Vol. 9 (June 1981), pp. 113–138.

DeAngelo, A., L. DeAngelo, and E. Rice. "Going Private: Minority Freezeouts and Shareholder Wealth." *Journal of Law and Economics*, Vol. 27 (Oct. 1984), pp. 367–401.

DeAngelo, H., and L. DeAngelo. "Managerial Ownership of Voting Rights: A Study of Public Corporations with Dual Classes of Common Stock." *Journal of Financial Economics*, Vol. 14 (Mar. 1985), pp. 33–69.

Denis, D. "Defensive Changes in Corporate Payout Policy: Share Repurchases and Special Dividends." *Journal of Finance*, Vol. 45 (Dec. 1990), pp. 1433–1456.

Hite, G., and J. Owers. "Security Price Reactions Around Corporate Spin-Off Announcements." *Journal of Financial Economics*, Vol. 12 (Dec. 1983), pp. 409–436.

Hite, G., J. Owers, and R. Rogers. "The Market for Interfirm Asset Sales: Partial Sell-Offs and Total Liquidations." *Journal of Financial Economics*, Vol. 18 (June 1987), pp. 229–252.

Hite, G., and M. Vetsuypens. "Management Buyouts of Divisions and Shareholder Wealth." *Journal of Finance*, Vol. 44 (Sept. 1989), pp. 953–970.

Hoskisson, R., and T. Turk. "Corporate Restructuring: Governance and Control Limits of the Internal Capital Market." *Academy of Management Review*, Vol. 15 (July 1990), pp. 459–477.

Jarrell, G., and A. Poulsen. "Dual-Class Recapitalizations as Antitakeover Mechanisms: The Recent Evidence." *Journal of Financial Economics*, Vol. 20 (Jan. 1988), pp. 129–152.

John, K., L. Lang, and J. Netter. "The Voluntary Restructuring of Large Firms in Response to Performance Decline." *Journal of Finance*, Vol. 47 (July 1992), pp. 891–917.

Kamma, S., G. Kanatas, and S. Raymar. "Dutch Auction vs. Fixed-Price Self-Tender Offers for Common Stock: An Empirical Examination." Unpublished manuscript, Indiana University, 1991.

Kaplan, S., and J. Stein. "How Risky Is the Debt in Highly Leveraged Transactions? Evidence From Public Recapitalizations." Unpublished manuscript, University of Chicago, 1991.

Kaplan, S., and M. Weisbach. "The Success of Acquisitions: Evidence From Divestitures." Unpublished manuscript, National Bureau of Economic Research.

Kim, E., and J. Schatzberg. "Voluntary Corporate Liquidations." *Journal of Financial Economics*, Vol. 19 (Dec. 1987), pp. 311–328.

Kleiman, R. "Shareholder Gains From Leveraged Cash-Outs." *Journal of Applied Corporate Finance*, Vol. 1 (Spring 1988), pp. 46–53.

Klein, A. "The Timing and Substance of Divestiture Announcements: Individual, Simultaneous, and Cumulative Effects." *Journal of Finance*, Vol. 41 (July 1986), pp. 685–695.

Lease, R., J. McConnell, and W. Mikkelson. "The Market Value of Control in Publicly Traded Corporations." *Journal of Financial Economics,* Vol. 11 (Apr. 1983), pp. 439–471.

Lehn, K., and A. Poulsen. "Free Cash Flow and Shareholder Gains in Going Private Transactions." Unpublished manuscript, Securities and Exchange Commission, 1990.

Masulis, R. "The Impact of Capital Structure Change on Firm Value: Some Estimates." *Journal of Finance,* Vol. 38 (Mar. 1983), pp. 107–126.

McConnell, J., and T. Nantell. "Corporate Combinations and Common Stock Returns: The Case of Joint Ventures." *Journal of Finance,* Vol. 40 (June 1985), pp. 519–536.

Miles, J., and J. Rosenfeld. "The Effect of Voluntary Spin-Off Announcements on Shareholder Wealth." *Journal of Finance,* Vol. 38 (Dec. 1983), pp. 1597–1606.

Muscarella, C. and M. Vetsuypens. "Efficiency and Organizational Structure: A Study of Reverse LBOs." *Journal of Finance,* Vol. 45 (Dec. 1990), pp. 1389–1413.

Nanda, V. "On the Good News in Equity Carve-Outs." *Journal of Finance,* Vol. 46 (Dec. 1991), pp. 1717–1737.

Partch, M. "The Creation of a Class of Limited Voting Common Stock and Shareholder Wealth." *Journal of Financial Economics,* Vol. 18 (June 1987), pp. 313–339.

Rosenfeld, J. "Additional Evidence on the Relation Between Divestiture Announcements and Shareholder Wealth." *Journal of Finance,* Vol. 39 (Dec. 1984), pp. 1437–1448.

Ruback, R. "Coercive Dual-Class Exchange Offers." *Journal of Financial Economics,* Vol. 20 (Jan. 1988), pp. 153–173.

Schipper, K., and A. Smith. "A Comparison of Equity Carve-Outs and Seasoned Equity Offerings: Share Price Effects and Corporate Restructuring." *Journal of Financial Economics,* Vol. 15 (Jan. 1986), pp. 153–186.

———. "Effects of Recontracting on Shareholder Wealth." *Journal of Financial Economics,* Vol. 12 (Dec. 1983), pp. 437–467.

———. "Equity Carve-Outs," *Corporate Restructuring and Executive Compensation,* Joel Stern, George Stewart, and Donald Chew, eds. Cambridge, Mass.: Ballinger, pp. 177–192.

Seward, J., and J. Walsh. "The Governance and Control of Voluntary Corporate Spin-Offs: An Investigation of the Contracting Efficiency Hypothesis." Unpublished manuscript. Amos Tuck School of Business, Dartmouth College.

Vermaelen, T. "Common Stock Repurchases and Market Signalling: An Empirical Study." *Journal of Financial Economics,* Vol. 9 (June 1981), pp. 139–183.

Walsh, J., and J. Seward. "On the Efficiency of Internal and External Corporate Control Mechanisms." *Academy of Management Review,* Vol. 15 (July 1990), pp. 421–458.

Weston, J. Fred, Kai Chung, and Susan Hoag. *Mergers, Restructuring and Corporate Control.* Englewood Cliffs, N.J.: Prentice-Hall, 1990.

Chapter 9

Executive Pay, Incentives, and Performance

JOHN D. ENGLAND

9.01 INTRODUCTION

Academicians, investors, and business planners are increasingly recognizing the importance of executive compensation as a key to successful implementation of business strategy. Executive compensation plans used to be designed with only tax and accounting issues in mind. However, today's compensation professionals, as well as today's board members, are less concerned with a compensation plan's impact on reported earnings and more concerned with its impact on shareholder value.

9.02 ATTRACTING AND RETAINING EXECUTIVES THROUGH COMPENSATION

When professional managers began to replace owner-managers at the helm of corporations, new motivational tools were required to keep executives working at their highest potential. Previously, an owner-manager's incentive to build a better company stemmed from the fact that the company was "his" or "hers"; family wealth depended on the owner's ability to maintain stock price and pay dividends. Professional managers, however, are hired hands, without the passion for excellence that comes from substantial ownership. Clearly, it is in today's shareholders' best interest to design a compensation system to replace ownership as the primary motivational device.

Just what should an executive compensation plan accomplish? First, it should attract individuals with the training and skills necessary for senior executive responsibilities. The casual observer of the U.S. business community may mistakenly believe that there are millions of appropriately trained managers just waiting for the chance to be a chief executive officer (CEO). However, just as not every lawyer aspires to become a member of the Supreme Court, nor every professor to become the president of a major university, not all managers have the desire to run a corporation. In addition, even fewer have the mix of skills required to do so. Therefore, an executive compensation program must first provide a reward system that will attract potential executives from within a company or from the business community outside.

Once attracted, the professional manager must be retained. Whereas the owner-manager would likely be deeply committed to the family corporation and very unlikely to leave it, the professional manager may not have the same type of altruistic devotion. Simply, a professional manager who perceives an imbalance in effort expended and rewards received may leave the company. Compensation surveys, attention given to executive compensation by the business press, and executive recruiters all provide information that can be used to weigh the effort-reward balance. Thus, executive compensation professionals must carefully monitor the external market for talent so that this balance between effort and reward is maintained.

A good compensation program may include features such as sign-on bonuses, perquisites, and so-called golden handcuffs, which attract and retain executives with desirable skills. However, a compensation program that includes only these features is not serving company shareholders as well as it might. A good compensation program should also let executives know what is expected of them and reward them accordingly when those expectations are achieved.

Companies have realized that one of the best ways to motivate managers is to underscore business plans and strategic corporate thrusts with incentive compensation. Human nature dictates that path A will be followed rather than paths B, C, and D if path A leads to appropriate rewards and the others do not.

FIGURE 9-1

CEO Total Executive Compensation

Source: Towers Perrin (1993)

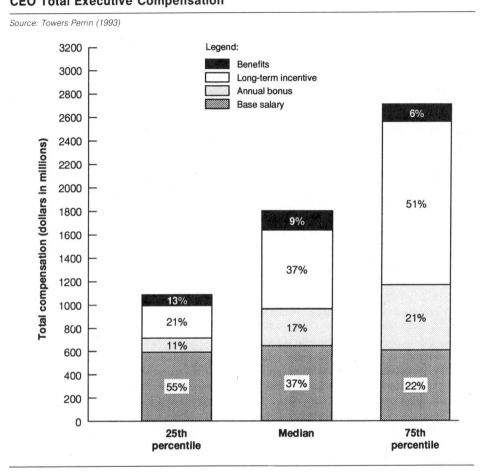

9.03 COMPONENTS OF EXECUTIVE COMPENSATION

The pay package received by today's professional manager is vastly differently from that of the owner-manager of the past. Although base salary remains the cornerstone of the executive pay package, compensation should not be mistaken as base salary alone. Executive paychecks are supplemented by short-term and long-term incentive compensation, executive benefits, and perquisites, creating what is known as total executive compensation.

Figure 9-1 illustrates a recent study by Towers Perrin, which found that base salary makes up only 37 percent of the median total compensation package of U.S. CEOs, down from 42 percent in 1984. Variable compensation, in the form of short-term and long-term incentives, makes up the largest portion of the total executive pay package.

[1] Base Salary

Base salary is the foundation of any compensation program for the following reasons:

- It is the most visible component of the total pay package.
- It influences the level and scope of many other compensation elements.
- It establishes an employee's standard of living and position within the organizational hierarchy, with attendant status implications.

Compensation theory states that an employee's base salary should be a function of external pay practices and incumbent characteristics such as performance and experience. Published salary surveys, as well as privately commissioned exchanges of competitive salary information, are typically used to determine competitive base salary levels, often called going rates. As defined by most companies, a going rate represents the typical salary paid to a hypothetical seasoned performer in a company or organization with similar characteristics. (Size, industry, and profitability are criteria often used in defining similar characteristics.)

In order to determine the going rate for the CEO position at Chrysler, for instance, surveys that include data from Ford and General Motors should be consulted, as well as information on other large industrial concerns. The Chrysler CEO's job responsibilities should then be compared with those of other CEOs included in the survey data and an appropriate going rate for the Chrysler position established.

Going rates are used to establish base salary midpoints, which, in turn, are used to determine base salary ranges. Each base salary range has a minimum, a midpoint (sometimes called a control point), and a maximum. The spread between the salary range minimum and maximum usually is a function of level. For lower-level jobs, where proficiency can be achieved quickly, the spread might only be 30 percent to 40 percent. For executive-level positions, however, one tends to find a much larger spread between salary range minimum and maximum, often 50 percent to 60 percent.

When base salary ranges are created for all positions, they are usually assigned hierarchical salary grades, and a salary grade structure is created. In an effort to recognize marketplace pay differentials between different positions, most organizations employ a 10 percent to 12 percent progression between salary grade midpoints. Figure 9-2 illustrates a sample company's annual salary structure.

Regardless of organizational level, an employee's salary should be not only within the base salary range established for the position but also within the range on the basis of the incumbent's experience and performance according to the following guidelines:

- A base salary minimum should be reserved for employees who are new to the position or those who meet the minimum requirements of the position.
- Given that the base salary midpoint is a function of the going rate, an employee's base salary should be comparable to a base salary midpoint when he or she is fully qualified for the position responsibilities and when his or her performance is fully competent. For lower-level positions, the level of proficient competency might be reached in one to two years; for higher-level jobs, however, it may take five to six years.
- Base salary maximums, which can be some 23 percent above fully competitive market rates of pay, should generally be reached only when an employee's performance and experience are far above the norm.

FIGURE 9-2

Sample Company Annual Salary Structure

Salary Grade	Minimum	Midpoint	Maximum	Spread
30	$183,180	$238,140	$293,090	60%
29	167,820	216,490	265,160	58
28	153,760	196,810	239,870	56
27	139,780	178,920	218,060	56
26	128,070	162,650	197,230	54
25	116,430	147,860	179,300	54
24	106,680	134,420	162,150	52
23	96,980	122,200	147,410	52
22	88,870	111,090	133,310	50
21	80,790	100,990	121,190	50
20	74,040	91,810	109,580	48
19	67,310	83,460	99,620	48
18	61,680	75,870	90,050	46
17	56,070	68,970	81,860	46
16	51,390	62,700	74,000	44
15	46,720	57,000	67,280	44
14	42,830	51,820	60,820	42
13	38,930	47,110	55,280	42
12	35,690	42,830	49,970	40
11	32,450	38,940	45,430	40
10	29,750	35,400	41,060	38
9	27,040	32,180	37,320	38
8	24,790	29,250	33,710	36
7	22,530	26,590	30,640	36
6	20,660	24,170	27,680	34
5	18,780	21,970	25,170	34
4	17,220	19,970	22,730	32
3	15,650	18,150	20,660	32
2	14,350	16,500	18,660	30
1	13,040	15,000	16,950	30

Like most rules, however, the theoretical relationship between actual base salary and the expected position within the range is often broken. Competitive premiums may have to be paid in order to entice an external candidate to accept a position at a new company. And sadly, because most companies' annual pay increases may not be sufficient for employees to make progress through their positions' base salary range, many employees never reach their salary grade midpoints, even after long years of experience and good performance.

Many companies find it difficult to measure the worth of an executive through base salary alone. For instance, how is the dollar value of an executive like Lee Iacocca determined, as opposed to the value of the position of Chrysler's CEO? Of what use is a competitive base salary range for the likes of Warren Buffett at Berkshire Hathaway? Further, pay-for-performance salary increases reward an executive over the long term

FIGURE 9-3

**Typical Annual Bonus and Incentive Schedule Awards
as a Percentage of Salary**

Position	Minimum	Target	Maximum
CEO	25	50	75
President	20	40	60
Chief financial officer	15	30	45
Business unit head	18	25	38
Staff vice-president	10	20	30
Manager	5	10	15

but do not tend to reward or motivate any specific actions that improve organizational performance. Thus, additional forms of total compensation, called annual and long-term incentive plans, have been designed to reward, at least in part the performance and personal qualities that a CEO or any other executive might bring to the job. And since most companies offer these kinds of arrangements, they have become a competitive necessity.

[2] Annual Incentives

Effective annual incentive programs generally have the following characteristics:

- They apply to executives whose duties and responsibilities allow them to affect goal attainment.
- Their award opportunities are of meaningful size.
- They are linked to objective measures of performance.
- They balance individual and team performance.

Most executives can remember the day they first became eligible to receive a bonus, and certainly they remember receiving their first bonus check. Since most companies limit participation in bonus plans to between 5 percent and 10 percent of their total employee population, eligibility for awards is akin to being formally recognized as a member of the management team.

Why do companies employ bonus programs? First, for many positions, eligibility for and, usually, receipt of an award is a competitive necessity. In fact, these types of programs are so institutionalized that many companies now speak in terms of competitive minimum, target, and maximum awards as a percent of salary that varies based on organizational level. For instance, a multi-billion-dollar company would probably use an award schedule resembling that found in Figure 9-3. Generally, over a 10-year period, most companies would pay an amount comparable to the target in 6 years and minimums and maximums might each be earned in 2 years.

The second reason many companies introduce these programs is that by putting more executive compensation at risk, they can often slow down the rate of increase in fixed base salaries and increase the variable component of bonus. It is hard to

FIGURE 9-4

Typical Incentive Plan Objectives Weighting

Position	Corporate Weighting	Group/Divison Weighting	Individual Weighting
CEO	100%	0	0
Chief financial officer	100	0	0
Division head	25	50%	25%
Corporate staff	25	50	25
Division staff	25	50	25
Plant manager	20	60	20

Note: Most common response from 1992 Towers Perrin survey of annual incentive practices of over 300 companies.

argue with a concept that only provides additional compensation when performance, however defined, is deemed to be acceptable.

The most important reason for companies to design and implement annual programs is that they focus executive attention on key goals. Unlike a productivity-oriented bonus, which can make workers work harder, annual incentive programs help participants "work smarter." In other words, an incentive plan will generally stipulate five or six key objectives that must be achieved if the executive is to earn various award levels. These may be corporate, business unit, or individual objectives. Often, depending on organizational level, the objectives might be weighted so that the executive knows the relative importance of each. A typical scheme is shown in Figure 9-4.

Most companies hold their top corporate executive officers accountable solely for corporate results. Staff officers' awards tend to be based largely on corporate results, with some portion of the award dependent on departmental goals. At the business unit level, the award focus tends to shift to the goals of the business unit itself, rather than corporate results over which the business unit manager may have little impact. Finally, at midmanagement levels, the objectives shift to those that are more specific to the position's accountabilities, with only modest weighting given to corporate and/or business unit goals.

Annual incentives and bonuses are typically paid in cash or in stock, and many companies allow executives to defer the earned awards until retirement. For example, according to a 1993 Towers Perrin study of 350 companies from the Fortune 1000, the median annual incentive was 75 percent of base salary, and the seventy-fifth percentile practice was 100 percent of base salary.

Annual awards can be a significant portion of an executive's income. As such, they are powerful instruments for motivating executives to accomplish particular objectives.

[3] Long-Term Incentives

Regardless of form, the basic reason for a long-term incentive plan is to motivate and reward management for a company's long-term growth and prosperity and to balance the inherently short-term orientation of annual incentive programs. Much has been

FIGURE 9-5

Prevalence of Long-Term Incentives

Source: Towers Perrin (1993)

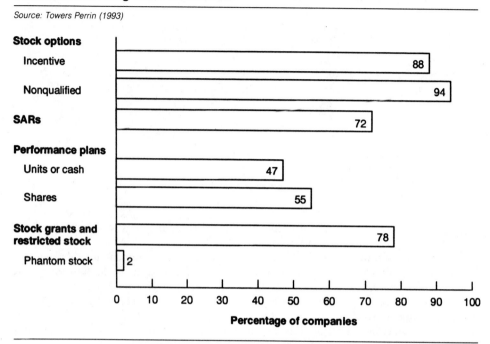

said about the short-term orientation of professional managers, who attempt to hold an operation together just until they are transferred or promoted or try to bring about short-term financial results at the expense of long-term success. Incentives, such as those shown in Figure 9-5 and described in Appendix 9.1, can ease this problem by linking executive rewards to long-term measures of performance.

[a] Stock-Based Incentives. Keeping in mind the motivation created by ownership, a vast majority of companies use stock-based incentives in their long-term incentive programs. The stated purposes of this approach include the following:

- Aligning professional managers more closely with the shareholder by giving them opportunities for stock ownership and price appreciation
- Giving a positive sign to Wall Street and the company shareholders that executives seek ownership in the business
- Encouraging managers to take a longer-term view of company performance

Although there is a cash opportunity cost associated with bargain purchases or grants of stock, and stock incentives can negatively affect earnings per share (EPS) calculations, companies tend to believe that these are outweighed by the positive identification and motivational considerations. Three broad types of long-term incentives deliver stock as their primary reward mechanism: (1) stock options; (2) restricted stock; and (3) performance shares.

Stock options. Stock options are by far the most prevalent long-term incentive device, allowing executives to "bet on the winning horse after the race has been run." Companies grant options to executives to buy shares at a stated price, typically the fair market price on the day of grant, for a period of years. These plans usually have vesting requirements that control the timing of option exercise and expiration dates that limit the life of an option. If the stock price rises, an executive may trade in or exercise each option plus the stated exercise price and receive a share of company stock in return. Because the option only has value to the executive if the market price of the underlying stock rises, the executive presumably has an incentive to increase shareholder value as measured by stock price. As Figure 9-5 shows, stock options (incentive and nonqualified) are the most prevalent form of long-term incentive plan.

Options come in various forms, the choice of which is largely dependent on the tax treatment. Nonqualified stock options (NQSOs) require an executive to pay ordinary income tax at the date of exercise on the price appreciation per share between the stated exercise price and the stock's fair market value at the time of exercise. Under certain strict Internal Revenue Code (IRC) provisions, incentive stock options (ISOs) may be awarded that offer capital gains tax treatment on the appreciation of the stock (if any) from the price at grant to the time of sale, thus avoiding the receipt of taxable income at time of exercise previously noted for NQSOs. However, providing capital gains treatment to the executive does not come without cost to the company: ISOs are substantially more dilutive and costly because, unlike the situation with NQSOs, the company may not deduct on its own tax return the value of the spread between the price the executive paid and the value of the stock at exercise.

Before the enactment of Tax Reform Act of 1986 (TRA 1986), many companies were willing to accept the nondeductibility of gains associated with ISOs in order to provide favorable capital gains tax treatment for their executives. However, there is only a modest difference in tax rates between ordinary income taxation and capital gains. Despite this, the company is still unable to deduct ISO gains because they continue to be capital gains.

Restricted stock. Restricted stock is typically an award of stock that is nontransferable and/or subject to substantial risk of forfeiture for a period of years. Only after all restrictions lapse does the executive unconditionally own the shares granted. The most prevalent restriction is one of continued employment, although performance-related conditions are sometimes applied. Restricted stock provides an effective set of "golden handcuffs" during the period of restrictions. Other advantages are the following:

- Dividends can be paid to the executive even when the shares are restricted.
- Shares are immediately assigned to the executive, usually with full dividend and voting rights, allowing earlier identification with the company.
- Restricted stock awards can be used to recognize and retain fast-track managerial talent.

As noted in Figure 9-5, 78 percent of large industrial companies use restricted stock. One reason restricted stock is less prevalent than stock options may be an adverse reaction to the "something for nothing" flavor of restricted stock grants to senior executives. Also, an executive may find the tax treatment of restricted stock burdensome. An executive can elect under IRC Section 83(b) to be taxed in the year of grant, despite the fact that the shares are not fully owned and are "restricted." An executive who elects to be taxed in the year of grant on the fair value of the stock without regard to the restrictions cannot recover the taxes paid if the stock is later forfeited. However, if the executive does not elect to be taxed in the year of grant, whenever the restrictions lapse on any of the restricted shares he or she must pay ordinary income tax on the then-current value of the stock.

Performance share plans. Performance shares are a contingent award of shares that are earned in whole or in part according to the degree of achievement of predetermined performance goals. Performance goals can be financial (e.g., EPS growth or return on equity (ROE) hurdles) or strategic (e.g., market share, reducing costs, or increasing quality). Of the 350 Fortune 1000 companies surveyed by Towers Perrin, 55 percent have instituted performance share plans that provide the following advantages:

- Reward is linked to a performance measure over which the executive has more direct control and is not linked solely to stock price movements.

- Performance share plans avoid the financing difficulties associated with option exercise.

- Performance share plans can communicate the importance of certain organizational goals while providing stock ownership opportunities.

Stock-based incentives play an important role in executive compensation plan design. While there is no perfect plan, stock option, restricted stock, and performance share programs can be effective in promoting stock ownership as well as meeting overall compensation objectives.

[b] Surrogate Stock Incentives. Owning stock in the enterprise for which one works is fundamental to an executive's compensation. In publicly held companies, the desire for executive stock ownership drives the design of many companies' long-term incentive plans. It is widely believed that the shareholders' interests will be served best if executive rewards are tied directly to increases in shareholder value, as measured by stock price.

But what long-term incentive alternatives are available to privately held companies, a recently acquired business that used to be publicly held, or a separate division or subsidiary of a holding company? Owning stock in the enterprise for which the executive works simply is not an alternative. And, somehow, performance plans tend not to be as emotionally satisfying as having an option on or earning stock.

Yet, the owner or owners of a privately held company or parent company shareholders still need executives to focus on increasing shareholder value. Thus, it became a challenge to compensation professionals to develop a long-term incentive that looked and acted like a stock-based incentive, i.e., that is, a surrogate stock incentive.

Capitalized stream of earnings. Early attempts to develop a surrogate stock incentive used a capitalized stream of earnings approach to creating a stock price. The concept is simple: A company's earnings are converted to a per-share basis by assuming a hypothetical number of shares outstanding. Then, a multiple, e.g., 10, is applied to EPS, and a stock price results.

When this approach is used for an incentive plan, executives are granted a certain number of "shares," which entitle them to receive the change in stock price over a designated period, typically three to five years.

A company that uses an approach similar to the one shown in Figure 9-6 is motivating growth in earnings. Often, however, earnings growth is only one critical financial measure. One method of using the capitalized stream of earnings approach to create

FIGURE 9-6

Capitalized Stream of Earnings Approach

	1991	1992	1993
Earnings	$50,000	$60,000	$70,000
Hypothetical shares	10,000	10,000	10,000
EPS	$ 5	$ 6	$ 7
Multiple	10	10	10
Stock price	$ 50	$ 60	$ 70
Gain per share	—	$ 10	$ 20

a stock price links the EPS multiple to another performance measure (for example, instead of using a multiple of 10, the multiple might be increased to 16 or decline to 6 at given levels of sales or capital efficiency performance).

Book value per share. A second approach to creating a surrogate stock price is to use the shareholders' equity section of the balance sheet rather than concentrating solely on the income statement. In this approach, a business's book value is converted to a per-share figure through the use of a hypothetical number of shares outstanding. Again, changes in book value per share typically determine incentive rewards.

This method is more conservative than using a capitalized stream of earnings stock price because radical changes in book value are rare. Also, unless a company has a net loss for the year or dividends exceed earnings, book value will always increase.

Of course, to use a book value approach, a company or division must have a book value. Many subsidiaries or divisions do not have an equity section on their balance sheets, and some privately held companies have unusual dividend policies that make book value growth unacceptable for incentive plan purposes.

Intrinsic value. While both the capitalized stream of earnings and book value approaches create figures that resemble stock prices, neither directly motivates increasing shareholder value. This does not mean that earnings or book value growth are not important; they are. But what is really needed is a measure designed both to parallel changes in shareholder value and to link those changes to specific measures of corporate performance.

Through research on the relationship between corporate performance and stock price movement in several industries, and by adapting a measure employed in basic security analysis, stock price movement has been related to two specific performance criteria:

- ROE in excess of the cost of equity
- When ROE is greater than the cost of equity, growth in equity

Earning an ROE in excess of a firm's cost of equity simply means that the company is earning a higher return than its shareholders should expect given the firm's risk. And when the return exceeds the cost of equity, the company should be reinvesting in the business so that shareholder returns can be maximized.

It has been shown that this relationship between growth in investment and returns

285

over the cost of equity affects a firm's market-to-book ratio. When a business is earning returns greater than the cost of equity and is reinvesting, investors will bid up the stock price so that it trades at a level above book value. If the business is disinvesting when it is earning returns in excess of the cost of equity, the multiple above book value will still be positive but will be at a much lower level than it could be with reinvestment. Finally, when a business is not earning enough to cover its cost of equity, its market-to-book ratio will be less than 1.0 (for example, the firm will trade at a discount to book). However, shareholder value can be increased through disinvestment (i.e., letting the shareholders take their money out of the company to invest elsewhere for a higher risk-adjusted return).

The intrinsic value of a company is often defined as its current book value plus the present value of an estimated stream of "real" future earnings. Real future earnings are earnings in excess of those required given the company's required ROE (as specified by the company's capital asset pricing model) and its future book values. The formula for intrinsic value is as follows:

$$\text{Intrinsic value} = \text{current book value} + \left[\text{future book value}_1 \times \left(\frac{\text{actual}}{\text{ROE}} - \frac{\text{required}}{\text{ROE}}\right)\right]$$

$$+ \left[\text{future book value}_2 \times \left(\frac{\text{actual}}{\text{ROE}} - \frac{\text{required}}{\text{ROE}}\right)\right] + \ldots$$

$$+ \left[\text{future book value}_n \times \left(\frac{\text{actual}}{\text{ROE}} - \frac{\text{required}}{\text{ROE}}\right)\right]$$

This formula can be rephrased by factoring out the current book value per share:

Intrinsic value = current book value × market-to-book ratio

As in the two earlier approaches, an intrinsic value per share is created at the beginning of the measurement period. Typically, an average of the past three years' growth in equity and returns in excess of the cost of equity are used to develop the theoretical market-to-book ratio. At the end of the measurement period, typically three to five years later, the change in intrinsic value is measured and incentive payments are made.

[c] Other Long-Term Incentive Devices. A number of other long-term incentive plans have been developed that use cash as reward mechanisms. Stock appreciation rights (SARs), often granted as companions to NQSOs or ISOs, were developed to ease the cash flow burden faced by executives upon the exercise of stock options. Instead of exercising the option and paying the stated exercise price, an executive can choose instead to receive an amount equal to the appreciation, paid in stock, cash, or both. Performance units are similar to performance shares except that the award may be made in cash rather than in stock. Phantom stock consists of units analogous to company shares; their value equals the appreciation in the market value of the stock underlying the units. Other equity plans that create separate and often subordinate classes of stock that may be converted to common shares are also used, although infrequently.

[4] Benefits and Perquisites

Although traditional employee benefits are still the main source of benefits for top management, many companies have special plans for their senior executives. The growth in the use of special plans has been driven by legislation called the Employee Retirement Income Security Act of 1974 (ERISA), which has placed statutory dollar limits on the benefits employers may provide under qualified retirement plans. Among the more common supplemental executive benefits are ERISA excess defined benefit and defined contribution supplements, supplemental executive retirement plans (SERPs), special death benefits, and postretirement medical plans.

Executive perquisites are used to supplement cash compensation and to further motivate and reward executives. Many companies offer perquisite programs that include company cars, first-class air travel, financial counseling, club memberships, and employment contracts.

9.04 PLANNING AND INCENTIVES

Executive compensation programs are fully effective only if they are appropriate to the business needs of the organization and if they help to highlight desired paths of executive action. These paths are a function of the strategic planning process, whether formal (as designed by platoons of MBAs or management consultants) or informal (e.g., a general notion in the CEO's mind about where the company should go and how it might get there). For development of the most effective combination of annual and long-term incentives, the executive incentive program must be linked to the strategic and operating plans of the business, as illustrated in Figure 9-7. Executives and managers must know what is expected of them, what resources will be available to them, and how their performance affects the entire organization.

[1] Mission

Corporate strategic planning begins by determining the company's mission, i.e., its reason for being or its enduring, long-term task. For a profit-making organization, the fundamental mission is always to increase the value of the business to the owners or the shareholders over time. The value of a publicly owned firm is most easily measured by long-term stock price appreciation and dividend growth. If making money were the only mission, the rest of the planning process would be quite simple. However, a company's mission may also include a definition of the market in which the company will operate, the types of businesses to be pursued, the kinds of customers it seeks to attract, and the work environment offered to its employees. Many firms expand their mission beyond the business world to include goals such as service to the community or being leaders in corporate responsibility. A privately held firm may have the mission of going public. Whatever the company's mission, it must be understood and articulated so that strategies can be developed to fulfill it. Because a business's mission is so closely tied to increasing shareholder value, stock-based incentives are often used to motivate indirectly executive actions that will fulfill the mission and thereby increase stock price and dividends.

FIGURE 9-7

Linkage of Planning and Incentive Systems

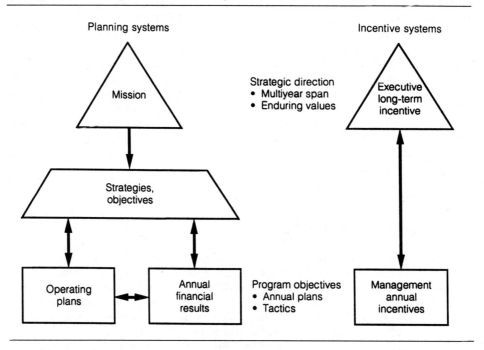

[2] Strategies

Corporate strategies help management understand how the organization's physical, financial, and human resources are to be used to best accomplish its mission. These strategies also allow executives and managers the luxury of a consistency check to ensure that the firm is moving towards its goals.

Corporate strategic development requires sweeping, penetrating business analyses detailing corporate strengths, weaknesses, opportunities, and threats. Competitors, both existing and potential, must be analyzed in terms of their future capabilities and probable reaction to the firm's strategic plan.

Corporate strategic development should provide a plan that illuminates (1) the direction in which the company is going; (2) how it is going to get there; and (3) what it needs to get there. For instance, a low-cost strategy might be contrasted with a niche strategy as follows:

1. Research and development:
   - *Low cost.* Develop products that can be produced at a low cost to satisfy the needs of the greatest number of customers.
   - *Niche.* Develop products that offer unique and perhaps patentable attributes that satisfy the needs of a specific group of existing and potential customers.

2. Marketing:

- *Low cost.* Withdraw from marginal markets with high delivery costs or those that demand custom products; concentrate on promoting standardized, off-the-shelf products.
- *Niche.* Seek areas where a significant group of customers is not being adequately served by existing products. The size of the niche is not as important as how well the firm can exploit it.

3. Manufacturing:

- *Low cost.* Develop production techniques and establish facilities to manufacture the product in long runs at the lowest possible cost.
- *Niche.* Use effective quality control procedures. Long production runs are not imperative. Locate manufacturing capacity in an area or areas where they can best serve customers.

Typically, strategic plans plot three to five years ahead, although management should carefully monitor the plan and readjust it when necessary. Any changes must be communicated to key executives and managers as soon as possible through the operating plan.

While stock-based incentives certainly play a role in helping to implement strategies, performance-related plans with cash or stock payouts are used more often. For instance, if the low-cost strategy of research and development is to develop products at a low cost, a cash award might be designed to promote the development of these types of ideas and products. Similarly, if the marketing strategy is to fill a particular market niche, a market share measure may drive incentive awards.

[3] Operating Plans

Operating plans translate broad strategies into steps of action. They combine internal and external information with strategic plans in order to develop specific programs, outline methods of resource use, and define performance objectives. Which programs or products should be introduced? Which markets should be expanded or contracted? What is feasible in light of the available resources of knowledge, cash, people, and technology? What are reasonable performance objectives and time frames? Answers to these kinds of questions help management transform broad strategic statements into plans that identify the specifics: who, what, where, and when.

Operating plans usually specify objectives to be achieved by year-end and the steps to be taken to achieve them. Communicating these steps to executives and managers is very important, because, without understanding the steps, it is difficult to reach the objective. Therefore, linking annual incentives to the successful implementation of operating plans can be an extremely effective way of communicating what is expected of management.

[4] Instrumental Versus Charitable Rewards

Reward systems that link mission, strategy, and operating plans with so-called instrumental rewards stand in contrast to those offering charitable rewards. Charitable or discretionary bonuses are handed out without regard to performance. To regain their competitive edge and to encourage longer-term thinking and growth, U.S. corporations must increasingly link reward systems to their missions, strategies, and operating plans through instrumental rewards. Charitable rewards should be limited to lower-level managers and prohibited for senior executives. Instead of giving charitable bonuses, which may not focus executive attention on activities that increase shareholder value, corporations should favor incentives that benefit shareholders and those that prompt executives to reach specific corporate goals.

9.05 MEASUREMENT OF PERFORMANCE

Thus far, this chapter has focused on the need to link executive compensation to performance through corporate strategic planning. In addition, however, a definition and measurement of performance must be developed.

[1] Performance as Viewed by Shareholders

To shareholders or investment managers, performance is usually a function of stock price and dividend growth. Individuals buy stock in a company and assume that management will do everything in its power to increase shareholder value.

Shareholders are not concerned only with absolute performance, however; they are also interested in relative performance. Relative performance, of course, can be defined in many ways. Investors may look at the performance of the Standard & Poor's 500, the Wilshire 5000, an industry grouping, or some alternative investment; the reference point for comparison depends on the perspective of the individual shareholder. Whatever that perspective is, a company must perform well compared with others in its group.

[2] Performance as Viewed by Management

To the U.S. manager, performance generally relates to size and profitability: "How much did we sell and how much did we earn?" While concepts such as strategic plan implementation (increasing market share, introducing new products, and improving quality) are important to most managers, they are often perceived as less important than profit growth.

Why? Managers are receiving a signal from somewhere that earnings growth is their most important goal. Although earnings and profitability growth are important, everyone is familiar with the story of the executive who cuts back on critical research and development expenditures in an effort to increase the earnings. Research expenses go down, earnings go up, and bonuses are paid; then the bottom drops out when a competitor introduces a new product based on the technology it had been researching. In this instance, the executive's concept of performance was linked to the incentive system, but the incentive system was not linked with the behavior that would increase long-term shareholder value.

[3] Traditional Accounting Measures

Many observers fault traditional accounting measures used in executive compensation plans for the short-term perspective of many U.S. managers. These observers point to such standard performance measures as target earnings growth rate, EPS, earnings as a percentage of equity, earnings as a percentage of capital, earnings as a percent of sales. If these accounting measures are the only hurdles used in both annual and long-term incentive plans, such criticism may be justified.

The real danger, however, is that accounting measures tend to drive many incentive plans; this responsibility to drive and manage incentive programs should rest with a committee of the board of directors. Often, however, accounting measures will not tell the true story behind management performance.

For instance, assume that General Products Company uses a peer group of 20 industry competitors in measuring its annual ROE for incentive plan purposes. While this company's ROE generally exceeds its cost of equity compared with its peer group, its ROE languishes somewhere around the average. A closer examination of the financial structures of many of the peer companies, however, shows a much greater proportion of debt in the capital structure than General Products has. When the peer group is pared to include only similarly capitalized companies, General Products' return on equity is in the top quartile every year. As a check, General Products' return on total capital is compared with the original group of peer companies. When the measure of investment is total capital rather than equity alone, the company's relative performance improves dramatically.

Changes in accounting principles can have a dramatic effect on accounting measures. In the past few years, companies have been adopting the Financial Accounting Standards Board (FASB) Statement of Financial Accounting Standards (SFAS) No. 87, which prescribes new pension accounting methods. Very few companies are unaffected by the transition; some report gains and others losses. The impact on the income statement (and thus any earnings-related measure) can be substantial. One large company reduced pension expense by $130 million the year it adopted SFAS No. 87, partially offsetting a considerable drop in operating performance that year. Had this company employed an unadjusted earnings-based incentive formula, executives might have enjoyed increased bonuses owing to an accounting rather than a performance change.

[4] Implications for Incentive Plan Design

This does not mean that earnings-related measures should not be used in the design of an incentive program. Profits are important, and long-term earnings growth should be emphasized in whatever format best captures the profit objectives in the strategic plan overall (e.g., ROE, return on common shareholders' equity, and EPS growth). However, accounting measures that emphasize earnings should not be used to the exclusion of other factors described in a company's strategic plan. If it is important to generate returns in excess of the cost of capital (as seems reasonable), this should be encouraged. If it is important to build market share, improve measurable quality, or surpass competitor performance, all of these should be encouraged as well. Far too much time is spent in careful crafting of intricate strategic and operating plans that leave out an important step in implementation: to provide executives with incentives to increase shareholder value, not just reported earnings.

To underscore the importance of not allowing accounting measures to drive incentive plans as though they were on autopilot, many plans include the following enabling legislation clause:

> At any time prior to the payment of performance awards, the compensation committee may adjust previously established performance targets and other terms and conditions, including the corporation's or other corporations' financial performance for plan purposes, to reflect major unforeseen events such as changes in laws, regulations, or accounting practices, mergers, acquisitions, divestitures, or extraordinary, unusual, or nonrecurring items or events.

9.06 DESIGNING SENSIBLE COMPENSATION PROGRAMS

Executive compensation is important because a company needs to attract qualified executive candidates. Further, once it has attracted these candidates, a company needs to make sure that the executives make a long-term commitment to it. Finally, a company needs to provide incentives that direct executive attention to accomplishing critical tasks and objectives. A sensible compensation program is developed by taking the following steps.

[1] Ask Questions

When reviewing its executive compensation program, a company should first ask the following questions:

- Is the total compensation package competitive?
- Does the package have an appropriate mix of guaranteed compensation (pay, benefits, and perquisites) and variable compensation (annual and long-term incentives)?
- Are the variable compensation elements sufficiently leveraged to make real reward opportunities possible?
- Are the reward opportunities instrumental or charitable?
- Does the incentive plan underscore operating and strategic plans and direct executive attention to the implementation of these plans?
- Are financial and nonfinancial goals tied into the incentive plan?
- Could there be any unintended consequences of the annual and long-term plans?

[2] Seek Information

To answer the previous questions, a number of sources may be tapped. Perhaps the best is the company's executives themselves. Interviewing the individuals who are affected by an executive compensation plan is critical to its effective design; the executives know the realities of their business situation and what goals are appropriate. By interviewing a number of executives, one can determine how well individual perceptions fit into the overall corporate consensus about business goals.

Information can also be obtained by analyzing planning documents. These provide the best sense of where the company wants to go and how it intends to get there. Board members may also be asked for their ideas; thus, shareholders, whom the board represents, can influence compensation plans. One often-overlooked source of information is Wall Street research analysts, whose livelihoods depend on understanding which performance resources are important to the companies they follow.

[3] Identify Critical Success Factors and Related Goals

Using input from management and board member interviews and the operating and strategic plans, the company can identify reasonable goals and suggest steps to achieve them. The temptation to set too many goals should be resisted. A general rule of thumb is that no more than three or four major goals should have to be met by an executive to achieve his or her performance objectives.

Some compensation plans may be related to the individual executive rather than to the company. Although stock ownership is usually an important aspect of most executive compensation plans, companies may also want to establish golden handcuffs so that younger executives will not leave for a competitor. In addition, cash or stock awards may be deferred until retirement, when, presumably, an executive's marginal tax rate will be lower. These design considerations are perfectly legitimate and should be used to the corporation's advantage.

[4] Run Projections

Although it is impossible to foresee all consequences, companies should try to test the effects of any proposed compensation plan. Spreadsheet software packages are available that make failure to run projections inexcusable. If an incentive plan is designed around particular performance features, testing its effects during both high and low levels of performance is very important. How much will the particular feature cost the company after tax? What will the size of the payouts be? Can those payouts be justified to the stockholders? Should there be caps on payout amounts? If the incentive plan uses stock-based incentives, what effect will the equity dilution have on EPS? If an executive compensation plan results in a totally unforeseen consequence, the plan cannot be considered a success. The company should have a good idea of what it is getting into before a plan is put into place.

[5] Communicate Objectives

If an executive compensation plan fails, the failure may not be due entirely to the plan's design. The problem could be a lack of communication within the organization itself. Sometimes a board of directors really does not understand a program's goals and is unpleasantly surprised when the results are announced. More often, the executives covered by a plan, the very ones who are supposed to be attracted, retained, and motivated by it, have not received adequate explanation of the opportunities available under their compensation program. Or they may be told about the plan's reward opportunities but not the near-term and long-term hurdles that must be overcome to reach them. Executive understanding and acceptance of a program is the essence of a sensible compensation package.

[6] Use Consultants

Although a company can do much of the incentive plan design itself, most find it useful to bring in an independent expert to help those responsible for compensation programs to think through the issues. A number of consulting firms, ranging from sole practitioners to large firms with huge research capabilities, specialize in executive compensation and offer a breadth of experience not typically found within corporations. In selecting a consultant, companies should consider other issues in addition to how well the consultant knows the particular tax and accounting regulations associated with executive compensation. While such knowledge is certainly necessary, a good consultant should also understand how important executive compensation is to the company's success and should be able to develop sensible programs that closely link operating and strategic plans.

Suggested Reading

Cheeks, James E., and Gordon D. Wolf, *How to Compensate Executives.* Homewood, Ill.: Dow Jones-Irwin, 1979.

Chingos, Peter T., et al. *Financial Considerations of Executive Compensation and Retirement Plans.* New York: John Wiley & Sons, Inc., 1984.

Crystal, Graef S. *Executive Compensation: Money, Motivation, and Imagination.* New York: AMACOM, 1978.

———. *Questions and Answers on Executive Compensation: How to Get What You're Worth.* Englewood Cliffs, N.J.: Prentice-Hall, Inc., 1984.

Ellig, Bruce R. *Executive Compensation—A Total Pay Perspective.* New York: McGraw-Hill, 1982.

———. "Incentive Plans: Over the Long Term." *Compensation and Benefit Review* (formerly *Compensation Review*), Vol. 16 (2nd Quarter 1984), p. 2.

England, J.D. "The Compensation Committee as a Payout 'Circuit Breaker.' " *Directors & Boards,* Vol. 12 (Fall 1987), p. 43.

———. "Developing a Total Compensation Philosophy Statement." *Personnel* (May 1988), p. 71.

Hurwich, Mark R. and Richard A. Furniss, Jr. "Measuring and Rewarding Strategic Performance." *Handbook of Business Strategy,* 2nd ed. New York: Warren Gorham Lamont, 1991.

Murthy, K., R. Srinivasa and M.S. Salter. "Should CEO Pay Be Linked to Results?" *Harvard Business Review,* Vol. 53 (May–June 1975), p. 3.

Redling, E.T. "Myths vs. Reality: The Relationship Between Top Executive Pay and Corporate Performance." *Compensation and Benefit Review* (formerly *Compensation Review*), Vol. 31 (4th Quarter 1981), p. 4.

Rappaport, Alfred. *Creating Shareholder Value: The New Standard for Business Performance.* New York: The Free Press, 1986.

Slona, Richard S. *How to Measure Managerial Performance.* New York: MacMillan, 1980.

Appendix 9.1 COMPARATIVE ANALYSIS OF LONG-TERM INCENTIVE DEVICES IN PUBLIC COMPANIES

NQSOs

Description and Common Features

Option to purchase shares of company stock at a stated price (option price) over a given period, frequently 10 years.

Option price normally equals 100 percent of the stock's fair market value on date of grant but may be set below or above this level (i.e., discount or premium).

NQSOs may be exercised by cash payment or by tendering previously owned shares of stock, depending on plan terms. NQSOs may be granted in tandem with SARs or other devices.

Tax Treatment

Executive

At exercise. Excess of the stock's fair market value over the option price is taxed as ordinary income and is subject to withholding.

At sale. Any appreciation occurring after calculation of the exercise tax obligation is taxed as either of the following:

- A long-term capital gain if the stock is held for more than one year
- A short-term capital gain for stock held for one year or less

Company

At exercise. Deduction allowed for the amount the executive recognizes as taxable income in the year the executive is taxed if withholding requirements are met.

At sale. No deduction allowed.

Accounting Treatment

Established by Accounting Principles Board Opinion No. 25.

No expense is recognizable if the following apply:

- Number and price of the optioned shares are fixed at the date of grant and no other terms are variable (e.g., based on future events or performance).
- Options are not discounted.
- Options are not exercisable by pyramiding (i.e., tendering previously owned shares of stock that have not been held for at least six months).
- Options are not issued with tandem SARs.

Appendix reprinted by permission of TPF&C, a Towers Perrin Company.

Discounted options. The discount amount at grant (a fixed amount) is accrued as an expense over the vesting period.

Options with tandem SARs, pyramiding, or variable terms. A compensation expense for the excess of the stock's fair market value over the option price is accrued over the period during which the options remain outstanding. Because such plans receive variable or SAR-type accounting, the plan's cost is unknown and open-ended when options are granted.

Any tax savings on postgrant appreciation generally bypass the income statement and are posted directly to the additional paid-in capital account on the balance sheet.

Insider Trading Treatment

At grant. Option grant will not be considered a purchase if the following apply:

- The plan meets certain requirements relating to disinterested administration, shareholder approval, limits on available shares, and nontransferability of options.
- Insiders do not sell shares acquired by exercising options until six months after option grant.

At exercise. Exercise will not be considered a purchase or a sale.

At sale. Sale of option stock will be considered a sale and will be matched with any purchase in the preceding or following six months.

Advantages

Executive

- Possibility of large gains; usually no limit on upside appreciation potential.
- Can time exercise to maximize gains.
- Can benefit from share appreciation before exercise without investing personal capital.
- If plan allows, the executive can do the following:
  —Exercise through stock-for-stock swaps.
  —Use broker loans for cashless exercises.
  —Have SARs attached (although this would worsen accounting treatment).
- No express limit or requirement (other than those imposed by plan) on the following:
  —Posttermination exercise periods.
  —Value of options that become exercisable each year for each executive.
  —Terms of option grants to major shareholders.
  —Ability to grant discounted options or amend options after they are granted without repricing.
  —Sequential option exercise.

Company

- Generally no income statement expense; provides a noncash means of compensating executives and a potential source of paid-in capital.
- Promotes shareholders' interests by facilitating executive stock ownership and ensuring that executive gains parallel shareholder gains.

Disadvantages

Executive

- Stock price changes may not parallel internal performance standards and/or actual management performance; no gain unless market value increases.
- Gain at exercise taxed as ordinary income, rather than as a capital gain.
- May need to borrow money or sell shares to finance option exercise and tax obligation. If shares are sold, future upside appreciation potential is lost.

Company

- Executive gains may not parallel internal performance standards and/or actual management performance.
- "In the money" options involve an opportunity cost and potentially dilute EPS, since they let executives buy shares at less than current value.

ISOs

Description and Common Features

Option to purchase shares of company stock at 100 percent (or more) of stock's fair market value on date of grant (option price) for a period of up to 10 years; designed to meet various other statutory requirements to qualify for ISO tax treatment, e.g.:

- $100,000 annual vesting limitation.
- Holding period (that is, stock cannot be sold until two years after option grant and one year after exercise)
- Limit on posttermination exercise (e.g., one year after disability terminations and three months after other terminations except for death)

ISOs may be exercised by cash payment or by tendering previously owned shares of stock, depending on plan terms. ISOs may be granted in tandem with SARs that have identical terms.

Tax Treatment

Established by IRC Section 422.

Executive

At exercise. No regular income tax is owed. However, the excess of the stock's fair market value over the option price (i.e., the spread) may trigger an alternative minimum tax obligation.

At sale. Gain (i.e., excess of sales price over option price) is taxed at long-term capital gains rate if shares are held at least two years from grant date and one year from exercise (qualifying disposition). If holding period requirements are not met and a disqualifying disposition occurs, the spread (from grant to exercise) is ordinary income; the remainder is capital gain.

Company

No tax deduction is allowed for an ISO (at either exercise or sale) unless a disqualifying disposition occurs. The company may deduct the spread at exercise in the year of the disqualifying disposition.

Accounting Treatment

Established by Accounting Principles Board Opinion No. 25.
No expense is recognizable if the following apply:

- Number and price of the optioned shares are fixed at the date of grant, and no other terms are variable (e.g., based on future events or performance).
- Options are not exercisable by pyramiding (i.e., tendering previously owned shares of stock that have not been held for at least six months).
- Options are not issued with tandem SARs.

Options with tandem SARs, pyramiding, or variable terms. A compensation expense for the excess of the stock's fair market value over the option price is accrued over the period during which the options remain outstanding. Because such plans receive variable or SAR-type accounting, the plan's cost is unknown and open-ended when options are granted.

Insider Trading Treatment

At grant. Option grant will not be considered a purchase if the following apply:

- The plan meets certain requirements relating to disinterested administration, shareholder approval, limits on available shares, and nontransferability of options.
- Insiders do not sell shares acquired by exercising options until six months after the option grant.

At exercise. Exercise will not be considered a purchase or a sale.

At sale. Sale of an option stock will be considered a sale and will be matched with any purchase in the preceding or following six months.

Advantages

Executive

- No tax at exercise (other than possible alternative minimum tax); taxation delayed until stock is sold.
- Possibility of large gains; usually no limit on upside appreciation potential.
- Can time exercise to maximize gains.
- Can benefit from share appreciation before exercise without personal investment.
- If plan allows, can do the following:
  —Exercise through stock-for-stock swaps.
  —Use broker loans for cashless exercises (although a disqualifying disposition would occur if holding periods are not met).
  —Have SARs attached with the same terms as the underlying option (although this would worsen accounting treatment).

Company

- Generally no income statement expense; provides a noncash means of compensating executives and a potential source of paid-in capital.
- Promotes shareholders' interests by facilitating stock ownership (especially owing to ISO holding periods) and ensuring that executive gains parallel shareholder gains.
- Favorable ISO tax treatment for executives may lessen pressure to help executives finance option exercises, since taxes are not owed until stock is sold (although exercise price is tied up during holding period).

Disadvantages

Executive

- Various restraints are imposed to realize ISO tax treatment, such as the following:
  —Limited time frame to exercise after employment terminates (especially the three-month limit after retirement).
  —Limit on annual vesting of $100,000 per executive.
  —Stricter rules for executives who are more than 10 percent owners.
  —Sequential exercise rules on pre-1987 grants.
  —Repricing of options where ISOs are materially amended after grant (with the exercise price adjusted to at least the stock's fair market value on the amendment date).
- Stock price changes may not parallel internal performance standards and/or actual management performance; no gain unless market value increases.
- May need to borrow money or sell shares to finance exercise. If shares are sold, future upside appreciation potential is lost.

Company

- No corporate tax deduction is allowed if executive makes a qualifying disposition of shares.
- Executive gains may not parallel internal performance standards and/or actual management performance.
- ''In the money'' options involve an opportunity cost and potentially dilute EPS, since they let executives buy shares at less than current value.

LIMITED SARS (LSARS)

Description and Common Features

Rights granted in tandem with stock options designed for use in the event of a change in the company's ownership or control. LSARs permit the executive to receive a payment equal to the excess of the stock's value at exercise over the option price, rather than exercising the underlying stock option.

Normally, such rights are granted only to Securities and Exchange Commission (SEC) insiders, which are prohibited from selling shares within six months of a share purchase, even in the midst of a tender offer or other change in control. Some plans permit insiders to exercise an LSAR (as opposed to the underlying stock option) only if there was another share purchase in the preceding 6 months that would preclude an immediate share sale upon exercise. LSARs usually remain in effect only for a limited period, such as 90 days from the change in control or other defined plan triggering event.

LSARs under some plans provide more favorable computational terms than might otherwise be achieved with a regular stock option. For example, LSAR payments might reflect the highest gain the executive could realize by exercising the option at any time during the three-month period following the change in control, rather than the gain on any specific date.

Payment is almost always in cash.

Tax Treatment

Executive

At exercise. Value of the rights is taxed as ordinary income and is subject to withholding.

Company

At exercise. Tax deduction is allowed for the amount of the executive's taxable income from the LSAR.

Accounting Treatment

Until a change in control occurs, triggering the LSAR, there is no effect on the accounting treatment for the underlying stock option. Consequently, according to Accounting

Principles Board Opinion No. 25, no expense is recognizable for stock options if the following apply:

- The number and price of the optioned shares are fixed at the date of grant, and no other terms are variable (e.g., based on future events or performance).
- Options are not discounted.
- Options are not exercisable by pyramiding (i.e., tendering previously owned shares of stock that have not been held for at least six months).

If and when a change in control occurs or is likely to occur, there is a presumption that the LSAR is more likely to be exercised than the underlying stock option. Then, the LSAR's current value (spread) would be expensed over the related period of service (normally the year in which the change in control occurs or is likely to occur). For any subsequent accounting periods in which the LSAR remains exercisable, any additional share appreciation would be expensed (or share depreciation would be recorded as a reduction of an expense).

If the LSAR expires before the underlying stock option, the previously accrued expense cannot be reversed.

Insider Trading Treatment

At grant. LSAR grant will not be considered a purchase if the plan meets certain requirements relating to disinterested administration, shareholder approval, limits on available securities, and nontransferability of options and LSARs.

At exercise. Automatic cash settlement will not be considered a purchase or a sale if the following apply:

- Plan sets forth right to receive cash upon occurrence of a triggering event.
- Six months elapse between grant and exercise.
- Triggering event is not within the insider's control.

Settlement is not limited to quarterly 10-day window periods.

Advantages

Executive

- Allows SEC insiders to realize a gain from their stock options in the event of a change in control, even if they had otherwise purchased stock in the preceding six months.
- Requires no personal investment and avoids cost of financing option exercises. Also avoids costs and risks of continuing to hold shares after exercise.
- Depending on the LSAR's terms, can eliminate the need for the executive to decide when to exercise and provide the highest possible gain during the change in control.

Company

- Promotes shareholders' interests by ensuring that executive gains parallel shareholder gains.

- No need to assist executives with financing, since no investment is required.
- Avoids the need to accrue an accounting expense (as for regular SARs) unless or until a change in control occurs.

Disadvantages

Executive

- Stock price changes may not parallel internal performance standards and/or actual management performance; no gain unless market value increases.
- No opportunity for capital gains.
- If options with LSARs vest upon a change in control, a portion of the gain will be a parachute subject to potential excise taxes under IRC Section 280G.
- For LSARs in tandem with ISOs, tax-imposed constraints apply.

Company

- Executive gains may not parallel internal performance standards and/or actual management performance.
- If LSARs become exercisable, accounting expenses are open-ended and cannot be predetermined. If the LSAR becomes exercisable owing to a change in control but is not exercised, accrued expenses cannot be recouped.
- If options with LSARs vest upon a change in control, a portion of the gain is potentially a nondeductible parachute under IRC Section 280G.

PERFORMANCE SHARES

Description and Common Features

A contingent grant of a fixed number of common shares at the beginning of a performance cycle, with the number of shares payable at the end of the cycle dependent on how well performance objectives are achieved. The ultimate value of the performance shares depends on both the number of shares earned and their market value at the end of the cycle.

Duration of performance cycles varies but is typically three to five years. Financial objectives may relate to such items as cumulative growth in earnings or improvements in rates of return.

At end of cycle, awards are paid in cash and/or stock according to the plan's earn-out provisions and actual company performance.

Tax Treatment

Executive

On payment date. Ordinary income tax is owed on the value of the award (whether paid in cash or unrestricted stock). This income is subject to withholding.

Company

On payment date. Tax deduction allowed for the amount of the executive's taxable income from the award.

Accounting Treatment

The estimated value of the shares is expensed over the period during which related services are performed. Changes in the market value of the stock are also reflected (which is not the case with performance unit plans).

Insider Trading Treatment

Performance shares settled only in cash have no insider trading ramifications. However, insider trading rules would apply if payments are accelerated upon a change in control. For other performance shares, the following apply:

At grant. Share grant will not be considered a purchase if the plan meets certain requirements relating to disinterested administration, shareholder approval, limits on available shares, and nontransferability of shares.

At settlement. Shares settled in stock will not be considered a purchase or a sale (although a sale will occur when the stock is sold; if shares are sold within six months of grant, grant will be considered a purchase).

Shares settled in cash will not be considered a purchase or a sale if any of the following applies to participant's election to receive cash:

- It is irrevocably made at least six months in advance.
- It occurs during or becomes effective in a quarterly ten-day window period.
- It is fixed or automatic (according to the terms of the plan) and out of the insider's control.

Advantages

Executive

- Possibility of large gains (including upside potential owing to share price appreciation).
- Reward partially related to a measure over which executive has some control.
- Requires no personal investment.
- Taxation delayed until end of performance cycle.
- No design limits imposed by IRC.

Company

- Promotes shareholders' interests, since executive gains are related to both internal measures of company performance and shareholder gains. Unlike purely stock-based devices, awards can also be linked to the planning process and attainment of strategic business goals.

- No need to assist executives with financing, since no investment is required.
- Forfeiture requirements for midcycle terminations can aid executive retention.
- Can facilitate executive stock ownership if awards are paid in stock.

Disadvantages

Executive

- Gains could be zero if performance targets are not met, even with share price appreciation.
- Gains may be capped by company-imposed maximums to limit accounting charges and cash flow drain.
- End of performance period may not be most advantageous timing in terms of stock price.
- No opportunity for capital gains.

Company

- Choice and design of financial targets may be difficult.
- Executive gains do not necessarily parallel shareholder returns (because of other performance objectives), which could create shareholder relations problems.
- Accounting expenses are open-ended and cannot be determined in advance.

PHANTOM STOCK

Description and Common Features

Units analogous to company shares, with a value generally equal to appreciation in the value of the underlying stock.

Phantom stock is valued at a fixed date, typically at retirement or 5 to 15 years after grant. Essentially, it is like an SAR with a fixed exercise time.

Payment may be in cash and/or stock.

Note: The term "phantom stock" is used in other contexts (e.g., formula or appraised value stock for nonpublic companies or divisions). The treatments described here reflect only the definition given above.

Tax Treatment

Executive

On payment date. Value of the units is taxed as ordinary income and is subject to withholding.

Company

On payment date. Tax deduction is allowed for the amount of the executive's tax liability from the units.

Accounting Treatment

The value of the units (i.e., the excess of the stock's value at the end of each accounting period over its value at the date of award) is expensed over the period during which the units remain outstanding.

Insider Trading Treatment

Phantom stock settled only in cash has no insider trading ramifications. (Insider trading rules would apply if payments are accelerated upon a change in control.) For other phantom stock:

At grant. Phantom share grant will not be considered a purchase if the plan meets certain requirements relating to disinterested administration, shareholder approval, limits on available securities, and nontransferability of phantom shares.

At exercise. Stock settlement will not be considered a purchase or a sale (although a sale will occur when the stock is sold, if shares are sold within six months of grant, grant will be considered a purchase).

Settlement in cash will not be considered a purchase or a sale if any of the following applies to the participant's election to receive cash:

- It is irrevocably made at least six months in advance.
- It occurs during or becomes effective in a quarterly 10-day window period and cash settlement is approved by committee.
- It is fixed or automatic (according to terms of the plan) and outside the insider's control.

Advantages

Executive

- Possibility of large gains.
- Taxation delayed until award is settled, which may be at retirement.
- Requires no personal investment.
- No design limits imposed by IRC.

Company

- Promotes shareholders' interests by facilitating executive stock ownership (assuming awards settled in stock) and by ensuring that executive gains parallel shareholder gains.
- Focuses executive attention on long-term growth in share value, since executive does not control when gain will be cashed out.
- No need to assist executives with financing, since no investment is required.
- Forfeiture requirements for terminations before settlement can aid executive retention.

Disadvantages

Executive

- Stock price changes may not parallel internal performance standards and/or actual management performance; no gain unless market value increases.
- Gains may be capped by company-imposed maximums designed to limit accounting charges and potential cash drain.
- No opportunity for capital gains.
- Cannot time exercise to maximize gains.

Company

- Executive gains may not parallel internal performance standards and/or actual management performance.
- Accounting expenses are open-ended and cannot be predetermined. In addition, since they reflect stock price changes, which may not always track with earnings or other performance indicators, expenses may be out of line with earnings and fluctuate significantly across accounting periods.
- Does not result in actual share ownership unless awards are settled in stock.

PERFORMANCE UNITS AND PERFORMING CASH

Description and Common Features

A grant of a contingent number of units or a contingent cash award. Units may have a fixed dollar value, with the number earned varying with performance. Alternatively, a fixed number of units may be granted, with the value varying on the basis of performance.

Duration of performance cycle varies, but is typically three to five years. Financial objectives may relate to such items as cumulative growth in earnings or improvements in rates of return.

At end of cycle, awards are paid in cash and/or stock according to the plan's earnout provisions and actual company performance.

Tax Treatment

Executive

On payment date. Ordinary income tax is owed on the value of the award (whether paid in cash or unrestricted stock). This income is subject to withholding.

Company

On payment date. Tax deduction is allowed for the amount of the executive's taxable income from the award.

Accounting Treatment

The estimated value of the units is expensed over the period during which related services are performed.

Insider Trading Treatment

No insider trading ramifications when units are granted or when units are settled in cash. (If shares are sold within six months of grant, grant will be considered a purchase.)

For awards settled only in stock (assumes that award constitutes a derivative security):

At grant. Award will not be considered a purchase if the plan meets certain requirements relating to disinterested administration, shareholder approval, limits on available shares, and nontransferability.

At settlement. Awards settled in stock will not be considered a purchase or a sale (although a sale will occur when the stock is sold).

For awards settled in either cash or stock, the treatment is similar to that for SARs.

Advantages

Executive

- Possibility of large gains.
- Reward related to a measure over which executive has some control.
- Requires no personal investment.
- Taxation delayed until end of performance cycle.
- No design limits imposed by IRC.

Company

- Establishes a direct relationship between executive gains and internal performance standards; awards can be linked to the planning process and attainment of strategic business goals.
- Because awards are not related to share price (over which the company has little control), accounting expense is more controllable.
- No need to assist executives with financing, since no investment is required.
- Forfeiture requirements for midcycle terminations can aid executive retention.
- Can facilitate executive stock ownership if awards are paid in stock.

Disadvantages

Executive

- Gains could be zero if performance targets are not met.

- Gains may be capped by company-imposed maximums to limit accounting charges and cash flow drain.
- End of performance cycle may not be most advantageous time to evaluate performance.
- No opportunity for capital gains.

Company

- Choice and design of financial targets may be difficult.
- Executive gains do not necessarily parallel shareholder returns, which could create shareholder relations problems.
- Executives do not have any direct financial interest in the company's share value during the performance cycle.
- Does not result in actual ownership of shares unless awards are settled in stock.
- Accounting expenses are potentially open-ended and cannot be determined in advance.

RESTRICTED STOCK

Description and Common Features

An award of stock with no or nominal cost to executives that is nontransferable and subject to a substantial risk of forfeiture. As owners of the shares, executives normally have voting and dividend rights even while the shares are subject to restrictions. These restrictions typically lapse over a period of three to five years.

Tax Treatment

Established by IRC Section 83.

Executive

Timing. Normally, the executive is taxed when the restrictions lapse (i.e., when the stock becomes transferable or is no longer subject to forfeiture). However, the executive may elect to pay taxes on the shares when they are awarded, so any postgrant appreciation can be taxed as a capital gain when stock is sold. Such Section 83(b) elections are quite uncommon, largely owing to the modest tax advantage of long-term capital gains treatment and the possibility of having to forfeit any taxes paid if the restrictions fail to lapse.

Amount. When restrictions lapse (or at the award date if early taxation is elected), the excess of the stock's fair market value over the price, if any, paid by the executive is taxed as ordinary income and is subject to withholding.

Dividends. Dividends are taxed as compensation income while restrictions on stock are in force, unless executive elects taxation at the time of the award. Where dividends are also restricted, tax is deferred until restrictions lapse.

Company

On date executive is taxed. Tax deduction in the amount of the executive's income from the award.

Dividends. Tax deduction for dividends paid while stock is subject to restrictions, unless executive elects taxation at time of award or unless dividends are also restricted.

Accounting Treatment

Established by Accounting Principles Board Opinion No. 25.

The excess of the stock's value at the time of award over the amount, if any, paid by the executive is expensed over the period for which the related service is performed (usually the restriction period).

Unless restrictions are performance-based (i.e., dependent on factors other than the passage of time), no expense is charged for any postgrant stock appreciation. The same treatment applies to Time Accelerated Restricted Stock Award Plan (TARSAP) grants, under which restrictions lapse after a set period of service but can potentially lapse sooner if certain performance goals are met.

Under either time-lapse or TARSAP approaches, any tax savings on postgrant appreciation are posted directly to the additional paid-in capital account on the balance sheet, bypassing the income statement.

If performance-based restrictions affect the number of shares awarded or the price paid for them, if any, an expense is also charged for any stock appreciation occurring during the performance period.

Insider Trading Treatment

At grant. Stock grant will not be considered a purchase if the following apply:

- The plan meets certain requirements relating to disinterested administration, shareholder approval and limits on available shares.
- Insiders do not sell the shares for six months after grant.

At vesting. Vesting is not considered a purchase or a sale.

At sale. Sale of stock will be considered a sale and will be matched with any purchase in the preceding or following six months.

Advantages

Executive

- Possibility of large gains (although typically less upside potential than with stock options owing to smaller number of shares awarded).
- Executive gets company stock, usually with voting and dividend rights without personal investment and has limited risk, since a decline in share price probably will not wipe out value (that is, gains will probably never be zero).
- Provides opportunity to delay taxation plus flexibility for taxation at grant if desired.

Company

- Promotes shareholders' interests by facilitating executive stock ownership and ensuring that gains parallel shareholder gains.
- Accounting expenses can be determined in advance (except under performance-based plans other than TARSAPs) and limited to share value at grant.
- No need to assist executives with financing, since no investment is required.
- Shares immediately owned by executives (but subject to forfeiture), so sense of ownership may be stronger than with other devices.
- Potential for forfeiture (if executive leaves before restrictions lapse) can significantly aid in executive retention.

Disadvantages

Executive

- Stock price changes may not parallel internal performance standards and/or actual management performance.
- Shares can be forfeited if early taxation is elected; taxes will be lost as well if shares are forfeited.
- Unless early taxation is elected, gain when restrictions lapse is taxed as ordinary income rather than as a capital gain.

Company

- Executive gains may not parallel internal performance standards and/or actual management performance.
- May create adverse shareholder reaction owing to appearance of getting something for nothing.
- Executive election regarding tax liability affects timing and amount of company tax deduction.

SARS

Description and Common Features

Rights, normally granted in tandem with stock options, that permit the executive to receive a payment equal to the excess of the stock's value at exercise over the option price in lieu of exercising the underlying stock option. Once exercisable, participants control when to exercise outstanding SARs during the SARs' term.

SARs may be attached to incentive stock options or nonqualified stock options or may be granted on a freestanding or independent basis without a tandem option.

Payment may be in cash and/or stock.

Tax Treatment

Executive

At exercise. Value of the rights is taxed as ordinary income and is subject to withholding.

Company

At exercise. Tax deduction is allowed for the amount of the executive's taxable income from SARs.

Accounting Treatment

Established by Accounting Principles Board Opinion No.25 and FASB Interpretation No. 28.

The SAR's value (i.e., the excess of the stock's market value at the end of each accounting period over the option price) must be expensed over the period during which the SAR is outstanding. This treatment applies to freestanding or independent SARs as well as most tandem SARs, since it is assumed that the SAR, rather than the underlying stock option, will be exercised.

Insider Trading Treatment

At grant. SAR grant will not be considered a purchase if the plan meets certain requirements relating to disinterested administration, shareholder approval, limits on available securities, and nontransferability of options and SARs.

At exercise. Cash settlement will not be considered a purchase or a sale if any of the following applies to exercise (and any election to receive cash):

- It is irrevocably elected six months in advance.
- It occurs during or becomes effective in a quarterly 10-day window period, and cash settlement is approved by committee.
- It is fixed or automatic (according to terms of the plan) and is outside the insider's control).

Stock settlement will not be considered a purchase or a sale (although a sale will occur when the stock is sold; if shares are sold within six months of grant, grant will be considered a purchase).

Freestanding or Independent Cash SARs

No insider trading ramifications if plan meets certain requirements relating to disinterested administration, limits on available securities, and nontransferability of SARs.

Advantages

Executive

- Possibility of large gains (although some plans cap gains).
- Requires no personal investment and avoids cost of financing option exercises. Also avoids costs and risks of continuing to hold shares after exercise.
- Can generally time exercise to maximize gains.
- For SARs attached to NQSOs, no design limits imposed by IRC.

Company

- Promotes shareholders' interests by facilitating executive ownership of company stock if awards are paid in stock and by ensuring that executive gains parallel shareholder gains.
- No need to assist executives with financing, since no investment is required.

Disadvantages

Executive

- Stock price changes may not parallel internal performance standards and/or actual management performance; no gain unless market value increases.
- Gains may be capped by company-imposed maximums designed to limit accounting charges and potential cash drain.
- No opportunity for capital gains.
- For SARs in tandem with ISOs, tax-imposed constraints also apply to the SARs.

Company

- Executive gains may not parallel internal performance standards and/or actual management performance.
- Accounting expenses are open-ended and cannot be predetermined. In addition, since they reflect stock price changes, which may not always track with earnings or other performance indicators, expenses may be out of line with earnings and fluctuate significantly across accounting periods.
- Does not result in actual share ownership unless awards are settled in stock.

Index

313